PENGUIN C

FIVE REVENGE TRAGEDIES

EMMA SMITH is Fellow and Tutor in English at Hertford College, Oxford. She has published widely on Shakespeare and on early modern drama, particularly on the plays in print and in performance. She is co-editor of *The Elizabethan Top Ten: Defining Print Popularity in Early Modern England* and is working on a book on the Shakespeare First Folio.

KYD, SHAKESPEARE, MARSTON, CHETTLE, MIDDLETON

Five Revenge Tragedies

The Spanish Tragedy, Hamlet (1603), Antonio's Revenge, The Tragedy of Hoffman, The Revenger's Tragedy

Edited and with an Introduction by
EMMA SMITH

PENGUIN BOOKS

PENGUIN CLASSICS

Published by the Penguin Group
Penguin Books Ltd, 80 Strand, London WC2R ORL, England
Penguin Group (USA) Inc., 375 Hudson Street, New York, New York 10014, USA
Penguin Group (Canada), 90 Eglinton Avenue East, Suite 700, Toronto, Ontario,
Canada M4P 2Y3 (a division of Pearson Penguin Canada Inc.)
Penguin Ireland, 25 St Stephen's Green, Dublin 2, Ireland (a division of Penguin Books Ltd)
Penguin Group (Australia), 250 Camberwell Road, Camberwell, Victoria 3124, Australia
(a division of Pearson Australia Group Pty Ltd)
Penguin Books India Pvt Ltd, 11 Community Centre, Panchsheel Park, New Delhi – 110 017, India
Penguin Group (NZ), 67 Apollo Drive, Rosedale, Auckland 0632, New Zealand
(a division of Pearson New Zealand Ltd)
Penguin Books (South Africa) (Pty) Ltd, Block D, Rosebank Office Park,
181 Jan Smuts Avenue, Parktown North, Gauteng 2193, South Africa

Penguin Books Ltd, Registered Offices: 80 Strand, London WC2R ORL, England

www.penguin.com

This edition first published in Penguin Classics 2012

015

Introduction and editorial matter copyright © Emma Smith, 2012
All rights reserved

The moral right of the author of the introduction and editorial material has been asserted

Set in 10.25/12.25pt Postscript Adobe Sabon
Typeset by Jouve (UK), Milton Keynes

Printed and bound in Great Britain by Clays Ltd, Elcograf S.p.A.

ISBN: 978-0-141-19227-7

www.greenpenguin.co.uk

Contents

FIVE REVENGE
TRAGEDIES

CONTENTS

Chronology

Dates of performance, usually conjectural, are taken from Alfred Harbage's *Annals of English Drama 975–1700*, rev. Sylvia Stoler Wagonheim (1989); '*c.*' indicates an approximate date; '?' indicates conjectural information.

	Revenge tragedies	Theatrical background	Historical background
1567		First purpose-built theatre in London	
1572			Attacks on Protestants in St Bartholomew's Day Massacre in Paris
1581	Publication of *Seneca his Ten Tragedies*		
1584			First English colony in America, Roanoke, founded by Ralegh
1587			Execution of Mary Queen of Scots
1588			Failure of Spanish Armada
c. 1590		Marlowe's *Dr Faustus* (Admiral's Men)	

	Revenge tragedies	Theatrical background	Historical background
1592	Kyd's *Spanish Tragedy* performed (Strange's Men at the Rose)		
1593		Theatres closed due to plague	
		Murder of Marlowe	
1594	Shakespeare's *Titus Andronicus*	Chamberlain's Men founded	Tyrone's rebellion in Ireland began Nine Years' War
	Death of Kyd		
1596		Shakespeare's *Romeo and Juliet* (Chamberlain's Men)	Riots against high food prices
1597			Failure of second Spanish Armada
1599		Opening of the Globe Theatre by Shakespeare's company, the Lord Chamberlain's Men	Bishops' Ban orders satires to be publicly burned
		Revival of boys' companies	Earl of Essex mounts (unsuccessful) expedition to quell Irish rebellion
		Beginning of 'Wars of the Theatres', particularly involving Jonson, Marston and Dekker	
1600	Marston's *Antonio's Revenge* (Children at St Paul's)		

	Revenge tragedies	Theatrical background	Historical background
c. 1600	Shakespeare's *Hamlet* (Chamberlain's Men)		
1601	Jonson paid for additions to *The Spanish Tragedy*		Earl of Essex's rebellion: he is executed for treason
1602	Chettle's *Tragedy of Hoffman* (Admiral's Men)		
1602	Publication of *The Spanish Tragedy* with additions		
1603		Lord Chamberlain's Men become King's Men	Death of Queen Elizabeth; accession of King James I
1604		Patent granted for indoor theatre at Blackfriars	Peace with Spain
1605	Middleton's *The Revenger's Tragedy* (King's Men)	Jonson's first court masque Shakespeare's *King Lear* (King's Men)	Gunpowder plot to blow up Parliament
1607			First settlement at Jamestown, Virginia
1610	Chapman's *The Revenge of Bussy D'Ambois* (Children of Whitefriars)		

	Revenge tragedies	Theatrical background	Historical background
1611	Tourneur, *The Atheist's Tragedy* (?King's Men)		
1612			Death of Prince Henry
1613	Webster, *The Duchess of Malfi* (King's Men)	Globe Theatre burns down during performance of Shakespeare's *All is True*	
1614		Hope Theatre built on Bankside for plays and bear-baiting	
		Jonson's *Bartholomew Fair* performed at Hope (Lady Elizabeth's Men)	
1616	Death of Shakespeare	Jonson's Folio of his plays and poems	
1620	Middleton, *Women Beware Women* (King's Men)		Pilgrim Fathers set out for America on the *Mayflower*
1623		Shakespeare's collected works published in Folio	
1625			Death of James I; accession of Charles I

Playwrights

Thomas Kyd (1558–94), *The Spanish Tragedy*

Kyd was the son of a London scrivener and attended Merchant
Taylors' School. There is no record of his having attended
university. His only other attested literary composition is a
translation of the tragedy *Cornelia* from the French (published
in 1594), although critics have suggested that he wrote the play
Soliman and Perseda, sharing its name with Hieronimo's playlet,
and an earlier, lost version of *Hamlet*, the so-called Ur-Hamlet.
He shared lodgings with fellow playwright Christopher Marlowe, and was imprisoned when atheistical papers, which Kyd
attributed to Marlowe, were found there.

The date of composition of *The Spanish Tragedy* is uncertain –
perhaps as early as 1587, since it does not mention the Spanish
Armada of the following year – and it is first recorded on stage
in February 1592 when Lord Strange's Men played at the Rose
Theatre. A further twenty-eight performances are recorded in
theatre proprietor Philip Henslowe's accounts between 1592
and 1597, making it an unprecedented success; a comic prequel
was commissioned called *The First Part of Jeronimo* (published
in 1605), and Ben Jonson was paid to write additional passages
to the original play in 1601. The play's popularity is corrobo-
rated by the large number of printed editions (eleven between
1592 and 1633) and an even larger body of allusions, parodies
and references in contemporary literature. The language, plot
and stagecraft of *The Spanish Tragedy* had a profound effect on
the early modern theatre, including on the other plays printed
in this volume. It has had some notable modern revivals, including
the National Theatre, London, directed by Michael Bogdanov

(1982), the Shakespeare Center in New York, directed by Ron Daley (1986), and at the Royal Shakespeare Company, Stratford-upon-Avon, directed by Michael Boyd (1997).

John Marston (1576–1634), *Antonio's Revenge*

Marston was born in Oxfordshire, and educated at Brasenose College and at the Middle Temple, where his father was a prominent lawyer. His early literary works include fashionable Ovidian love poetry and satires, which fell foul of the Bishops' Ban on satire in 1599. His dramatic works for the Children at St Paul's, a successful children's company, include *Antonio and Mellida* (1600), part one of *Antonio's Revenge* (1600). Later Marston wrote for the Children of the Blackfriars, including *The Malcontent* (1604) and *The Dutch Courtesan* (1604), and he collaborated with his rival Jonson and George Chapman on *Eastward Ho* (1605). By the end of the decade he was ordained a priest and withdrew from theatrical life.

Antonio's Revenge was printed in 1602, and its chronology in relation to that of *Hamlet*, with which it clearly shares a good deal, is contested. It has never had a professional stage revival since Elizabethan times.

William Shakespeare (1564–1616), *Hamlet (1603)*

Shakespeare was born in Stratford-upon-Avon and he had moved to London and begun a career as an actor and playwright by the beginning of the 1590s. He was a sharer (part-owner) in the Chamberlain's Men from 1594, and wrote exclusively for the company (later named the King's Men) until his retirement in around 1611. By the time of *Hamlet*, written around 1600 and first published in 1603, he had written in a range of genres from romantic comedy to narrative poetry. *Hamlet* is often seen to mark a transition from the comedies and histories of the 1590s towards the more tragic plays of the new century.

The earliest printed text (1603) is the one used in this edition. It was followed in 1604 by a second, much longer version of the play, and in Shakespeare's posthumously printed collected dramatic works, the Folio of 1623, by a third version (see Appendix). Disparaged by bibliographers as a corrupted version of Shakespeare's intentions, *Hamlet (1603)* has gradually gained more acceptance, and has had a particular impact in the theatre, where its unfamiliar take on a sometimes over-familiar play has been highly successful: the Nottingham Playhouse, directed by Andrew McKinnon (1983), the Orange Tree in Richmond, directed by Sam Walters (1985), the Oregon Shakespeare Festival directed by Barry Kraft (1994), and as the two-handed play *Kupenga Kwa Hamlet* (*The Madness of Hamlet*), directed by Arne Pohlmeier for Two Gents Productions on UK tour (2010).

Henry Chettle (died between 1603 and 1607), *The Tragedy of Hoffman*

Much about Henry Chettle's life is unknown, including his dates of birth and death. Initially trained as a printer, he was a prolific playwright working, almost always in collaboration with other writers, for Philip Henslowe at the Admiral's Men throughout the 1590s, although little of his work reached print. *The Tragedy of Hoffman, or The Revenge for a Father* seems to be Chettle's attempt to rework the popular Hamlet themes for the Chamberlain's Men's great rivals, probably in 1602. It was not published until 1631, when it was described 'as it hath bin diuers times acted with great applause, at the Phenix in Druery-lane'; there is no modern stage history although a semi-staged reading, directed in Oxford by Elisabeth Dutton under the auspices of the Malone Society in 2010, is recorded online [via http://bit.ly/hoffman2010].

Thomas Middleton (1580–1627), *The Revenger's Tragedy*

Middleton was a Londoner who attended Queen's College, Oxford, but seems to have preferred writing to study, leaving without a degree and publishing poetry and satire before turning to drama and comic pamphlets. His extensive corpus of plays ranges across genres, from city comedy to Italianate tragedy,

from political satire to Lord Mayors' pageants; he collaborated
with Shakespeare on the satirical *Timon of Athens* and with
other writers, including Thomas Dekker and William Rowley;
and he wrote for a number of different theatre companies, including, for *The Revenger's Tragedy*, the King's Men, performed
1605. His work has been published in *Thomas Middleton: The
Collected Works* (ed. Gary Taylor and John Lavagnino, 2007).

Middleton's authorship of *The Revenger's Tragedy* has only
recently been accepted; anonymous editions were printed without authorial attribution in 1607 and 1608. During much of
the twentieth century it was asserted that Cyril Tourneur, the
author of *The Atheist's Tragedy*, had written it. Recent productions have been the Royal Shakespeare Company, directed by
Di Trevis (1987), the Manchester Royal Exchange, directed
by Jonathan Moore (2008), and the National Theatre, London,
directed by Melly Stills (2008). In 2002 Alex Cox released
his film *The Revengers Tragedy*, set in a futuristic dystopian
Liverpool.

Introduction

The quest for retribution can seem a timeless, cross-cultural phenomenon, from Greek drama to soap opera, from urban myths of wronged wives cutting up expensive suits to retaliatory military action on an international scale. But it is also true that revenge as a shaping motif in tragic drama has some specific historical instances, and particularly in the late Elizabethan and early Jacobean period. The plays included in this edition are part of a wider dramatic phenomenon which, while it draws some of its inventive energy from broader cultural mythemes of vengeance, also responds to the circumstances of its own moment in three distinct ways: in its depiction and interrogation of justice, in its analysis of death and in its playful engagement with theatricality.

In its representation of a man seeking justice for a murder to which the institutions of the state seem powerless to respond, Kyd's *The Spanish Tragedy* initiated a pattern followed by subsequent revenge tragedies. As knight marshal, Hieronimo's judicial role in the Spanish court multiplies the ironies of his own legal impotence, and when he meets the petitioners desperate for his help in pursuing their own cases, he '*Tear[s] the papers*' (3.13): the letter of the law is, quite literally, shredded. Unable to seek redress through legal means, Hieronimo instead turns to private revenge, although he describes the operations of legal process in terms strikingly similar to those of the revenge quest: 'For blood with blood, shall while I sit as judge, / Be satisfied, and the law discharged' (3.6). Characteristically in these plays, the ruling figures are actively or passively implicated in the crimes which must be revenged. The indifferent

Spanish king, the regicide king in *Hamlet (1603)* and the feebly vicious duke in *The Revenger's Tragedy* are all culpable, and thus the genre seems to head off any possibility of legal redress, giving rather a kind of licence to the necessarily ingenious methods of the revenger. Law courts in *The Revenger's Tragedy* and in *The Spanish Tragedy* are shown to be infected with unrepentant wit, as Junior and Pedringano each show their disregard for the institutions of civil society. Instead, 'the stage is the courtroom in which the case is tried', as Sartre puts it.[1] Revenge tragedies do not exactly portray legal problems; instead, they supplant such a representational regime with their own savage, ritualized forms of justice.

The Elizabethan juror Francis Bacon's remarks on revenge are often-quoted: 'revenge is a kind of wild justice, which the more man's nature runs to, the more ought law to weed it out. For as for the first wrong, it doth but offend the law; but the revenge of that wrong putteth the law out of office.'[2] Bacon's opposition between revenge and the law has been an important one for discussions of the genre in its historical context. In a landmark study of *Elizabethan Revenge Tragedy, 1587–1642* (1940), Fredson Bowers used extensive contemporary legal cases to pinpoint Elizabethan attitudes to revenge, and noted that the law 'punished an avenger who took justice into his own hands just as heavily as the original murderer', even though there was a kind of cultural sympathy for those who took on the burden of blood revenge for the murder of a relative.[3] Bowers suggested that this paradox was enacted in the revenge genre, where revengers often set out with the audience's sympathy, which they gradually forfeited as their lust for blood exceeded the original crime.

In many ways, however, revenge plays seem designedly structured to compromise the status of the revengers, even by placing the nature of that original crime under suspicion. The deaths of Andrea in the battle with the Portuguese (*The Spanish Tragedy*), or of the king in his orchard (*Hamlet (1603)*), or of the chaste Gloriana (*The Revenger's Tragedy*) or Mellida (*Antonio's Revenge*) are the precondition for the revenge plays but are not depicted within them. Their status is contested and subject to rewritings by the living. In Chettle's *Tragedy of Hoffman*, the execution of Hans Hoffman for piracy appears to have been an entirely legal, if merciless, course, and the a priori unsuitability of this death for Hoffman's own revenge quest sets this whole play off at an ethically oblique angle. Or rather, perhaps, it suggests what may also be true elsewhere: that the original crime is to revenge tragedy rather as the MacGuffin is to Hitchcock – an initial spur that is largely irrelevant once the dynamic of the plot and characters has been established. For example, Vindice gains his fiendishly appropriate revenge on the duke for the death of Gloriana in Act 3 of *The Revenger's Tragedy*: thereafter his avenging energy is more fundamentalist in its pursuit of general depravity rather than personal wrong, and Gloriana's role seems thus to have been to prompt, rather than pre-empt, his course of action.

Eric Hobsbawm has identified a cross-cultural phenomenon he calls 'banditry': a mode of ambivalent popular lawlessness in which individuals are set at odds with their rulers or institutions but retain the sympathy of their class as folk heroes.[4] The revenger–bandit in these plays occupies an equivocal ethical position. On the one hand, his agency and his pursuit of duty can be admirable, and his grief powerfully articulated. The simplicity of Hoffman's cry of anguish 'You killed my father' (5.3), or of Hieronimo's 'as dear to me was my Horatio / As yours, or yours, or yours, my lords to you' (4.4), seems to emphasize that revengers are shaped by monstrous and unearned injustices. On the other hand, however, the revenger tends to be characterized by increasing savagery. As John Kerrigan identifies, in taking revenge the revenger effects an exchange with his adversary: 'when B, injured by A, does to A what A did to him, he makes himself resemble the opponent he has blamed, while he transforms his enemy into the kind of victim he once was'.[5] The moral disturbance of this transference gives the revenge genre its queasy narrative energy. *Antonio's Revenge* visualizes the interplay, moving from the opening image of Piero *'unbraced, his arms bare, smeared in blood, a poniard in one hand, bloody, and a torch in the other'* to its echo in Antonio *'his arms bloody, a torch and a poniard'* (3.5). For Hoffman the overlap is psychic, as he takes on the identity of Otho, the man he murdered; Vindice experiences the same uncanny recognition when Lussurioso dispatches him to kill – himself; Hamlet is both subject (in relation to his father) and object (in relation to the death of Corambis) of that play's revenge quests.

Revengers thus both enact and compromise systems of ethical and legal justice, and they take their ethical bearings less from audience experiences of the law or of ethics and more from previous plays in the genre. As Robert Warshow writes of a modern genre often associated with the early modern revenge plays, the cinematic Western – both are preoccupied with the isolated, self-reliant individual with his own moral code inhabiting a contested space which plays out its contradictions in the ultimate destruction of the hero – 'it appeals to the previous experience of the type itself; it creates its own field of reference'.[6] Revenge tragedies are less concerned with the external field of law and justice than they might seem, and more concerned, perhaps, with their own generic dramaturgy.

If revenge tragedies do not reflect, in any simple way, early modern attitudes to justice, they do have affinities with legal procedures and methodologies, in their investigation of detection, proof and punishment. Introducing an Elizabethan translation of the Roman Stoic philosopher and playwright Seneca, to whom Kyd and other revenge tragedians are heavily indebted and from whom Marston, in particular, often quotes, T. S. Eliot observes that 'The Spanish Tragedy, like the series of Hamlet plays, including Shakespeare's, has an affinity to our own contemporary detective drama'.[7] Lorna Hutson has explored the ways in which ethical questions of violence and retribution are played out procedurally, as revenge plays gather and test evidence and probability.[8] Here we might consider the delay of the revenger less as a psychological barrier and more as an investigative necessity: Hieronimo needs Bel-imperia's witness statement, delivered in a bloody letter, to be sure of the identity of his son's murderers and vows 'by circumstances [to] try, / What I can gather to confirm this writ' (3.2). Hamlet uses the play as 'the thing / Wherein I'll catch the conscience of the king' (scene 7). As Hoffman's plot unravels in The Tragedy of

Hoffman, the play's detectives multiply: Hoffman eschews stran-
gulation, worrying that 'Circles of purple blood' (4.2) will proclaim foul play to even the most cursory autopsy; an alibi for the
relevant hour proves Rodorick the hermit could not have lured
Lodowick and Lucibella to their doom; Martha notes that her
son's costume, worn by Lucibella, 'is not sea-wet: if my son
were drowned / Then why thus dry is his apparel found?' (5.1).
Processes of revenge and mourning are here folded in with the
forensic assessment of death's causes – and consequences.

The outcome of these investigations is to attach direct culpability for deaths to specific human agents: Horatio was killed
by Lorenzo and Balthazar; Feliche by Piero, Julio by Antonio;
the duke by Vindice; the old king by his successor. But these
direct lines of culpability stand in here, as in the modern detective story, for existential questions of causation that are more
difficult to articulate. Like bandits, revengers are 'symptoms of
crisis and tension in their society'.[9] The anxieties which they
embody, however, have been seen by recent critics as less concerned with matters of temporal justice and law – the ethics of
revenge in contemporary society – and instead related to the
post-Reformation religious context and to contested attitudes
to the dead. Crucial among the ritual and doctrinal differences
between the unreformed and reformed religions – between
Catholicism and Protestantism – were their understandings of
death and of relations between the living and the dead. Requiem
masses and prayers for the dead had given Catholic liturgy rituals of connection and agency in which the dead were not
beyond the help of the living, and those mourning had an active
role towards those who had died. The existence of Purgatory
within Catholic practice as a third, intermediate post-mortem
destination that was not heaven or hell, allowed for the tropes
of ghostly return, as in *Hamlet (1603)*:

> I am thy father's spirit, doomed for a time
> To walk the night, and all the day
> Confined in flaming fire,
> Till the foul crimes done in my days of nature
> Are purged and burnt away. (5)

By contrast, reformed religion's reimagining of the afterlife demanded, as Peter Marshall has explored, 'a far-reaching re-configuration of the cultural and emotional nexus that bound the living to the dead ... well beyond the boundaries of academic theology'.[10] The stage was one of the dominant spaces of this cultural work.

Revenge tragedies present their dead as insistently demanding of the living that they remember through retributive violence. Some of these ghosts return from the dead, like Hamlet's father, Andrea in *The Spanish Tragedy* or Andrugio in *Antonio's Revenge*; others are present in grim bony relics ventriloquized by the living, as in the addresses by Vindice to the skull of his betrothed at the start of *The Revenger's Tragedy* or Hoffman to the 'anatomy' or skeleton of his father. In all these cases the dead have a mnemonic function, and this role is taken up by other props too: Hieronimo offers his double Bazulto, weeping over his own murdered son, a handkerchief to wipe his eyes, but as the stage direction makes clear, '*He draweth out a bloody napkin*', a 'token' from Horatio 'That of thy death revenged I should be' (3.13). Ultimately this play reveals Horatio's body as its ultimate mnemonic device: the 1997 RSC production had the court recoil in disgust at the smell of Horatio's unburied body. Keeping him unburied is a prompt to revenge, but it may also be an attempt to keep him in the world of the living: the early modern period did not always consider a person dead until buried, as suggested by contemporary arrests of corpses for debt on their way to the graveyard.[11] As Bacon observes, the 'man that studieth revenge keepeth his own wounds green, that otherwise would heal and do well'.[12] Revenge stands in for, and defers, funeral rituals, and in their repeated inscription of disrupted, incomplete or postponed burials, these plays allude to the contested understandings of the appropriate treatment of the departed, just as contemporaries argued over the legitimacy of prayers for the dead, the tolling of bells and the erection of graveyard crosses. As Thomas Anderson puts it, by 'registering a generation's inability to move beyond the loss of the community of the dead, the revenge stage offers its vision of early modern communities – peopled with body parts, skeletons, bastards, corpses, and disembodied

voices – that try to compensate for, even as they repeat, the trau-
matic loss of the place of the dead'.[13]

By this analysis, it is not so much the criminalized human
agents of death within the plays that are significant, but the
unknowable mystery of death itself. The Elizabethan liturgy for
the burial of the dead included 1 Corinthians 15:26: 'The last
enemy that shall be destroyed is death' (King James Version).
Lorenzo in *The Spanish Tragedy* or Piero in *Antonio's Revenge*
thus become merely the personification of an impersonal fatal
force that can, within the fiction of the genre, be humanized and
thus defeated. Revengers attempt, in Robert Watson's words,
to 'convert the villain into a scapegoat for mortality itself' in an
'absurd version of homeopathic medicine – death curing death'.[14]
Many of the images of revenge tragedies recall the visual iconography of the *danse macabre*, in which Death, a grimly jovial
skeleton, twines implacably among the living as they feast or
embrace: the bony sentinels of *The Tragedy of Hoffman*, for
example, or the skulls of Gloriana and Yorick, or the festivities
usurped by mortality in *Antonio's Revenge* and *The Spanish Tragedy*. Just as sixteenth-century medics explored the body's hidden
mysteries in the new science of anatomy, and just as contemporary
divines explored the *ars moriendi*, or art of dying well, so too the
stage, in its unflinching depiction of mortality, approached existential questions of life, death and the inexplicable passage between.

The understanding of these issues in the drama is visceral. First
Otho, then Ferdinand and finally Hoffman in *The Tragedy of
Hoffman* narrate the physiological processes of their dying. Hamlet's preoccupation with the fate of the soul after death does not
preclude an abiding interest in the vermiculating or decaying
body: the murdered courtier Corambis is 'At supper, not where
he is eating, but / Where he is eaten: a certain company of politic
worms are even now at him' (11). But revenge, too, and its companion emotion grief are seen as physiological. Antonio, impatient
with his courtiers' attempts at stoical comfort, demands:

> Are thy moist entrails crumpled up with grief
> Of parching mischiefs? Tell me, does thy heart
> With punching anguish spur thy galled ribs? (1.5)

Hieronimo experiences his grief as a sympathetic injury: 'They murdered me that made these fatal marks' (4.4), and, indeed, the life of the revenger is itself usually sacrificed to his quest. If revengers make themselves resemble their victims, they usually also become their own final victims. Vindice recognizes, having given away their plots to a horrified Antonio at the end of *The Revenger's Tragedy*, that ''Tis time to die, when we ourselves our foes' (5.3), and the logic of the genre makes it clear that he should not survive his crimes. Only Antonio of *Antonio's Revenge* outlives his vengeance, vowing a 'virgin bed' as he continues to mourn for his lost love (5.6).

In ending the play, Antonio also acknowledges its theatricality, closing the 'last act' of his own revenge and bidding any future playwright who would attempt to write about Mellida to present 'some black tragedy': 'may his style be decked / With freshest blooms of purest elegance'. The self-reflexive turn at the end of the play is clear in its references to Marston's own highly unusual vocabulary. Revenge tragedies exhibit a high degree of self-consciousness, both about their own theatrical status and about previous plays in the genre. Hoffman gleefully describes the murder of Otho as 'but the prologue to the ensuing play'; when the stoical Pandulpho asks rhetorically, 'Would'st have me cry, run raving up and down. / For my son's loss?' (1.5), the recollection is of Hieronimo mourning Horatio; Vindice uses the prop of the skull to quote Hamlet's most iconic moment in the graveyard; Antonio, like Hamlet and Hieronimo, enters reading a book. When the young actor playing Balurdo in *Antonio's Revenge* enters with his beard half off, he recalls Balthazar preparing for the playlet in 'Soliman and Perseda' at the end of *The Spanish Tragedy*. What has changed, however, is that in Kyd's play the character Balthazar is playing an actor at this point, putting on a beard to play the Turkish emperor Soliman. In *Antonio's Revenge* there is no such intermediary: Balurdo's imperfect costume is to play – to *be* – Balurdo himself, and thus we cannot suppress the knowledge that this is a play. Writing of the studio system in the classic Hollywood period – perhaps our nearest analogy to the commercial world of the early modern theatre – Thomas Schatz discusses a 'genre's

progression from transparency to opacity – from straightfor-
ward storytelling to self-conscious formalism' as a way in which
it can 'evaluate its very status as a popular form'.[15] Revenge
tragedy, that is to say, becomes more opaque, more self-conscious,
more knowing, and to an extent that is indeed what happens to
this type of play in the fifteen or so years between *The Spanish
Tragedy* and *The Revenger's Tragedy*. When Vindice calls for
thunder to accompany his deeds, he knows he is operating
within a fictional genre and has no identity outside it (Vindice =
revenge). As Susan Sontag's celebrated 'Notes on Camp' recognizes, he understands 'Being-as-Playing-a-Role': one of the key
elements of a camp aesthetic is 'love of the unnatural: of artifice
and exaggeration',[16] and it is a love fully embraced by Vindice
and the play.

But early modern revenge tragedy was, from its outset,
marked by an affinity between retribution and theatre. Kerrigan
notes that the sequence action + revenge is one of the simplest
units of drama, and Hieronimo, as author of 'Soliman and
Perseda', is only the most literal version of the thoroughgoing
equivalence between revenger and playwright. As 'surrogate
artist', the revenger excels in designing and executing his own
play-within-a-play, from Hamlet's 'The Mousetrap' to the usurped
accession rites of Lussurioso at the end of *The Revenger's Tragedy*.[17] And just as revenge plays create their own internal
tension through the chain of action and retaliation, so the series of plays within the genre are interconnected as dramatic
acts of (sometimes violent) statement and response. *Antonio's
Revenge* darkens the comic ending of *Antonio and Mellida* just
as the anonymous prequel to *The Spanish Tragedy*, *The First
Part of Jeronimo*, sought to excavate a happier past for Andrea
and Bel-imperia. *Hamlet (1603)* discusses different acting styles
and acknowledges, in a topical reference, that audiences 'are
turned to private plays, / And to the humour of children' (7) – the
Children at St Paul's performing the similar and contemporaneous *Antonio's Revenge*. Quarrels between different theatre
companies over the performing rights to the popular *The Spanish Tragedy*, and the tit-for-tat writing sequence of additional
passages to this old stager in response to *Hamlet*, *Antonio's*

Revenge and *The Tragedy of Hoffman* (see Chronology) impli-
cate the revenge tragedy genre in the rivalries of the commercial
theatre and turn its stock vengeance plot into a metaphor for
dramatic competition. The so-called Wars of the Theatres, a
sequence of connected, antagonistic plays by different writers
for different companies, turn revenge plot into dramatic rivalry,
or vice versa. In Ben Jonson's *Poetaster* (1601) Marston is rep-
resented by the character Crispinus, who, in a dramatically apt
form of restitution for his linguistic crimes familiar from the
revenge tragedy genre, is forced to vomit up some of his newly
coined words. If Hieronimo used theatre as a vehicle for his
revenge in the Spanish court, so later writers use revenge as a
vehicle for theatre. The self-consciousness always associated
with revenge tragedy becomes an end in itself, an intense,
knowing meditation on the power of theatre to create fictions
of being, agency and control.

NOTES

1. John Kerrigan, *Revenge Tragedy: Aeschylus to Armageddon*
   (1996), p. 28.
2. Francis Bacon, *The Essays*, ed. John Pitcher (1985), p. 72.
3. Fredson Bowers, *Elizabethan Revenge Tragedy, 1587–1642* (1940),
   p. 11.
4. Eric Hobsbawn, *Bandits*, new edn (2001).
5. Kerrigan, *Revenge Tragedy*, p. 6.
6. Robert Warshow, *The Immediate Experience* (1962), p. 130.
7. T. S. Eliot, Introduction, in *Seneca his Tenne Tragedies* (1927),
   p. xxv.
8. Lorna Hutson, *The Invention of Suspicion: Law and Mimesis in
   Shakespeare and Renaissance Drama* (2007), especially chapter 6.
9. Hobsbawn, *Bandits*, p. 29.
10. Peter Marshall, *Beliefs and the Dead in Reformation England*
    (2002), p. 188.
11. Robert N. Watson, *The Rest is Silence: Death as Annihilation in
    the English Renaissance* (1994), p. 4.
12. Bacon, *Essays*, p. 73.
13. Thomas Anderson, *Performing Early Modern Trauma from
    Shakespeare to Milton* (2006), p. 127.

14. Watson, *Rest is Silence*, p. 56.
15. Thomas Schatz, *Hollywood Genres: Formulas, Filmmaking and the Studio System* (1981), p. 38.
16. Susan Sontag, 'Notes on Camp', in *Against Interpretation and Other Essays* (2009), pp. 280, 275.
17. Kerrigan, *Revenge Tragedy*, pp. 4, 17.

Further Reading

John Kerrigan's *Revenge Tragedy: Aeschylus to Armageddon* (1996) ranges with lucid erudition from Greek tragedy to Sherlock Holmes, via *Hamlet* and *The Spanish Tragedy*. More specifically on early modern drama is Michael Neill's *Issues of Death: Mortality and Identity in English Renaissance Tragedy* (1997), which develops the compelling thesis that 'tragedy ... was among the principal instruments by which the culture of early modern England reinvented death' (p. 3). Thomas Rist's *Revenge Tragedy and the Drama of Commemoration in Reforming England* (2008) focuses the association, making revenge tragedy in particular a ritual of mourning and remembrance. For a collection of critical essays, including important work on gender and sexuality, see Stevie Simkin (ed.), *New Casebooks: Revenge Tragedy* (2001). Janet Clare's *Revenge Tragedies of the Renaissance* (2006) includes a number of plays not in this volume, and is recommended as a guide to further exploration.

The Spanish Tragedy

Dillon, Janette, 'The Spanish Tragedy and Staging Languages in Renaissance Drama', *Research Opportunities in Renaissance Drama* 34 (1995), 14–40.

Erne, Lukas, *Beyond the Spanish Tragedy: A Study of the Works of Thomas Kyd* (2001).

Griffin, Eric, 'Nationalism, the Black Legend, and the Revised *Spanish Tragedy*', *English Literary Renaissance* 39:2 (2009), 336–70.

Hartley, Andrew James, 'Social Consciousness: Spaces for Characters in *The Spanish Tragedy*', *Cahiers Elisabéthains* 58 (2000), 1–14.

Semenza, Gregory M., '*The Spanish Tragedy* and Metatheatre', in Emma Smith and Garrett J. Sullivan (eds.), *The Cambridge Companion to English Renaissance Tragedy* (2010).

Watson, Robert N., *The Rest is Silence: Death as Annihilation in the English Renaissance* (1994), chapter 2.

Antonio's Revenge

Ayres, Philip J., 'Marston's *Antonio's Revenge*: The Morality of the Revenging Hero', *Studies in English Literature, 1500–1900* 12:2 (1972), 359–74.

Baines, Barbara J., '*Antonio's Revenge*: Marston's Play on Revenge Plays', *Studies in English Literature, 1500–1900* 23:2 (1983), 277–94.

Burnett, Mark Thornton, ' "I Will Not Swell like a Tragedian": Marston's *Antonio's Revenge* in Performance', *Neuphilologische Mitteilungen* 90 (1989), 311–20.

Loewenstein, Joseph, 'Marston's Gorge and the Question of Formalism', in Mark David Rasmussen (ed.), *Renaissance Literature and Its Formal Engagements* (2002), pp. 89–114.

Spinrad, Phoebe S., 'The Sacralization of Revenge in *Antonio's Revenge*', *Comparative Drama* 39:2 (2005), 169–85.

Hamlet (1603)

Clayton, Thomas (ed.), *The 'Hamlet' First Published (Q1, 1603): Origins, Form, Intertextualities* (1992).

Irace, Kathleen O., *The First Quarto of Hamlet* (1998).

Sams, Eric, 'Taboo or Not Taboo? The Text, Dating and Authorship of *Hamlet*, 1589–1623', *Hamlet Studies* 10 (1988), 12–46.

Thompson, Ann, and Neil Taylor, *William Shakespeare: Hamlet*, 2 vols. (1995).

The Tragedy of Hoffman

Brucher, Richard, 'Piracy and Parody in Chettle's *Hoffman*', *Ben Jonson Journal* 6 (1999), 209–22.
Jowett, John (ed.), *Henry Chettle: The Tragedy of Hoffman* (1983).
Pesta, Duke, 'Articulating Skeletons: Hamlet, Hoffman, and the Anatomical Graveyard', *Cahiers Elisabéthains* 69 (2006), 21–39.

The Revenger's Tragedy

Coddon, Karin S., ' "For Show or Useless Property": Necrophilia and *The Revenger's Tragedy*', *English Literary History* 61 (1994), 71–88 (reprinted in Simkin, *New Casebooks: Revenge Tragedy.*)
Dollimore, Jonathan, *Radical Tragedy: Religion, Ideology and Power in the Drama of Shakespeare and his Contemporaries* (1984), chapter 9.
McMillin, Scott, 'Acting and Violence: *The Revenger's Tragedy* and Its Departures from *Hamlet*', *Studies in English Literature* 24:2 (1984), 275–91.
Mullaney, Steven, 'Mourning and Misogyny: *Hamlet, The Revenger's Tragedy*, and the Final Progress of Elizabeth I, 1600–1607', *Shakespeare Quarterly* 45 (1994), 139–62.

Note on the Texts

This is intended as a reader's, rather than a scholar's, edition. The plays are printed according to my estimate of their chronological order. While they have been newly edited from the earliest printed texts, I have tried to strike a balance between readability and excessive intervention. Spelling has been silently modernized, punctuation only lightly changed, and the few substantive emendations are all indicated in the notes, where 'Q' signals a reading from the first text. Stage directions in square brackets are my additions: I have kept these to a minimum to preserve the flexibility of performance choices. For ease of understanding I have added '[*Aside*]', even though it rarely appears in early modern printed plays and can seem to superimpose a normative, realist stage architecture on to the different spatial imagination of Elizabethan and Jacobean theatres. Also, I have added a list of characters, now conventional but rarely provided in printed plays from this period. I have not undertaken any relineation to regularize the appearance of the texts.

Notes acknowledge at least some of my significant and grateful debts to the plays' previous editors, as listed below. I have made grateful use of Emily Wilson's excellent translations in her *Seneca: Six Tragedies* (2010). Translations are from Latin, unless the language is otherwise specified.

The Spanish Tragedy

Edited from the earliest quarto, which is undated but generally assumed, following the entry in the Stationers' Register, to be 1592. Previous editions by Frederick S. Boas, *The Works of*

Thomas Kyd (Oxford: Clarendon Press, 1955), Philip Edwards, *The Spanish Tragedy* (Manchester: Revels Plays/Manchester University Press, 1959), and J. R. Mulryne, *The Spanish Tragedy* (London: New Mermaids/Benn, 1970; 2nd edn, 1989).

Hamlet (1603)

Edited from the 1603 quarto in the British Library. Previous editions by Graham Holderness and Bryan Loughrey, *The Tragicall Historie of Hamlet Prince of Denmarke* (Hemel Hempstead: Harvester Wheatsheaf, 1992), Kathleen O. Irace, *The First Quarto of Hamlet* (Cambridge: Cambridge University Press, 1998), and Ann Thompson and Neil Taylor, *Hamlet*, 2 vols. (London: Arden Shakespeare, 2006).

Antonio's Revenge

Edited from the 1602 quarto. Previous editions by G. K. Hunter, *Antonio's Revenge* (Lincoln, Nebraska: Regents Renaissance Drama, 1965), and W. Reavley Gair, *Antonio's Revenge* (Manchester: Revels Plays/Manchester University Press, 1978).

The Tragedy of Hoffman

Edited from the 1631 quarto. Previous editions by Harold Jenkins, *The Tragedy of Hoffman* (London: Malone Society Reprints, 1951), and John Jowett, *The Tragedy of Hoffman* (Nottingham: Nottingham Drama Texts, 1983).

The Revenger's Tragedy

Edited from the uncorrected and corrected states of the 1607/8 quarto. Previous editions by Brian Gibbons, *The Revenger's Tragedy* (London: Ernest Benn, 1967; 2nd edn, 1989), R. A. Foakes, *The Revenger's Tragedy* (Manchester: Revels Plays/Manchester University Press, 1980), and MacDonald P. Jackson for *Thomas Middleton: The Collected Works*, ed. Gary Taylor and John Lavagnino (Oxford: Clarendon Press, 2007).

THOMAS KYD

THE SPANISH TRAGEDY

LIST OF CHARACTERS

GHOST *of Don Andrea*
REVENGE
KING *of Spain*
Ciprian *duke of* CASTILE, *his brother*
LORENZO *son of Ciprian*
CHRISTOPHIL *Lorenzo's servant*
BEL-IMPERIA *daughter of Ciprian*
PEDRINGANO *her servant*
GENERAL
VICEROY *of Portugal*
BALTHAZAR *his son*
SERBERINE *Balthazar's servant*
ALEXANDRO
VILLUPPO
AMBASSADOR *of Portugal*
HIERONIMO *knight marshal of Spain*
ISABELLA *his wife*
HORATIO *his son*
PAGE
3 WATCHMEN
MAID
DEPUTY
HANGMAN
2 PORTINGALES
BAZULTO *an old man*
Citizens, Attendants, Halberdiers, Noblemen, Servant

ACT 1

Scene 1

Enter the Ghost of Andrea, and with him Revenge.

Ghost. When this eternal substance of my soul
  Did live imprisoned in my wanton flesh,
  Each in their function serving other's need,
  I was a courtier in the Spanish court.
  My name was Don Andrea, my descent,
  Though not ignoble, yet inferior far
  To gracious fortunes of my tender youth:
  For there in prime and pride of all my years,
  By duteous service and deserving love,
  In secret I possessed a worthy dame,   10
  Which hight sweet Bel-imperia by name.
  But in the harvest of my summer joys,
  Death's winter nipped the blossoms of my bliss,
  Forcing divorce betwixt my love and me.
  For in the late conflict with Portingale,
  My valour drew me into danger's mouth.
  Till life to death made passage through my wounds.
  When I was slain, my soul descended straight
  To pass the flowing stream of Acheron:
  But churlish Charon, only boatman there,   20
  Said that my rites of burial not performed,
  I might not sit among his passengers.
  Ere Sol had slept three nights on Thetis' lap,
  And slaked his smoking chariot in her flood:
  By Don Horatio our knight marshal's son,

11 *hight*: was called
19 *Acheron*: river of the lower world. The description of the underworld here is derived from Virgil's *Aeneid*, Book VI
20 *Charon*: ferryman across the River Styx in the underworld
23 *Sol*: the sun   *Thetis*: daughter of the sea god Nereus
25 *knight marshal*: officer in the English royal household with jurisdiction within 12 miles (20 km) of the palace

My funerals and obsequies were done.
Then was the ferryman of hell content
To pass me over to the slimy strond,
That leads to fell Avernus' ugly waves:
30   There pleasing Cerberus with honied speech,
I passed the perils of the foremost porch,
Not far from hence amidst ten thousand souls,
Sat Minos, Aeacus and Rhadamanth,
To whom no sooner 'gan I make approach,
To crave a passport for my wandering ghost,
But Minos' engraven leaves of lottery,
Drew forth the manner of my life and death.
'This knight,' quoth he, 'both lived and died in love:
And for his love tried fortune of the wars.
40   And by wars' fortune lost both love and life.'
'Why then,' said Aeacus, 'convey him hence,
To walk with lovers in our fields of love,
And spend the course of everlasting time,
Under green myrtle trees and cypress shades.'
'No, no,' said Rhadamanth, 'it were not well,
With loving souls to place a martialist:
He died in war, and must to martial fields
Where wounded Hector lives in lasting pain,
And Achilles' Myrmidons do scour the plain.'
50   Then Minos, mildest censor of the three,
Made this device to end the difference.
'Send him,' quoth he, 'to our infernal king
To doom him as best seems his majesty.'
To this effect my passport straight was drawn.
In keeping on my way to Pluto's court,
Through dreadful shades of ever-glooming night,

28 *strond*: strand, shore
29 *fell*: savage   *Avernus*: lake entrance to the underworld
30 *Cerberus*: three-headed guard dog of the underworld
33 *Minos, Aeacus and Rhadamanth*: judges of the underworld
36 *leaves of lottery*: in Virgil, lots were drawn to judge the destination of the
dead in the underworld
46 *martialist*: soldier   49 *Myrmidons*: Achilles' followers in Homer's *Iliad*
49 *scour*: move quickly   55 *Pluto*: king of the underworld

I saw more sights than thousand tongues can tell,
Or pens can write, or mortal hearts can think.
Three ways there were: that on the right-hand side
Was ready way unto the foresaid fields   60
Where lovers live and bloody martialists,
But either sort contained within his bounds.
The left-hand path declining fearfully,
Was ready downfall to the deepest hell,
Where bloody Furies shake their whips of steel,
And poor Ixion turns an endless wheel;
Where usurers are choked with melting gold,
And wantons are embraced with ugly snakes,
And murderers groan with never-killing wounds,
And perjured wights scalded in boiling lead,   70
And all foul sins with torments overwhelmed.
'Twixt these two ways, I trod the middle path,
Which brought me to the fair Elysian green,
In midst whereof there stands a stately tower,
The walls of brass, the gates of adamant.
Here finding Pluto with his Proserpine,
I showed my passport humbled on my knee;
Whereat fair Proserpine began to smile,
And begged that only she might give my doom.
Pluto was pleased and sealed it with a kiss.   80
Forthwith, Revenge, she rounded thee in th'ear,
And bade thee lead me through the gates of horn,
Where bad dreams have passage in the silent night.
No sooner had she spoke but we were here,
I wot not how, in twinkling of an eye.

65 *Furies*: in Greek mythology, the angry avengers of crimes
66 *Ixion*: punished by Zeus for lusting after his wife Hera, by being bound
to an ever-spinning wheel
67 *usurers*: money lenders   70 *wights*: men
73 *Elysian*: Elysium was the resting place for heroes and the virtuous
75 *adamant*: hard stone or diamond
76 *Proserpine*: Pluto's consort, also known as Persephone
79 *doom*: judgement
82 *gates of horn*: in the *Aeneid*, the entrance for true visions or dreams
85 *wot*: know

Revenge. Then know, Andrea, that thou art arrived
 Where thou shalt see the author of thy death,
 Don Balthazar, the prince of Portingale,
 Deprived of life by Bel-imperia:
90 Here sit we down to see the mystery,
 And serve for Chorus in this tragedy.

[ACT 1

Scene 2]

Enter Spanish King, General, Castile, Hieronimo.

King. Now say, lord general, how fares our camp?
General. All well, my sovereign liege, except some few
 That are deceased by fortune of the war.
King. But what portends thy cheerful countenance,
 And posting to our presence thus in haste?
 Speak man, hath fortune given us victory?
General. Victory, my liege, and that with little loss.
King. Our Portingales will pay us tribute then.
General. Tribute and wonted homage therewithal.
10 *King.* Then blest be heaven, and guider of the heavens,
 From whose fair influence such justice flows.
Castile. *O multum dilecte Deo, tibi militat aether,*
 Et conjuratae curvato poplite gentes
 Succumbunt: recti soror est victoria juris.
King. Thanks to my loving brother of Castile.
 But general, unfold in brief discourse
 Your form of battle and your war's success,
 That adding all the pleasure of thy news

90 *mystery*: hidden or secret thing 1 *camp*: army
8 *tribute*: 'tax . . . in acknowledgement of submission' (*OED*)
12–14 *O multum . . . juris*: address derived from Roman poet Claudian:
'O one much loved of God, for thee the heavens contend, and the united
peoples fall down on bended knee: victory is sister to just right' (Boas)

Unto the height of former happiness,
With deeper wage and greater dignity,   20
We may reward thy blissful chivalry.
General. Where Spain and Portingale do jointly knit
  Their frontiers, leaning on each other's bound,
  There met our armies in their proud array:
  Both furnished well, both full of hope and fear,
  Both menacing alive with daring shows,
  Both vaunting sundry colours of device,
  Both cheerly sounding trumpets, drums and fifes,
  Both raising dreadful clamours to the sky,
  That valleys, hills and rivers made rebound,   30
  And heaven itself was frighted with the sound.
  Our battles both were pitched in squadron form,
  Each corner strongly fenced with wings of shot,
  But ere we joined and came to push of pike,
  I brought a squadron of our readiest shot
  From out our rearward to begin the fight.
  They brought another wing to encounter us:
  Meanwhile our ordnance played on either side,
  And captains strove to have their valours tried.
  Don Pedro, their chief horsemen's colonel   40
  Did with his cornet bravely make attempt,
  To break the order of our battle ranks.
  But Don Rogero, worthy man of war
  Marched forth against him with our musketeers,
  And stopped the malice of his fell approach.
  While they maintain hot skirmish to and fro,
  Both battles join and fall to handy blows,
  Their violent shot resembling th'ocean's rage,
  When roaring loud and with a swelling tide,

---

20 *deeper wage*: more reward   21 *chivalry*: gallant horsemanship
23 *bound*: border   27 *colours*: flags or banners
30 *rebound*: echo   32 *squadron form*: square formation
33 *wings of shot*: armed troops on the outside of the formation
34 *push of pike*: close combat   38 *ordnance*: artillery
41 *cornet*: wing of soldiers   47 *handy*: hand-to-hand

50   It beats upon the rampiers of huge rocks,
     And gapes to swallow neighbour-bounding lands.
     Now while Bellona rageth here and there,
     Thick storms of bullets rain like winter's hail,
     And shivered lances dark the troubled air.
        Pede pes and cuspide cuspis,
        Arma sonant armis, vir petiturque viro.
     On every side drop captains to the ground,
     And soldiers, some ill-maimed, some slain outright:
     Here falls a body scindered from his head;
60   There legs and arms lie bleeding on the grass,
     Mingled with weapons and unbowelled steeds,
     That scattering overspread the purple plain.
     In all this turmoil three long hours and more,
     The victory to neither part inclined,
     Till Don Andrea with his brave lanciers,
     In their main battle made so great a breach,
     That half dismayed, the multitude retired:
     But Balthazar the Portingales' young prince,
     Brought rescue and encouraged them to stay.
70   Here-hence the fight was eagerly renewed,
     And in that conflict was Andrea slain:
     Brave man-at-arms, but weak to Balthazar.
     Yet while the prince insulting over him
     Breathed out proud vaunts, sounding to our reproach,
     Friendship and hardy valour joined in one,
     Pricked forth Horatio our knight marshal's son,
     To challenge that prince in single fight.

50 *rampiers*: ramparts   52 *Bellona*: Roman goddess of war
53 *rain*: Q ran   54 *shivered*: shattered
55–6 *Pede pes . . . viro*: 'Foot against foot, spear against spear, arms clash on
arms and man is assailed by man' (not a direct quotation: Boas notes sources
in Virgil and Curtius)
56 *Arma*: Q *Anni*   *armis*: Q *annis*
59 *scindered*: sundered   61 *unbowelled*: disembowelled
62 *purple*: blood-soaked   70 *Here-hence*: As a result
73 *insulting*: scornfully triumphing over
74 *vaunts*: brags   76 *Pricked forth*: Spurred on

Not long between these twain the fight endured,
But straight the prince was beaten from his horse,
And forced to yield him prisoner to his foe.   80
When he was taken, all the rest they fled,
And our carbines pursued them to the death,
Till Phoebus waning to the western deep,
Our trumpeters were charged to sound retreat.
King. Thanks, good lord general, for these good news.
And for some argument of more to come,
Take this, and wear it for thy sovereign's sake.
     Give him his chain.
But tell me now, hast thou confirmed a peace?
General. No peace, my liege, but peace conditional,
That if with homage tribute be well paid.   90
The fury of your forces will be stayed.
And to this peace their viceroy hath subscribed.
     Give the King a paper.
And made a solemn vow that during life,
His tribute shall be truly paid to Spain.
King. These words, these deeds, become thy person well.
But now knight marshal, frolic with thy king,
For 'tis thy son that wins this battle's prize.
Hieronimo. Long may he live to serve my sovereign liege,
And soon decay unless he serve my liege.
     A tucket afar off.
King. Not thou nor he shall die without reward.   100
What means this warning of this trumpet's sound?
General. This tells me that your grace's men of war,
Such as war's fortune hath reserved from death,
Come marching on towards your royal seat,
To show themselves before your majesty,
For so I gave in charge at my depart.
Whereby by demonstration shall appear,
That all (except three hundred or few more)

---

82 *carbines*: cavalry
83 *Phoebus*: the sun   *waning*: Q wauing   86 *argument*: token
96 *frolic*: rejoice   99 *tucket*: trumpet flourish instructing troops to march

Are safe returned, and by their foes enriched.

The army enters, Balthazar, between Lorenzo
and Horatio, captive.

110 *King.* A gladsome sight, I long to see them here.

They enter and pass by.

Was that the warlike prince of Portingale,
That by our nephew was in triumph led?

General. It was, my liege, the prince of Portingale.

King. But what was he that on the other side,
Held him by th'arm as partner of the prize?

Hieronimo. That was my son, my gracious sovereign,
Of whom, though from his tender infancy
My loving thoughts did never hope but well,
He never pleased his father's eyes till now,
120 Nor filled my heart with overcloying joys.

King. Go let them march once more about these walls.
That staying them we may confer and talk
With our brave prisoner and his double guard.
Hieronimo, it greatly pleaseth us,
That in our victory thou have a share,
By virtue of thy worthy son's exploit.

Enter [the army] again.

Bring hither the young prince of Portingale,
The rest march on, but ere they be dismissed,
We will bestow on every soldier two ducats,
130 And on every leader ten, that they may know
Our largess welcomes them.

Exeunt [army].

Welcome, Don Balthazar, welcome nephew,
And thou, Horatio, thou art welcome too.
Young prince, though thy father's hard misdeeds
In keeping back the tribute that he owes
Deserve but evil measure at our hands,
Yet shalt thou know that Spain is honourable.

120 *overcloying*: excessively moving   122 *staying*: stopping
131 *largess*: generosity

Balthazar. The trespass that my father made in peace,
   Is now controlled by fortune of the wars:
   And cards once dealt, it boots not ask why so.   140
   His men are slain, a weakening to his realm,
   His colours seized, a blot unto his name,
   His son distressed, a corsive to his heart,
   These punishments may clear his late offence.
King. Ay, Balthazar, if he observe this truce
   Our peace will grow the stronger for these wars:
   Meanwhile live thou, though not in liberty,
   Yet free from bearing any servile yoke.
   For in our hearing thy deserts were great,
   And in our sight thyself art gracious.   150
Balthazar. And I shall study to deserve this grace.
King. But tell me, for their holding makes me doubt,
   To which of these twain art thou prisoner?
Lorenzo. To me, my liege.
Horatio. To me, my sovereign.
Lorenzo. This hand first took his courser by the reins.
Horatio. But first my lance did put him from his horse.
Lorenzo. I seized his weapon and enjoyed it first.
Horatio. But first I forced him lay his weapons down.
King. Let go his arm upon our privilege.   160
     Let him go.
   Say worthy prince, to whether didst thou yield?
Balthazar. To him in courtesy, to this perforce;
   He spake me fair, this other gave me strokes;
   He promised life, this other threatened death;
   He won my love, this other conquered me;
   And truth to say, I yield myself to both.
Hieronimo. But that I know your grace for just and wise,
   And might seem partial in this difference,
   Enforced by nature and by law of arms,

---

140 *boots*: profits   142 *colours*: standards   143 *corsive*: corrosive
156 *courser*: horse   160 *privilege*: sovereign authority   161 *whether*: which
168 *partial*: biased   *difference*: disagreement

170   My tongue should plead for young Horatio's right.
      He hunted well that was a lion's death.
      Not he that in a garment wore his skin:
      So hares may pull dead lions by the beard.
King. Content thee marshal, thou shalt have no wrong,
      And for thy sake thy son shall want no right.
      Will both abide the censure of my doom?
Lorenzo. I crave no better than your grace awards.
Horatio. Nor I, although I sit beside my right.
King. Then by my judgement thus your strife shall end,
180   You both deserve and both shall have reward.
      Nephew, thou took'st his weapon and his horse,
      His weapons and his horse are thy reward.
      Horatio, thou didst force him first to yield.
      His ransom therefore is thy valour's fee:
      Appoint the sum as you shall both agree.
      But nephew, thou shalt have the prince in guard,
      For thine estate befitteth such a guest.
      Horatio's house were small for all his train,
      Yet in regard thy substance passeth his,
190   And that just guerdon may befall desert,
      To him we yield the armour of the prince.
      How likes Don Balthazar of this device?
Balthazar. Right well my liege, if this proviso were,
      That Don Horatio bear us company,
      Whom I admire and love for chivalry.
King. Horatio, leave him not that loves thee so.
      Now let us hence to see our soldiers paid,
      And feast our prisoner as our friendly guest.
          Exeunt.

---

171 *lion's death*: proverbial, 'the braver hunter is the one to kill the lion,
rather than simply wear his pelt'
176 *censure*: judgement
178 *sit beside*: possibly set aside, forgo (Edwards)
190 *guerdon*: reward

[ACT 1

Scene 3]

Enter Viceroy, Alexandro, Villuppo.

Viceroy. Is our ambassador dispatched for Spain?
Alexandro. Two days, my liege, are past since his depart.
Viceroy. And tribute payment gone along with him?
Alexandro. Ay, my good lord.
Viceroy. Then rest we here a while in our unrest,
   And feed our sorrows with some inward sighs,
   For deepest cares break never into tears.
   But wherefore sit I in a regal throne?
   This better fits a wretch's endless moan.
   Yet this is higher than my fortunes reach,   10
   And therefore better than my state deserves.
    Falls to the ground.
   Ay, ay, this earth, image of melancholy,
   Seeks him whom fates adjudge to misery:
   Here let me lie, now am I at the lowest,
    Qui jacet in terra, non habet unde cadat.
    In me consumpsit vires fortuna nocendo,
    Nil superest ut jam possit obesse magis.
   Yes, Fortune may bereave me of my crown:
   Here take it now; let Fortune do her worst,
   She will not rob me of this sable weed.   20
   O no, she envies none but pleasant things,
   Such is the folly of despiteful chance.
   Fortune is blind and sees not my deserts,

15–17 *Qui jacet . . . magis*: collage from Alanus de Insulis, Seneca and Kyd's
own composition: 'If one lies on the ground, one has no further to fall;
towards me Fortune has exhausted her power to injure; there is nothing more
that can happen to me'
20 *sable weed*: black clothing   22 *despiteful*: cruel
23 *blind*: the visual iconography of Fortune had her blind (thus indifferent to
merit) and standing on a rolling stone (thus mutable)

So is she deaf and hears not my laments;
And could she hear, yet is she wilful mad,
And therefore will not pity my distress.
Suppose that she could pity me, what then?
What help can be expected at her hands,
Whose foot standing on a rolling stone,
30   And mind more mutable than fickle winds?
Why wail I then where's hope of no redress?
O yes, complaining makes my grief seem less.
My late ambition hath distained my faith,
My breach of faith occasioned bloody wars,
Those bloody wars have spent my treasure,
And with my treasure my people's blood,
And with their blood, my joy and best beloved,
My best beloved, my sweet and only son.
O wherefore went I not to war myself?
40   The cause was mine, I might have died for both:
My years were mellow, his but young and green,
My death were natural, but his was forced.
Alexandro. No doubt my liege, but still the prince survives.
Viceroy. Survives? Ay where?
Alexandro. In Spain, a prisoner by mischance of war.
Viceroy. Then have they slain him for his father's fault.
Alexandro. That were a breach to common law of arms.
Viceroy. They reck no laws that meditate revenge.
Alexandro. His ransom's worth will stay from foul revenge.
50   *Viceroy.* No, if he lived, the news would soon be here.
Alexandro. Nay, evil news fly faster still than good.
Viceroy. Tell me no more of news, for he is dead.
Villuppo. My sovereign, pardon the author of ill news,
And I'll bewray the fortune of thy son.
Viceroy. Speak on, I'll guerdon thee whate'er it be,
Mine ear is ready to receive ill news,
My heart grows hard 'gainst mischief's battery.
Stand up I say and tell thy tale at large.

33 *distained*: sullied   48 *reck*: care for
54 *bewray*: reveal   57 *mischief*: misfortune

Villuppo. Then hear that truth which these mine eyes have seen.
  When both the armies were in battle joined,   60
  Don Balthazar, amidst the thickest troops,
  To win renown did wondrous feats of arms:
  Amongst the rest I saw him hand to hand
  In single fight with their lord general.
  Till Alexandro that here counterfeits
  Under the colour of a duteous friend,
  Discharged his pistol at the prince's back,
  As though he would have slain their general.
  But therewithal Don Balthazar fell down:
  And when he fell then we began to fly,   70
  But had he lived the day had sure been ours.
Alexandro. O wicked forgery! O traitorous miscreant!
Viceroy. Hold thou thy peace! But now Villuppo say,
  Where then became the carcass of my son?
Villuppo. I saw them drag it to the Spanish tents.
Viceroy. Ay, ay, my nightly dreams have told me this:
  Thou false, unkind, unthankful, traitorous beast,
  Wherein had Balthazar offended thee,
  That thou shouldst thus betray him to our foes?
  Was't Spanish gold that bleared so thine eyes,   80
  That thou could'st see no part of our deserts?
  Perchance because thou art Terceira's lord,
  Thou hadst some hope to wear this diadem,
  If first my son and then myself were slain:
  But thy ambitious thought shall break thy neck.
  Ay, this was it that made thee spill his blood
    Take the crown and put it on again.
  But I'll now wear it till thy blood be spilt.
Alexandro. Vouchsafe, dread sovereign, to hear me speak.
Viceroy. Away with him, his sight is second hell.
                            [Exit Alexandro.]
  Keep him till we determine of his death;   90
  If Balthazar be dead, he shall not live.
  Villuppo, follow us for thy reward.   *Exit Viceroy.*

82 *Terceira*: an island in the Azores

Villuppo. Thus have I with an envious, forged tale
　　Deceived the king, betrayed mine enemy,
　　And hope for guerdon of my villainy.　　*Exit.*

[ACT 1

Scene 4]

Enter Horatio and Bel-imperia.

Bel-imperia. Signior Horatio, this is the place and hour,
　　Wherein I must entreat thee to relate
　　The circumstances of Don Andrea's death,
　　Who, living, was my garland's sweetest flower,
　　And in his death hath buried my delights.
Horatio. For love of him and service to yourself,
　　I nill refuse this heavy doleful charge,
　　Yet tears and sighs, I fear, will hinder me.
　　When both our armies were enjoined in fight,
10　　Your worthy chevalier amidst the thick'st,
　　For glorious cause still aiming at the fairest,
　　Was at the last by young Don Balthazar
　　Encountered hand to hand: their fight was long,
　　Their hearts were great, their clamours menacing,
　　Their strength alike, their strokes both dangerous.
　　But wrathful Nemesis that wicked power,
　　Envying at Andrea's praise and worth,
　　Cut short his life to end his praise and worth.
　　She, she herself disguised in armour's mask,
20　　(As Pallas was before proud Pergamus)
　　Brought in a fresh supply of halberdiers,

93 *envious*: malicious　7 *nill*: will not
10 *chevalier*: gallant　11 *glorious cause*: for love of Bel-imperia
16 *Nemesis*: goddess of divine retribution
20 *Pallas*: Pallas Athene, goddess patron of Athens　*Pergamus*: Troy
21 *halberdiers*: soldiers armed with halberds or long spears mounted with axes

Which pauncht his horse and dinged him to the ground.
Then young Don Balthazar with ruthless rage,
Taking advantage of his foe's distress,
Did finish what his halberdiers begun,
And left not till Andrea's life was done.
Then, though too late, incensed with just remorse,
I with my band set forth against the prince,
And brought him prisoner from his halberdiers.
Bel-imperia. Would thou had slain him that so slew my love.   30
    But then was Don Andrea's carcass lost?
Horatio. No, that was it for which I chiefly strove,
    Nor stepped I back till I recovered him.
    I took him up and wound him in mine arms,
    And welding him unto my private tent,
    There laid him down and dewed him with my tears,
    And sighed and sorrowed as became a friend.
    But neither friendly sorrow, sighs nor tears,
    Could win pale death from his usurped right.
    Yet this I did, and less I could not do: 40
    I saw him honoured with due funeral.
    This scarf I plucked from off his lifeless arm,
    And wear it in remembrance of my friend.
Bel-imperia. I know the scarf, would he had kept it still.
    For had he lived he would have kept it still,
    And worn it for his Bel-imperia's sake:
    For 'twas my favour at his last depart.
    But now wear thou it both for him and me,
    For after him thou hast deserved it best.
    But for thy kindness in his life and death,   50
    Be sure while Bel-imperia's life endures,
    She will be Don Horatio's thankful friend.
Horatio. And, madam, Don Horatio will not slack,
    Humbly to serve fair Bel-imperia.
    But now if your good liking stand thereto,
    I'll crave your pardon to go seek the prince,

22 *pauncht*: stabbed in the belly   *dinged*: knocked
34 *wound*: embraced   35 *welding*: carrying, wielding
47 *favour*: item worn as a token of affection

For so the duke your father gave me charge.   *Exit*.
Bel-imperia. Ay, go Horatio, leave me here alone.
For solitude best fits my cheerless mood.
60   Yet what avails to wail Andrea's death,
From whence Horatio proves my second love?
Had he not loved Andrea as he did,
He could not sit in Bel-imperia's thoughts.
But how can love find harbour in my breast,
Till I revenge the death of my beloved?
Yes, second love shall further my revenge.
I'll love Horatio, my Andrea's friend,
The more to spite the prince that wrought his end.
And where Don Balthazar that slew my love,
70   Himself now pleads for favour at my hands,
He shall in rigour of my just disdain,
Reap long repentance for his murderous deed:
For what was't else but murderous cowardice,
So many to oppress one valiant knight.
Without respect of honour in the fight?
And here he comes that murdered my delight.
       Enter Lorenzo and Balthazar.
Lorenzo. Sister, what means this melancholy walk?
Bel-imperia. That for a while I wish no company.
Lorenzo. But here the prince is come to visit you.
80   *Bel-imperia*. That argues that he lives in liberty.
Balthazar. No madam, but in pleasing servitude.
Bel-imperia. Your prison then belike is your conceit.
Balthazar. Ay, by conceit my freedom is enthralled.
Bel-imperia. Then with conceit enlarge yourself again.
Balthazar. What if conceit have laid my heart to gage?
Bel-imperia. Pray that you borrowed and recover it.
Balthazar. I die if it return from whence it lies.
Bel-imperia. A heartless man, and live? A miracle!
Balthazar. Ay, lady, love can work such miracles.
90   *Lorenzo*. Tush, tush, my lord, let go these ambages,

83 *conceit*: thought, imagination   85 *gage*: ransom
90 *Tush*: Expression of contempt or disapproval
90 *ambages*: indirect speeches, ambiguities

And in plain terms acquaint her with your love.

Bel-imperia. What boots complaint, when there's no remedy?

Balthazar. Yes, to your gracious self must I complain,
In whose fair answer lies my remedy,
On whose perfection all my thoughts attend,
On whose aspect mine eyes find beauty's bower,
In whose translucent breast my heart is lodged.

Bel-imperia. Alas my lord, these are but words of course,
And but devise to drive me from this place.
*She in going in lets fall her glove, which Horatio coming
out takes up.*

Horatio. Madam: your glove.   100

Bel-imperia. Thanks good Horatio, take it for thy pains.

Balthazar. Signior Horatio stooped in happy time.

Horatio. I reaped more grace than I deserved or hoped.

Lorenzo. My lord, be not dismayed for what is past,
You know that women oft are humorous.
These clouds will overblow with little wind.
Let me alone, I'll scatter them myself.
Meanwhile let us devise to spend the time
In some delightful sports and revelling.

Horatio. The king, my lords, is coming hither straight,   110
To feast the Portingale ambassador.
Things were in readiness before I came.

Balthazar. Then here it fits us to attend the king,
To welcome hither our ambassador,
And learn my father and my country's health.
Enter the banquet, trumpets, the King and Ambassador.

King. See lord ambassador, how Spain entreats
Their prisoner Balthazar, thy viceroy's son:
We pleasure more in kindness than in wars.

Ambassador. Sad is our king, and Portingale laments,
Supposing that Don Balthazar is slain.   120

Balthazar. So am I slain by beauty's tyranny.
You see, my lord, how Balthazar is slain.

96 *aspect*: form   98 *words of course*: formulaic speeches
105 *humorous*: temperamental

I frolic with the duke of Castile's son,
Rapt every hour in pleasures of the court,
And graced with favours of his majesty.
King. Put off your greetings till our feast be done.
Now, come and sit with us and taste our cheer.
    Sit to the banquet.
Sit down, young prince, you are our second guest;
Brother, sit down, and nephew take your place,
130 Signior Horatio, wait thou upon our cup,
For well thou hast deserved to be honoured.
Now lordings, fall to: Spain is Portugal,
And Portugal is Spain; we both are friends,
Tribute is paid, and we enjoy our right.
But where is old Hieronimo our marshal?
He promised us in honour of our guest,
To grace our banquet with some pompous jest.
    Enter Hieronimo with a drum, three knights, each his
    scutcheon, then he fetches three kings, they take their
    crowns and them captive.
Hieronimo, this masque contents mine eye,
Although I sound not well the mystery.
140 *Hieronimo.* The first armed knight that hung his scutcheon up,
    He takes the scutcheon and gives it to the King.
Was English Robert, earl of Gloucester,
Who when King Stephen bore sway in Albion,
Arrived with five and twenty thousand men,
In Portingale, and by success of war,
Enforced the king, then but a Saracen,
To bear the yoke of the English monarchy.
King. My lord of Portingale, by this you see
That which may comfort both your king and you,
And make your late comfort seem the less.
150 But say Hieronimo, what was the next?
Hieronimo. The second knight that hung his scutcheon up,

124 *Rapt*: Entranced   132 *fall to*: begin eating   137 *pompous*: stately
137SD *scutcheon*: shield   139 *sound*: fathom, understand
139 *mystery*: hidden significance   142 *Albion*: England
145 *Saracen*: Muslim, Arabic (with connection to the Crusades)

    He doth as he did before.
   Was Edmond, earl of Kent in Albion,
   When English Richard wore the diadem.
   He came likewise and razed Lisbon's walls,
   And took the king of Portingale in fight:
   For which, and other such like service done,
   He after was created duke of York.
King. This is another special argument,
   That Portingale may deign to bear our yoke,
   When it by little England hath been yoked.   160
   But now Hieronimo, what were the last?
Hieronimo. The third and last not least in our account,
    Doing as before.
   Was as the rest a valiant Englishman:
   Brave John of Gaunt, the duke of Lancaster,
   As by his scutcheon plainly may appear.
   He with a puissant army came to Spain,
   And took our king of Castile prisoner.
Ambassador. This is an argument for our viceroy
   That Spain may not insult for her success,
   Since English warriors likewise conquered Spain,   170
   And made them bow their knees to Albion.
King. Hieronimo, I drink to thee for this device,
   Which hath pleased both the ambassador and me.
   Pledge me Hieronimo, if thou love the king.
    Takes the cup of Horatio.
   My lord, I fear we sit but overlong,
   Unless our dainties were more delicate,
   But welcome are you to the best we have.
   Now let us in, that you may be dispatched,
   I think our council is already set.
    Exeunt omnes.

166 *puissant*: powerful   176 *Unless*: Unless it were that

[ACT 1

Scene 5]

Ghost. Come we for this from depth of underground,
    To see him feast that gave me my death's wound?
    These pleasant sights are sorrow to my soul,
    Nothing but league and love and banqueting?
Revenge. Be still Andrea; ere we go from hence,
    I'll turn their friendship into fell despite,
    Their love to mortal hate, their day to night,
    Their hope into despair, their peace to war,
    Their joys to pain, their bliss to misery.

ACT 2

Scene 1

Enter Lorenzo and Balthazar.

Lorenzo. My lord, though Bel-imperia seem thus coy,
    Let reason hold you in your wonted joy:
    In time the savage bull sustains the yoke,
    In time all haggard hawks will stoop to lure,
    In time small wedges cleave the hardest oak,
    In time the flint is pierced with softest shower,
    And she in time will fall from her disdain,
    And rue the sufferance of your friendly pain.
Balthazar. No, she is wilder and more hard withal,
10   Than beast, or bird, or tree, or stony wall.

3–10 *In time the savage ... stony wall*: quoted from Watson's sonnet in his
Hecatompathia
4 *haggard*: untrained
4 *stoop to lure*: technical term from falconry: to come down for food

But wherefore blot I Bel-imperia's name?
It is my fault, not she that merits blame.
My feature is not to content her sight,
My words are rude and work her no delight.
The lines I send her are but harsh and ill,
Such as do drop from Pan and Marsyas' quill.
My presents are not of sufficient cost,
And being worthless all my labour's lost.
Yet might she love me for my valiancy,
Ay, but that's slandered by captivity.   20
Yet might she love me to content her sire,
Ay, but her reason masters his desire.
Yet might she love me as her brother's friend,
Ay, but her hopes aim at some other end.
Yet might she love me to uprear her state,
Ay, but perhaps she hopes some nobler mate.
Yet might she love me as her beauty's thrall,
Ay, but I fear she cannot love at all.
Lorenzo. My lord, for my sake leave these ecstasies,
And doubt not but we'll find some further remedy.   30
Some cause there is that lets you not be loved:
First that must needs be known and then removed.
What if my sister love some other knight?
Balthazar. My summer's day will turn to winter's night.
Lorenzo. I have already found a stratagem,
To sound the bottom of this doubtful theme.
My lord, for once you shall be ruled by me,
Hinder me not whate'er you hear or see.
By force or fair means will I cast about,
To find the truth of all this question out.   40

13 *feature*: shape, proportions
16 *Pan and Marsyas*: gods punished after challenging Apollo in contests of
flute-playing; see also *Tragedy of Hoffman*, 1.3.2–3 and note
16 *quill*: pen; reed pipe   20 *slandered*: brought into disrepute
21 *sire*: father   25 *uprear*: raise   27 *beauty's*: Q beauteous
27 *thrall*: slave or captive   29 *ecstasies*: outbursts
36 *sound the bottom*: discover

Ho Pedringano!
Pedringano. Signior.
Lorenzo. Vien qui presto.
        Enter Pedringano.
Pedringano. Hath your lordship any service to command me?
Lorenzo. Ay, Pedringano, service of import:
    And not to spend the time in trifling words,
    Thus stands the case; it is not long, thou knowest,
    Since I did shield thee from my father's wrath,
    For thy conveyance in Andrea's love,
50 For which thou wert adjudged to punishment.
    I stood betwixt thee and thy punishment:
    And since, thou knowest how I have favoured thee.
    Now to these favours will I add reward,
    Not with fair words, but store of golden coin,
    And lands and living joined with dignities,
    If thou but satisfy my just demand.
    Tell truth and have me for thy lasting friend.
Pedringano. Whate'er it be your lordship shall demand,
    My bounden duty bids me tell the truth.
    If case it lie in me to tell the truth.
Lorenzo. Then Pedringano, this is my demand,
60 Whom loves my sister Bel-imperia?
    For she reposeth all her trust in thee.
    Speak man, and gain both friendship and reward,
    I mean, whom loves she in Andrea's place?
Pedringano. Alas my lord, since Don Andrea's death,
    I have no credit with her as before,
    And therefore know not if she love or no.
Lorenzo. Nay if thou dally, then I am thy foe.
    And fear shall force what friendship cannot win.
                                    [*Threatens him with violence.*]
    Thy death shall bury what thy life conceals,
70 Thou diest for more esteeming her than me.
Pedringano. O stay, my lord!

43 *Vien qui presto*: 'Come here quickly' (Italian)
49 *conveyance*: acting as go-between

Lorenzo. Yet speak the truth and I will guerdon thee,
  And shield thee from whatever can ensue.
  And will conceal whate'er proceeds from thee,
  But if thou dally once again, thou diest.
Pedringano. If Madam Bel-imperia be in love –
Lorenzo. What villain, ifs and ands?
Pedringano. O stay my lord, she loves Horatio.
      Balthazar starts back.
Lorenzo. What, Don Horatio our knight marshal's son?
Pedringano. Even him, my lord.   80
Lorenzo. Now say, but how knowest thou he is her love?
  And thou shalt find me kind and liberal:
  Stand up I say, and fearless tell the truth.
Pedringano. She sent him letters which myself perused,
  Full fraught with lines and arguments of love,
  Preferring him before Prince Balthazar.
Lorenzo. Swear on this cross, that what thou sayest is true,
  And that thou wilt conceal what thou hast told.
Pedringano. I swear to both by him that made us all.
Lorenzo. In hope thine oath is true, here's thy reward.   90
  But if I prove thee perjured and unjust,
  This very sword whereon thou took'st thine oath,
  Shall be the worker of thy tragedy.
Pedringano. What I have said is true, and shall for me
  Be still concealed from Bel-imperia.
  Besides your honour's liberality
  Deserves my duteous service even till death.
Lorenzo. Let this be all that thou shalt do for me,
  Be watchful when and where these lovers meet,
  And give me notice in some secret sort.   100
Pedringano. I will, my lord.
Lorenzo. Then shalt thou find that I am liberal,
  Thou knowest that I can more advance thy state
  Than she, be therefore wise, and fail me not.
  Go and attend her as thy custom is,

---

82 *liberal*: generous   85 *fraught*: loaded   91 *unjust*: dishonest

Lest absence make her think thou dost amiss.
   Exit Pedringano.
Why so: *tam armis quam ingenio*:
Where words prevail not, violence prevails,
But gold doth more than either of them both.
110   How likes Prince Balthazar this stratagem?
Balthazar. Both well, and ill: it makes me glad and sad.
Glad, that I know the hinderer of my love,
Sad, that I fear she hates me whom I love.
Glad, that I know on whom to be revenged,
Sad, that she'll fly me if I take revenge.
Yet must I take revenge or die myself,
For love resisted grows impatient.
I think Horatio be my destined plague.
First in his hand he brandished a sword,
120   And with that sword he fiercely waged war,
And in that war he gave me dangerous wounds,
And by those wounds he forced me to yield,
And by my yielding I became his slave.
Now in his mouth he carries pleasing words,
Which pleasing words do harbour sweet conceits,
Which sweet conceits are limed with sly deceits,
Which sly deceits smooth Bel-imperia's ears,
And through her ears dive down into her heart,
And in her heart set him where I should stand.
130   Thus has he ta'en my body by his force,
And now by sleight would captivate my soul:
But in his fall I'll tempt the destinies,
And either lose my life, or win my love.
Lorenzo. Let's go my lord, your staying stays revenge,
Do you but follow me and gain your love,
Her favour must be won by his remove.   *Exeunt.*

107 *tam armis quam ingenio*: 'by equal parts of force and skill' (Mulryne)
126 *limed*: baited   127 *smooth*: flatter   131 *sleight*: trickery

[ACT 2

Scene 2]

Enter Horatio and Bel-imperia.

Horatio. Now madam, since by favour of your love,
    Our hidden smoke is turned to open flame:
    And that with looks and words we feed our thoughts –
    Two chief contents, where more cannot be had –
    Thus in the midst of love's fair blandishments,
    Why show you sign of inward languishments?
      Pedringano showeth all to [Balthazar] and Lorenzo,
      placing them in secret.
Bel-imperia. My heart, sweet friend, is like a ship at sea,
    She wisheth port, where riding all at ease
    She may repair what stormy times have worn,
    And leaning on the shore may sing with joy,   10
    That pleasure follows pain, and bliss annoy.
    Possession of thy love is th'only port,
    Wherein my heart with fears and hopes long tossed,
    Each hour doth wish and long to make resort,
    There to repair the joys that it hath lost:
    And sitting safe, to sing in Cupid's choir,
    That sweetest bliss is crown of love's desire.
      Balthazar above.
Balthazar. O sleep, mine eyes, see not my love profaned;
    Be deaf, my ears, hear not my discontent;
    Die heart, another joys what thou deservest.   20
Lorenzo. Watch still, mine eyes, to see this love disjoined,
    Hear still, mine ears, to hear them both lament,
    Live heart, to joy at fond Horatio's fall.
Bel-imperia. Why stands Horatio speechless all this while?
Horatio. The less I speak, the more I meditate.

4 *contents*: sources of contentment   9 *may*: Q mad
17SD *Balthazar above*: indicating his place over the stage in the gallery
21 *disjoined*: separated

Bel-imperia. But whereon dost thou chiefly meditate?
Horatio. On dangers past, and pleasures to ensue.
Balthazar. On pleasures past, and dangers to ensue.
Bel-imperia. What dangers, and what pleasures dost thou
    mean?
30 *Horatio.* Dangers of war, and pleasures of our love.
Lorenzo. Dangers of death, but pleasures none at all.
Bel-imperia. Let dangers go, thy war shall be with me,
    But such a warring as breaks no bond of peace.
    Speak thou fair words, I'll cross them with fair words.
    Send thou sweet looks, I'll meet them with sweet looks,
    Write loving lines, I'll answer loving lines,
    Give me a kiss, I'll countercheck thy kiss,
    Be this our warring peace, or peaceful war.
Horatio. But gracious madam, then appoint the field,
40   Where trial of this war shall first be made.
Balthazar. Ambitious villain, how his boldness growest.
Bel-imperia. Then be thy father's pleasant bower the field,
    Where first we vowed a mutual amity:
    The court were dangerous, that place is safe.
    Our hour shall be when Vesper 'gins to rise.
    That summons home distressful travellers.
    There none shall hear us but the harmless birds.
    Happily the gentle nightingale
    Shall carol us asleep ere we be ware.
50   And singing with the prickle at her breast,
    Tell our delight and mirthful dalliance.
    Till then each hour will seem a year and more.
Horatio. But honey sweet and honourable love,
    Return we now unto your father's sight:
    Dangerous suspicion waits on our delight.
Lorenzo. Ay, danger mixed with jealous despite,
    Shall send thy soul into eternal night.   *Exeunt.*

37 *countercheck*: reply, rebuke   42 *bower*: arbour
45 *Vesper*: the morning star   46 *travellers*: labourers   49 *ware*: watchful
50 *prickle*: thorn

[ACT 2

Scene 3]

Enter King of Spain, Portingale ambassador, Don Ciprian [Castile], &c [and attendants].

King. Brother of Castile, to the prince's love
   What says your daughter Bel-imperia?
Castile. Although she coy it as becomes her kind,
   And yet dissemble that she loves the prince,
   I doubt not I, but she will stoop in time.
   And were she froward, which she will not be,
   Yet herein shall she follow my advice,
   Which is to love him or forgo my love.
King. Then lord ambassador of Portingale,
   Advise thy king to make this marriage up,   10
   For strengthening of our late-confirmed league,
   I know no better means to make us friends.
   Her dowry shall be large and liberal:
   Besides that she is daughter and half-heir
   Unto our brother here Don Ciprian,
   And shall enjoy the moiety of his land,
   I'll grace her marriage with an uncle's gift,
   And this it is: in case the match go forward,
   The tribute which you pay shall be released,
   And if by Balthazar she have a son,   20
   He shall enjoy the kingdom after us.
Ambassador. I'll make the motion to my sovereign liege,
   And work it if my counsel may prevail.
King. Do so, my lord, and if he give consent,
   I hope his presence here will honour us
   In celebration of the nuptial day,
   And let himself determine of the time.

---

3 *coy it*: behave modestly   6 *froward*: difficult, uncontrollable
16 *moiety*: half-share   22 *motion*: proposal

Ambassador. Will't please your grace command me aught beside?
King. Commend me to the king and so farewell.
30   But where's Prince Balthazar to take his leave?
Ambassador. That is performed already, my good lord.
King. Amongst the rest of what you have in charge,
    The prince's ransom must not be forgot:
    That's none of mine, but his that took him prisoner,
    And well his forwardness deserves reward.
    It was Horatio our knight marshal's son.
Ambassador. Between us there's a price already pitched,
    And shall be sent with all convenient speed.
King. Then once again, farewell my lord.
40   *Ambassador.* Farewell my lord of Castile and the rest.   *Exit.*
King. Now brother, you must take some little pains
    To win fair Bel-imperia from her will:
    Young virgins must be ruled by their friends.
    The prince is amiable and loves her well,
    If she neglect him and forgo his love,
    She both will wrong her own estate and ours:
    Therefore whiles I do entertain the prince
    With greatest pleasure that our Court affords,
    Endeavour you to win your daughter's thought,
50   If she give back, all this will come to naught.   *Exeunt.*

[ACT 2

Scene 4]

Enter Horatio, Bel-imperia, and Pedringano.

Horatio. Now that the night begins with sable wings
    To overcloud the brightness of the sun,
    And that in darkness pleasures may be done,

34 *forwardness*: eagerness   36 *pitched*: agreed   42 *will*: wilfulness
43 *friends*: relatives   50 *back*: back-word, refusal

Come Bel-imperia, let us to the bower,
And there in safety pass a pleasant hour.
Bel-imperia. I follow thee my love, and will not back,
Although my fainting heart controls my soul.
Horatio. Why, make you doubt of Pedringano's faith?
Bel-imperia. No he is as trusty as my second self.
  Go Pedringano, watch about the gate,   10
And let us know if any make approach.
Pedringano. [*Aside*] Instead of watching I'll deserve more gold
By fetching Don Lorenzo to this match.   *Exit Pedringano.*
Horatio. What means my love?
Bel-imperia. I know not what myself,
And yet my heart foretells me some mischance.
Horatio. Sweet, say not so, fair Fortune is our friend,
And heavens have shut up day to pleasure us.
The stars thou see'st hold back their twinkling shine,
And Luna hides herself to pleasure us.   20
Bel-imperia. Thou hast prevailed, I'll conquer my misdoubt,
And in thy love and counsel drown my fear:
I fear no more, love now is all my thoughts,
Why sit we not, for pleasure asketh ease?
Horatio. The more thou sit'st within these leafy bowers,
The more will Flora deck it with her flowers.
Bel-imperia. I – but if Flora spy Horatio here,
Her jealous eye will think I sit too near.
Horatio. Hark madam, how the birds record by night,
For joy that Bel-imperia sits in sight.   30
Bel-imperia. No Cupid counterfeits the nightingale,
To frame sweet music to Horatio's tale.
Horatio. If Cupid sing, then Venus is not far,
Ay, thou art Venus or some fairer star.
Bel-imperia. If I be Venus thou must needs be Mars,
And where Mars reigneth there must needs be war.
Horatio. Then thus begin our wars: put forth thy hand,

---

8 *faith*: faithfulness 13 *match*: meeting 20 *Luna*: moon
26 *Flora*: goddess of flowers and of spring 29 *record*: sing
33 *Venus*: goddess of love 35 *Mars*: god of war, lover of Venus

That it may combat with my ruder hand.
Bel-imperia. Set forth thy foot to try the push of mine.
40 *Horatio.* But first my looks shall combat against thine.
Bel-imperia. Then ward thyself: I dart this kiss at thee.
Horatio. Thus I retort the dart thou threw'st at me.
Bel-imperia. Nay then to gain the glory of the field,
    My twining arms shall yoke and make you yield.
Horatio. Nay then my arms are large and strong withal;
    Thus elms by vines are compassed till they fall.
Bel-imperia. O let me go, for in my troubled eyes
    Now may'st thou read that life in passion dies.
Horatio. O stay a while and I will die with thee,
50   So shalt thou yield, and yet have conquered me.
Bel-imperia. Who's there Pedringano? We are betrayed!
    Enter Lorenzo, Balthazar, Serberine, Pedringano,
    disguised.
Lorenzo. My lord, away with her, take her aside,
    O sir forbear, your valour is already tried.
    Quickly: dispatch, my masters.
    They hang him in the arbour.
Horatio. What, will you murder me?
Lorenzo. Ay, thus and thus, these are the fruits of love.
    They stab him.
Bel-imperia. O save his life and let me die for him,
    O save him, brother, save him Balthazar:
    I loved Horatio but he loved not me.
60 *Balthazar.* But Balthazar loves Bel-imperia.
Lorenzo. Although his life were still ambitious proud,
    Yet is he at the highest now he is dead.
Bel-imperia. Murder, murder! Help, Hieronimo, help!
Lorenzo. Come, stop her mouth: away with her.   *Exeunt.*

38 *ruder*: coarser 41 *ward*: guard 42 *retort*: turn back
45 *withal*: Q with 49 *die*: punning: achieve orgasm

[ACT 2

Scene 5]

Enter Hieronimo in his shirt, &c.

Hieronimo. What outcries pluck me from my naked bed,
    And chill my throbbing heart with trembling fear,
    Which never danger yet could daunt before?
    What calls Hieronimo? Speak, here I am:
    I did not slumber, therefore 'twas no dream,
    No, no, it was some woman cried for help,
    And here within this garden did she cry,
    And in this garden must I rescue her.
    But stay, what murderous spectacle is this?
    A man hanged up and all the murderers gone,   10
    And in my bower to lay the guilt on me.
    This place was made for pleasure not for death.
    He cuts him down.
    Those garments that he wears I oft have seen,
    Alas, it is Horatio, my sweet son!
    O no, but he that whilom was my son.
    O was it thou that call'st me from my bed?
    O speak, if any spark of life remain!
    I am thy father, who hath slain my son?
    What savage monster, not of human kind
    Hath here been glutted with thy harmless blood,   20
    And left thy bloody corpse dishonoured here,
    For me amidst this dark and dreadful shades,
    To drown thee with an ocean of my tears?
    O heavens, why made you night to cover sin?
    By day this deed of darkness had not been.
    O earth, why didst thou not in time devour,
    The vile profaner of this sacred bower?

OSD *shirt*: nightshirt 15 *whilom*: formerly

O poor Horatio, what hadst thou misdone?
To lose thy life ere life was new begun.
30   O wicked butcher, whatsoe'er thou wert,
How could thou strangle virtue and desert?
Ay me, most wretched, that have lost my joy,
In losing my Horatio my sweet boy.
    Enter Isabella.
Isabella. My husband's absence makes my heart to throb.
    Hieronimo!
Hieronimo. Here Isabella, help me to lament,
For sighs are stopped, and all my tears are spent.
Isabella. What world of grief: my son Horatio?
O where's the author of this endless woe?
40   *Hieronimo.* To know the author were some ease of grief,
For in revenge my heart would find relief.
Isabella. Then is he gone? And is my son gone too?
O gush out tears, fountains and floods of tears!
Blow sighs and raise an everlasting storm,
For outrage fits our cursed wretchedness.
Hieronimo. Sweet lovely rose, ill-plucked before thy time,
Fair worthy son, not conquered but betrayed:
I'll kiss thee now, for words with tears are stained.
Isabella. And I'll close up the glasses of his sight,
50   For once these eyes were only my delight.
Hieronimo. See'st thou this handkercher besmeared with
    blood?
It shall not from me till I take revenge.
Seest thou those wounds that yet are bleeding fresh?
I'll not entomb them till I have revenged.
Then will I joy amidst my discontent,
Till then my sorrow never shall be spent.
Isabella. The heavens are just, murder cannot be hid;
Time is the author both of truth and right
And time will bring this treachery to light.
60   *Hieronimo.* Meanwhile good Isabella cease thy plaints,
Or at the least dissemble them awhile.

28 *misdone*: done wrong   39 *author*: perpetrator

So shall we sooner find the practice out,
And learn by whom all this was brought about.
Come Isabel now let us take him up.
  They take him up.
And bear him in from out this cursed place,
I'll say his dirge, singing fits not this case.
O aliquis mihi quas pulchrum ver educat herbas
  Hieronimo sets his breast unto his sword.
Misceat, et nostro detur, medicina dolori;
Aut, si qui faciunt animis oblivia, succos,
Praebeat; ipse metam magnum quaecunque per orbem,   70
Gramina Sol pulchras effert in luminis oras;
Ipse bibam quicquid meditatur saga veneni,
Quicquid et herbarum vi caeca nenia nectit.
Omnia perpetiar, lethum quoque, dum semel omnis,
Noster in extincto moriatur pectore sensus
Ergo tuos oculos nunquum mea vita, videbo,
Et tua perpetuus sepelivet lumina somnus?
Emoriar tecum: sic, sic juvat ire sub umbras.
At tamen absistam properato cedere letho,
Ne mortem vindicta tuam tum nulla sequatur.   80
  Here he throws it from him and bears the body away.

---

62 *practice*: treachery   66 *dirge*: funeral song
67–80 *aliquis . . . sequatur*: Kyd's compilation of bits of Lucretius, Virgil and
Ovid: 'Let someone mix for me the herbs that the beautiful spring brings
forth, and let a medicine be given for our pain: or let him offer juices, if there
are any that will bring oblivion to our minds. I shall myself gather whatever
herbs the sun brings forth, throughout the mighty world, into the fair realms
of light. I shall myself drink whatever poison the sorceress contrives,
whatever herbs too, the goddess of spells weaves together by her secret
power. All things I shall essay, death even, until all feeling dies at once in my
dead heart. Shall I never again, my life, see your face, and has eternal sleep
buried your light? I shall die with you – so, so would I rejoice to go to the
shades below. But nonetheless, I shall keep myself from a hasty death, in case
then no revenge should follow your death' (Edwards)
73 *herbarum*: Q *irraui* (emendation Edwards, Mulryne)

[ACT 2

Scene 6]

Ghost. Brought'st thou me hither to increase my pain?
  I looked that Balthazar should have been slain:
  But 'tis my friend Horatio that is slain,
  And they abuse fair Bel-imperia
  On whom I doted more than all the world,
  Because she loved me more than all the world.
Revenge. Thou talkest of harvest when the corn is green,
  The end is crown of every work well done;
  The sickle comes not till the corn be ripe.
10 Be still, and ere I lead thee from this place,
  I'll show thee Balthazar in heavy case.

ACT 3

Scene 1

Enter Viceroy of Portingale, Nobles, Villuppo.

Viceroy. Infortunate condition of kings,
  Seated amidst so many helpless doubts!
  First we are placed upon extremest height,
  And oft supplanted with exceeding heat,
  But ever subject to the wheel of chance.
  And at our highest, never joy we so,
  As we both doubt and dread our overthrow.
  So striveth not the waves with sundry winds,
  As Fortune toileth in the affairs of kings.
10 That would be feared, yet fear to be beloved,
  Sith fear or love to kings is flattery.

---

2 *looked*: anticipated, expected 1 *Infortunate*: Subject to Fortune

For instance, lordings, look upon your king,
By hate deprived of his dearest son,
The only hope of our successive line.
[1] Nobleman. I had not thought that Alexandro's heart
    Hath been envenomed with such extreme hate:
    But now I see that words have several works,
    And there's no credit in that countenance.
Villuppo. No, for my lord, had you beheld the train
    That feigned love had coloured in his looks,   20
    When he in camp consorted Balthazar:
    Far more inconstant had you thought the sun,
    That hourly coasts the centre of the earth,
    Than Alexandro's purpose to the prince.
Viceroy. No more Villuppo, thou hast said enough,
    And with thy words thou slayest our wounded thoughts.
    Nor shall I longer dally with the world,
    Procrastinating Alexandro's death:
    Go some of you and fetch the traitor forth.
    That as he is condemned he may die.   30
        Enter Alexandro with a Nobleman and halberds.
2 Nobleman. In such extremes will naught but patience serve.
Alexandro. But in extremes, what patience shall I use?
    Not discontents it me to leave the world
    With whom there nothing can prevail but wrong.
2 Nobleman. Yet hope the best.
Alexandro.   'Tis heaven is my hope,
    As for the earth it is too much infect
    To yield me hope of any of her mould.
Viceroy. Why linger ye? Bring forth that daring fiend,
    And let him die for his accursed deed.
Alexandro. Not that I fear the extremity of death,   40
    For nobles cannot stoop to servile fear
    Do I, O king, thus discontented live.
    But this, O this, torments my labouring soul.
    That thus I die suspected of a sin.
    Whereof, as heavens have known my secret thoughts,

18 *credit*: belief   37 *mould*: earth, character

So am I free from this suggestion.
Viceroy. No more I say, to the tortures! when!
   Bind him and burn his body in those flames.
        They bind him to the stake.
   That shall prefigure those unquenched fires
50 Of Phlegethon prepared for his soul.
Alexandro. My guiltless death will be avenged on thee,
   On thee, Villuppo, that hath maliced thus,
   Or for thy meed hast falsely me accused.
Villuppo. Nay Alexandro if thou menace me,
   I'll lend a hand to send thee to the lake,
   Where those thy words shall perish with thy works,
   Injurious traitor, monstrous homicide.
        Enter Ambassador.
Ambassador. Stay hold a while and here, with pardon of his
        majesty,
   Lay hands upon Villuppo.
60 *Viceroy.* Ambassador, what news hath urged this sudden
        entrance?
Ambassador. Know sovereign lord, that Balthazar doth live!
Viceroy. What sayest thou? Liveth Balthazar our son?
Ambassador. Your highness' son Lord Balthazar doth live,
   And well entreated in the court of Spain,
   Humbly commends him to your majesty.
   These eyes beheld, and these my followers,
   With these the letters of the king's commends,
        Gives him letters.
   Are happy witnesses of his highness' health.
        The King looks on the letters and proceeds.
Viceroy. 'Thy son doth live, thy tribute is received,
70 Thy peace is made, and we are satisfied:
   The rest resolve upon as things proposed,
   For both our honours and thy benefit.'
Ambassador. These are his highness' further articles.
        He gives him more letters.

46 *suggestion*: accusation   50 *Phlegethon*: infernal river of fire
53 *meed*: reward   55 *lake*: Acheron, the lake of hell
64 *entreated*: treated   65 *commends*: sends greetings

Viceroy. Accursed wretch to intimate these ills
   Against the life and reputation
   Of noble Alexandro. Come my lord, unbind him,
   Let him unbind thee that is bound to death,
   To make a quittal for thy discontent.
     They unbind him.
Alexandro. Dread lord, in kindness you could do no less
   Upon report of such a damned fact.   80
   But thus we see our innocence hath saved
   The hopeless life which thou, Villuppo, sought,
   By thy suggestions to have massacred.
Viceroy. Say, false Villuppo? wherefore didst thou thus
   Falsely betray Lord Alexandro's life?
   Him whom thou knowest, that no unkindness else
   But even the slaughter of our dearest son,
   Could once have moved us to have misconceived.
Alexandro. Say, treacherous Villuppo, tell the king,
   Or wherein hath Alexandro used thee ill?   90
Villuppo. Rent with remembrance of so foul a deed,
   My guilty soul submits me to thy doom:
   For not for Alexandro's injuries,
   But for reward and hope to be preferred:
   Thus have I shamelessly hazarded his life.
Viceroy. Which, villain, shall be ransomed with thy death,
   And not so mean a torment as we here
   Devised for him, who thou saidst slew our son:
   But with the bitterest torments and extremes,
   That may be yet invented for thine end.   100
     Alexandro seems to entreat.
   Entreat me not, go take the traitor hence.
               Exit Villuppo.

   And Alexandro let us honour thee,
   With public notice of thy loyalty.
   To end those things articulated here,
   By our great lord the mighty king of Spain,

78 *quittal*: repayment   81 *But*: Except
88 *misconceived*: mistakenly suspected   101 *entreat*: plead

We with our council will deliberate:
Come, Alexandro, keep us company.   *Exeunt.*

[ACT 3

Scene 2]

Enter Hieronimo.

Hieronimo. Oh eyes, no eyes, but fountains fraught with tears;
Oh life, no life, but lively form of death;
Oh world, no world, but mass of public wrongs,
Confused and filled with murder and misdeeds;
Oh sacred heavens! if this unhallowed deed,
If this inhuman and barbarous attempt,
If this incomparable murder, thus
Of mine but now no more my son,
Shall unrevealed and unrevenged pass,
How should we term your dealings to be just,
If you unjustly deal with those that in your justice trust?
That night, sad secretary to my moans,
With direful visions wake my vexed soul,
And with the wounds of my distressful son,
Solicit me for notice of his death.
The ugly fiends do sally forth of hell,
And frame my steps to unfrequented paths,
And fear my heart with fierce inflamed thoughts.
The cloudy day my discontents records,
Early begins to register my dreams,
And drive me forth to seek the murderer.
Eyes, life, world, heavens, hell, night and day,
See, search, show, send, some man
Some mean, that may –
    A letter falleth.

12 *secretary*: confidant

What's here? A letter, tush, it is not so,
A letter written to Hieronimo?   *Red ink.*
'Bel-imperia: For want of ink receive this bloody writ,
Me hath my hapless brother hid from thee,
Revenge thyself on Balthazar and him,
For these were they that murdered thy son.   30
Hieronimo, revenge Horatio's death,
And better fare than Bel-imperia doth.'
What means this unexpected miracle?
My son slain by Lorenzo and the prince:
What cause had they Horatio to malign?
Or what might move thee Bel-imperia,
To accuse thy brother, had he been the mean?
Hieronimo beware, thou art betrayed,
And to entrap thy life this train is laid.
Advise thee therefore, be not credulous: 40
This is devised to endanger thee,
That thou by this Lorenzo shouldst accuse,
And he for thy dishonour done, should draw
Thy life in question, and thy name in hate.
Dear was the life of my beloved son,
And of his death behoves me be revenged:
Then hazard not thine own, Hieronimo,
But live t'effect thy resolution.
I therefore will by circumstances try,
What I can gather to confirm this writ,   50
And harkening near the duke of Castile's house,
Close if I can with Bel-imperia,
To listen more, but nothing to bewray.
      Enter Pedringano.
Now Pedringano.
Pedringano. Now Hieronimo.
Hieronimo. Where's thy lady?
Pedringano. I know not, here's my lord.
      Enter Lorenzo.

26 *Red ink*: presumably a note for the stagehands about the appearance of
the bloody letter
37 *mean*: means   39 *train*: trap   52 *Close*: Meet   53 *bewray*: disclose

Lorenzo. How now, who's this, Hieronimo?

Hieronimo. My lord.

60 *Pedringano.* He asketh for my lady Bel-imperia.

Lorenzo. What to do, Hieronimo? The duke my father hath
 Upon some disgrace a while removed her hence,
 But if it be aught I may inform her of,
 Tell me Hieronimo and I'll let her know it.

Hieronimo. Nay, nay my lord, I thank you, it shall not need.
 I had a suit unto her, but too late,
 And her disgrace makes me unfortunate.

Lorenzo. Why so Hieronimo? Use me?

Hieronimo. Oh no, my lord, I dare not, it must not be.

70 I humbly thank your lordship.

Lorenzo. Why then, farewell.

Hieronimo. My grief no heart, my thoughts no tongue can tell.

               Exit.

Lorenzo. Come hither Pedringano, see'st thou this?

Pedringano. My lord, I see it and suspect it too.

Lorenzo. This is that damned villain Serberine,
 That hath I fear revealed Horatio's death.

Pedringano. My lord, he could not, 'twas so lately done,
 And since he hath not left my company.

Lorenzo. Admit he have not, his condition's such,

80 As fear or flattering words may make him false.
 I know his humour, and therewith repent,
 That ere I used him in this enterprise.
 But Pedringano to prevent the worst,
 And 'cause I know thee secret as my soul,
 Here for thy further satisfaction take thou this.
  Gives him more gold.
 And harken to me, thus it is devised:
 This night thou must, and prithee so resolve,
 Meet Serberine at St Luigi's park,
 Thou knowest 'tis here hard by behind the house.

---

79 *condition*: character 81 *humour*: disposition
87 *prithee*: I pray thee

There take thy stand, and see thou strike him sure.   90
For die he must, if we do mean to live.
Pedringano. But how shall Serberine be there my lord?
Lorenzo. Let me alone, I'll send to him to meet
The prince and me, where thou must do this deed.
Pedringano. It shall be done, my lord, it shall be done,
And I'll go arm myself to meet him there.
Lorenzo. When things shall alter, as I hope they will,
Then shalt thou mount for this: thou knowest my mind.
   Exit Pedringano.
Che le Ieron!
   Enter Page.
Page. My Lord?   100
Lorenzo. Go, sirrah, to Serberine, and bid him forthwith,
Meet the prince and me at St Luigi's park
Behind the house this evening, boy.
Page. I go, my lord.
Lorenzo. But, sirrah, let the hour be eight o'clock.
Bid him not fail.
Page. I fly my lord.   *Exit.*
Lorenzo. Now to confirm the complot thou hast cast
Of all these practices, I'll spread the watch,
Upon precise commandment from the king,   110
Strongly to guard the place where Pedringano
This night shall murder hapless Serberine.
Thus must we work that will avoid distrust,
Thus must we practise to prevent mishap,
And thus one ill another must expulse.
This sly inquiry of Hieronimo for Bel-imperia breeds suspi-
   cion,
And this suspicion bodes a further ill.
As for myself, I know my secret fault;
And so do they, but I have dealt for them.
They that for coin their souls endangered   120

98 *mount*: rise (punning on the gallows)
99 *Che le Ieron*: unclear: perhaps a corruption of the page's name
108 *complot*: conspiracy   109 *watch*: constables   115 *expulse*: expel

To save my life, for coin shall venture theirs:
And better it's that base companions die,
Than by their life to hazard our good haps.
Nor shall they live for me, to fear their faith:
I'll trust myself, myself shall be my friend,
For die they shall, slaves are ordained to no other end.

                                                                            Exit.

[ACT 3

Scene 3]

Enter Pedringano with a pistol.

Pedringano. Now Pedringano, bid thy pistol hold,
    And hold on, Fortune: once more favour me,
    Give but success to mine attempting spirit,
    And let me shift for taking of mine aim.
    Here is the gold, this is the gold proposed,
    It is no dream that I adventure for,
    But Pedringano is possessed thereof.
    And he that would not strain his conscience,
    For him that thus his liberal purse hath stretched,
10 Unworthy such a favour may he fail,
    And wishing, want when such as I prevail.
    As for the fear of apprehension,
    I know, if need should be, my noble lord
    Will stand between me and ensuing harms.
    Besides, this place is free from all suspect:
    Here therefore will I stay and take my stand.
        Enter the Watch.
1 *[Watch].* I wonder much to what intent it is,
    That we are thus expressly charged to watch?

123 *haps*: fortunes   4 *shift*: succeed

2 [Watch]. 'Tis by commandment in the king's own name.
3 [Watch]. But we were never wont to watch and ward,   20
    So near the duke his brother's house before.
2 [Watch]. Content yourself, stand close, there's somewhat in't.
    Enter Serberine.
Serberine. Here, Serberine, attend and stay thy pace,
    For here did Don Lorenzo's page appoint,
    That thou by his command shouldst meet with him.
    How fit a place, if one were so disposed,
    Methinks this corner is, to close with one.
Pedringano. Here comes the bird that I must seize upon,
    Now, Pedringano, or never play the man.
Serberine. I wonder that his lordship stays so long   30
    Or wherefore should he send for me so late?
Pedringano. For this, Serberine, and thou shalt ha't.
    Shoots the dag.
    So there he lies, my promise is performed.
    The Watch.
1 [Watch]. Hark gentlemen, this is a pistol shot.
2 [Watch]. And here's one slain: stay the murderer.
Pedringano. Now by the sorrows of the souls in hell.
    He strives with the Watch.
    Who first lays hands on me, I'll be his priest.
3 [Watch]. Sirrah confess, and therein play the priest,
    Why hast thou thus unkindly killed the man?
Pedringano. Why, because he walked abroad so late.   40
3 [Watch]. Come sir, you had been better kept your bed,
    Than have committed this misdeed so late.
2 [Watch]. Come, to the marshal's with the murderer.
1 [Watch]. On to Hieronimo, help me here,
    To bring the murdered body with us too.
Pedringano. Hieronimo – carry me before whom you will.
    Whate'er he be I'll answer him and you,
    And do your worst, for I defy you all.   *Exeunt.*

---

20 *watch and ward*: patrol   32SD *dag*: gun   36SD *strives*: struggles

[ACT 3

Scene 4]

Enter Lorenzo and Balthazar.

Balthazar. How now, my lord, what makes you rise so soon?
Lorenzo. Fear of preventing our mishaps too late.
Balthazar. What mischief is it that we not mistrust?
Lorenzo. Our greatest ills we least mistrust, my lord,
  And inexpected harms do hurt us most.
Balthazar. Why tell me, Don Lorenzo, tell me, man,
  If aught concerns our honour and your own?
Lorenzo. Not you nor me, my lord, but both in one,
  For I suspect, and the presumption's great,
10 That by those base confederates in our fault,
  Touching the death of Don Horatio,
  We are betrayed to old Hieronimo.
Balthazar. Betrayed, Lorenzo? tush, it cannot be.
Lorenzo. A guilty conscience urged with the thought
  Of former evils, easily cannot err:
  I am persuaded, and dissuade me not,
  That all's revealed to Hieronimo.
  And therefore know that I have cast it thus:
  But here's the page. How now, what news with thee?
20 *Page.* My lord, Serberine is slain.
Balthazar. Who? Serberine, my man?
Page. Your highness' man, my lord.
Lorenzo. Speak page, who murdered him?
Page. He that is apprehended for the fact.
Lorenzo. Who?
Page. Pedringano.
Balthazar. Is Serberine slain that loved his lord so well?
  Injurious villain, murderer of his friend.
Lorenzo. Hath Pedringano murdered Serberine?

3 *mistrust*: anticipate   24 *fact*: crime

My lord, let me entreat you to take the pains   30
To exasperate and hasten his revenge,
With your complaints unto my lord the king.
This their dissension breeds a greater doubt.
Balthazar. Assure thee, Don Lorenzo, he shall die.
  Or else his highness hardly shall deny.
  Meanwhile, I'll haste the marshal sessions,
  For die he shall for this his damned deed.   *Exit Balthazar.*
Lorenzo. Why so, this fits our former policy,
  And thus experience bids the wise to deal.
  I lay the plot, he prosecutes the point,   40
  I set the trap, he breaks the worthless twigs,
  And sees not that wherewith the bird was limed.
  Thus hopeful men that mean to hold their own,
  Must look like fowlers to their dearest friends.
  He runs to kill whom I have holp to catch,
  And no man knows it was my reaching fatch.
  'Tis hard to trust unto a multitude,
  Or anyone in my opinion,
  When men themselves their secrets will reveal.
    Enter a messenger with a letter.
  Boy?   50
Page. My lord.
Lorenzo. What's he?
Messenger. I have a letter to your lordship.
Lorenzo. From whence?
Messenger. From Pedringano that's imprisoned.
Lorenzo. So he is in prison then?
Messenger. Ay, my good lord.
Lorenzo. What would he with us?
  He writes us here to stand good lord and help him in distress.
  Tell him I have his letters, know his mind,   60
  And what we may, let him assure him of.
  Fellow, begone: my boy shall follow thee.

31 *exasperate*: render more severe   38 *policy*: course of action; trick
40 *prosecutes*: brings about
42 *limed*: trapped (by being stuck in bird-lime)   45 *holp*: helped
46 *fatch*: stratagem   59 *stand*: stand fast

Exit Messenger.
This works like wax, yet once more try thy wits.
Boy, go convey this purse to Pedringano.
Thou knowest the prison, closely give it him:
And be advised that none be there about.
Bid him be merry still, but secret;
And though the marshal sessions be today,
Bid him not doubt of his delivery.
70   Tell him his pardon is already signed,
And thereon bid him boldly to be resolved:
For were he ready to be turned off,
(As 'tis my will the uttermost be tried)
Thou with his pardon shall attend him still,
Show him this box, tell him his pardon's in't:
But let him wisely keep his hopes unknown,
He shall not want while Don Lorenzo lives: away.
Page. I go my lord, I run.
Lorenzo. But sirrah, see that this be cleanly done.
       Exit Page.
80   Now stands our fortune on a tickle point,
And now or never ends Lorenzo's doubts.
One only thing is uneffected yet,
And that's to see the executioner.
But to what end? I list not trust the air
With utterance of our pretence therein,
For fear the privy whispering of the wind
Convey our words amongst unfriendly ears,
That lie too open to advantages.
       Et quel que voglio io, nessun lo sa,
90   *Intendo io: quel mi bastera.*   *Exit.*

72 *turned off*: executed   80 *tickle*: insecure   82 *uneffected*: not done
84 *list not*: do not wish to   88 *advantages*: taking advantage
89–90 *Et quel . . . bastera*: 'And what I want, nobody knows; I know, and
that's enough for me' (Italian)

[ACT 3

Scene 5]

Enter Boy with the box.

Page. My master hath forbidden me to look in this box, and by
my troth 'tis likely, if he had not warned me, I should not
have had so much idle time: for we men-kind in our minority
are like women in their uncertainty, that they are most
forbidden, they will soonest attempt: so I now. By my bare
honesty here's nothing but the bare empty box: were it not
sin against secrecy, I would say it were a piece of gentleman-
like knavery. I must go to Pedringano and tell him his pardon
is in this box – nay, I would have sworn it, had I not seen the
contrary. I cannot choose but smile to think, how the villain   10
will flout the gallows, scorn the audience, and descant on the
hangman, and all presuming of his pardon from hence. Will't
not be an odd jest, for me to stand and grace every jest he
makes, pointing my finger at this box: as who would say,
mock on, here's thy warrant? Is't not a scurvy jest, that a man
should jest himself to death? Alas poor Pedringano, I am in
a sort sorry for thee, but if I should be hanged with thee,
I cannot weep.   *Exit.*

[ACT 3

Scene 6]

Enter Hieronimo and the Deputy.

Hieronimo. Thus must we toil in other men's extremes,
      That know not how to remedy our own,

---

3 *minority*: under age   4 *uncertainty*: irresolution   11 *descant*: criticize

And do them justice, when unjustly we,
For all our wrongs, can compass no redress.
But shall I never live to see the day
That I may come, by justice of the heavens,
To know the cause that may my cares allay?
This toils my body, this consumeth age,
That only I to all men just must be,
10   And neither gods nor men be just to me.
Deputy. Worthy Hieronimo, your office asks
     A care to punish such as do transgress.
Hieronimo. So is't my duty to regard his death,
     Who when he lived deserved my dearest blood:
     But come: for that we came for, let's begin.
     For here lies that which bids me to be gone.
          Enter Officers, Boy and Pedringano, with a letter in his
          hand, bound.
Deputy. Bring forth the prisoner for the court is set.
Pedringano. Gramercy, boy, but it was time to come,
     For I had written to my lord anew,
20   A nearer matter that concerneth him,
     For fear his lordship had forgotten me.
     But sith he hath remembered me so well,
     Come, come, come on, when shall we to this gear?
Hieronimo. Stand forth, thou monster, murderer of men,
     And here for satisfaction of the world,
     Confess thy folly and repent thy fault,
     For there's thy place of execution.
Pedringano. This is short work, well to your marshalship.
     First I confess, nor fear I death therefore,
30   I am the man, 'twas I slew Serberine.
     But sir, then you think this shall be the place,
     Where we shall satisfy you for this gear?
Deputy. Ay, Pedringano.
Pedringano. Now I think not so.
Hieronimo. Peace, impudent, for thou shalt find it so.

8 *consumeth*: wears out   13 *regard*: care about   18 *Gramercy*: Thank you
20 *nearer*: more serious   23 *gear*: business; gallows

51

For blood with blood shall, while I sit as judge,
Be satisfied, and the law discharged.
And though myself cannot receive the like,
Yet will I see that others have their right.
Dispatch, the fault's approved and confessed,   40
And by our law he is condemned to die.
Hangman. Come on sir, are you ready?
Pedringano. To do what, my fine officious knave?
Hangman. To go to this gear.
Pedringano. O sir, you are too forward, thou wouldst fain
furnish me with a halter, to disfurnish me of my habit. So I
should go out of this gear my raiment, into that gear the rope.
But hangman, now I spy your knavery, I'll not change without
boot, that's flat.
Hangman. Come sir.   50
Pedringano. So then I must up.
Hangman. No remedy.
Pedringano. Yes, but there shall be for my coming down.
Hangman. Indeed, here's a remedy for that.
Pedringano. How? be turned off?
Hangman. Ay truly: come are you ready?
I pray sir, dispatch, the day goes away.
Pedringano. What do you hang by the hour. If you do, I may
chance to break your old custom.
Hangman. Faith you have reason, for I am like to break your   60
young neck.
Pedringano. Dost thou mock me hangman? pray God I be not
preserved to break your knave's pate for this.
Hangman. Alas sir, you are a foot too low to reach it, and
I hope you will never grow so high while I am in the office.
Pedringano. Sirrah, dost see yonder boy with the box in his
hand?
Hangman. What, he that points to it with his finger?
Pedringano. Ay, that companion.

40 *approved*: proved
46 *disfurnish*: by custom, a hangman got the clothes of an executed criminal
49 *boot*: purpose, recompense   57 *dispatch*: do it quickly

70 *Hangman.* I know him not, but what of him?

Pedringano. Doest thou think to live till his old doublet will make thee a new truss?

Hangman. Ay, and many a fair year after, to truss up many an honester man than either thou or he.

Pedringano. What hath he in his box as thou think'st?

Hangman. 'Faith, I cannot tell, nor I care not greatly. Methinks you should rather harken to your soul's health.

Pedringano. Why, sirrah hangman? I take it, that that is good for the body, is likewise good for the soul: and it may be in

80   that box is balm for both.

Hangman. Well, thou art even the merriest piece of man's flesh that e'er groaned at my office door.

Pedringano. Is your roguery become an office with a knave's name?

Hangman. Ay, and that shall all they witness that see you seal it with a thief's name.

Pedringano. I prithee request this good company to pray with me.

Hangman. Ay marry sir, this is a good motion: my masters, you see here's a good fellow.

90 *Pedringano.* Nay, nay, now I remember me, let them alone till some other time, for now I have no great need.

Hieronimo. I have not seen a wretch so impudent.

O monstrous times where murder's set so light,

And where the soul that should be shrined in heaven,

Solely delights in interdicted things,

Still wandering in the thorny passages,

That intercepts itself of happiness.

Murder, O bloody monster, God forbid

A fault so foul should 'scape unpunished.

100   Dispatch and see this execution done,

This makes me to remember thee, my son.

        Exit Hieronimo.

Pedringano. Nay soft, no haste.

Deputy. Why, wherefore stay you, have you hope of life?

72 *truss*: close-fitting jacket; to hang
88 *marry*: expression of surprise or outrage   *motion*: proposal
95 *interdicted*: forbidden   97 *intercepts*: prevents

Pedringano. Why, ay.
Hangman. As how?
Pedringano. Why rascal, by my pardon from the king.
Hangman. Stand you on that, then you shall off with this.
    He turns him off.
Deputy. So executioner, convey him hence.
  But let his body lie unburied.
  Let not the earth be choked or infect   110
  With that which heavens condemns and men neglect.

                                      Exeunt.

[ACT 3

Scene 7]

Enter Hieronimo.

Hieronimo. Where shall I run to breathe abroad my woes,
  My woes, whose weight hath wearied the earth?
  Or mine exclaims that have surcharged the air,
  With ceaseless plaints for my deceased son?
  The blustering winds conspiring with my words,
  At my lament have moved the leafless trees,
  Disrobed the meadows of their flowered green,
  Made mountains marsh with spring tides of my tears,
  And broken through the brazen gates of hell.
  Yet still tormented is my tortured soul,   10
  With broken sighs and restless passions,
  That winged mount, and hovering in the air,
  Beat at the windows of the brightest heavens,
  Soliciting for justice and revenge:
  But they are placed in those empyreal heights,
  Where countermured with walls of diamond,

---

107 *Stand*: Depend   15 *empyreal*: the highest heavens
16 *countermured*: defensively double-walled

I find the place impregnable, and they
Resist my woes, and give my words no way.
    Enter Hangman with a letter.
Hangman. O lord sir, God bless you sir, the man Sir Petergade.
20   Sir, he that was so full of merry conceits.
Hieronimo. Well, what of him?
Hangman. O lord sir, he went the wrong way, the fellow had
    a fair commission to the contrary. Sir, here is his passport,
    I pray you sir, we have done him wrong.
Hieronimo. I warrant thee, give it me.
Hangman. You will stand between the gallows and me?
Hieronimo. Ay, ay.
Hangman. I thank your lord worship.
    Exit Hangman.
Hieronimo. And yet though somewhat nearer me concerns,
30   I will to ease the grief that I sustain,
    Take truce with sorrow while I read on this.
    'My lord, I writ as mine extremes required,
    That you would labour my delivery:
    If you neglect, my life is desperate,
    And in my death I shall reveal the truth.
    You know my lord I slew him for your sake,
    And was confederate with the prince and you,
    Won by rewards and hopeful promises,
    I holp to murder Don Horatio too.'
40   Holp he to murder mine Horatio?
    And actors in th'accursed tragedy,
    Wast thou Lorenzo, Balthazar, and thou,
    Of whom my son, my son deserved so well?
    What have I heard, what have mine eyes beheld?
    O sacred heavens, may it come to pass,
    That such a monstrous and detested deed,
    So closely smothered and so long concealed,
    Shall thus by this be venged or revealed!
    Now see I what I durst not then suspect,

19 *Petergade*: apparently the hangman's version of Pedringano
23 *commission*: authority   32 *writ*: Q write

That Bel-imperia's letter was not feigned,   50
Nor feigned she, though falsely they have wronged
Both her, myself, Horatio, and themselves.
Now may I make compare 'twixt hers and this,
Of every accident; I ne'er could find
Till now, and now I feelingly perceive,
They did what heaven unpunished would not leave.
O false Lorenzo, are these thy flattering looks?
Is this the honour that thou didst my son?
And Balthazar, bane to thy soul and me,
Was this the ransom he reserved thee for?   60
Woe to the cause of these constrained wars,
Woe to thy baseness and captivity,
Woe to thy birth, thy body and thy soul,
Thy cursed father, and thy conquered self.
And banned with bitter execrations be
The day and place where he did pity thee.
But wherefore waste I mine unfruitful words
When naught but blood will satisfy my woes?
I will go plain me to my lord the king,
And cry aloud for justice through the court.   70
Wearing the flints with these my withered feet,
And either purchase justice by entreats,
Or tire them all with my revenging threats.   *Exit.*

[ACT 3

Scene 8]

Enter Isabella and her maid.

Isabella. So that you say this herb will purge the eye
   And this the head: ah, but none of them will purge the heart:

---

54 *accident*: circumstance   61 *constrained*: forced
65 *banned*: cursed   69 *plain*: complain   1 *purge*: heal

No, there's no medicine left for my disease,
Nor any physic to recure the dead.
   She runs lunatic.
Horatio, O where's Horatio?
Maid. Good madam, affright not thus yourself,
   With outrage for your son Horatio.
   He sleeps in quiet in the Elysian fields.
Isabella. Why, did I not give you gowns and goodly things,
10   Bought you a whistle and a whipstalk too,
   To be revenged on their villainies?
Maid. Madam, these humours do torment my soul.
Isabella. My soul, poor soul thou talks of things
   Thou know'st not what: my soul hath silver wings,
   That mounts me up into the highest heavens,
   To heaven, ay, there sits my Horatio,
   Backed with a troop of fiery cherubins,
   Dancing about his newly-healed wounds
   Singing sweet hymns and chanting heavenly notes,
20   Rare harmony to greet his innocence,
   That died, ay died a mirror in our days.
   But say, where shall I find the men, the murderers,
   That slew Horatio, whither shall I run
   To find them out, that murdered my son?   *Exeunt.*

[ACT 3

Scene 9]

Bel-imperia at a window.

Bel-imperia. What means this outrage that is offered me?
   Why am I thus sequestered from the court?
   No notice? shall I not know the cause

7 *outrage*: unrestrained behaviour
10 *whipstalk*: whip handle (here, a toy)   21 *mirror*: model, paragon
2 *sequestered*: kept apart

Of this my secret and suspicious ills?
Accursed brother, unkind murderer,
Why bends thou thus thy mind to martyr me?
Hieronimo, why writ I of thy wrongs?
Or why art thou so slack in thy revenge?
Andrea, O Andrea, that thou sawest,
Me for thy friend Horatio handled thus.   10
And him for me thus causeless murdered.
Well, force perforce, I must constrain myself,
To patience, and apply me to the time,
Till heaven, as I have hoped, shall set me free.
      Enter Christophil.
Christophil. Come Madam Bel-imperia, this may not be.
                                              Exeunt.

[ACT 3

Scene 10]

Enter Lorenzo, Balthazar and the Page.

Lorenzo. Boy, talk no further, thus far things go well,
    Thou art assured that thou sawest him dead?
Page. Or else my lord I live not.
Lorenzo. That's enough.
    As for his resolution to his end,
    Leave that to him with whom he sojourns now.
    Here, take my ring and give it Christophil,
    And bid him let my sister be enlarged,
    And bring her hither straight.   *Exit Page.*
    This that I did was for a policy,   10
    To smooth and keep the murder secret,
    Which as a nine-days' wonder being o'erblown

---

4 *suspicious*: arousing suspicion   12 *force perforce*: of necessity
8 *enlarged*: released   12 *o'erblown*: blown over

My gentle sister will I now enlarge.

Balthazar. And time, Lorenzo, for my lord the duke,
You heard, inquired for her yesternight.

Lorenzo. Why, and my lord, I hope you heard me say,
Sufficient reason, why she kept away.
But that's all one: my lord, you love her?

Balthazar. Ay.

20 *Lorenzo.* Then in your love beware, deal cunningly,
Salve all suspicions, only soothe me up,
And if she hap to stand on terms with us,
As for her sweetheart, and concealment so,
Jest with her gently: under feigned jest
Are things concealed, that else would breed unrest.
But here she comes.

                              Enter Bel-imperia.
                              Now, sister –

Bel-imperia. Sister, no, thou art no brother, but an enemy.
Else wouldst thou not have used thy sister so.
First, to affright me with thy weapons drawn,
30 And with extremes abuse my company;
And then to hurry me like whirlwind's rage,
Amidst a crew of thy confederates,
And clap me up where none might come at me,
Nor I at any, to reveal my wrongs.
What madding fury did possess thy wits?
Or wherein is't that I offended thee?

Lorenzo. Advise you better Bel-imperia,
For I have done you no disparagement;
Unless, by more discretion than deserved,
40 I sought to save your honour and mine own.

Bel-imperia. Mine honour, why Lorenzo, wherein is't
That I neglect my reputation so,
As you, or any need to rescue it?

Lorenzo. His highness and my father were resolved,
To come confer with old Hieronimo,

21 *Salve*: Allay *soothe*: agree   33 *clap me up*: imprison me
38 *disparagement*: humiliation

Concerning certain matters of estate,
That by the viceroy was determined.
Bel-imperia. And wherein was mine honour touched in that?
Balthazar. Have patience, Bel-imperia: hear the rest.
Lorenzo. Me next in sight as messenger they sent.   50
    To give him notice that they were so nigh:
    Now when I came, consorted with the prince,
    And, unexpected in an arbour there,
    Found Bel-imperia with Horatio.
Bel-imperia. How then?
Lorenzo. Why, then remembering that old disgrace,
    Which you for Don Andrea hath endured,
    And now, were likely longer to sustain,
    By being found so meanly accompanied:
    Thought rather, for I knew no readier mean,   60
    To thrust Horatio forth my father's way.
Balthazar. And carry you obscurely somewhere else,
    Lest that his highness should have found you there.
Bel-imperia. Even so my lord, and you are witness,
    That this is true which he entreateth of?
    You, gentle brother, forged this for my sake,
    And you, my lord, were made his instrument:
    A work of worth, worthy the noting too!
    But what's the cause that you concealed me since?
Lorenzo. Your melancholy, sister, since the news   70
    Of your first favourite Don Andrea's death,
    My father's old wrath hath exasperate.
Balthazar. And better was't for you, being in disgrace,
    To absent yourself and give his fury place.
Bel-imperia. But why had I no notice of his ire?
Lorenzo. That were to add more fuel to your fire,
    Who burnt like Etna for Andrea's loss.
Bel-imperia. Hath not my father then inquired for me?
Lorenzo. Sister, he hath, and thus excused I thee.
    He whispereth in her ear.

46 *estate*: state   59 *meanly*: of low birth   66 *forged*: contrived
72 *exasperate*: made more severe   77 *Etna*: volcano in Sicily

80   But Bel-imperia, see the gentle prince:
        Look on thy love, behold young Balthazar,
        Whose passions by thy presence are increased,
        And in whose melancholy thou mayest see,
        Thy hate, his love; thy flight, his following thee.
    Bel-imperia. Brother, you are become an orator –
        I know not, I, by what experience –
        Too politic for me, past all compare
        Since last I saw you: but content yourself,
        The prince is meditating higher things.
90   *Balthazar.* 'Tis of thy beauty that conquers kings.
        Of those thy tresses Ariadne's twines.
        Wherewith my liberty thou has surprised.
        Of that thine ivory front, my sorrows' map,
        Wherein I see no haven to rest my hope.
    Bel-imperia. To love and fear and both at once, my lord,
        In my conceit are things of more import
        Than women's wits are to be busied with.
    Balthazar. 'Tis I that love.
    Bel-imperia. Whom?
100 *Balthazar.* Bel-imperia.
    Bel-imperia. But I that fear.
    Balthazar. Whom?
    Bel-imperia. Bel-imperia.
    Lorenzo. Fear yourself?
    Bel-imperia. Ay, brother.
    Lorenzo. How?
    Bel-imperia. As those, that what they love are loath and fear to
        lose.
    Balthazar. Then fair, let Balthazar your keeper be.
    Bel-imperia. No, *Balthazar* doth fear as well as we,
110   *Et tremulo metui pavidum junxere timorem*
      Et vanum stolidae proditionis opus.   *Exit.*
    Lorenzo. Nay, and you argue things so cunningly,

---

91 *Ariadne*: used a thread to guide Theseus through the labyrinth
92 *surprised*: taken prisoner   93 *front*: forehead   96 *conceit*: mind
110–11 *Et tremulo . . . opus*: obscure: 'They joined dismayed dread to
quaking fear, a futile deed of sottish betrayal' (Edwards)

We'll go continue this discourse at court.
Balthazar. Lead by the lodestar of her heavenly looks,
  Wends poor oppressed Balthazar,
  As o'er the mountains walks the wanderer,
  Incertain to effect his pilgrimage.   *Exeunt.*

[ACT 3

Scene 11]

Enter two Portingales, and Hieronimo meets them.

1 [Portingale]. By your leave sir.
Hieronimo. Good leave have you, nay, I pray you go.
  For I'll leave you, if you can leave me, so.
2 [Portingale]. Pray you which is the next way to my lord the
  duke's?
Hieronimo. The next way from me.
1 [Portingale]. To his house we mean.
Hieronimo. O hard by, 'tis yon house you see.
2 [Portingale]. You could not tell us if his son were there?
Hieronimo. Who, my lord Lorenzo?
1 [Portingale]. Ay sir.   10
    He goeth in at one door and comes out at another.
Hieronimo. Oh forbear, for other talk for us far fitter were.
  But if you be importunate to know
  The way to him, and where to find him out,
  Then list to me, and I'll resolve your doubt.
  There is a path upon your left-hand side,
  That leadeth from a guilty conscience,
  Unto a forest of distrust and fear.
  A darksome place, and dangerous to pass:
  There shall you meet with melancholy thoughts,

114 *lodestar*: navigational star   117 *Incertain*: Doubtful

20   Whose baleful humours if you but uphold,
        It will conduct you to despair and death;
        Whose rocky cliffs, when you have once beheld,
        Within a hugy dale of lasting night,
        That, kindled with the world's iniquities,
        Doth cast up filthy and detested fumes,
        Not far from thence, where murderers have built
        A habitation for their cursed souls.
        There in a brazen cauldron fixed by Jove,
        In his fell wrath upon a sulphur flame,
30   Yourselves shall find Lorenzo bathing him
        In boiling lead and blood of innocents.
    1 [Portingale]. Ha, ha, ha!
    Hieronimo. Ha, ha, ha! why, ha, ha, ha! Farewell, good ha, ha,
        ha!   *Exit.*
    2 [Portingale]. Doubtless this man is passing lunatic,
        Or imperfection of his age doth make him dote.
        Come, let's away to seek my lord the duke.

[ACT 3

Scene 12]

*Enter Hieronimo with a poniard in one hand and a rope in the
other.*

Hieronimo. Now sir, perhaps I come and see the king.
        The king sees me, and fain would hear my suit:
        Why is this not a strange and seld-seen thing
        That standers-by with toys should strike me mute?
        Go to, I see their shifts, and say no more.
        Hieronimo, 'tis time for thee to trudge.

20 *uphold:* persist   23 *hugy:* huge   35 *passing:* very
3 *seld-seen:* seldom-seen   4 *toys:* trivial matters
5 *Go to:* expression of impatience   *shifts:* tricks
6 *trudge:* get moving

Down by the dale that flows with purple gore,
Standeth a fiery tower; there sits a judge,
Upon a seat of steel and molten brass;
And 'twixt his teeth he holds a fire-brand,   10
That leads unto the lake where hell doth stand.
Away Hieronimo, to him be gone:
He'll do thee justice for Horatio's death.
Turn down this path, thou shalt be with him straight,
Or this, and even thou need'st not take thy breath.
This way or that way? soft and fair, not so:
For if I hang or kill myself, let's know
Who will revenge Horatio's murder then?
No, no, fie, no. Pardon me: I'll none of that.
    He flings away the dagger and halter.
This way I'll take, and this way comes the king.   20
    He takes them up again.
And here I'll have a fling and him that's flat.
And Balthazar, I'll be with thee to bring,
And thee, Lorenzo. Here's the king, nay, stay,
And here, ay here, there goes the hare away.
    Enter King, Ambassador, Castile and Lorenzo.
King. Now show, ambassador, what our viceroy sayeth,
    Hath he received the articles we sent?
Hieronimo. Justice, O justice to Hieronimo!
Lorenzo. Back, see'st thou not the king is busy?
Hieronimo. O is he so?
King. Who is he that interrupts our business?   30
Hieronimo. Not I. Hieronimo, beware, go by, go by.
Ambassador. Renowned king, he hath received and read
    Thy kingly proffers, and thy promised league,
    And as a man extremely overjoyed,
    To hear his son so princely entertained,
    Whose death he had so solemnly bewailed,
    This for thy further satisfaction
    And kingly love, he kindly lets thee know:
    First, for the marriage of his princely son,

21 *flat*: settled   24 *hare*: quarry, game   31 *go by*: be careful

40   With Bel-imperia thy beloved niece,
      The news are more delightful to his soul,
      Than myrrh or incense to the offended heavens.
      In person therefore will he come himself,
      To see the marriage rites solemnized,
      And in the presence of the court of Spain,
      To knit a sure inextricable band,
      Of kingly love and everlasting league,
      Betwixt the crowns of Spain and Portingale.
      There will he give his crown to Balthazar,
50   And make a queen of Bel-imperia.
King. Brother, how like you this our viceroy's love?
Castile. No doubt my lord, it is an argument
      Of honourable care to keep his friend,
      And wondrous zeal to Balthazar his son:
      Nor am I least indebted to his grace,
      That bends his liking to my daughter thus.
Ambassador. Now last, dread lord, here hath his highness sent,
      Although he send not that his son return,
      His ransom due to Don Horatio.
60 *Hieronimo.* Horatio, who calls Horatio?
King. And well remembered, thank his majesty.
      Here, see it given to Horatio.
Hieronimo. Justice, O justice, justice, gentle king!
King. Who is that, Hieronimo?
Hieronimo. Justice, O justice, O my son, my son,
      My son whom naught can ransom or redeem!
Lorenzo. Hieronimo, you are not well-advised.
Hieronimo. Away Lorenzo, hinder me no more,
      For thou hast made me bankrupt of my bliss:
70   Give me my son, you shall not ransom him.
      Away, I'll rip the bowels of the earth,
          He diggeth with his dagger.
      And ferry over to th'Elysian plains,
      And bring my son to show his deadly wounds.
      Stand from about me, I'll make a pick-axe of my poniard.

46 *inextricable*: Q inexecrable; indissoluble

    And here surrender up my marshalship:
    For I'll go marshal up the fiends in hell,
    To be avenged on you all for this.
King. What means this outrage? will none of you restrain
    his fury?
Hieronimo. Nay soft and fair, you shall not need to strive,
    Needs must he go that the devils drive.   *Exit.*   80
King. What accident hath happed Hieronimo?
    I have not seen him to demean him so.
Lorenzo. My gracious Lord, he is with extreme pride,
    Conceived of young Horatio his son,
    And, covetous of having to himself
    The ransom of the young prince Balthazar,
    Distract, and in a manner lunatic.
King. Believe me nephew, we are sorry for't.
    This is the love that fathers bear their sons.
    But gentle brother, go give to him this gold,   90
    The prince's ransom, let him have his due,
    For what he hath Horatio shall not want.
    Haply Hieronimo hath need thereof.
Lorenzo. But if he be thus helplessly distract,
    'Tis requisite his office be resigned,
    And given to one of more discretion.
King. We shall increase his melancholy so.
    'Tis best that we see further in it first:
    Till when, ourself will not exempt the place.
    And brother, now bring in the ambassador,   100
    That he may be a witness of the match
    'Twixt Balthazar and Bel-imperia.
    And that we may prefix a certain time
    Wherein the marriage shall be solemnized,
    That we may have thy lord the viceroy here.
Ambassador. Therein your highness highly shall content
    His majesty, that longs to hear from hence.
King. On then, and hear you, lord ambassador.   *Exeunt.*

81 *happed*: happened to   93 *Haply*: Perhaps
99 *exempt the place*: obscure: the context would suggest 'suspend the office'

[ACT 3

Scene 13]

Enter Hieronimo with a book in his hand.

Hieronimo. *Vindicta mihi.*
　　Ay, heaven will be revenged of every ill,
　　Nor will they suffer murder unrepaid.
　　Then stay, Hieronimo, attend their will,
　　For mortal men may not appoint their time.
　　Per scelus semper tutum est sceleribus iter.
　　Strike and strike home, where wrong is offered thee,
　　For evils unto ills conductors be.
　　And death's the worst of resolution.
10　　For he that thinks with patience to contend
　　To quiet life, his life shall easily end.
　　Fata si miseros juvant, habes salutem:
　　Fata si vitam negant, habes sepulchrum.
　　If destiny thy miseries do ease,
　　Then hast thou health, and happy shalt thou be;
　　If destiny deny thee life, Hieronimo,
　　Yet shalt thou be assured of a tomb.
　　If neither, yet let this thy comfort be,
　　Heaven covereth him that hath no burial,
20　　And to conclude, I will revenge his death.
　　But how? not as the vulgar wits of men,
　　With open, but inevitable ills;
　　As by a secret, yet a certain mean,
　　Which under kindship will be cloaked best.
　　Wise men will take their opportunity,

osd *book*: Hieronimo quotes from both the Bible and Seneca
1 *Vindicta mihi*: 'Vengeance is mine' (Romans 12:19)
6 *Per scelus . . . iter*: 'The safe way for crime is always through crime'
(Seneca)
12–13 *Fata si . . . sepulchrum*: translated in lines 14–17 (Seneca)
22 *inevitable*: successful　24 *kindship*: kindness

Closely and safely fitting things to time:
But in extremes, advantage hath no time,
And therefore all times fit not for revenge:
Thus therefore will I rest me in unrest,
Dissembling quiet in unquietness,   30
Not seeming that I know their villainies:
That my simplicity may make them think,
That ignorantly I will let all slip
For ignorance I wot, and well they know,
Remedium malorum iners est.
Nor aught avails it me to menace them,
Who as a wintry storm upon a plain,
Will bear me down with their nobility.
No, no, Hieronimo, thou must enjoin
Thine eyes to observation, and thy tongue   40
To milder speeches than thy spirit affords;
Thy heart to patience, and thy hands to rest,
Thy cap to courtesy, and thy knee to bow,
Till to revenge thou know when, where, and how.
How now, what noise, what coil is that you keep?
    A noise within.
    Enter a servant.
Servant. Here are a sort of poor petitioners
    That are importunate, and it shall please you sir,
    That you should plead their cases to the king.
Hieronimo. That I should plead their several actions –
    Why, let them enter, and let me see them.   50
    Enter three citizens and an old man.
1 [Citizen]. So I tell you this for learning and for law,
    There's not any advocate in Spain.
    That can prevail, or will take half the pain,
    That he will in pursuit of equity.
Hieronimo. Come near, you men that thus importune me.
    Now must I bear a face of gravity,
    For thus I used before my marshalship,

---

35 *Remedium . . . est*: 'Is an idle remedy for ills' (Seneca)
45 *coil*: disturbance   46 *sort*: crowd

To plead in causes as corrigedor.
Come on sirs, what's the matter?
60 2 *[Citizen]*. Sir, an action.
Hieronimo. Of battery?
1 *[Citizen]*. Mine of debt.
Hieronimo. Give place.
2 *[Citizen]*. No sir, mine's an action of the case.
3 *[Citizen]*. Mine an ejectione firmae by a lease.
Hieronimo. Content you sirs, are you determined,
That I should plead your several actions?
1 *[Citizen]*. Ay sir, and here's my declaration,
2 *[Citizen]*. And here is my bond.
70 3 *[Citizen]*. And here is my lease.
        They give him papers.
Hieronimo. But wherefore stands yon silly man so mute,
With mournful eyes and hands to heaven upreared?
Come hither father, let me know thy cause.
Senex. O worthy sir, my cause but slightly known.
May move the hearts of warlike Myrmidons,
And melt the Corsic rocks with ruthful tears.
Hieronimo. Say father, tell me what's thy suit?
Senex. No sir, could my woes
Give way unto my most distressful words,
80   Then should I not in paper as you see,
With ink bewray what blood began in me.
Hieronimo. What's here? the humble supplication
Of Don Bazulto for his murdered son.
Senex. Ay sir.
Hieronimo. No sir, it was my murdered son, oh my son.
My son, oh my son Horatio.
But mine, or thine, Bazulto be content.
Here, take my handkerchief and wipe thine eyes,
Whiles wretched I, in thy mishaps may see,
90   The lively portrait of my dying self.

58 *corrigedor*: advocate or magistrate   60 *action*: legal case
65 *ejectione firmae*: writ to eject a tenant   76 *Corsic*: Corsican
81 *blood*: passion   90 *lively*: living

He draweth out a bloody napkin.
O no, not this, Horatio this was thine,
And when I dyed it in thy dearest blood,
This was a token 'twixt my soul and me,
That of thy death revenged I should be.
But here, take this, and this, what, my purse?
Ay, this and that, and all of them are thine,
For all as one are our extremities.
1 [Citizen]. O, see the kindness of Hieronimo.
2 [Citizen]. This gentleness shows him a gentleman.
Hieronimo. See, see, o see thy shame Hieronimo,   100
See here a loving father to his son.
Behold the sorrows and the sad laments,
That he delivereth for his son's decease.
If love's effects so strives in lesser things,
If love enforce such moods in meaner wits,
If love express such power in poor estates –
Hieronimo, when as a raging sea
Tossed with the wind and tide o'erturnest then
The upper billows, course of waves to keep,
Whilst lesser waters labour in the deep;   110
Then shamest thou not, Hieronimo, to neglect,
The sweet revenge of thy Horatio?
Though on this earth justice will not be found,
I'll down to hell and in this passion,
Knock at the dismal gates of Pluto's court,
Getting by force as once Alcides did,
A troop of Furies and tormenting hags,
To torture Don Lorenzo and the rest.
Yet lest the triple-headed porter should
Deny my passage to the slimy strond,   120

107 *as a raging sea*: this extended image is confused and difficult to make
complete sense of: Hieronimo berates himself for not doing as the raging sea,
when his social inferiors, 'lesser waters', do their labouring
116 *Alcides*: Hercules, who descended to the underworld as his twelfth
labour
119 *triple-headed porter*: Cerberus; see also 1.1.30 note above

The Thracian poet thou shalt counterfeit:
Come on, old father, be my Orpheus,
And if thou canst no notes upon the harp,
Then sound the burden of thy sore heart's grief,
Till we do gain that Proserpine may grant
Revenge on them that murdered my son.
Then will I rent and tear them thus and thus,
Shivering their limbs in pieces with my teeth.
         Tear the papers.
1 [*Citizen*]. O sir, my declaration!
         Exit Hieronimo and they after.
130 2 [*Citizen*]. Save my bond!
         Enter Hieronimo.
Save my bond!
3 [*Citizen*]. Alas my lease! it cost me ten pound,
And you my lord have torn the same.
Hieronimo. That cannot be, I gave it never a wound,
Show me one drop of blood fall from the same.
How is it possible I should slay it then?
Tush no, run after, catch me if you can.
         Exeunt all but the old man.
         Bazulto remains until Hieronimo enters again, who
         staring him in the face speaks.
Hieronimo. And art thou come, Horatio, from the depth
To ask for justice in this upper earth?
140 To tell thy father thou art unrevenged,
To wring more tears from Isabella's eyes
Whose lights are dimmed with overlong laments?
Go back my son, complain to Aeacus,
For here's no justice: gentle boy, be gone.
For justice is exiled from the earth.
Hieronimo will bear thee company.
Thy mother cries on righteous Rhadamanth

121–2 *Thracian poet . . . Orpheus*: Orpheus, the Thracian poet-musician,
persuaded Persephone/Proserpine by his playing to let his dead wife Eurydice
leave the underworld
124 *burden*: refrain or chorus

For just revenge against the murderers.
Senex. Alas my lord, whence springs this troubled speech?
Hieronimo. But let me look on my Horatio: 150
    Sweet boy, how art thou changed in death's black shade?
    Had Proserpine no pity on thy youth?
    But suffered thy fair crimson-coloured spring,
    With withered winter to be blasted thus?
    Horatio, thou art older than thy father.
    Ah ruthless fate, that favour thus transforms.
Senex. Ah, my good lord, I am not your young son.
Hieronimo. What, not my son? thou then a Fury art,
    Sent from the empty kingdom of black night,
    To summon me to make appearance   160
    Before grim Minos and just Rhadamanth,
    To plague Hieronimo that is remiss,
    And seeks not vengeance for Horatio's death.
Senex. I am a grieved man and not a ghost,
    That came for justice for my murdered son.
Hieronimo. Ay, now I know thee, now thou nam'st my son,
    Thou art the lively image of my grief,
    Within thy face my sorrows I may see.
    Thy eyes are gummed with tears, thy cheeks are wan,
    Thy forehead troubled, and thy muttering lips   170
    Murmur sad words abruptly broken off;
    By force of windy sighs thy spirit breathes,
    And all this sorrow riseth for thy son:
    And selfsame sorrow feel I for my son.
    Come in old man, thou shalt to Isabel,
    Lean on my arm, I thee, thou me shalt stay,
    And thou, and I, and she will sing a song:
    Three parts in one, but all of discords framed,
    Talk not of cords, but let us now be gone,
    For with a cord Horatio was slain.   *Exeunt.*   180

154 *blasted*: blighted, parched   176 *stay*: support

[ACT 3

Scene 14]

Enter King of Spain, the Duke, Viceroy and Lorenzo, Baltha-
zar, Don Pedro, and Bel-imperia.

King. Go brother, it is the duke of Castile's cause, salute the
    viceroy in our name.
Castile. I go.
Viceroy. Go forth, Don Pedro for thy nephew's sake,
    And greet the duke of Castile.
Pedro. It shall be so.
King. And now to meet these Portuguese,
    For as we now are, so sometimes were these,
    Kings and commanders of the western Indies.
10   Welcome, brave viceroy to the court of Spain,
    And welcome all his honourable train.
    'Tis not unknown to us, for why you come,
    Or have so kingly crossed the seas:
    Sufficeth it in this we note the troth
    And more than common love you lend to us.
    So is it that mine honourable niece,
    For it beseems us now that it be known,
    Already is betrothed to Balthazar:
    And by appointment and our condescent,
20   Tomorrow are they to be married.
    To this intent, we entertain thyself,
    Thy followers, their pleasure, and our peace:
    Speak men of Portingale, shall it be so?
    If ay, say so: if not say flatly no.
Viceroy. Renowned king, I come not as thou think'st,
    With doubtful followers, unresolved men,
    But such as have upon thine articles,
    Confirmed thy motion and contented me.

11 *train*: attendants   14 *troth*: loyalty   19 *condescent*: agreement

Know, sovereign, I come to solemnize
The marriage of thy beloved niece,   30
Fair Bel-imperia with my Balthazar.
With thee my son, whom sith I live to see,
Here take my crown, I give it her and thee,
And let me live a solitary life,
In ceaseless prayers,
To think how strangely heaven hath thee preserved.
King. See, brother, see how nature strives in him,
   Come, worthy viceroy, and accompany
   Thy friend, with thine extremities:
   A place more private fits this princely mood.   40
Viceroy. Or here or where your highness thinks it good.
   Exeunt all but Castile and Lorenzo.
Castile. Nay, stay Lorenzo, let me talk with you.
   Seest thou this entertainment of these kings?
Lorenzo. I do my lord, and joy to see the same.
Castile. And knowest thou why this meeting is?
Lorenzo. For her my lord, whom Balthazar doth love,
   And to confirm their promised marriage.
Castile. She is thy sister?
Lorenzo. Who, Bel-imperia? Ay, my gracious lord,
   And this is the day, that I have longed so happily to see. 50
Castile. Thou wouldst be loath that any fault of thine,
   Should intercept her in her happiness.
Lorenzo. Heavens will not let Lorenzo err so much.
Castile. Why then Lorenzo, listen to my words:
   It is suspected and reported too,
   That thou, Lorenzo, wronged Hieronimo,
   And in his suits towards his majesty,
   Still keep'st him back and seeks to cross his suit.
Lorenzo. That I, my lord?
Castile. I tell thee son, myself I have heard it said,   60
   When to my sorrow I have been ashamed
   To answer for thee, though thou art my son,

32 *sith*: then, next   39 *extremities*: extreme emotions
52 *intercept*: disrupt   57 *suits*: requests

Lorenzo, knowest thou not the common love,
And kindness that Hieronimo hath won
By his deserts within the court of Spain?
Or seest thou not the king my brother's care,
In his behalf, and to procure his health?
Lorenzo, should'st thou thwart his passions,
And he exclaim against thee to the king,
70   What honour wer't in this assembly,
Or what a scandal wer't among the kings,
To hear Hieronimo exclaim on thee?
Tell me, and look thou tell me truly too,
Whence grows the ground of this report in court?
Lorenzo. My lord, it lies not within power
To stop the vulgar, liberal of their tongues:
A small advantage makes a water breach,
And no man lives that long contenteth all.
Castile. Myself have seen thee busy to keep back
80   Him and his supplications from the king.
Lorenzo. Yourself, my lord, hath seen his passions,
That ill-beseemed the presence of a king,
And, for I pitied him in his distress,
I held him thence with kind and courteous words,
As free from malice to Hieronimo,
As to my soul, my lord.
Castile. Hieronimo, my son, mistakes thee then.
Lorenzo. My gracious father, believe me so he doth,
But what's a silly man distract in mind,
90   To think upon the murder of his son.
Alas, how easy is it for him to err?
But for his satisfaction and the world's,
'Twere good my lord that Hieronimo and I
Were reconciled if he misconstrue me.
Castile. Lorenzo thou hast said, it shall be so,
Go one of you and call Hieronimo.
       Enter Balthazar and Bel-imperia.
Balthazar. Come Bel-imperia, Balthazar's content,

87 *mistakes*: misinterprets

   My sorrow's ease and sovereign of my bliss:
   Sith heaven hath ordained thee to be mine,
   Disperse those clouds and melancholy looks,   100
   And clear them up with those thy sun-bright eyes,
   Wherein my hope and heaven's fair beauty lies.
Bel-imperia. My looks, my lord, are fitting for my love,
   Which new begun, can show brighter yet.
Balthazar. New-kindled flames should burn as morning sun.
Bel-imperia. But not too fast, lest heat and all be done.
   I see my lord my father.
Balthazar. Truce my love, I will go salute him.
Castile. Welcome Balthazar, welcome brave prince,
   The pledge of Castile's peace: 110
   And welcome Bel-imperia, how now girl?
   Why comest thou sadly to salute us thus?
   Content thyself, for I am satisfied,
   It is not now as when Andrea lived,
   We have forgotten and forgiven that,
   And thou art graced with a happier love.
   But Balthazar, here comes Hieronimo,
   I'll have a word with him.
     Enter Hieronimo and a servant.
Hieronimo. And where's the duke?
Servant. Yonder.   120
Hieronimo. Even so: what new device have they devised, trow?
   Poco palabras, mild as the lamb,
   Is't I will be revenged? no, I am not the man.
Castile. Welcome Hieronimo.
Lorenzo. Welcome Hieronimo.
Balthazar. Welcome Hieronimo.
Hieronimo. My lords, I thank you for Horatio.
Castile. Hieronimo, the reason that I sent
   To speak with you, is this –
Hieronimo. What, so short?   130
   Then I'll be gone, I thank you for't.
Castile. Nay, stay Hieronimo! go call him, son.

121 *trow*: do you think   122 *Poco palabras*: 'Few words' (Spanish)

Lorenzo. Hieronimo, my father craves a word with you.

Hieronimo. With me sir? Why my lord, I thought you had
    done.

Lorenzo. No, would he had.

Castile. Hieronimo, I hear you find yourself aggrieved at
    my son,
  Because you have not access unto the king,
  And say 'tis he that intercepts your suits.

Hieronimo. Why, is not this a miserable thing my lord?

140 *Castile.* Hieronimo, I hope you have no cause,
  And would be loath that one of your deserts,
  Should once have reason to suspect my son,
  Considering how I think of you myself.

Hieronimo. Your son Lorenzo, whom, my noble lord?
  The hope of Spain, mine honourable friend?
  Grant me the combat of them, if they dare.
    Draws out his sword.
  I'll meet him face to face to tell me so.
  These be the scandalous reports of such
  As loves not me, and hate my lord too much.

150 Should I suspect Lorenzo would prevent
  Or cross my suit, that loved my son so well,
  My lord, I am ashamed it should be said.

Lorenzo. Hieronimo, I never gave you cause.

Hieronimo. My good lord, I know you did not.

Castile. Then there pause, and for the satisfaction of the world,
  Hieronimo, frequent my homely house,
  The Duke of Castile Ciprian's ancient seat,
  And when thou wilt, use me, my son, and it.
  But, here before Prince Balthazar and me,

160 Embrace each other and be perfect friends.

Hieronimo. Ay marry, my lord, and shall.
  Friends, quoth he, see, I'll be friends with you all.
  Specially with you, my lovely lord,
  For diverse causes is fit for us,
  That we be friends, the world is suspicious,
  And men may think what we imagine not.

Balthazar. Why this is friendly done, Hieronimo.
Lorenzo. And that I hope: old grudges are forgot.
Hieronimo. What else, it were a shame it should not be so.
Castile. Come on, Hieronimo, at my request,   170
   Let us entreat your company today.
    Exeunt.
Hieronimo. Your lordship's to command,
   Pha! keep your way.
   Chi mi fa piu carezze che non suole
   Tradito mi ha, o tradirmi vuole.   *Exit.*

[ACT 3

Scene 15]

Ghost and Revenge [sleeping].

Ghost. Awake, Erichtho, Cerberus awake,
   Solicit Pluto, gentle Proserpine;
   To combat, Acheron and Erebus in hell,
   For nearby Styx and Phlegethon:
   Nor ferried Charon to the fiery lakes
   Such fearful sights, as poor Andrea see?
   Revenge, awake!
Revenge. Awake, for why?
Ghost. Awake Revenge, for thou art ill-advised
   To sleep away what thou art warned to watch.   10
Revenge. Content thyself and do not trouble me.
Ghost. Awake Revenge, if love, as love hath had,

174–5 *Chi mi . . . vuole*: 'He who shows unusual fondness to me has or
wishes to betray me' (Italian)
1–5 *Awake . . . lakes*: editors usually, following Edwards, suggest a line has
been lost here that would make sense of Andrea's vision: that infernal sights
cannot compare to what is being played out in front of him
1 *Erichtho*: a sorceress

Have yet the power or prevalence in hell,
Hieronimo with Lorenzo is joined in league,
And intercepts our passage to revenge:
Awake Revenge, or we are woebegone.
Revenge. Thus worldlings ground, what they have dreamed, upon,
Content thyself Andrea, though I sleep,
Yet is my mood soliciting their souls.
20   Sufficeth thee that poor Hieronimo,
Cannot forget his son Horatio?
Nor dies Revenge although he sleep awhile,
For in unquiet, quietness is feigned:
And slumbering is a common worldly wile,
Behold, Andrea, for an instance how
Revenge hath slept, and then imagine thou,
What 'tis to be subject to destiny.
        Enter a dumbshow.
Ghost. Awake Revenge, reveal this mystery.
Revenge. The two first the nuptial torches bear,
30   As brightly burning as the midday's sun:
But after them doth Hymen hie as fast,
Clothed in sable and a saffron robe,
And blows them out, and quencheth them with blood,
As discontent that things continue so.
Ghost. Sufficeth me thy meaning's understood,
And thanks to thee and those infernal powers,
That will not tolerate a lover's woe,
Rest thee, for I will sit to see the rest.
Revenge. Then argue not, for thou hast thy request.
        Exeunt.

17 *ground . . . upon*: base their beliefs on dreams
31 *Hymen*: god of marriage   *hie*: run

ACT 4

Scene 1

Enter Bel-imperia and Hieronimo.

Bel-imperia. Is this the love thou bear'st Horatio?
  Is this the kindness that thou counterfeits?
  Are these the fruits of thine incessant tears?
  Hieronimo, are these thy passions,
  Thy protestations and thy deep laments
  That thou wert wont to weary men withal?
  O unkind father, O deceitful world,
  With what excuses can'st thou show thyself?
  With what dishonour, and the hate of men,
  From this dishonour and the hate of men: 10
  Thus to neglect the loss and life of him,
  Whom both my letters, and thine own belief,
  Assures thee to be causeless slaughtered.
  Hieronimo, for shame Hieronimo:
  Be not a history to aftertimes,
  Of such ingratitude unto thy son.
  Unhappy mothers of such children then,
  But monstrous fathers, to forget so soon
  The death of those, whom they with care and cost
  Have tendered so, thus careless should be lost,   20
  Myself a stranger in respect of thee,
  So loved his life, as still I wish their deaths;
  Nor shall his death be unrevenged by me.
  Although I bear it out for fashion's sake.
  For here I swear in sight of heaven and earth,
  Should'st thou neglect the love thou should'st retain,
  And give it over and devise no more,
  Myself should send their hateful souls to hell,

10 *From this . . . of men*: this repetition may well be a compositorial error,
but if any text was lost it cannot be recovered
15 *history*: admonitory tale or example   24 *fashion*: appearance

That wrought his downfall with extremest death.
30 *Hieronimo.* But may it be that Bel-imperia
Vows such revenge as she hath deigned to say:
Why then I see that heaven applies our drift,
And all the saints do sit soliciting
For vengeance on those cursed murderers,
Madam 'tis true, and now I find it so,
I found a letter, written in your name,
And in that letter, how Horatio died.
Pardon, O pardon, Bel-imperia,
My fear and care in not believing it;
40 Nor think, I thoughtless think upon a mean,
To let his death be unrevenged at full.
And here I vow, so you but give consent,
And will conceal my resolution,
I will ere long determine of their deaths,
That causeless thus have murdered my son.
Bel-imperia. Hieronimo, I will consent, conceal,
And aught that may effect for thine avail,
Join with thee to revenge Horatio's death.
Hieronimo. On then, whatsoever I devise,
50 Let me entreat you grace my practices.
For why, the plot's already in mine head,
Here they are.
        Enter Balthazar and Lorenzo.
Balthazar. How now, Hieronimo? what courting Bel-imperia?
Hieronimo. Ay, my lord, such courting as I promise you,
She hath my heart, but you, my lord, have hers.
Lorenzo. But now Hieronimo, or never we are to entreat your help.
Hieronimo. My help, why my good lords, assure yourselves of
me, for you have given me cause, ay, by my faith have you.
Balthazar. It pleased you at the entertainment of the ambassador,
60 To grace the king so much as with a show.
Now were your study so well furnished,
As for the passing of the first night's sport,
To entertain my father with the like,

32 *drift*: intention   39 *care*: caution   47 *avail*: help   50 *grace*: support

Or any suchlike pleasing motion,
Assure yourself, it would content them well.
Hieronimo. Is this all?
Balthazar. Ay, this is all.
Hieronimo. Why then I'll fit you, say no more.
    When I was young, I gave my mind
    And 'plied myself to fruitless poetry,   70
    Which though it profit the professor naught,
    Yet is it passing pleasing to the world.
Lorenzo. And how for that?
Hieronimo. Marry, my good lord, thus.
    And yet methinks you are too quick with us.
    When in Toledo there I studied,
    It was my chance to write a tragedy:
    See here, my lords.
       He shows them a book.
    Which long forgot, I found this other day,
    Now: would your lordships favour me so much,   80
    As but to grace me with your acting it?
    I mean each one of you to play a part,
    Assure you it will prove most passing strange,
    And wondrous plausible to that assembly.
Balthazar. What would you have us play a tragedy?
Hieronimo. Why Nero thought it no disparagement,
    And kings and emperors have ta'en delight,
    To make experience of their wits in plays.
Lorenzo. Nay, be not angry, good Hieronimo,
    The prince but asked a question.   90
Balthazar. In faith Hieronimo, and you be in earnest,
    I'll make one.
Lorenzo. And I another.
Hieronimo. Now my good lord, could you entreat
    Your sister Bel-imperia to make one,
    For what's a play without a woman in it?

64 *motion*: entertainment
68 *fit you*: get what you want; requite you; do as is fit
75 *quick*: impatient
86 *Nero*: Roman emperor; see also *Hamlet*, scene 9.233 and note

Bel-imperia. Little entreaty shall serve me, Hieronimo,
　For I must needs be employed in your play.
Hieronimo. Why this is well. I tell you, lordings,
It was determined to have been acted
By gentlemen and scholars too,
Such as could tell what to speak.
Balthazar. And now it shall be played by princes and courtiers
Such as can tell how to speak,
If, as it is our country manner,
You will but let us know the argument.
Hieronimo. That shall I roundly: the chronicles of Spain
Record this written of a knight of Rhodes,
He was betrothed and wedded at the length
To one Perseda an Italian dame,
Whose beauty ravished all that her beheld,
Especially the soul of Soliman,
Who at the marriage was the chiefest guest.
By sundry means sought Soliman to win
Perseda's love, and could not gain the same.
Then 'gan he break his passions to a friend,
One of his bashaws whom he held full dear;
Her had this bashaw long solicited,
And saw she was not otherwise to be won
But by her husband's death this knight of Rhodes,
Whom presently by treachery he slew.
She, stirred with an exceeding hate therefore,
As cause of this slew Soliman,
And to escape the bashaw's tyranny,
Did stab herself, and this the tragedy.
Lorenzo. O excellent!
Bel-imperia. But say, Hieronimo, what then became of him

100
110
120

---

100 *determined*: designed　106 *argument*: synopsis　107 *roundly*: plainly
110–12 *Perseda . . . Soliman*: a play called *Soliman and Perseda*, closely
based on Henry Wotton's *Courtlie Controversie of Cupid's Cautels* (1578)
and published in 1592, has often been attributed to Kyd, but its echo of this
playlet is the only evidence for his authorship; see also Playwrights
117 *bashaws*: courtiers or officers in the Turkish court

That was the bashaw?
Hieronimo. Marry thus, moved with remorse of his misdeeds
   Ran to a mountain-top and hung himself.   130
Balthazar. But which of us is to perform that part?
Hieronimo. O that will I, my lords, make no doubt of it,
   I'll play the murderer, I warrant you,
   For I already have conceited that.
Balthazar. And what shall I?
Hieronimo. Great Soliman the Turkish emperor.
Lorenzo. And I?
Hieronimo. Erastus, the knight of Rhodes.
Bel-imperia. And I?
Hieronimo. Perseda, chaste and resolute.   140
   And here, my lords, are several abstracts drawn,
   For each of you to note your parts,
   And act it as occasion's offered you.
   You must provide a Turkish cap,
   A black mustachio and a fauchion.
     Gives a paper to Balthazar.
   You with a cross like to a knight of Rhodes.
     Gives another to Lorenzo.
   And madam, you must attire yourself,
     He giveth Bel-imperia another.
   Like Phoebe, Flora, or the huntress,
   Which to your discretion shall seem best.
   And as for me, my lords, I'll look to one,   150
   And with the ransom that the viceroy sent
   So furnish and perform this tragedy,
   As all the world shall say Hieronimo
   Was liberal in gracing of it so.
Balthazar. Hieronimo, methinks a comedy were better.
Hieronimo. A comedy, fie, comedies are fit for common wits!
   But to present a kingly troupe withal,
   Give me a stately written tragedy,

134 *conceited*: imagined   141 *abstracts*: outlines
145 *fauchion*: broad curved sword
148 *huntress*: the chaste goddess of hunting, Diana

     Tragedia cothurnata, fitting kings,
160   Containing matter, and not common things.
     My lords, all this must be performed
     As fitting for the first night's revelling.
     The Italian tragedians were so sharp of wit,
     That in one hour's meditation,
     They would perform anything in action.
Lorenzo. And well it may, for I have seen the like
     In Paris, 'mongst the French tragedians.
Hieronimo. In Paris? mass and well remembered,
     There's one thing more that rests for us to do.
170 *Balthazar.* What's that, Hieronimo? forget not anything.
Hieronimo. Each one of us must act his part
     In unknown languages,
     That it may breed the more variety.
     As you my lord in Latin, I in Greek,
     You in Italian, and for because I know
     That Bel-imperia hath practised the French
     In courtly French shall all her phrases be.
Bel-imperia. You mean to try my cunning then, Hieronimo.
Balthazar. But this will be a mere confusion,
180   And hardly shall we all be understood.
Hieronimo. It must be so, for the conclusion
     Shall prove the invention, and all was good:
     And I myself in an oration,
     That I will have there behind a curtain,
     And with a strange and wondrous show besides,
     Assure yourself shall make the matter known.
     And all shall be concluded in one scene,
     For there's no pleasure ta'en in tediousness.
Balthazar. How like you this?
190 *Lorenzo.* Why thus, my lord, we must resolve,
     To soothe his humours up.
Balthazar. On then, Hieronimo, farewell till soon.

159 *Tragedia cothurnata*: Buskined tragedy, the most serious sort in ancient
Greece
160 *matter*: serious material   168 *mass*: used in oaths
172 *unknown*: foreign   178 *cunning*: knowledge

Hieronimo. You'll ply this gear.
Lorenzo. I warrant you.
　　Exeunt all but Hieronimo.
Hieronimo. Why so, now shall I see the fall of Babylon,
　　Wrought by the heavens in this confusion.
　　And if the world like not this tragedy,
　　Hard is the hap of old Hieronimo.　　*Exit.*

[ACT 4

Scene 2]

Enter Isabella with a weapon.

Isabella. Tell me no more, O monstrous homicides!
　　Since neither piety nor pity moves
　　The king to justice or compassion,
　　I will revenge myself upon this place,
　　Where thus they murdered my beloved son.
　　　　She cuts down the arbour.
　　Down with these branches and those loathsome boughs
　　Of this unfortunate and fatal pine:
　　Down with them, Isabella, rent them up,
　　And burn the roots from whence the rest is sprung:
　　I will not leave a root, a stalk, a tree,   10
　　A bough, a branch, a blossom, nor a leaf,
　　No, not a herb within this garden plot.
　　Accursed complot of my misery,
　　Fruitless for ever may this garden be.
　　Barren the earth and blissless whosoever
　　Imagines not to keep it unmanured.
　　An eastern wind commixed with noisome airs,

195 *Babylon*: both the biblical Tower of Babel, associated with a confusion
of languages, and the wicked city of Babylon
8 *rent*: tear　16 *unmanured*: uncultivated
17 *noisome*: harmful

Shall blast the plants and the young saplings;
The earth with serpents shall be plastered
20   And passengers for fear to be infect,
Shall stand aloof and looking at it, tell
There murdered died the son of Isabel.
Ay, here he died, and here I him embrace.
See where his ghost solicits with his wounds,
Revenge on her that should revenge his death.
Hieronimo, make haste to see thy son,
For sorrow and despair hath cited me,
To hear Horatio plead with Rhadamanth.
Make haste, Hieronimo, to hold excused
30   Thy negligence in pursuit of their deaths
Whose hateful wrath bereaved him of his breath.
Ah nay, thou dost delay their deaths,
Forgives the murderers of thy noble son.
And none but I bestir me to no end.
And as I curse this tree from further fruit,
So shall my womb be cursed for his sake,
And with this weapon will I wound the breast,
The hapless breast that gave Horatio suck.
        She stabs herself. [Exit.]

[ACT 4

Scene 3]

Enter Hieronimo, he knocks up the curtain.
Enter the Duke of Castile.

Castile. How now Hieronimo, where's your fellows,
    That you take all this pain?
Hieronimo. O sir, it is for the author's credit,
    To look that all things may go well:

---

20 *passengers*: passers-by   27 *cited*: summoned   OSD *knocks up*: hangs up

But good my lord, let me entreat your grace,
To give the king the copy of the play:
This is the argument of what we show.
Castile. I will, Hieronimo.
Hieronimo. One thing more, my good lord.
Castile. What's that?   10
Hieronimo. Let me entreat your grace,
    That when the train are passed into the gallery,
    You would vouchsafe to throw me down the key.
Castile. I will, Hieronimo.   *Exit Castile.*
Hieronimo. What, are you ready Balthazar?
    Bring a chair and a cushion for the king.
        Enter Balthazar with a chair.
    Well done Balthazar, hang up the title:
    Our scene is Rhodes. What, is your beard on?
Balthazar. Half on, the other is in my hand.
Hieronimo. Dispatch for shame, are you so long?   20
        Exit Balthazar.
    Bethink thyself, Hieronimo.
    Recall thy wits, recompt thy former wrongs
    Thou hast received by murder of thy son.
    And lastly, not least, how Isabel,
    Once his mother and thy dearest wife,
    All woebegone for him hath slain herself.
    Behoves thee then, Hieronimo, to be revenged.
    The plot is laid of dire revenge.
    On then, Hieronimo, pursue revenge,
    For nothing wants but acting of revenge.   30
        Exit Hieronimo.

17 *title*: board to indicate location   22 *recompt*: recall

[ACT 4

Scene 4]

Enter Spanish King, Viceroy, the Duke of Castile, and their train.

King. Now, viceroy, shall we see the tragedy
    Of Soliman the Turkish emperor,
    Performed of pleasure by your son the prince,
    My nephew Don Lorenzo and my niece.
Viceroy. Who, Bel-imperia?
King. Ay, and Hieronimo our marshal,
    At whose request they deign to do't themselves.
    These be our pastimes in the court of Spain.
    Here brother, you shall be the book-keeper.
10   This is the argument of that they show.
        He giveth him a book.
        Gentlemen, this play of Hieronimo in sundry languages was
        thought good to be set down in English more largely, for
        the easier understanding to every public reader.
        Enter Balthazar, Bel-imperia and Hieronimo.
Balthazar. Bashaw, that Rhodes is ours, yield heavens the honour,
    And holy Mahomet our sacred Prophet:
    And be thou graced with every excellence
    That Soliman can give or thou desire.
    But thy desert in conquering Rhodes is less,
    Than in reserving this fair Christian nymph
    Perseda, blissful lamp of excellence:
    Whose eyes compel like powerful adamant
    The warlike heart of Soliman to wait.
20 *King.* See, viceroy, that is Balthazar, your son,
    That represents the Emperor Soliman.
    How well he acts his amorous passion!
Viceroy. Ay, Bel-imperia hath taught him that.
Castile. That's because his mind runs all on Bel-imperia.

---

9 *book-keeper*: prompter

Hieronimo. Whatever joy earth yields betide your majesty.
Balthazar. Earth yields no joy without Perseda's love.
Hieronimo. Let then Perseda on your grace attend.
Balthazar. She shall not wait on me, but I on her,
 Drawn by the influence of her lights, I yield,
 But let my friend the Rhodean knight come forth,   30
 Erasto, dearer than my life to me,
 That he may see Perseda my beloved.
  Enter Erasto.
King. Here comes Lorenzo: look upon the plot,
 And tell me brother, what part plays he?
Bel-imperia. Ah my Erasto, welcome to Perseda.
Lorenzo. Thrice happy is Erasto, that thou lives,
 Rhodes' loss is nothing to Erasto's joy:
 Sith his Perseda lives, his life survives.
Balthazar. Ah bashaw, here is love between Erasto
 And fair Perseda sovereign of my soul.   40
Hieronimo. Remove Erasto mighty Soliman,
 And then Perseda will be quickly won.
Balthazar. Erasto is my friend, and while he lives,
 Perseda never will remove her love.
Hieronimo. Let not Erasto live, to grieve great Soliman.
Balthazar. Dear is Erasto in our princely eye.
Hieronimo. But if he be your rival, let him die.
Balthazar. Why let him die, so love commandeth me.
 Yet grieve I that Erasto should so die.
Hieronimo. Erasto, Soliman saluteth thee   50
 And lets thee wit by me his highness' will:
 Which is, thou should'st be thus employed. *Stab him.*
Bel-imperia. Ay me Erasto, see Soliman, Erasto's slain.
Balthazar. Yet liveth Soliman to comfort thee
 Fair queen of beauty, let not favour die,
 But with a gracious eye behold his grief,
 That with Perseda's beauty is increased.
 If by Perseda's grief be not released.
Bel-imperia. Tyrant, desist soliciting vain suits,
 Relentless are mine ears to thy laments   60

As thy butcher is pitiless and base,
Which seized on my Erasto, harmless knight.
Yet by thy power thou thinkest to command,
And to thy power Perseda doth obey,
But were she able, thus she would revenge
Thy treachery on thee ignoble prince: *Stab him.*
And on herself she would be thus revenged.   *Stab herself.*
King. Well said old marshal, this was bravely done.
Hieronimo. But Bel-imperia plays Perseda well.
70 *Viceroy.* Were this in earnest, Bel-imperia,
You would be better to my son than so.
King. But now what follows for Hieronimo?
Hieronimo. Marry, this follows for Hieronimo.
Here break we off our sundry languages,
And thus conclude I in our vulgar tongue.
Haply you think, but bootless are your thoughts,
That this is fabulously counterfeit,
And that we do as all tragedians do,
To die today for, fashioning our scene,
80 The death of Ajax or some Roman peer,
And in a minute starting up again,
Revive to please tomorrow's audience.
No princes, know that I am Hieronimo,
The hopeless father of a hapless son,
Whose tongue is tuned to tell his latest tale,
Not to excuse gross errors in the play.
I see your looks urge instance of these words,
Behold the reason urging me to this.
    Shows his dead son.
See here my show, look on this spectacle:
90 Here lay my hope, and here my hope hath end;
Here lay my heart, and here my heart was slain;
Here lay my treasure, here my treasure lost;
Here lay my bliss, and here my bliss bereft.
But hope, heart, treasure, joy and bliss:
All fled, failed, died, yea, all decayed with this.
From forth these wounds came breath that gave me life,

They murdered me that made these fatal marks.
The cause was love, whence grew this mortal hate.
The hate Lorenzo and young Balthazar:
The love, my son to Bel-imperia.   100
But night, the coverer of accursed crimes,
With pitchy silence hushed these traitors' harms,
And lent them leave, for they had sorted leisure,
To take advantage in my garden plot,
Upon my son, my dear Horatio.
There merciless they butchered up my boy,
In black, dark night, to pale, dim, cruel death.
He shrieks, I heard, and yet methinks I hear
His dismal outcry echo in the air.
With soonest speed I hasted to the noise,   110
Where hanging on a tree, I found my son,
Through-girt with wounds, and slaughtered as you see,
And grieved I, think you, at this spectacle?
Speak Portuguese, whose loss resembles mine,
If thou canst weep upon thy Balthazar,
'Tis like I wailed for my Horatio.
And you, my lord, whose reconciled son,
Marched in a net, and thought himself unseen,
And rated me for brainsick lunacy,
With 'God amend that mad Hieronimo!' –   120
How can you brook our play's catastrophe?
And here behold this bloody handkercher,
Which at Horatio's death I, weeping, dipped
Within the river of his bleeding wounds.
It as propitious, see I have reserved,
And never hath it left my bloody heart,
Soliciting remembrance of my vow.
With these, O these accursed murderers,
Which now performed, my heart is satisfied.
And to this end, the bashaw I became,   130
That might revenge me on Lorenzo's life,

102 *pitchy*: black   118 *Marched in a net*: Concealed himself
119 *rated*: berated

Who therefore was appointed to the part
And was to represent the knight of Rhodes.
That I might kill him more conveniently.
So, viceroy, was this Balthazar, thy son,
That Soliman, which Bel-imperia,
In person of Perseda murdered:
Solely appointed to that tragic part,
That she might slay him that offended her.
140   Poor Bel-imperia missed her part in this,
For though the story saith she should have died,
Yet I of kindness and of care to her,
Did otherwise determine of her end:
But love of him whom they did hate too much,
Did urge her resolution to be such.
And princes, now behold Hieronimo,
Author and actor in this tragedy:
Bearing his latest fortune in his fist:
And will as resolute conclude his part,
150   As any of the actors gone before.
And gentles, thus I end my play,
Urge no more words, I have no more to say.
        He runs to hang himself.
King. O harken, viceroy, hold Hieronimo!
Brother, my nephew and thy son are slain.
Viceroy. We are betrayed, my Balthazar is slain,
Break ope the doors, run, save Hieronimo.
Hieronimo, do but inform the king of these events,
Upon mine honour thou shalt have no harm.
Hieronimo. Viceroy, I will not trust thee with my life
160   Which I this day have offered to my son:
Accursed wretch, why stayest thou him that was resolved to die?
King. Speak traitor, damned bloody murderer speak.
For now I have thee I will make thee speak.
Why hast thou done this undeserving deed?
Viceroy. Why hast thou murdered my Balthazar?

140 *missed*: departed from   156 *ope*: open

Castile. Why hast thou butchered both my children thus?
Hieronimo. O good words: as dear to me was my Horatio
    As yours, or yours, or yours, my lords to you.
    My guiltless son was by Lorenzo slain,
    And by Lorenzo and that Balthazar,   170
    Am I at last revenged thoroughly,
    Upon whose souls may heavens be yet avenged,
    With greater far than these afflictions.
Castile. But who were thy confederates in this?
Viceroy. That was thy daughter Bel-imperia,
    For by her hand my Balthazar was slain.
    I saw her stab him.
King. Why speakest not thou?
Hieronimo. What lesser liberty can kings afford,
    Than harmless silence? then afford it me: 180
    Sufficeth I may not, nor I will not tell thee.
King. Fetch forth the tortures.
    Traitor as thou art, I'll make thee tell.
Hieronimo. Indeed, thou mayest torment me, as his wretched son
    Hath done in murdering my Horatio.
    But never shalt thou force me to reveal
    The thing which I have vowed inviolate:
    And therefore in despite of all thy threats,
    Pleased with their deaths, and eased with their revenges,
    First take my tongue, and afterwards my heart.   190
                      [*He bites out his tongue.*]
King. O monstrous resolution of a wretch,
    See viceroy, he hath bitten forth his tongue,
    Rather than to reveal what we required!
Castile. Yet can he write.
King. And if in this he satisfy us not,
    We will devise the extremest kind of death,
    That ever was invented for a wretch.
    Then he makes signs for a knife to mend his pen.
Castile. O, he would have a knife to mend his pen.
Viceroy. Here, and advise him that thou write the truth,
King. Look to my brother, save Hieronimo.   200

He with a knife stabs the Duke and himself.

King. What age hath ever heard such monstrous deeds?
My brother and the whole succeeding hope
That Spain expected after my decease.
Go bear his body hence that we may mourn
The loss of our beloved brother's death,
That he may be entombed whate'er befall.
I am the next, the nearest, the last of all.

Viceroy. And thou Don Pedro do the like for us:
Take up our hapless son untimely slain.
Set me with him, and he with woeful me,
Upon the mainmast of a ship unmanned,
And let the wind and tide haul me along,
To Scylla's barking and untamed grief,
Or to the loathsome pool of Acheron,
To weep my want for my sweet Balthazar.
Spain hath no refuge for a Portingale.

*The trumpets sound a dead march, the King of Spain
mourning after his brother's body, and the [Viceroy] of
Portingale bearing the body of his son.*

[ACT 4

Scene 5]

Enter Ghost and Revenge.

Ghost. Ay, now my hopes have end in their effects,
When blood and sorrow finish my desires:
Horatio murdered in his father's bower,
Vile Serberine by Pedringano slain,
False Pedringano hanged by quaint device,
Fair Isabella by herself misdone,

213 *Scylla*: a dangerous rock, paired with Charybdis
213 *grief*: often emended to 'gulf'   5 *quaint*: strange

Prince Balthazar by Bel-imperia stabbed,
The duke of Castile and his wicked son
Both done to death by old Hieronimo.
My Bel-imperia fallen as Dido fell,   10
And good Hieronimo slain by himself:
Ay, these were spectacles to please my soul.
Now will I beg at lovely Proserpine,
That by the virtue of her princely doom,
I may consort my friends in pleasing sort,
And on my foes work just and sharp revenge.
I'll lead my friend Horatio through those fields
Where never-dying wars are still inured.
I'll lead fair Isabella to that train
Where pity weeps but never feeleth pain.   20
I'll lead my Bel-imperia to those joys
That vestal virgins and fair queens possess,
I'll lead Hieronimo where Orpheus plays
Adding sweet pleasure to eternal days.
But say Revenge, for thou must help or none,
Against the rest how shall my hate be shown?
Revenge. This hand shall haul them down to deepest hell,
    Where none but Furies, bugs, and tortures dwell.
Ghost. Then sweet Revenge, do this at my request,
    Let me be judge and doom them to unrest.   30
    Let loose poor Tityus from the vulture's grip,
    And let Don Ciprian supply his room.
    Place Don Lorenzo on Ixion's wheel,
    And let the lover's endless pains surcease:
    Juno forgets old wrath and grants him ease.
    Hang Balthazar around Chimera's neck,
    And let him there bewail his bloody love,
    Repining at our joys that are above.

10 *Dido*: killed herself when her lover Aeneas left Carthage
14 *doom*: judgement   28 *bugs*: objects of terror
31 *Tityus*: tortured for lustfulness by having vultures peck his liver
34 *lover*: Ixion *surcease*: cease
36 *Chimera*: mythological monster with the head of a lion, body of a goat
and tail of a dragon

      Let Serberine go roll the fatal stone,
40   And take from Sisyphus his endless moan.
      False Pedringano for his treachery,
      Let him be dragged through boiling Acheron.
      And there live dying still in endless flames,
      Blaspheming gods and all their holy names.
Revenge. Then haste we down to meet thy friends and foes,
      To place thy friends in ease, the rest in woes.
      For here, though death hath end their misery,
      I'll there begin their endless tragedy.

FINIS

40 *Sisyphus*: condemned to push a huge stone uphill

WILLIAM SHAKESPEARE

HAMLET

(1603)

LIST OF CHARACTERS

HAMLET *prince of Denmark*
GHOST *of Hamlet's father, late King Hamlet of Denmark*
KING *Hamlet's uncle*
QUEEN *Gertred, Hamlet's mother*
CORAMBIS *councillor*
LEARTES *son of Corambis*
OFELIA *daughter of Corambis*
HORATIO *Hamlet's friend*
ROSSENCRAFT and GILDERSTONE *Hamlet's friends*
VOLTEMAR and CORNELIA *Danish ambassadors*
BARNARDO and MARCELLUS *watchmen*
MONTANO *Corambis' agent*
FORTENBRASSE *prince of Norway*
PLAYERS
SENTINEL
BRAGGART
1 CLOWN *gravedigger*
2 CLOWN
PRIEST
LORDS
AMBASSADORS
ATTENDANTS

[SCENE 1]

Enter [Sentinel and Barnardo].

Sentinel. Stand, who is that?
Barnardo. 'Tis I.
Sentinel. O, you come most carefully upon your watch.
Barnardo. And if you meet Marcellus and Horatio,
   The partners of my watch, bid them make haste.
Sentinel. I will. See, who goes there?
    Enter Horatio and Marcellus.
Horatio. Friends to this ground.
Marcellus. And liegemen to the Dane,
   O farewell, honest soldier. Who hath relieved you?
Sentinel. Barnardo hath my place. Give you good night. [*Exit.*]   10
Marcellus. Holla, Barnardo.
Barnardo. Say, is Horatio there?
Horatio. A piece of him.
Barnardo. Welcome Horatio, welcome good Marcellus.
Marcellus. What, hath this thing appeared again tonight?
Barnardo. I have seen nothing.
Marcellus. Horatio says 'tis but our fantasy,
   And will not let belief take hold of him
   Touching this dreaded sight twice seen by us.
   Therefore I have entreated him along with us   20
   To watch the minutes of this night,
   That if again this apparition come,
   He may approve our eyes, and speak to it.
Horatio. Tut, 'twill not appear.
Barnardo. Sit down, I pray, and let us once again
   Assail your ears that are so fortified,
   What we have two nights seen.

---

11 *Holla*: Exclamation meaning 'stop!'
17 *fantasy*: imagination 26 *fortified*: defended

Horatio. Well, sit we down, and let us hear Barnardo speak of
   this.

30 *Barnardo.* Last night of all, where yonder star that's westward
   from the pole had made his course to illumine that part of
   heaven where now it burns, the bell then tolling one –
      Enter Ghost.

Marcellus. Break off your talk, see where it comes again!

Barnardo. In the same figure like the king that's dead.

Marcellus. Thou art a scholar, speak to it, Horatio.

Barnardo. Looks it not like the king?

Horatio. Most like. It horrors me with fear and wonder.

Barnardo. It would be spoke to.

Marcellus. Question it, Horatio.

40 *Horatio.* What art thou that thus usurp the state, in
   Which the majesty of buried Denmark did some times
   Walk? By heaven, I charge thee, speak.

Marcellus. It is offended.
      Exit Ghost.

Barnardo. See, it stalks away.

Horatio. Stay, speak, speak, by heaven, I charge thee speak!

Marcellus. 'Tis gone and makes no answer.

Barnardo. How now Horatio, you tremble and look pale.
   Is this not something more than fantasy?
   What think you on't?

50 *Horatio.* Afore my God, I might not this believe, without the
   sensible and true avouch of my own eyes.

Marcellus. Is it not like the king?

Horatio. As thou art to thy self.
   Such was the very armour he had on,
   When he the ambitious Norway combated.
   So frowned he once, when in an angry parle
   He smote the sleaded poleaxe on the ice:
   'Tis strange.

---

37 *horrors*: horrifies   51 *sensible*: of the senses   *avouch*: proof
56 *parle*: meeting to discuss armistice
57 *sleaded poleaxe*: obscure, perhaps 'sledded Polacks' (Poles on sleds), or
'leaded pole-axe'

Marcellus. Thus twice before, and jump at this dead hour
  With martial stalk he passed through our watch.   60
Horatio. In what particular to work, I know not,
  But in the thought and scope of my opinion,
  This bodes some strange eruption to the state.
Marcellus. Good, now sit down and tell me he that knows
  Why this same strict and most observant watch
  So nightly toils the subject of the land,
  And why such daily cost of brazen cannon
  And foreign mart for implements of war,
  Why such impress of shipwrights, whose sore task
  Does not divide the Sunday from the week?   70
  What might be toward, that this sweaty march
  Doth make the night joint labourer with the day?
  Who is't that can inform me?
Horatio. Marry that I can, at least the whisper goes so:
  Our late king, who as you know was by Fortenbrasse of Norway
  Thereto pricked on by a most emulous cause, dared to
  The combat, to which our valiant Hamlet –
  For so this side of our known world esteemed him –
  Did slay this Fortenbrasse
  Who by a sealed compact well ratified by law   80
  And heraldry, did forfeit with his life all those
  His lands which he stood seized of by the conqueror,
  Against the which, a moiety competent,
  Was gaged by our king:
  Now sir, young Fortenbrasse,
  Of inapproved mettle hot and full
  Hath in the skirts of Norway here and there,
  Sharked up a fight of lawless resolutes
  For food and diet to some enterprise

59 *jump*: exactly   63 *eruption*: revolt   68 *mart*: merchandise
69 *impress*: enforced service   71 *toward*: anticipated
74 *Marry*: Expression of surprise or outrage   76 *pricked*: spurred
76 *emulous*: rivalrous   80 *sealed*: Q seale   *compact*: agreement
83 *moiety competent*: half or equal share   84 *gaged*: wagered
86 *inapproved*: unproved   88 *Sharked*: Seized

90   That hath a stomach in't: and this, I take it, is the
      Chief head and ground of this our watch.
          Enter the Ghost.
      But lo, behold, see where it comes again!
      I'll cross it, though it blast me. Stay, illusion!
      If there be any good thing to be done
      That may do ease to thee and grace to me,
      Speak to me.
      If thou art privy to thy country's fate,
      Which haply foreknowing may prevent, O speak to me,
      Or if thou hast extorted in thy life
100   Or hoarded treasure in the womb of earth,
      For which they say you spirits walk in death, speak to me.
      Stay and speak, speak, stop it, Marcellus!   [*A cock crows.*]
Barnardo. 'Tis here.   *Exit Ghost.*
Horatio. 'Tis here.
Marcellus. 'Tis gone. O we do it wrong, being so majestical, to
          offer it the show of violence,
      For it is as the air invulnerable
      And our vain blows malicious mockery.
Barnardo. It was about to speak when the cock crew.
Horatio. And then it faded like a guilty thing,
110   Upon a fearful summons. I have heard
      The cock, that is the trumpet to the morning,
      Doth with his early and shrill-crowing throat
      Awake the god of day, and at his sound,
      Whether in earth or air, in sea or fire,
      The stravagant and erring spirit hies
      To his confines, and of the truth hereof
      This present object made probation.
Marcellus. It faded on the crowing of the cock.
      Some say, that ever 'gainst that season comes
120   Wherein our Saviour's birth is celebrated,
      The bird of dawning singeth all night long,
      And then, they say, no spirit dare walk abroad,

106 *invulnerable*: Q invelmorable   115 *stravagant*: extravagant, wandering
117 *probation*: examination, trial

The nights are wholesome, then no planet strikes,
No fairy takes, nor witch hath power to charm,
So gracious and so hallowed is that time.
Horatio. So have I heard, and do in part believe it.
But see, the sun in russet mantle clad,
Walks o'er the dew of yon high mountain top.
Break we our watch up, and by my advice,
Let us impart what we have seen tonight   130
Unto young Hamlet: for upon my life,
This spirit, dumb to us, will speak to him.
Do you consent, we shall acquaint him with it,
As needful in our love, fitting our duty?
Marcellus. Let's do't I pray, and I this morning know
Where we shall find him most conveniently.   [*Exeunt.*]

[SCENE 2]

Enter King, Queen, Hamlet, Leartes, Corambis, and the two
ambassadors [Cornelia and Voltemar], with attendants.

King. Lords, we here have writ to Fortenbrasse,
Nephew to old Norway, who impotent
And bed-rid, scarcely hears of this his
Nephew's purpose: and we here dispatch
Young good Cornelia, and you, Voltemar
For bearers of these greetings to old
Norway, giving to you no further personal power
To business with the king,
Than those related articles do show.
Farewell, and let your haste commend your duty.   10
Cornelia and Voltemar. In this and all things we show our duty.
King. We doubt nothing: heartily farewell.
And now Leartes. What's the news with you?
You said you had a suit: what is't, Leartes?

123 *strikes*: Q frikes   2 *impotent*: Q impudent

Leartes. My gracious lord, your favourable licence,
  Now that the funeral rites are all performed,
  I may have leave to go again to France,
  For though the favour of your grace might stay me,
  Yet something is there whispers in my heart,
20 Which makes my mind and spirits bend all for France.
King. Have you your father's leave, Leartes?
Corambis. He hath, my lord, wrung from me a forced grant,
  And I beseech you grant your highness' leave.
King. With all our heart. Leartes, fare thee well.
Leartes. I in all love and duty take my leave.
King. And now, princely son Hamlet.   *Exit.*
  What means these sad and melancholy moods?
  For your intent in going to Wittenberg,
  We hold it most unmeet and unconvenient,
30 Being the joy and half-heart of your mother.
  Therefore let me entreat you stay in court.
  All Denmark's hope, our cousin and dearest son.
Hamlet. My lord, 'tis not the sable suit I wear,
  No nor the tears that still stand in my eyes,
  Nor the distracted haviour in the visage,
  Nor all together mixed with outward semblance,
  Is equal to the sorrow of my heart.
  Him have I lost I must of force forgo,
  These but the ornaments and suits of woe.
40 *King.* This shows a loving care in you, son Hamlet:
  But you must think, your father lost a father,
  That father dead, lost his, and so shall be until the
  General ending. Therefore cease laments.
  It is a fault against heaven, fault against the dead,
  A fault 'gainst nature, and in reason's
  Common course most certain:
  None lives on earth, but he is born to die.
Queen. Let not thy mother lose her prayers, Hamlet.
  Stay here with us, go not to Wittenberg.

15 *licence*: permission 29 *unmeet*: improper 33 *sable*: black
35 *haviour*: bearing, manner 38 *of force*: necessarily

Hamlet. I shall in all my best obey you, madam.   50
King. Spoke like a kind and most loving son.
   And there's no health the king shall drink today,
   But the great cannon to the clouds shall tell
   The rouse the king shall drink unto Prince Hamlet.
     Exeunt all but Hamlet.
Hamlet. O, that this too much grieved and sallied flesh
   Would melt to nothing, or that the universal
   Globe of heaven would turn all to a chaos!
   O God, within two months; no, not two: married
   Mine uncle! O let me not think of it,
   My father's brother – but no more like   60
   My father, than I to Hercules.
   Within two months, ere yet the salt of most
   Unrighteous tears had left their flushing
   In her galled eyes: she married – O God, a beast
   Devoid of reason would not have made
   Such speed! Frailty, thy name is woman.
   Why she would hang on him, as if increase
   Of appetite had grown by what it looked on.
   O wicked, wicked speed, to make such
   Dexterity to incestuous sheets,   70
   Ere yet the shoes were old,
   The which she followed my dead father's corse
   Like Niobe, all tears! Married! Well, it is not,
   Nor it cannot come to good.
   But break my heart, for I must hold my tongue.
     Enter Horatio and Marcellus.
Horatio. Health to your lordship.

54 *rouse*: toast
61 *Hercules*: virile god in Roman mythology; see also *Antonio's Revenge*,
prologue, 11 and 5.6.14–15 and note
64 *galled*: sore
70 *incestuous*: according to the 'Table of Kindred and Affinity' in the Book
of Common Prayer, a man was forbidden to marry his brother's widow
72 *corse*: corpse
73 *Niobe*: in mythology, Niobe wept incessantly for the death of her
children; see also *Tragedy of Hoffman*, 5.2.134 and note

Hamlet. I am very glad to see you. Horatio, or I much forget
    myself.

Horatio. The same my lord, and your poor servant ever.

80 *Hamlet.* O my good friend, I change that name with you: but
    what make you from Wittenberg, Horatio? Marcellus?

Marcellus. My good lord.

Hamlet. I am very glad to see you, good even, sirs.
    But what is your affair in Elsenour?
    We'll teach you to drink deep ere you depart.

Horatio. A truant disposition, my good lord.

Hamlet. Nor shall you make me truster
    Of your own report against yourself:
    Sir, I know you are no truant:

90   But what is your affair in Elsenour?

Horatio. My good lord, I came to see your father's funeral.

Hamlet. O, I pray thee do not mock me, fellow student.
    I think it was to see my mother's wedding.

Horatio. Indeed my lord, it followed hard upon.

Hamlet. Thrift, thrift, Horatio: the funeral baked meats
    Did coldly furnish forth the marriage tables.
    Would I had met my dearest foe in heaven
    Ere ever I had seen that day, Horatio.
    O my father, my father; me thinks I see my father.

100 *Horatio.* Where, my lord?

Hamlet. Why, in my mind's eye, Horatio.

Horatio. I saw him once. He was a gallant king.

Hamlet. He was a man, take him for all in all,
    I shall not look upon his like again.

Horatio. My lord, I think I saw him yesternight.

Hamlet. Saw, who?

Horatio. My lord, the king your father.

Hamlet. Ha ha, the king my father, kee you?

Horatio. Cease your admiration for a while

110   With an attentive ear, till I may deliver,
    Upon the witness of these gentlemen,
    This wonder to you.

94 *hard upon*: promptly   108 *kee*: say   109 *Cease*: Q Ceasen

Hamlet. For God's love, let me hear it.
Horatio. Two nights together had these gentlemen,
　　Marcellus and Barnardo, on their watch,
　　In the dead vast and middle of the night.
　　Been thus encountered by a figure like your father.
　　Armed to point, exactly cap-à-pié,
　　Appears before them thrice. He walks
　　Before their weak and fear-oppressed eyes   120
　　Within his truncheon's length,
　　While they distilled almost to jelly
　　With the act of fear, stands dumb,
　　And speak not to him. This to me
　　In dreadful secrecy impart they did,
　　And I with them the third night kept the watch,
　　Where as they had delivered form of the thing,
　　Each part made true and good,
　　The apparition comes. I knew your father:
　　These hands are not more like.   130
Hamlet. 'Tis very strange.
Horatio. As I do live, my honoured lord, 'tis true,
　　And we did think it right done,
　　In our duty to let you know it.
Hamlet. Where was this?
Marcellus. My lord, upon the platform where we watched.
Hamlet. Did you not speak to it?
Horatio. My lord we did, but answer made it none.
　　Yet once methought it was about to speak,
　　And lifted up his head to motion,   140
　　Like as he would speak, but even then
　　The morning cock crew loud, and in all haste,
　　It shrunk in haste away, and vanished
　　Our sight.
Hamlet. Indeed, indeed sirs, but this troubles me:
　　Hold you the watch to night?
All. We do my lord.

118 *cap-à-pié*: Q Capapea; from head to toe   127 *form*: visible aspect
136 *platform*: battlements

Hamlet. Armed, say ye?
All. Armed, my good lord.
150   *Hamlet.* From top to toe?
All. My good lord, from head to foot.
Hamlet. Why, then saw you not his face?
Horatio. O yes, my lord, he wore his beaver up.
Hamlet. How looked he: frowningly?
Horatio. A countenance more in sorrow than in anger.
Hamlet. Pale, or red?
Horatio. Nay, very pale.
Hamlet. And fixed his eyes upon you?
Horatio. Most constantly.
160   *Hamlet.* I would I had been there.
Horatio. It would 'a much amazed you.
Hamlet. Yea, very like, very like: stayed it long?
Horatio. While one with moderate pace
        Might tell a hundred.
Marcellus. O longer, longer.
Hamlet. His beard was grizzled, no?
Horatio. It was as I have seen it in his life,
        A sable silver.
Hamlet. I will watch tonight. Perchance 'twill walk again.
170   *Horatio.* I warrant it will.
Hamlet. If it assume my noble father's person,
        I'll speak to it, if hell itself should gape,
        And bid me hold my peace. Gentlemen,
        If you have hither concealed this sight,
        Let it be tenable in your silence still,
        And whatsoever else shall chance tonight,
        Give it an understanding, but no tongue.
        I will requite your loves, so fare you well.
        Upon the platform, 'twixt eleven and twelve,
180   I'll visit you.
All. Our duties to your honour.   *Exeunt.*
Hamlet. O your loves, your loves, as mine to you,

153 *beaver*: helmet face-guard   164 *tell*: count
168 *sable silver*: black and silver   175 *tenable*: capable of being kept in
177 *understanding*: meaning, sense

Farewell. My father's spirit in arms:
Well, all's not well. I doubt some foul play.
Would the night were come,
Till then, sit still my soul. Foul deeds will rise,
Though all the world o'erwhelm them to men's eyes.

Exit.

[*SCENE 3*]

Enter Leartes and Ofelia.

Leartes. My necessaries are embarked, I must aboard.
  But ere I part, mark what I say to thee:
  I see Prince Hamlet makes a show of love.
  Beware Ofelia, do not trust his vows.
  Perhaps he loves you now, and now his tongue
  Speaks from his heart, but yet take heed, my sister.
  The chariest maid is prodigal enough,
  If she unmask her beauty to the moon.
  Virtue itself 'scapes not calumnious thoughts.
  Believ't, Ofelia. Therefore keep aloof   10
  Lest that he trip thy honour and thy fame.
Ofelia. Brother, to this I have lent attentive ear,
  And doubt not, but to keep my honour firm,
  But my dear brother, do not you,
  Like to a cunning sophister,
  Teach me the path and ready way to heaven.
  While you forgetting what is said to me,
  Yourself, like to a careless libertine
  Doth give his heart, his appetite at full,
  And little recks how that his honour dies?   20
Leartes. No, fear it not, my dear Ofelia.

---

184 *doubt*: suspect 7 *chariest*: most cautious
9 *calumnious*: slanderous 11 *trip*: cause to fall
15 *sophister*: one who deploys specious arguments 20 *recks*: cares

Here comes my father, occasion smiles upon a second leave.
    Enter Corambis.
Corambis. Yet here Leartes? Aboard, aboard, for shame,
    The wind sits in the shoulder of your sail,
    And you are stayed for. There, my blessing with thee –
    And these few precepts in thy memory:
    Be thou familiar, but by no means vulgar;
    Those friends thou hast, and their adoptions tried,
    Grapple them to thee with a hoop of steel,
30 But do not dull the palm with entertain
    Of every new unfledg'd courage;
    Beware of entrance into a quarrel; but being in,
    Bear it that the opposed may beware of thee;
    Costly thy apparel, as thy purse can buy,
    But not expressed in fashion,
    For the apparel oft proclaims the man,
    And they of France of the chief rank and station
    Are of a most select and general chief in that;
    This above all, to thy own self be true,
40 And it must follow, as the night the day,
    Thou canst not then be false to any one,
    Farewell, my blessing with thee.
Leartes. I humbly take my leave; farewell Ofelia,
    And remember well what I have said to you.   *Exit.*
Ofelia. It is already locked within my heart,
    And you yourself shall keep the key of it.
Corambis. What is't, Ofelia, he hath said to you?
Ofelia. Something concerning the Prince Hamlet.
Corambis. Marry, well thought on: 'tis given me to understand,
50 That you have been too prodigal of your maiden presence
    Unto Prince Hamlet. If it be so,
    As so 'tis given to me, and that in way of caution
    I must tell you: you do not understand yourself
    So well as befits my honour and your credit.

22 *occasion*: opportunity   25 *stayed for*: awaited
28 *adoptions*: suitability as friends   29 *Grapple*: Fasten
30 *entertain*: greeting   49 *Marry*: Expression of surprise or outrage
49 *understand*: appreciate

Ofelia. My lord, he hath made many tenders of his love to me.
Corambis. Tenders? ay, ay, tenders you may call them.
Ofelia. And withal, such earnest vows.
Corambis. Springes to catch woodcocks,
    What, do I not know when the blood doth burn,
    How prodigal the tongue lends the heart vows?   60
    In brief, be more scanter of your maiden presence,
    Or tendering thus you'll tender me a fool.
Ofelia. I shall obey, my lord, in all I may.
Corambis. Ofelia, receive none of his letters,
    For lovers' lines are snares to entrap the heart;
    Refuse his tokens, both of them are keys
    To unlock chastity unto desire.
    Come in Ofelia: such men often prove
    Great in their words, but little in their love.
Ofelia. I will, my lord.   *Exeunt.*   70

[SCENE 4]

Enter Hamlet, Horatio, and Marcellus.

Hamlet. The air bites shrewd; it is an eager and
    A nipping wind. What hour is't?
Horatio. I think it lacks of twelve.   *Sound Trumpets.*
Marcellus. No, 'tis struck.
Horatio. Indeed, I heard it not. What doth this mean, my lord?
Hamlet. O, the king doth wake tonight, and takes his rouse,
    Keeps wassail, and the swaggering upspring reels;
    And as he dreams his draughts of Rhenish down,
    The kettle, drum, and trumpet thus bray out
    The triumphs of his pledge.   10
Horatio. Is it a custom here?
Hamlet. Ay marry is't, and though I am

58 *Springes*: Traps   61 *scanter*: more limited
1 *shrewd*: bitter   7 *upspring*: a kind of dance
8 *Rhenish*: wine from the Rhine in Germany

Native here, and to the manner born,
It is a custom more honoured in the breach
Than in the observance.
   Enter the Ghost.

Horatio. Look my lord, it comes!
Hamlet. Angels and ministers of grace defend us.
  Be thou a spirit of health, or goblin damned,
  Bring with thee airs from heaven, or blasts from hell,
20 Be thy intents wicked or charitable,
  Thou comest in such questionable shape,
  That I will speak to thee.
  I'll call thee Hamlet, King, Father, royal Dane.
  O answer me: let me not burst in ignorance,
  But say why thy canonized bones hearsed in death
  Have burst their ceremonies: why thy sepulchre,
  In which we saw thee quietly interred,
  Hath burst his ponderous and marble jaws,
  To cast thee up again? What may this mean,
30 That thou, dead corse, again in complete steel
  Revisits thus the glimpses of the moon,
  Making night hideous, and we fools of nature,
  So horridly to shake our disposition,
  With thoughts beyond the reaches of our souls?
  Say, speak, wherefore, what may this mean?
Horatio. It beckons you, as though it had something
  To impart to you alone.
Marcellus. Look with what courteous action
  It waves you to a more removed ground.
40 But do not go with it.
Horatio. No, by no means, my lord.
Hamlet. It will not speak. Then will I follow it.
Horatio. What if it tempt you toward the flood, my lord,
  That beckles o'er his base into the sea,
  And there assume some other horrid shape,
  Which might deprive your sovereignty of reason,

---

18 *goblin*: demon   39 *removed*: secluded, private
44 *beckles*: obscure, perhaps 'beckons' or 'beetles'

And drive you into madness? Think of it.
Hamlet. Still am I called: go on, I'll follow thee.
Horatio. My lord, you shall not go.
Hamlet. Why, what should be the fear?   50
  I do not set my life at a pin's fee,
  And for my soul, what can it do to that
  Being a thing immortal, like itself?
  Go on: I'll follow thee.
Marcellus. My lord, be ruled: you shall not go.
Hamlet. My fate cries out, and makes each petty artery
  As hardy as the Nemean lion's nerve.
  Still am I called. Unhand me, gentlemen;
  By heaven, I'll make a ghost of him that lets me.
  Away, I say – go on, I'll follow thee.   60
Horatio. He waxeth desperate with imagination.
Marcellus. Something is rotten in the state of Denmark.
Horatio. Have after. To what issue will this sort?
Marcellus. Let's follow: 'tis not fit thus to obey him.   *Exit.*

[SCENE 5]

Enter Ghost and Hamlet.

Hamlet. I'll go no further: whither wilt thou lead me?
Ghost. Mark me.
Hamlet. I will.
Ghost. I am thy father's spirit, doomed for a time
  To walk the night, and all the day
  Confined in flaming fire,
  Till the foul crimes done in my days of nature
  Are purged and burnt away.
Hamlet. Alas, poor ghost.

51 *pin's fee*: the (low) value of a pin   56 *artery*: Q Artiue
57 *Nemean lion*: renowned beast strangled by Hercules as one of his labours
59 *lets*: hinders   61 *waxeth*: grows

10 *Ghost.* Nay, pity me not, but to my unfolding
      Lend thy listening ear. But that I am forbid
      To tell the secrets of my prisonhouse,
      I would a tale unfold whose lightest word
      Would harrow up thy soul, freeze thy young blood,
      Make thy two eyes like stars start from their spheres,
      Thy knotted and combined locks to part,
      And each particular hair to stand on end
      Like quills upon the fretful porpentine.
      But this same blazon must not be, to ears of flesh and blood.
20   Hamlet, if ever thou didst thy dear father love –
Hamlet. O God –
Ghost. Revenge his foul and most unnatural murder.
Hamlet. Murder?
Ghost. Yea, murder in the highest degree,
      As in the least, 'tis bad,
      But mine most foul, beastly, and unnatural.
Hamlet. Haste me to know it, that with wings as swift as
      meditation, or the thought of it, may sweep to my revenge.
Ghost. O I find thee apt, and duller shouldst thou be
30   Than the fat weed that roots itself in ease
      On Lethe wharf: brief let me be.
      'Tis given out, that sleeping in my orchard,
      A serpent stung me, and so the whole ear of Denmark
      Is with a forged process of my death rankly abused.
      But know, thou noble youth: he that did sting
      Thy father's heart now wears his crown.
Hamlet. O my prophetic soul! My uncle, my uncle!
Ghost. Yea he, that incestuous wretch, won to his will with gifts –
      O wicked will, and gifts that have the power
40   So to seduce – my most seeming virtuous queen.
      But virtue, as it never will be moved,
      Though lewdness court it in a shape of heaven,

10 *unfolding*: revelation, tale   18 *porpentine*: porcupine
19 *blazon*: public description
30–31 *fat weed . . . wharf*: the weed has not been identified; Lethe is a river
in the classical underworld; see also *Antonio's Revenge*, 4.3.198 note
34 *forged*: invented

So lust, though to a radiant angel linked,
Would sate itself from a celestial bed,
And prey on garbage: but soft, methinks
I scent the morning's air, brief let me be.
Sleeping within my orchard, my custom always
In the afternoon, upon my secure hour
Thy uncle came, with juice of hebona
In a vial, and through the porches of my ears   50
Did pour the leprous distilment, whose effect
Hold such an enmity with blood of man,
That swift as quicksilver, it posteth through
The natural gates and alleys of the body,
And turns the thin and wholesome blood
Like eager droppings into milk.
And all my smooth body, barked and tettered over.
Thus was I, sleeping, by a brother's hand
Of crown, of queen, of life, of dignity,
At once deprived. No reckoning made of,   60
But sent unto my grave,
With all my accompts and sins upon my head.
O horrible, most horrible!
Hamlet. O God!
Ghost. If thou hast nature in thee, bear it not,
    But howsoever, let not thy heart
    Conspire against thy mother aught,
    Leave her to heaven
    And to the burden that her conscience bears.
    I must be gone: the glow-worm shows the matin   70
    To be near and 'gins to pale his uneffectual fire:
    Hamlet, adieu, adieu, adieu: remember me.   *Exit.*
Hamlet. O all you host of heaven! O earth, what else?
    And shall I couple hell? Remember thee?

43 *angel*: Q angle   48 *secure*: safe, unworried   49 *hebona*: poison
53 *quicksilver*: mercury (poisonous)
57 *barked and tettered*: encrusted with pustules   62 *accompts*: accounts
70 *matin*: morning

Yes, thou poor ghost. From the tables
Of my memory, I'll wipe away all saws of books,
All trivial fond conceits
That ever youth, or else observance noted,
And thy remembrance all alone shall sit.
80   Yes, yes, by heaven! A damned pernicious villain,
Murderous, bawdy, smiling damned villain!
My tables – meet it is I set it down,
That one may smile, and smile, and be a villain.
At least I am sure, it may be so in Denmark.
So uncle, there you are, there you are.
Now to the words: it is adieu, adieu, remember me.
So 'tis, enough, I have sworn.
    Enter Horatio, and Marcellus.
Horatio. My lord, my lord!
Marcellus. Lord Hamlet.
90   *Hamlet.* Illo, lo, ho, ho!
Marcellus. Illo, lo, so, ho, so, come boy, come!
Horatio. Heavens secure him.
Marcellus. How is't, my noble lord?
Horatio. What news, my lord?
Hamlet. O wonderful, wonderful.
Horatio. Good my lord, tell it.
Hamlet. No not I: you'll reveal it.
Horatio. Not I, my lord, by heaven.
Marcellus. Nor I, my lord.
100   *Hamlet.* How say you then? Would heart of man
    Once think it? But you'll be secret?
Both. Ay, by heaven, my lord.
Hamlet. There's never a villain dwelling in all Denmark,
    But he's an arrant knave.
Horatio. There need no ghost come from the grave to tell you this.
Hamlet. Right, you are in the right, and therefore

75 *tables*: writing tablets or notebook
76 *saws*: commonplaces or sayings from books
90 *Illo*: Greeting, related to 'hello' or 'holla'

I hold it meet without more circumstance at all,
We shake hands and part, you as your business
And desires shall lead you: for look you,
Every man hath business, and desires, such   110
As it is, and for my own poor part, I'll go pray.
Horatio. These are but wild and whirling words, my lord.
Hamlet. I am sorry they offend you; heartily, yes 'faith, heartily.
Horatio. There's no offence, my lord.
Hamlet. Yes, by Saint Patrick, but there is, Horatio,
And much offence too. Touching this vision,
It is an honest ghost, that let me tell you.
For your desires to know what is between us,
O'ermaster it as you may:
And now kind friends, as you are friends,   120
Scholars and gentlemen:
Grant me one poor request.
Both. What is't, my lord?
Hamlet. Never make known what you have seen tonight.
Both. My lord, we will not.
Hamlet. Nay, but swear.
Horatio. In faith, my lord, not I.
Marcellus. Nor I, my lord, in faith.
Hamlet. Nay, upon my sword, indeed upon my sword.
Ghost. Swear.   130
     The Ghost under the stage.
Hamlet. Ha, ha! Come you here, this fellow in the cellarage,
Here consent to swear.
Horatio. Propose the oath, my lord.
Hamlet. Never to speak what you have seen tonight,
Swear by my sword.
Ghost. Swear.
Hamlet. Hic et ubique? Nay then, we'll shift our ground.
Come hither gentlemen, and lay your hands
Again upon this sword: never to speak

131 *cellarage*: underground cellar
138 *Hic et ubique*: Here and everywhere

140   Of that which you have seen, swear by my sword.
      Ghost. Swear.
      Hamlet. Well said old mole, can'st work in the earth? So fast, a
        worthy pioneer, once more, remove.
      Horatio. Day and night, but this is wondrous strange.
      Hamlet. And therefore as a stranger give it welcome.
        There are more things in heaven and earth, Horatio,
        Than are dreamt of in your philosophy,
        But come here, as before, you never shall,
        How strange or odd soe'er I bear myself,
150   As I perchance hereafter shall think meet,
        To put an antic disposition on,
        That you at such times seeing me, never shall
        With arms, encumbered thus, or this head shake,
        Or by pronouncing some undoubtful phrase,
        As well, well, we know, or we could and if we would,
        Or there be, and if they might, or such ambiguous
        Giving out, to note that you know aught of me.
        This not to do, so grace and mercy
        At your most need help you, swear.
160   *Ghost.* Swear.
      Hamlet. Rest, rest, perturbed spirit! So, gentlemen,
        In all my love I do commend me to you,
        And what so poor a man as Hamlet may
        To pleasure you, God willing shall not want.
        Nay come, let's go together.
        But still your fingers on your lips, I pray,
        The time is out of joint: O cursed spite,
        That ever I was born to set it right,
        Nay come, let's go together.   *Exeunt.*

---

143 *pioneer*: soldier specializing in digging mines
151 *antic*: bizarre, incongruous   154 *undoubtful*: doubtful

[SCENE 6]

Enter Corambis, and Montano.

Corambis. Montano, here, these letters to my son,
   And this same money with my blessing to him,
   And bid him ply his learning, good Montano.
Montano. I will, my lord.
Corambis. You shall do very well, Montano, to say thus:
   'I knew the gentleman', or 'know his father',
   To inquire the manner of his life,
   As thus: being amongst his acquaintance,
   You may say, you saw him at such a time, mark you me,
   At game, or drinking, swearing, or drabbing,   10
   You may go so far.
Montano. My lord, that will impeach his reputation.
Corambis. Ay faith, not a whit, no, not a whit,
   Now happily he closeth with you in the consequence,
   As you may bridle it, not disparage him a jot.
   What was I about to say . . . ?
Montano. He closeth with him in the consequence.
Corambis. Ay, you say right, he closeth with him thus,
   This will he say – let me say, what he will say –
   Marry this, 'I saw him yesterday', or 't'other day',   20
   Or then, or 'at such a time a-dicing',
   Or 'at tennis', aye, or 'drinking drunk', or 'entering
   Of a house of lightness' – *viz.* brothel –
   Thus sir, do we that know the world, being men of reach,
   By indirections, find directions forth,
   And so shall you my son. You ha' me, ha' you not?
Montano. I have, my lord.
Corambis. Well, fare you well, commend me to him.
Montano. I will, my lord.
Corambis. And bid him ply his music.   30

---

10 *drabbing*: visiting prostitutes   14 *closeth*: becomes more confiding
23 *viz.*: namely (abbreviation of *videlicet*)   24 *reach*: understanding

Montano. My lord, I will.   *Exit.*
      Enter Ofelia.
Corambis. Farewell. How now, Ofelia, what's the news with you?
Ofelia. O my dear father: such a change in nature,
     So great an alteration in a prince,
     So pitiful to him, fearful to me,
     A maiden's eye ne'er looked on.
Corambis. Why, what's the matter, my Ofelia?
Ofelia. O young Prince Hamlet, the only flower of Denmark,
     He is bereft of all the wealth he had,
40   The jewel that adorned his feature most
     Is filched and stolen away: his wit's bereft him.
     He found me walking in the gallery all alone,
     There comes he to me, with a distracted look,
     His garters lagging down, his shoes untied,
     And fixed his eyes so steadfast on my face,
     As if they had vowed this is their latest object.
     Small while he stood, but grips me by the wrist,
     And there he holds my pulse till with a sigh
     He doth unclasp his hold, and parts away
50   Silent, as is the mid-time of the night.
     And as he went, his eye was still on me,
     For thus his head over his shoulder looked,
     He seemed to find the way without his eyes,
     For out of doors he went without their help,
     And so did leave me.
Corambis. Mad for thy love.
     What, have you given him any cross words of late?
Ofelia. I did repel his letters, deny his gifts,
     As you did charge me.
60 *Corambis.* Why that hath made him mad.
     By heaven, 'tis as proper for our age to cast
     Beyond ourselves as 'tis for the younger sort
     To leave their wantonness. Well, I am sorry
     That I was so rash: but what remedy?

     41 *filched*: stolen   44 *lagging*: drooping   47 *Small*: Short

Let's to the king: this madness may prove,
Though wild a while, yet more true to thy love.
    Exeunt.

[*SCENE 7*]

Enter King and Queen, Rossencraft and Gilderstone.

King. Right noble friends, that our dear cousin Hamlet
    Hath lost the very heart of all his sense,
    It is most right, and we most sorry for him.
    Therefore we do desire, even as you tender
    Our care to him, and our great love to you,
    That you will labour but to wring from him
    The cause and ground of his distemperancy.
    Do this: the king of Denmark shall be thankful.
Rossencraft. My lord, whatsoever lies within our power
    Your majesty may more command in words   10
    Than use persuasions to your liegemen, bound
    By love, by duty and obedience.
Gilderstone. What we may do for both your majesties
    To know the grief troubles the prince your son,
    We will endeavour all the best we may,
    So in all duty do we take our leave.
King. Thanks Gilderstone, and gentle Rossencraft.
Queen. Thanks Rossencraft, and gentle Gilderstone.
    [Exeunt.] Enter Corambis and Ofelia.
Corambis. My lord, the ambassadors are joyfully
    Returned from Norway.   20
King. Thou hast been the father of good news.
Corambis. Have I, my lord? I assure your grace,
    I hold my duty as I hold my life,
    Both to my God and to my sovereign king:

7 *distemperancy*: disordered mental state

And I believe, or else this brain of mine
Hunts not the train of policy so well
As it had wont to do, but I have found
The very depth of Hamlet's lunacy.
Queen. God grant he hath.
    Enter the Ambassadors [Voltemar and Cornelia].
30 *King.* Now Voltemar, what from our brother Norway?
Voltemar. Most fair returns of greetings and desires.
    Upon our first he sent forth to suppress
    His nephew's levies, which to him appeared
    To be a preparation against the Polack,
    But better looked into, he truly found
    It was against your highness; whereat grieved,
    That so his sickness, age, and impotence,
    Was falsely born in hand, sends out arrests
    On Fortenbrasse, which he in brief obeys;
40 Receives rebuke from Norway: and in fine,
    Makes vow before his uncle, never more
    To give the assay of arms against your majesty.
    Whereon old Norway overcome with joy,
    Gives him three thousand crowns in annual fee,
    And his commission to employ those soldiers,
    So levied as before, against the Polack,
    With an entreaty herein further show,
    That it would please you to give quiet pass
    Through your dominions, for that enterprise
50 On such regards of safety and allowances
    As therein are set down.
King. It likes us well, and at fit time and leisure
    We'll read and answer these his articles.
    Meantime we thank you for your well-
    Took labour: go to your rest, at night we'll feast together.
    Right welcome home.
    Exeunt Ambassadors.
Corambis. This business is very well dispatched.
    Now my lord, touching the young Prince Hamlet.

33 *levies*: enrolments of soldiers   34 *Polack*: Pole

Certain it is that he is mad: mad let us grant him then.
Now to know the cause of this effect –   60
Or else to say the cause of this defect,
For this effect defective comes by cause –
Queen. Good my lord, be brief.
Corambis. Madam, I will: my lord, I have a daughter –
    Have while she's mine, for that we think
    Is surest, we often lose – now to the prince.
    My lord, but note this letter,
    The which my daughter in obedience
    Delivered to my hands.
King. Read it, my lord.   70
Corambis. Mark, my lord.
    'Doubt that in earth is fire,
    Doubt that the stars do move,
    Doubt truth to be a liar,
    But do not doubt I love.
    To the beautiful Ofelia:
    Thine ever the most unhappy prince Hamlet.'
    My lord, what do you think of me?
    Ay, or what might you think when I saw this?
King. As of a true friend and a most loving subject.   80
Corambis. I would be glad to prove so.
    Now when I saw this letter, thus I bespake my maiden:
    Lord Hamlet is a prince out of your star,
    And one that is unequal for your love.
    Therefore I did command her refuse his letters,
    Deny his tokens, and to absent herself;
    She as my child obediently obeyed me.
    Now since which time, seeing his love thus crossed –
    Which I took to be idle, and but sport –
    He straightway grew into a melancholy,   90
    From that unto a fast, then unto a distraction,
    Then into a sadness, from that unto a madness,
    And so by continuance, and weakness of the brain
    Into this frenzy, which now possesseth him:
    And if this be not true, take this from this.

King. Think you 'tis so?

Corambis. How? So my lord, I would very fain know
    That thing that I have said is so, positively,
    And it hath fallen out otherwise.
100   Nay, if circumstances lead me on,
    I'll find it out, if it were hid
    As deep as the centre of the earth.

King. How should we try this same?

Corambis. Marry, my good lord, thus:
    The prince's walk is here in the gallery,
    There let Ofelia walk until he comes.
    Yourself and I will stand close in the study.
    There shall you hear the effect of all his heart,
    And if it prove any otherwise than love,
110   Then let my censure fail another time.

King. See where he comes, poring upon a book.

    Enter Hamlet.

Corambis. Madam, will it please your grace
    To leave us here?

Queen. With all my heart.   *Exit.*

Corambis. And here Ofelia, read you on this book,
    And walk aloof: the king shall be unseen.

Hamlet. To be, or not to be, aye, there's the point.
    To die, to sleep, is that all? Ay, all.
    No, to sleep, to dream – ay marry, there it goes:
120   For in that dream of death, when we awake,
    And borne before an everlasting judge,
    From whence no passenger ever returned,
    The undiscovered country, at whose sight
    The happy smile, and the accursed damned –
    But for this, the joyful hope of this,
    Who'd bear the scorns and flattery of the world,
    Scorned by the right rich, the rich cursed of the poor?
    The widow being oppressed, the orphan wronged,
    The taste of hunger, or a tyrant's reign,
130   And thousand more calamities besides,

97 *fain*: gladly   110 *censure*: judgement

To grunt and sweat under this weary life,
When that he may his full quietus make,
With a bare bodkin? Who would this endure,
But for a hope of something after death,
Which puzzles the brain, and doth confound the sense,
Which makes us rather bear those evils we have,
Than fly to others that we know not of.
Ay that, O that conscience makes cowards of us all.
Lady in thy orisons be all my sins remembered.

Ofelia. My lord, I have sought opportunity, which now I have,   140
   to redeliver to your worthy hands, a small remembrance,
   such tokens which I have received of you.

Hamlet. Are you fair?

Ofelia. My lord?

Hamlet. Are you honest?

Ofelia. What means my lord?

Hamlet. That if you be fair and honest,
   Your beauty should admit no discourse to your honesty.

Ofelia. My lord, can beauty have better privilege than with honesty?

Hamlet. Yea marry, may it; for beauty may transform   150
   Honesty from what she was into a bawd.
   Then honesty can transform beauty:
   This was sometimes a paradox,
   But now the time gives it scope.
   I never gave you nothing.

Ofelia. My lord, you know right well you did,
   And with them such earnest vows of love,
   As would have moved the stoniest breast alive.
   But now too true I find:
   Rich gifts wax poor, when givers grow unkind.   160

Hamlet. I never loved you.

Ofelia. You made me believe you did.

Hamlet. O, thou shouldst not 'a believed me!
   Go to a nunnery, go: why shouldst thou
   Be a breeder of sinners? I am myself indifferent honest,

132 *quietus*: 'a release or respite from life' (*OED*)   133 *bodkin*: dagger
139 *orisons*: prayers

But I could accuse myself of such crimes
It had been better my mother had ne'er borne me.
O, I am very proud, ambitious, disdainful,
With more sins at my beck than I have thoughts
170   To put them in. What should such fellows as I
Do, crawling between heaven and earth?
To a nunnery go! We are arrant knaves all,
Believe none of us – to a nunnery go.
Ofelia. O heavens secure him.
Hamlet. Where's thy father?
Ofelia. At home, my lord.
Hamlet. For God's sake let the doors be shut on him,
He may play the fool nowhere but in his
Own house: to a nunnery go.
180   *Ofelia.* Help him, good God.
Hamlet. If thou dost marry, I'll give thee
This plague to thy dowry:
Be thou as chaste as ice, as pure as snow,
Thou shalt not 'scape calumny, to a nunnery go.
Ofelia. Alas, what change is this?
Hamlet. But if thou wilt needs marry, marry a fool.
For wise men know well enough,
What monsters you make of them: to a nunnery go.
Ofelia. Pray God restore him.
190   *Hamlet.* Nay, I have heard of your paintings too,
God hath given you one face,
And you make yourselves another.
You fig and you amble and you nickname God's creatures,
Making your wantonness your ignorance.
A pox, 'tis scurvy, I'll no more of it,
It hath made me mad. I'll no more marriages.
All that are married but one, shall live.
The rest shall keep as they are: to a nunnery go,
To a nunnery go.   *Exit.*

169 *beck*: command
188 *monsters*: referring to the proverbial horns of the cuckold
190 *paintings*: cosmetics   193 *fig*: trot about
195 *A pox*: Expression of irritation or impatience

Ofelia. Great God of heaven, what a quick change is this?   200
   The courtier, scholar, soldier, all in him
   All dashed and splintered thence, O woe is me,
   To 'a seen what I have seen, see what I see.   *Exit.*
    Enter King and Corambis.
King. Love? No, no, that's not the cause,
   Some deeper thing it is that troubles him.
Corambis. Well, something it is: my lord, content you a while,
   I will myself go feel him. Let me work.
   I'll try him every way: see, where he comes.
   Send you those gentlemen, let me alone
   To find the depth of this. Away, be gone.   *Exit King.*   210
   Now my good lord, do you know me?   *Enter Hamlet.*
Hamlet. Yea, very well, y'are a fishmonger.
Corambis. Not I, my lord.
Hamlet. Then sir, I would you were so honest a man,
   For to be honest, as this age goes,
   Is one man to be picked out of ten thousand.
Corambis. What do you read, my lord?
Hamlet. Words, words.
Corambis. What's the matter, my lord?
Hamlet. Between who?   220
Corambis. I mean, the matter that you read, my lord.
Hamlet. Marry, most vile heresy:
   For here the satirical satyr writes,
   That old men have hollow eyes, weak backs,
   Grey beards, pitiful weak hams, gouty legs,
   All which, sir, I most potently believe not:
   For sir, yourself shall be old as I am,
   If like a crab, you could go backward.
Corambis. How pregnant his replies are, and full of wit:
   Yet first he took me for a fishmonger.   230
   All this comes by love, the vehemency of love.
   And when I was young, I was very idle,
   And suffered much ecstasy in love, very near this.

225 *hams*: the back of the knee   229 *pregnant*: full of meaning
232 *idle*: foolish

Will you walk out of the air, my lord?

Hamlet. Into my grave.

Corambis. By the mass, that's out of the air indeed.
   Very shrewd answers.
   My lord I will take my leave of you.
      Enter Gilderstone and Rossencraft.

Hamlet. You can take nothing from me sir,
240   I will more willingly part withal.
   Old doting fool.

Corambis. You seek Prince Hamlet: see, there he is.   *Exit.*

Gilderstone. Health to your lordship.

Hamlet. What, Gilderstone and Rossencraft,
   Welcome, kind school-fellows, to Elsenour.

Gilderstone. We thank your grace, and would be very glad
   You were as when we were at Wittenberg.

Hamlet. I thank you, but is this visitation free of
   Yourselves, or were you not sent for?
250   Tell me true. Come, I know the good king and queen
   Sent for you: there is a kind of confession in your eye.
   Come, I know you were sent for.

Gilderstone. What say you?

Hamlet. Nay, then I see how the wind sits.
   Come, you were sent for.

Rossencraft. My lord, we were, and willingly if we might
   Know the cause and ground of your discontent.

Hamlet. Why, I want preferment.

Rossencraft. I think not so, my lord.

260 *Hamlet.* Yes, faith, this great world you see, contents me not,
   No, nor the spangled heavens, nor earth nor sea,
   No, nor man that is so glorious a creature,
   Contents me not, no nor woman too, though you laugh.

Gilderstone. My lord, we laugh not at that.

Hamlet. Why did you laugh then
   When I said, man did not content me?

Gilderstone. My lord, we laughed when you said man did not
      content you:

236 *mass*: used in oaths

What entertainment the players shall have,
We boarded them a' the way: they are coming to you.
Hamlet. Players? What players be they?   270
Rossencraft. My lord, the tragedians of the city,
   Those that you took delight to see so often.
Hamlet. How comes it that they travel? Do they grow resty?
Gilderstone. No my lord, their reputation holds as it was wont.
Hamlet. How then?
Gilderstone. I'faith my lord, novelty carries it away,
   For the principal public audience that
   Came to them, are turned to private plays,
   And to the humour of children.
Hamlet. I do not greatly wonder of it.   280
   For those that would make mops and mows
   At my uncle, when my father lived,
   Now give a hundred, two hundred pounds
   For his picture: but they shall be welcome.
   He that plays the king shall have tribute of me,
   The venturous knight shall use his foil and target,
   The lover shall sigh gratis,
   The clown shall make them laugh
   That are tickled in the lungs, or the blank verse shall halt for't,
   And the lady shall have leave to speak her mind freely.   290
        The trumpets sound. Enter Corambis.
   Do you see yonder great baby?
   He is not yet out of his swaddling clouts.
Gilderstone. That may be, for they say an old man
   Is twice a child.
Hamlet. I'll prophesy to you, he comes to tell me a' the players,
   You say true, o'Monday last, 'twas so indeed.
Corambis. My lord, I have news to tell you.
Hamlet. My lord, I have news to tell you:

269 *boarded*: met   273 *resty*: inactive
279 *children*: the newly fashionable children's acting company of Blackfriars
281 *mops and mows*: grimaces   286 *foil*: weapon   *target*: round shield
289 *halt*: falter, wait

When Roscius was an actor in Rome –

300 *Corambis.* The actors are come hither, my lord.

Hamlet. Buzz, buzz.

Corambis. The best actors in Christendom,
Either for comedy, tragedy, history, pastoral,
Pastoral historical, historical comical,
Comical historical, pastoral tragedy historical.
Seneca cannot be too heavy, nor Plato too light,
For the law hath writ those are the only men.

Hamlet. O Jephtha judge of Israel! What a treasure hadst thou?

Corambis. Why, what a treasure had he, my lord?

310 *Hamlet.* Why, one fair daughter, and no more,
The which he loved passing well.

Corambis. Ah, still harping a' my daughter! Well, my lord,
If you call me Jephtha, I have a daughter that
I love passing well.

Hamlet. Nay, that follows not.

Corambis. What follows then, my lord?

Hamlet. Why, 'by lot, or God wot', 'as it came to pass,
And so it was', the first verse of the godly ballad
Will tell you all: for look you where my abridgement comes:
Enter Players.

320 Welcome masters, welcome all.
What, my old friend, thy face is vallanced
Since I saw thee last: com'st thou to beard me in Denmark?
My young lady and mistress, by'r lady but your
Ladyship is grown by the altitude of a chopine higher than
you were:

299 *Roscius*: Roman actor
306 *Seneca*: Roman philosopher and playwright, very influential on revenge tragedy
306 *Plato*: classical Greek philosopher, hence inappropriate here: perhaps Corambis', or someone's, mistake for the comic playwright Plautus
308 *Jephtha*: father forced to sacrifice his daughter, having promised God to offer whoever first greeted him on his return from battle with the Ammonites (Judges 10)
319 *abridgement*: that which will shorten my speech
321 *vallanced*: fringed
324 *chopine*: exaggeratedly raised shoe

Pray God sir, your voice, like a piece of uncurrent
Gold, be not cracked in the ring: come on, masters,
We'll even to't, like French falconers,
Fly at anything we see: come, a taste of your
Quality, a speech, a passionate speech.
Players. What speech, my good lord?   330
Hamlet. I heard thee speak a speech once,
  But it was never acted: or if it were,
  Never above twice, for as I remember,
  It pleased not the vulgar: it was caviar
  To the million: but to me
  And others that received it in the like kind,
  Cried in the top of their judgements an excellent play,
  Set down with as great modesty as cunning.
  One said there was no sallets in the lines to make them savoury,
  But called it an honest method, as wholesome as sweet.   340
  Come, a speech in it I chiefly remember
  Was Aeneas' tale to Dido,
  And then especially where he talks of princes' slaughter.
  If it live in the memory begin at this line –
  Let me see:
  'The rugged Pyrrhus, like th'Hyrcanian beast –'
  No, 'tis not so, it begins with Pyrrhus.
  O I have it:
  'The rugged Pyrrhus, he whose sable arms,
  Black as his purpose did the night resemble,   350
  When he lay couched in the ominous horse,
  Hath now his black and grim complexion smeared
  With heraldry more dismal, head to foot,
  Now is he total guise, horridly tricked

---

325 *uncurrent*: not in circulation, not current   339 *sallets*: salads
342 *Aeneas' tale to Dido*: In Virgil's *Aeneid*, Aeneas tells Dido the story of
Troy's destruction
346 *Pyrrhus*: revenging son of Achilles
346 *Hyrcanian*: Q arganian; from Hyrcania, known for its tigers
351 *ominous horse*: the Trojan horse, secretly filled with Greek soldiers,
which broke the siege of Troy
354 *guise*: disguise, masked

With blood of fathers, mothers, daughters, sons,
Baked and imparched in coagulate gore,
Rifted in earth and fire, old grandsire Priam seeks –'
So go on.
Corambis. Afore God, my lord, well spoke, and with good accent.
360 *Player.* 'Anon he finds him striking too short at Greeks,
His antique sword rebellious to his arm,
Lies where it falls, unable to resist.
Pyrrhus at Priam drives, but all in rage,
Strikes wide, but with the whiff and wind
Of his fell sword, th'unnerved father falls.'
Corambis. Enough, my friend, 'tis too long.
Hamlet. It shall to the barbers with your beard:
A pox, he's for a jig, or a tale of bawdry,
Or else he sleeps. Come on, to Hecuba, come.
370 *Player.* 'But who, O who had seen the mobled queen?'
Corambis. Mobled queen is good, faith, very good.
Player. 'All in the alarum and fear of death rose up,
And o'er her weak and all o'er-teeming loins, a blanket
And a kercher on that head, where late the diadem stood,
Who this had seen with tongue-envenomed speech
Would treason have pronounced;
For if the gods themselves had seen her then,
When she saw Pyrrhus with malicious strokes,
Mincing her husband's limbs,
380 It would have made milch the burning eyes of heaven,
And passion in the gods.'
Corambis. Look my lord, if he hath not changed his colour,
And hath tears in his eyes: no more good heart, no more.
Hamlet. 'Tis well, 'tis very well. I pray my lord,
Will you see the players well bestowed?
I tell you they are the chronicles
And brief abstracts of the time.

356 *imparched*: dry, roasted
357 *Priam*: king of Troy; see also *Tragedy of Hoffman*, 2.2.14–15 and note
364 *whiff*: puff of wind   365 *unnerved*: 'rendered nerveless or weak' (*OED*)
369 *Hecuba*: wife of Priam   370 *mobled*: muffled
374 *kercher*: handkerchief   380 *milch*: milk

After your death I can tell you,
You were better have a bad epitaph,
Than their ill report while you live.   390
Corambis. My lord, I will use them according to their deserts.
Hamlet. O far better, man: use every man after his deserts
    Then who should 'scape whipping?
    Use them after your own honour and dignity,
    The less they deserve, the greater credit's yours.
Corambis. Welcome, my good fellows.   *Exit.*
Hamlet. Come hither, masters: can you not play the murder of
    Gonzago?
Players. Yes, my lord.
Hamlet. And could'st not thou for a need study me   400
    Some dozen or sixteen lines,
    Which I would set down and insert?
Players. Yes, very easily, my good lord.
Hamlet. 'Tis well, I thank you: follow that lord,
    And do you hear, sirs? Take heed you mock him not.
    Gentlemen, for your kindness I thank you,
    And for a time I would desire you leave me.
Gilderstone. Our love and duty is at your command.
        Exeunt all but Hamlet.
Hamlet. Why, what a dunghill idiot slave am I?
    Why these players here draw water from their eyes,   410
    For Hecuba: why, what is Hecuba to him, or he to Hecuba?
    What would he do an if he had my loss?
    His father murdered, and a crown bereft him?
    He would turn all his tears to drops of blood,
    Amaze the standers-by with his laments,
    Strike more than wonder in the judicial ears,
    Confound the ignorant and make mute the wise.
    Indeed his passion would be general.
    Yet I, like to an ass and John-a-dreams,
    Having my father murdered by a villain,   420
    Stand still, and let it pass: why sure, I am a coward.

389 *epitaph*: Q Epiteeth
419 *John-a-dreams*: dreamy fellow

Who plucks me by the beard, or twits my nose,
Gives me the lie i'th'throat down to the lungs,
Sure I should take it, or else I have no gall,
Or by this I should 'a fatted all the region kites
With this slave's offal, this damned villain,
Treacherous, bawdy, murderous villain!
Why, this is brave, that I the son of my dear father,
Should like a scullion, like a very drab

430   Thus rail in words. About my brain:
I have heard that guilty creatures sitting at a play
Hath, by the very cunning of the scene, confessed a murder
Committed long before.
The spirit that I have seen may be the devil.
And out of my weakness and my melancholy
As he is very potent with such men.
Doth seek to damn me: I will have sounder proofs.
The play's the thing,
Wherein I'll catch the conscience of the king.   *Exit.*

[SCENE 8]

Enter King, Queen, and Lords [Rossencraft and Gilderstone].

King. Lords, can you by no means find
    The cause of our son Hamlet's lunacy?
    You being so near in love, even from his youth,
    Methinks should gain more than a stranger should.
Gilderstone. My lord, we have done all the best we could
    To wring from him the cause of all his grief,
    But still he puts us off, and by no means
    Would make an answer to that we exposed.
Rossencraft. Yet was he something more inclined to mirth
10   Before we left him, and I take it

425 *kites:* carrion-eating birds of prey
429 *scullion:* Q scalion; low-ranking servant

He hath given order for a play tonight,
At which he craves your highness' company.
King. With all our heart, it likes us very well.
    Gentlemen, seek still to increase his mirth,
    Spare for no cost, our coffers shall be open,
    And we unto yourselves will still be thankful.
Both. In all we can, be sure you shall command.
Queen. Thanks, gentlemen, and what the queen of Denmark
    May pleasure you, be sure you shall not want.
Gilderstone. We'll once again unto the noble prince.   20
King. Thanks to you both: Gertred, you'll see this play?
Queen. My lord, I will, and it joys me at the soul
    He is inclined to any kind of mirth.
Corambis. Madam, I pray be ruled by me:
    And my good sovereign, give me leave to speak,
    We cannot yet find out the very ground
    Of his distemperance, therefore
    I hold it meet, if so it please you,
    Else they shall not meet, and thus it is.
King. What is't, Corambis?   30
Corambis. Marry my lord, this: soon, when the sports are done,
    Madam, send you in haste to speak with him,
    And I myself will stand behind the arras.
    There question you the cause of all his grief,
    And then in love and nature unto you, he'll tell you all:
    My lord, how think you on it?
King. It likes us well: Gertred, what say you?
Queen. With all my heart, soon will I send for him.
Corambis. Myself will be that happy messenger,
    Who hopes his grief will be revealed to her.   40
                                       Exeunt omnes.

33 *arras*: tapestry curtain or screen

[SCENE 9]

Enter Hamlet and the Players.

Hamlet. Pronounce me this speech trippingly a' the tongue as I
    taught thee,
    Marry, an you mouth it, as many of your players do.
    I'd rather hear a town bull bellow,
    Than such a fellow speak my lines.
    Nor do not saw the air thus with your hands,
    But give everything his action with temperance.
    O it offends me to the soul, to hear a rumbustious periwig
    fellow,
    To tear a passion in tatters, into very rags,
    To split the ears of the ignorant, who for the
10   Most part are capable of nothing but dumbshows and noises.
    I would have such a fellow whipped, for o'erdoing termagant.
    It out-Herods Herod.
Player. My lord, we have indifferently reformed that among us.
Hamlet. The better, the better, mend it altogether!
    There be fellows that I have seen play –
    And heard others commend them, and that highly too –
    That having neither the gait of Christian, pagan,
    Nor Turk, have so strutted and bellowed,
    That you would 'a thought, some of nature's journeymen
20   Had made men, and not made them well,
    They imitated humanity so abominable.
    Take heed, avoid it.
Player. I warrant you, my lord.
Hamlet. And do you hear? Let not your clown speak

---

7 *periwig*: stylized wig, theatrical rather than everyday
11 *termagant*: imaginary deity then believed to be worshipped by Muslims,
presented in the mystery plays as 'a violent overbearing personage' (*OED*)
12 *Herod*: king of Judea who ordered the massacre of the innocents to try to
kill the infant Jesus; played in medieval plays as a ranting tyrant
19 *journeymen*: hired men   23 *warrant*: promise, guarantee as true

More than is set down: there be some of them I can tell you
That will laugh themselves, to set on some
Quantity of barren spectators to laugh with them,
Albeit there is some necessary point in the play
Then to be observed: O 'tis vile, and shows
A pitiful ambition in the fool that useth it.   30
And then you have some again, that keeps one suit
Of jests, as a man is known by one suit of
Apparel, and gentlemen quotes his jests down
In their tables, before they come to the play, as thus:
'Cannot you stay 'til I eat my porridge?' And, 'you owe me
A quarter's wages': and, 'my coat wants a cullison':
And, 'your beer is sour': and blabbering with his lips
And this keeping in his cinque-a-pace of jests,
When, God knows, the warm clown cannot make a jest
Unless by chance, as the blind man catches a hare.   40
Masters, tell him of it.
Player. We will, my lord.
Hamlet. Well, go make you ready.
                              Exeunt players. [Enter Horatio.]
Horatio. Here, my lord.
Hamlet. Horatio, thou art even as just a man.
  As e'er my conversation coped withal.
Horatio. O, my lord!
Hamlet. Nay, why should I flatter thee?
  Why should the poor be flattered?
  What gain should I receive by flattering thee,   50
  That nothing hath but thy good mind?
  Let flattery sit on those time-pleasing tongues,
  To gloze with them that loves to hear their praise,
  And not with such as thou, Horatio.
  There is a play tonight, wherein one scene they have
  Comes very near the murder of my father.
  When thou shalt see that act afoot,
  Mark thou the king: do but observe his looks,

25 *set*: written   36 *cullison*: employer's badge
38 *cinque-a-pace*: dance, hence comic routine   53 *gloze*: talk speciously

For I mine eyes shall rivet to his face.

60   And if he do not bleach, and change at that,

It is a damned ghost that we have seen.

Horatio, have a care: observe him well.

Horatio. My lord, mine eyes shall still be on his face,

And not the smallest alteration

That shall appear in him, but I shall note it.

Hamlet. Hark, they come.

    Enter King, Queen, Corambis, [Ofelia,] and other Lords.

King. How now son Hamlet, how fare you: shall we have a
play?

Hamlet. I'faith, the chameleon's dish, not capon crammed, feed

70   a' the air.

Ay, father. My lord, you played in the university?

Corambis. That I did, my lord, and I was counted a good actor.

Hamlet. What did you enact there?

Corambis. My lord, I did act Julius Caesar, I was killed in the
Capitol: Brutus killed me.

Hamlet. It was a brute part of him,

To kill so capital a calf.

Come, be these players ready?

Queen. Hamlet, come sit down by me.

80   *Hamlet.* No, by my faith mother, here's a metal more attractive.

Lady, will give you me leave, and so forth,

To lay my head in your lap?

Ofelia. No, my lord.

Hamlet. Upon your lap. What did you think I meant, contrary
matters?

    *Enter a Dumb Show, the King and Queen. He sits down
    in an arbour, she leaves him. Then enters Lucianus with
    poison in a vial, and pours it in his ears, and goes away.
    Then the Queen cometh and finds him dead, and goes
    away with the other.*

Ofelia. What means this, my lord?   *Enter the Prologue.*

60 *bleach*: blanch, go pale
69 *chameleon's dish*: the chameleon was rumoured to live on air
69 *crammed*: stuffed
74 *Julius Caesar*: Shakespeare's previous play in 1599

Hamlet. This is miching mallico, that means mischief.
Ofelia. What doth this mean, my lord?
Hamlet. You shall hear anon: this fellow will tell you all.
Ofelia. Will he tell us what this show means?   90
Hamlet. Ay, or any show you'll show him,
   Be not afeared to show, he'll not be afeared to tell.
   O, these players cannot keep counsel, they'll tell all.
Prologue. For us and for our tragedy
   Here stooping to your clemency,
   We beg your hearing patiently.
Hamlet. Is't a prologue, or a poesy for a ring?
Ofelia. 'Tis short, my lord.
Hamlet. As women's love.
    Enter the Duke and Duchess.
Duke. Full forty years are past, their date is gone   100
   Since happy time joined both our hearts as one.
   And now the blood that filled my youthful veins
   Runs weakly in their pipes, and all the strains
   Of music, which whilom pleased mine ear,
   Is now a burden that age cannot bear.
   And therefore sweet nature must pay his due,
   To heaven must I, and leave the earth with you.
Duchess. O say not so, lest that you kill my heart.
   When death takes you, let life from me depart.
Duke. Content thyself: when ended is my date,   110
   Thou mayest, perchance, have a more noble mate,
   More wise, more youthful, and one –
Duchess. O speak no more, for then I am accursed,
   None weds the second, but she kills the first:
   A second time I kill my lord that's dead,
   When second husband kisses me in bed.
Hamlet. O wormwood, wormwood!
Duke. I do believe you, sweet, what now you speak,
   But what we do determine oft we break,

87 *miching mallico*: obscure, Hamlet apparently glosses as 'mischief'
95 *stooping*: bowing   104 *whilom*: formerly
117 *wormwood*: bitter-tasting plant used in medicine
119 *determine*: decide

120   For our demises still are overthrown,
         Our thoughts are ours, their end's none of our own:
         So think you will no second husband wed,
         But die thy thoughts, when thy first lord is dead.
      Duchess. Both here and there pursue me lasting strife,
         If once a widow, ever I be wife.
      Hamlet. If she should break now.
      Duke. 'Tis deeply sworn, sweet. Leave me here awhile,
         My spirits grow dull, and fain I would beguile the tedious time
            with sleep.
      Duchess. Sleep rock thy brain,
130   And never come mischance between us twain.   *Exit Lady.*
      Hamlet. Madam, how do you like this play?
      Queen. The lady protests too much.
      Hamlet. O, but she'll keep her word.
      King. Have you heard the argument: is there no offence in it?
      Hamlet. No offence in the world: poison in jest, poison in jest.
      King. What do you call the name of the play?
      Hamlet. Mousetrap: marry, how tragically – this play is
         The image of a murder done in Guyana. Albertus
         Was the Duke's name, his wife Baptista.
140   Father, it is a knavish piece a' work, but what
         A' that, it toucheth not us, you and I that have free
         Souls: let the galled jade wince. This is one
         Lucianus, nephew to the king.
      Ofelia. Y'are as good as a Chorus, my lord.
      Hamlet. I could interpret the love you bear, if I saw the poopies
         dallying.
      Ofelia. Y'are very pleasant, my lord.
      Hamlet. Who I, your only jigmaker? Why, what should a man
         do but be merry? For look how cheerfully my mother looks:
150   my father died within these two hours.
      Ofelia. Nay, it is twice two months, my lord.
      Hamlet. Two months, nay, then let the devil wear black,
         For I'll have a suit of sables. Jesus, two months dead,
         And not forgotten yet? Nay then, there's some

142 *jade*: 'inferior or worn-out horse' (*OED*)   145 *poopies*: puppets

Likelihood a gentleman's death may outlive memory,
But by my faith he must build churches then,
Or else he must follow the old epitaph:
With ho, with ho, the hobby-horse is forgot.
Ofelia. Your jests are keen, my lord.
Hamlet. It would cost you a groaning to take them off.   160
Ofelia. Still better and worse.
Hamlet. So you must take your husband, begin. Murderer
  Begin, a pox, leave thy damnable faces and begin,
  Come: the croaking raven doth bellow for revenge.
Murderer. Thoughts black, hands apt, drugs fit, and time agreeing.
  Confederate season, else no creature seeing:
  Thou mixture rank, of midnight weeds collected,
  With Hecate's bane thrice-blasted, thrice-infected,
  Thy natural magic and dire property,
  One wholesome life usurps immediately.   *Exit.*   170
Hamlet. He poisons him for his estate.
King. Lights, I will go to bed.
Corambis. The king rises: lights, ho!
    Exeunt King and Lords.
Hamlet. What, frighted with false fires?
  Then let the stricken deer go weep,
  The hart ungalled play,
  For some must laugh, while some must weep,
  Thus runs the world away.
Horatio. The king is moved, my lord.
Hamlet. Ay, Horatio: I'll take the ghost's word   180
  For more than all the coin in Denmark.
    Enter Rossencraft and Gilderstone.
Rossencraft. Now my lord, how is't with you?
Hamlet. And if the king like not the tragedy,
  Why then belike he likes it not, perdy.
Rossencraft. We are very glad to see your grace so pleasant.
  My good lord, let us again entreat

---

158 *hobby-horse*: horse costume worn by morris dancer
168 *Hecate*: goddess of witchcraft
184 *belike*: probably *perdy*: certainly

To know of you the ground and cause of your distemperature.
Gilderstone. My lord, your mother craves to speak with you.
Hamlet. We shall obey, were she ten times our mother.
190 *Rossencraft.* But my good lord, shall I entreat thus much?
Hamlet. I pray, will you play upon this pipe?
Rossencraft. Alas, my lord, I cannot.
Hamlet. Pray, will you?
Gilderstone. I have no skill, my lord.
Hamlet. Why look, it is a thing of nothing.
   'Tis but stopping of these holes,
   And with a little breath from your lips,
   It will give most delicate music.
Gilderstone. But this cannot we do, my lord.
200 *Hamlet.* Pray now, pray heartily, I beseech you.
Rossencraft. My lord, we cannot.
Hamlet. Why, how unworthy a thing would you make of me?
   You would seem to know my stops, you would play upon me,
   You would search the very inward part of my heart,
   And dive into the secret of my soul.
   Zounds, do you think I am easier to be played
   On, than a pipe? Call me what instrument
   You will, though you can fret me, yet you cannot
   Play upon me! Besides, to be demanded by a sponge –
210 *Rossencraft.* How, a sponge, my lord?
Hamlet. Ay sir, a sponge, that soaks up the king's
   Countenance, favours, and rewards, that makes
   His liberality your storehouse: but such as you
   Do the king, in the end, best service.
   For he doth keep you as an ape doth nuts,
   In the corner of his jaw; first mouths you,
   Then swallows you, so, when he hath need
   Of you, 'tis but squeezing of you.
   And sponge, you shall be dry again, you shall.
220 *Rossencraft.* Well my lord, we'll take our leave.
Hamlet. Farewell, farewell, God bless you.

191 *pipe*: woodwind instrument
203 *stops*: using a finger to cover the holes in a woodwind instrument
206 *Zounds*: From 'God's wounds' (oath)   208 *fret*: rub

Exit Rossencraft and Gilderstone.
Enter Corambis.

Corambis. My lord, the queen would speak with you.
Hamlet. Do you see yonder cloud in the shape of a camel?
Corambis. 'Tis like a camel indeed.
Hamlet. Now methinks it's like a weasel.
Corambis. 'Tis backed like a weasel.
Hamlet. Or like a whale.
Corambis. Very like a whale.   *Exit Corambis.*
Hamlet. Why then, tell my mother I'll come by and by.
   Goodnight, Horatio.   230
Horatio. Goodnight unto your lordship.   *Exit Horatio.*
Hamlet. My mother she hath sent to speak with me:
   O God, let ne'er the heart of Nero enter
   This soft bosom.
   Let me be cruel, not unnatural.
   I will speak daggers: those sharp words being spent,
   To do her wrong my soul shall ne'er consent.   *Exit.*

[SCENE 10]

Enter the King.

King. O that this wet that falls upon my face
   Would wash the crime clear from my conscience!
   When I look up to heaven, I see my trespass,
   The earth doth still cry out upon my fact,
   Pay me the murder of a brother and a king,
   And the adulterous fault I have committed.
   O these are sins that are unpardonable:
   Why say thy sins were blacker than is jet,
   Yet may contrition make them as white as snow:
   Ay, but still to persever in a sin,   10

233 *Nero*: tyrannical Roman emperor, who had his mother (among many
others) executed

It is an act against the universal power.
Most wretched man, stoop, bend thee to thy prayer,
Ask grace of heaven to keep thee from despair.
   He kneels. Enter Hamlet.
Hamlet. Ay so, come forth and work thy last,
And thus he dies, and so I am revenged.
No, not so. He took my father sleeping, his sins brimful,
And how his soul stood to the state of heaven
Who knows, save the immortal powers.
And shall I kill him now,
20   When he is purging of his soul,
Making his way for heaven? This is a benefit
And not revenge. No, get thee up again,
When he's at game, swearing, taking his carouse, drinking
   drunk,
Or in the incestuous pleasure of his bed,
Or at some act that hath no relish
Of salvation in't, then trip him
That his heels may kick at heaven,
And fall as low as hell. My mother stays:
This physic but prolongs thy weary days.   *Exit Hamlet.*
30 *King.* My words fly up, my sins remain below:
No king on earth is safe, if God's his foe.   *Exit King.*

[SCENE 11]

Enter Queen and Corambis.

Corambis. Madam, I hear young Hamlet coming.
   I'll shroud myself behind the arras.   *Exit Corambis.*
Queen. Do so my lord.   *[Enter Hamlet.]*
Hamlet. Mother, mother. O are you here?
   How is't with you, mother?
Queen. How is't with you?

28 *stays*: awaits   29 *physic*: medicine

Hamlet. I'll tell you, but first we'll make all safe.
Queen. Hamlet, thou hast thy father much offended.
Hamlet. Mother, you have my father much offended.
Queen. How now, boy?   10
Hamlet. How now, mother? Come here, sit down, for you shall
  hear me speak.
Queen. What wilt thou do? Thou wilt not murder me? Help, ho!
Corambis. Help for the queen!
                            [*Hamlet stabs him through the arras.*]
Hamlet. Ay, a rat, dead for a ducat.
  Rash intruding fool, farewell.
  I took thee for thy better.
Queen. Hamlet, what hast thou done?
Hamlet. Not so much harm, good mother.
  As to kill a king, and marry with his brother.   20
Queen. How! Kill a king!
Hamlet. Ay, a king: nay, sit you down, and ere you part,
  If you be made of penetrable stuff,
  I'll make your eyes look down into your heart,
  And see how horrid there and black it shows.
Queen. Hamlet, what meanst thou by these killing words?
Hamlet. Why this I mean: see here, behold this picture.
  It is the portraiture of your deceased husband.
  See here a face to outface Mars himself;
  An eye, at which his foes did tremble at;   30
  A front wherein all virtues are set down
  For to adorn a king and gild his crown,
  Whose heart went hand in hand even with that vow
  He made to you in marriage, and he is dead.
  Murdered, damnably murdered. This was your husband,
  Look you now, here is your husband,
  With a face like Vulcan;
  A look fit for a murder and a rape,
  A dull, dead hanging look and a hell-bred eye,
  To affright children and amaze the world.   40

17 *better*: social superior (the King)   29 *Mars*: Roman god of war
31 *front*: forehead
37 *Vulcan*: Roman god of fire and metal-working

And this same have you left to change with this.
What devil thus hath cozened you at hob-man blind?
Ah! Have you eyes, and can you look on him
That slew my father, and your dear husband,
To live in the incestuous pleasure of his bed?
Queen. O Hamlet, speak no more.
Hamlet. To leave him that bore a monarch's mind,
For a king of clouts, of very threads.
Queen. Sweet Hamlet, cease.
50 *Hamlet.* Nay, but still to persist and dwell in sin,
To sweat under the yoke of infamy,
To make increase of shame, to seal damnation.
Queen. Hamlet, no more.
Hamlet. Why appetite with you is in the wane,
Your blood runs backward now from whence it came.
Who'd chide hot blood within a virgin's heart
When lust shall dwell within a matron's breast?
Queen. Hamlet, thou cleaves my heart in twain.
Hamlet. O throw away the worser part of it, and keep the
      better.
      Enter the Ghost in his nightgown.
60 Save me, save me, you gracious
Powers above, and hover over me
With your celestial wings.
Do you not come your tardy son to chide,
That I thus long have let revenge slip by?
O do not glare with looks so pitiful!
Lest that my heart of stone yield to compassion,
And every part that should assist revenge,
Forgo their proper powers, and fall to pity.
Ghost. Hamlet, I once again appear to thee,
70 To put thee in remembrance of my death.
Do not neglect, nor long time put it off.
But I perceive by thy distracted looks,
Thy mother's fearful, and she stands amazed.

42 *cozened*: cheated   *hob-man blind*: game of blind man's buff
48 *clouts*: cloths, patches

Speak to her, Hamlet, for her sex is weak.
Comfort thy mother, Hamlet: think on me.
Hamlet. How is't with you, lady?
Queen. Nay, how is't with you
   That thus you bend your eyes on vacancy,
   And hold discourse with nothing but with air?
Hamlet. Why, do you nothing hear?   80
Queen. Not I.
Hamlet. Nor do you nothing see?
Queen. No, neither.
Hamlet. No, why see the king my father, my father, in the habit
   As he lived, look you how pale he looks,
   See he steals away out of the portal,
   Look, there he goes.   *Exit Ghost.*
Queen. Alas, it is the weakness of thy brain,
   Which makes thy tongue to blazon thy heart's grief.
   But as I have a soul, I swear by heaven,   90
   I never knew of this most horrid murder.
   But Hamlet, this is only fantasy,
   And for my love forget these idle fits.
Hamlet. Idle? No mother, my pulse doth beat like yours,
   It is not madness that possesseth Hamlet.
   O mother, if ever you did my dear father love.
   Forbear the adulterous bed tonight.
   And win yourself by little as you may.
   In time it may be you will loathe him quite:
   And mother, but assist me in revenge,   100
   And in his death your infamy shall die.
Queen. Hamlet, I vow by that majesty
   That knows our thoughts, and looks into our hearts,
   I will conceal, consent, and do my best,
   What stratagem soe'er thou shalt devise.
Hamlet. It is enough, mother, good night.
   Come sir, I'll provide for you a grave,
   Who was in life a foolish prating knave.
      Exit Hamlet with the dead body.
      Enter the King and Lords [Rossencraft and Gilderstone].
King. Now Gertred, what says our son? How do you find him?

110   *Queen.* Alas, my lord, as raging as the sea:
          Whenas he came, I first bespake him fair,
          But then he throws and tosses me about
          As one forgetting that I was his mother.
          At last I called for help, and as I cried, Corambis
          Called, which Hamlet no sooner heard, but whips me
          Out his rapier, and cries 'a Rat, a Rat', and in his rage
          The good old man he kills.
       King. Why this his madness will undo our state.
          Lords, go to him: inquire the body out.
120   *Gilderstone.* We will, my lord.   *Exeunt Lords.*
       King. Gertred, your son shall presently to England.
          His shipping is already furnished,
          And we have sent by Rossencraft and Gilderstone,
          Our letters to our dear brother of England,
          For Hamlet's welfare and his happiness.
          Haply the air and climate of the country
          May please him better than his native home:
          See, where he comes.
              Enter Hamlet and the Lords.
       Gilderstone. My lord, we can by no means
130   Know of him where the body is.
       King. Now son Hamlet, where is this dead body?
       Hamlet. At supper, not where he is eating, but
          Where he is eaten: a certain company of politic worms are
             even now at him.
          Father, your fat king and your lean beggar
          Are but variable services: two dishes to one mess.
          Look you, a man may fish with that worm
          That hath eaten of a king,
          And a beggar eat that fish,
          Which that worm hath caught.
140   *King.* What of this?
       Hamlet. Nothing, father, but to tell you, how a king
          May go a progress through the guts of a beggar.
       King. But son Hamlet, where is this body?

       133 *politic*: shrewd, cunning   142 *progress*: royal journey

Hamlet. In heaven: if you chance to miss him there,
    Father, you had best look in the other parts below
    For him, and if you cannot find him there,
    You may chance to nose him as you go up the lobby.
King. Make haste and find him out.
Hamlet. Nay, do you hear? Do not make too much haste.
    I'll warrant you he'll stay till you come.   150
King. Well, son Hamlet, we in care of you, but specially in
    tender preservation of your health,
    The which we prize even as our proper self,
    It is our mind you forthwith go for England,
    The wind sits fair, you shall aboard tonight.
    Lord Rossencraft and Gilderstone shall go along with you.
Hamlet. O with all my heart: farewell, mother.
King. Your loving father, Hamlet.
Hamlet. My mother I say: you married my mother,
    My mother is your wife, man and wife is one flesh,   160
    And so, my mother, farewell: for England ho!
        Exeunt all but the King.
King. Gertred, leave me,
    And take your leave of Hamlet.
    To England is he gone, ne'er to return.
    Our letters are unto the king of England,
    That on the sight of them, on his allegiance
    He presently without demanding why
    That Hamlet lose his head, for he must die.
    There's more in him than shallow eyes can see:
    He once being dead, why then our state is free.   *Exit.*   170

[SCENE 12]

Enter Fortenbrasse, Drum and Soldiers.

Fortenbrasse. Captain, from us go greet

145 *below*: in hell   147 *nose*: smell

The king of Denmark:
Tell him that Fortenbrasse, nephew to old Norway,
Craves a free pass and conduct over his land,
According to the articles agreed on.
You know our rendezvous: go, march away.   *Exeunt all.*

[SCENE 13]

Enter King and Queen.

King. Hamlet is shipped for England: fare him well,
    I hope to hear good news from thence ere long,
    If everything fall out to our content,
    As I do make no doubt but so it shall.
Queen. God grant it may: heavens keep my Hamlet safe.
    But this mischance of old Corambis' death
    Hath pierced so the young Ofelia's heart,
    That she, poor maid, is quite bereft her wits.
King. Alas, dear heart! And on the other side,
10 We understand her brother's come from France,
    And he hath half the heart of all our land,
    And hardly he'll forget his father's death,
    Unless by some means he be pacified.
Queen. O see, where the young Ofelia is!
    Enter Ofelia playing on a lute, and her hair down,
    singing.
Ofelia. How should I your true love know
    From another man?
    By his cockle-hat, and his staff,
    And his sandal shoon.
    White his shroud as mountain snow,
20 Larded with sweet flowers,

17 *cockle-hat*: a hat worn by pilgrims from the shrine of St James at
Compostella and marked with his symbol of a scallop shell
18 *shoon*: shoes   20 *Larded*: Strewn

That bewept to the grave did not go
With true lovers' showers:
He is dead and gone, lady,
He is dead and gone.
At his head a grass-green turf
At his heels a stone.
King. How is't with you, sweet Ofelia?
Ofelia. Well, God yield you.
  It grieves me to see how they laid him in the cold ground,
  I could not choose but weep: 30
  And will he not come again?
  And will he not come again?
  No, no, he's gone, and we cast away moan,
  And he never will come again.
  His beard as white as snow:
  All flaxen was his poll,
  He is dead, he is gone,
  And we cast away moan.
  God 'a mercy on his soul.
  And of all Christian souls, I pray God.   40
  God be with you, ladies, God be with you.   *Exit Ofelia.*
King. A pretty wretch! This is a change indeed:
  O Time, how swiftly runs our joys away!
  Content on earth was never certain bred,
  Today we laugh and live, tomorrow dead.
  How now, what noise is that?
       A noise within. Enter Leartes.
Leartes. Stay there until I come,
  O thou vile king, give me my father.
  Speak, say, where's my father?
King. Dead.   50
Leartes. Who hath murdered him? Speak, I'll not
  Be juggled with, for he is murdered.
Queen. True, but not by him.
Laertes. By whom? By heaven, I'll be resolved.

36 *poll:* head   44 *certain:* dependable   52 *juggled:* cheated

King. Let him go, Gertred. Away, I fear him not.
   There's such a divinity doth wall a king,
   That treason dares not look on.
   Let him go, Gertred: that your father is murdered,
   'Tis true, and we most sorry for it,
60   Being the chiefest pillar of our state:
   Therefore will you like a most desperate gamester,
   Swoopstake-like, draw at friend and foe and all?
Leartes. To his good friends thus wide I'll ope mine arms,
   And lock them in my heart; but to his foes,
   I will no reconcilement but by blood.
King. Why now you speak like a most loving son.
   And that in soul we sorrow for his death,
   Yourself ere long shall be a witness:
   Meanwhile be patient, and content yourself.
     Enter Ofelia as before.
70 *Leartes.* Who's this, Ofelia? O my dear sister!
   Is't possible a young maid's life
   Should be as mortal as an old man's saw?
   O heavens themselves! How now, Ofelia?
Ofelia. Well, God amercy, I 'a been gathering of flowers:
   Here, here is rue for you,
   You may call it herb-a-grace o'Sundays,
   Here's some for me too: you must wear your rue
   With a difference. There's a daisy.
   Here love, there's rosemary for you
80   For remembrance: I pray, love, remember.
   And there's pansy for thoughts.
Leartes. A document in madness, thoughts, remembrance:
   O God, O God!
Ofelia. There is fennel for you, I would 'a given you
   Some violets, but they all withered, when
   My father died: alas, they say the owl was
   A baker's daughter, we see what we are,
   But cannot tell what we shall be.

56 *wall*: protect 61 *gamester*: gambler
62 *Swoopstake-like*: As in a sweepstake 63 *ope*: open
72 *saw*: saying, maxim 75 *rue*: herb (sorrow)

For bonny sweet Robin is all my joy.
Leartes. Thoughts and afflictions, torments worse than hell!   90
Ofelia. Nay love, I pray you make no words of this now:
    I pray now, you shall sing 'a-down',
    And you 'a-down-a', 'tis o'the king's daughter
    And the false steward, and if anybody
    Ask you of anything, say you this:
    Tomorrow is Saint Valentine's day,
    All in the morning betime,
    And a maid at your window,
    To be your Valentine:
    The young man rose, and donned his clothes,   100
    And dupped the chamber door,
    Let in the maid, that out a maid,
    Never departed more.
    Nay I pray mark now,
    By Gis and by Saint Charity,
    Away, and fie for shame:
    Young men will do't when they come to't:
    By cock they are to blame.
    Quoth she, 'before you tumbled me,
    You promised me to wed'.   110
    So would I a' done, by yonder sun,
    If thou hadst not come to my bed.
    So God be with you all, God be with you, ladies.
    God be with you love.   *Exit Ofelia.*
Leartes. Grief upon grief: my father murdered,
    My sister thus distracted.
    Cursed be his soul that hath wrought this wicked act.
King. Content you, good Leartes, for a time,
    Although I know your grief is as a flood,
    Brimful of sorrow, but forbear a while,
    And think already the revenge is done
    On him that makes you such a hapless son.   120
Leartes. You have prevailed my lord. Awhile I'll strive,

101 *dupped*: opened 105 *Gis*: Oath, derived from 'Jesu'
113 *be with you, ladies*: Q bwy, ladies

To bury grief within a tomb of wrath
Which once unhearsed, then the world shall hear
Leartes had a father he held dear.
King. No more of that, ere many days be done,
    You shall hear that you do not dream upon.

Exeunt omnes.

[SCENE 14]

Enter Horatio and the Queen.

Horatio. Madam, your son is safe arrived in Denmark,
    This letter I even now received of him,
    Whereas he writes how he escaped the danger
    And subtle treason that the king had plotted.
    Being crossed by the contention of the winds,
    He found the packet sent to the king of England,
    Wherein he saw himself betrayed to death.
    As at his next conversion with your grace,
    He will relate the circumstance at full.
10 *Queen.* Then I perceive there's treason in his looks
    That seeemed to sugar o'er his villainy.
    But I will soothe and please him for a time,
    But murderous minds are always jealous.
    But know not you, Horatio, where he is?
Horatio. Yes madam, and he hath appointed me
    To meet him on the east side of the city
    Tomorrow morning.
Queen. O fail not, good Horatio, and withal, commend me
    A mother's care to him, bid him a while
20 Be wary of his presence, lest that he
    Fail in that he goes about.
Horatio. Madam, never make doubt of that:

8 *conversion:* conversation
20 *presence:* 'the immediate vicinity of a person; the company or society of someone' (*OED*)

I think by this the news be come to court:
He is arrived, observe the king, and you shall
Quickly find, Hamlet being here,
Things fell not to his mind.
Queen. But what became of Gilderstone and Rossencraft?
Horatio. He being set ashore, they set for England,
   And in the packet there writ down that doom
   To be performed on them 'pointed for him.   30
   And by great chance he had his father's seal,
   So all was done without discovery.
Queen. Thanks be to heaven for blessing of the prince.
   Horatio once again I take my leave,
   With thousand mother's blessings to my son.
Horatio. Madam, adieu.

[SCENE 15]

Enter King and Leartes.

King. Hamlet from England! Is it possible?
   What chance is this? they are gone, and he come home.
Leartes. O he is welcome, by my soul he is.
   At it my jocund heart doth leap for joy,
   That I shall live to tell him, thus he dies.
King. Leartes, content yourself: be ruled by me,
   And you shall have no let for your revenge.
Leartes. My will, not all the world.
King. Nay, but Leartes, mark the plot I have laid.
   I have heard him often with a greedy wish,   10
   Upon some praise that he hath heard of you
   Touching your weapon, which with all his heart,
   He might be once tasked for to try your cunning.
Leartes. And how for this?

7 *let*: hindrance   13 *cunning*: skill

King. Marry, Leartes, thus: I'll lay a wager –
   Shall be on Hamlet's side, and you shall give the odds –
   The which will draw him with a more desire,
   To try the master: that in twelve venies
   You gain not three of him. Now this being granted,
20   When you are hot in midst of all your play,
   Among the foils shall a keen rapier lie,
   Steeped in a mixture of deadly poison,
   That if it draws but the least dram of blood,
   In any part of him, he cannot live.
   This being done will free you from suspicion,
   And not the dearest friend that Hamlet loved
   Will ever have Leartes in suspect.
Leartes. My lord, I like it well.
   But say Lord Hamlet should refuse this match?
30 *King.* I'll warrant you, we'll put on you
   Such a report of singularity,
   Will bring him on, although against his will.
   And lest all that should miss,
   I'll have a potion that shall ready stand,
   In all his heat when he that calls for drink,
   Shall be his period and our happiness.
Leartes. 'Tis excellent, O, would the time were come!
   Here comes the queen.   *Enter the Queen.*
King. How now Gertred, why look you heavily?
40 *Queen.* O my lord, the young Ofelia
   Having made a garland of sundry sorts of flowers,
   Sitting upon a willow by a brook,
   The envious sprig broke, into the brook she fell.
   And for a while her clothes spread wide abroad,
   Bore the young lady up: and there she sat smiling,
   Even mermaid-like, 'twixt heaven and earth,

18 *venies*: fencing bouts
21 *foils*: fencing weapons with blunt edge and a button at the point
21 *rapier*: thin, sharp-pointed sword
31 *singularity*: distinction, excellence
33 *miss*: miscarry 36 *period*: ending

Chanting old sundry tunes uncapable
As it were of her distress. But long it could not be
Till that her clothes, being heavy with their drink,
Dragged the sweet wretch to death.   50
Leartes. So, she is drowned.
  Too much of water has thou, Ofelia,
  Therefore I will not drown thee in my tears.
  Revenge it is must yield this heart relief,
  For woe begets woe, and grief hangs on grief.   *Exeunt.*

[SCENE 16]

Enter [1] Clown and an other [2 Clown].

1 Clown. I say no, she ought not to be buried
  In Christian burial.
2 Clown. Why sir?
1 Clown. Marry, because she's drowned.
2 Clown. But she did not drown herself.
1 Clown. No, that's certain, the water drowned her.
2 Clown. Yea but it was against her will.
1 Clown. No, I deny that, for look you sir: I stand here,
  If the water comes to me, I drown not myself,
  But if I go to the water, and am there drowned,   10
  Ergo I am guilty of my own death.
  Y'are gone, go y'are gone sir.
2 Clown. I but see, she hath Christian burial,
  Because she is a great woman.
1 Clown. Marry more's the pity, that great folk
  Should have more authority to hang or drown
  Themselves, more than other people.
  Go fetch me a stoup of drink, but before thou

47 *uncapable*: insensible, unable to take in
1 *Clown*: Countryman, peasant   11 *Ergo*: Therefore
14 *great*: high-born   18 *stoup*: drinking cup

Goest, tell me one thing. Who builds strongest,
20   Of a mason, a shipwright, or a carpenter?
   2 Clown. Why a mason, for he builds all of stone,
      And will endure long.
   1 Clown. That's pretty. To't again, to't again.
   2 Clown. Why then a carpenter, for he builds the gallows,
      And that brings many a one to his long home.
   1 Clown. Pretty again, the gallows doth well, marry how does it
      well? the gallows does well to them that do ill, go get thee
      gone:
      And if anyone asks thee hereafter, say,
30   A grave-maker, for the houses he builds
      Last till doomsday. Fetch me a stoup of beer, go.
         Enter Hamlet and Horatio.
      A pick-axe and a spade,
      A spade for and a winding sheet,
      Most fit it is, for t'will be made,   *He throws up a shovel.*
      For such a guest most meet.
   Hamlet. Hath this fellow any feeling of himself,
      That is this merry in making of a grave?
      See how the slave jowls their heads against the earth.
   Horatio. My lord, custom hath made it in him seem nothing.
40   *1 Clown.* A pick-axe and a spade, a spade,
      For and a winding sheet,
      Most fit it is for to be made,
      For such a guest most meet.
   Hamlet. Look you, there's another Horatio.
      Why may't not be the skull of some lawyer?
      Methinks he should indict that fellow
      Of an action of battery, for knocking
      Him about the pate with a shovel: now where is your
      Quirks and quillets now, your vouchers and

34SD *shovel*: sometimes emended to 'skull': clearly skulls are unearthed
during this conversation
47 *battery*: assault
49 *Quirks*: Arguments   *quillets*: small plot of land
49 *vouchers*: 'summoning of a person into court to warrant the title to a
property' (*OED*)

Double vouchers, your leases and freehold,   50
And tenement? Why that same box there will scarce
Hold the conveyance of his land, and must
The honour lie there? O pitiful transformance!
I prithee tell me, Horatio,
Is parchment made of sheepskins?
Horatio. Ay, my lord, and of calfskins too.
Hamlet. I'faith, they prove themselves sheep and calves
That deal with them, or put their trust in them.
There's another, why may not that be such a one's
Skull, that praised my lord such a one's horse,   60
When he meant to beg him? Horatio, I prithee
Let's question yonder fellow.
Now my friend, whose grave is this?
1 Clown. Mine sir.
Hamlet. But who must lie in it?
1 Clown. If I should say, I should, I should lie in my throat sir.
Hamlet. What man must be buried here?
1 Clown. No man sir.
Hamlet. What woman?
1 Clown. No woman neither sir, but indeed   70
One that was a woman.
Hamlet. An excellent fellow, by the Lord, Horatio.
This seven years have I noted it: the toe of the peasant
Comes so near the heel of the courtier,
That he galls his kibe. I prithee, tell me one thing:
How long will a man lie in the ground before he rots?
1 Clown. I'faith sir, if he be not rotten before
He will be laid in, as we have many pocky corpses,
He will last you, eight years, a tanner
Will last you eight years full out, or nine.   80
Hamlet. And why a tanner?
1 Clown Why his hide is so tanned with his trade,
That it will hold out water, that's a parlous
Devourer of your dead body, a great soaker.

---

52 *conveyance*: legal transference of property   75 *kibe*: chilblain or blister
75 *prithee*: I pray thee   78 *pocky*: marked with pocks, syphilitic
79 *tanner*: leatherworker

Look you, here's a skull hath been here this dozen year,
Let me see, ay ever since our last king Hamlet
Slew Fortenbrasse in combat, young Hamlet's father,
He that's mad.

Hamlet. Ay marry, how came he mad?

90 *1 Clown.* I'faith, very strangely, by losing of his wits.

Hamlet. Upon what ground?

1 Clown. A' this ground, in Denmark.

Hamlet. Where is he now?

1 Clown. Why now they sent him to England.

Hamlet. To England! Wherefore?

1 Clown. Why they say he shall have his wits there,
Or if he have not, 'tis no great matter there,
It will not be seen there.

Hamlet. Why not there?

100 *1 Clown.* Why there they say the men are as mad as he.

Hamlet. Whose skull was this?

1 Clown. This, a plague on him, a mad rogue's it was,
He poured once a whole flagon of Rhenish of my head,
Why, do not you know him? this was one Yorick's skull.

Hamlet. Was this? I prithee let me see it, alas, poor Yorick,
I knew him, Horatio. A fellow of infinite mirth, he hath carried me twenty times upon his back. Here hung those lips
that I have kissed a hundred times, and to see, now they
abhor me: where's your jests now, Yorick? your flashes of

110 merriment? Now go to my lady's chamber, and bid her paint
herself an inch thick, to this she must come, Yorick. Horatio,
I prithee tell me one thing, dost thou think that Alexander
looked thus?

Horatio. Even so, my lord.

Hamlet. And smelt thus?

Horatio. Ay, my lord, no otherwise.

Hamlet. No, why might not imagination work, as thus of
Alexander. Alexander died, Alexander was buried, Alexander

---

109 *abhor*: fill with horror and disgust
112 *Alexander*: legendary Greek imperial leader

became earth, of earth we make clay, and Alexander being
but clay, why might not time bring to pass, that he might   120
stop the bunghole of a beer barrel?
Imperious Caesar dead and turned to clay,
Might stop a hole to keep the wind away.

> *Enter King and Queen, Leartes, and other Lords, with a*
> *Priest after the coffin.*

What funeral's this, that all the court lament?
It shows to be some noble parentage.
Stand by a while.

Leartes. What ceremony else? say, what ceremony else?

Priest. My Lord, we have done all that lies in us,
And more than well the church can tolerate.
She hath a dirge sung for her maiden soul: 130
And but for favour of the king, and you,
She had been buried in the open fields,
Where now she is allowed Christian burial.

Leartes. So, I tell thee churlish priest, a ministering angel shall
my sister be, when thou liest howling.

Hamlet. The fair Ofelia dead!

Queen. Sweets to the sweet, farewell:
I had thought to adorn thy bridal bed, fair maid,
And not to follow thee unto thy grave.

Leartes. Forbear the earth a while: sister, farewell: 140

> *Leartes leaps into the grave.*

Now pour your earth on, Olympus high,
And make a hill to o'ertop Pelion:

> *Hamlet leaps in after Leartes.*

What's he that conjures so?

Hamlet. Behold 'tis I, Hamlet the Dane.

Leartes. The devil take thy soul.

Hamlet. O thou prayest not well.
I prithee take thy hand from off my throat,
For there is something in me dangerous,

127 *else*: more   141 *Olympus*: mountain home of the Greek Gods
142 *Pelion*: mountain in Greece in mythology; it was piled on top of Ossa in
an attempt to storm Olympus

Why let thy wisdom fear. Hold off thy hand!
150   I loved Ofelia as dear as twenty brothers could.
Show me what thou wilt do for her:
Wilt fight? wilt fast? wilt pray?
Wilt drink up vessels? eat a crocodile? I'll do't.
Com'st thou here to whine?
And where thou talk'st of burying thee alive,
Here let us stand: and let them throw on us.
Whole hills of earth, till with the heighth thereof,
Make Ossa as a wart.
King. Forbear Leartes; now is he mad, as is the sea,
160   Anon as mild and gentle as a dove:
Therefore a while give his wild humour scope.
Hamlet. What is the reason sir that you wrong me thus?
I never gave you cause: but stand away,
A cat will mew, a dog will have a day.
     Exit Hamlet and Horatio.
Queen. Alas, it is his madness makes him thus,
And not his heart, Leartes.
King. My lord, 'tis so: but we'll no longer trifle.
This very day shall Hamlet drink his last,
For presently we mean to send to him.
170   Therefore Leartes be in readiness.
Leartes. My lord, till then my soul will not be quiet.
King. Come Gertred, we'll have Leartes, and our son
Made friends and lovers, as befits them both,
Even as they tender us, and love their country.
Queen. God grant they may.   *Exeunt omnes.*

[SCENE 17]

Enter Hamlet and Horatio.

Hamlet. Believe me, it grieves me much, Horatio,

158 *Ossa*: Q Oosell; mountain in Greece

That to Leartes I forgot myself:
For by myself methinks I feel his grief,
Though there's a difference in each other's wrong.
  Enter a Braggart Gentleman.
Horatio, but mark yon water-fly,
The Court knows him, but he knows not the court.
Gentleman. Now God save thee, sweet Prince Hamlet.
Hamlet. And you sir: foh, how the musk-cod smells!
Gentleman. I come with an embassage from his majesty to
  you.
Hamlet. I shall give you attention: 10
  By my troth methinks it is very cold.
Gentleman. It is indeed very rawish cold.
Hamlet. 'Tis hot methinks.
Gentleman. Very sweltery hot:
  The king, sweet prince, hath laid a wager on your side,
  Six Barbary horse, against six French rapiers,
  With all their accoutrements too, o'the carriages:
  In good faith they are very curiously wrought.
Hamlet. The carriages sir, I do not know what you mean.
Gentleman. The girdles, and hangers sir, and such like.   20
Hamlet. The word hath been more cousin-german to the
  phrase, if he could have carried the cannon by his side.
  And how's the wager? I understand you now.
Gentleman. Marry sir, that young Leartes in twelve venies
  At rapier and dagger do not get three odds of you,
  And on your side the king hath laid,
  And desires you to be in readiness.
Hamlet. Very well, if the king dare venture his wager,
  I dare venture my skull. When must this be?
Gentleman. My lord, presently, the king and her majesty,   30

4SD *Braggart*: Boastful, vain   5 *water-fly*: pestering insect
8 *musk-cod*: perfumed fop
16 *Barbary horse*: valuable horses from North Africa
18 *wrought*: designed
20 *girdles, and hangers*: loops or straps designed to hold swords
21 *cousin-german*: close relative (literally, first cousin)
26 *laid*: bet

With the rest of the best judgement in the court,
Are coming down into the outward palace.
Hamlet. Go tell his majesty, I will attend him.
Gentleman. I shall deliver your most sweet answer.   *Exit.*
Hamlet. You may sir, none better, for y'are spiced,
Else he had a bad nose could not smell a fool.
Horatio. He will disclose himself without inquiry.
Hamlet. Believe me, Horatio, my heart is on the sudden
Very sore, all hereabout.
40 *Horatio.* My lord, forbear the challenge then.
Hamlet. No Horatio, not I, if danger be now
Why then it is not to come, there's a predestinate providence
in the fall of a sparrow: here comes the king.
    Enter King, Queen, Leartes, Lords.
King. Now son Hamlet, we have laid upon your head,
And make no question but to have the best.
Hamlet. Your majesty hath laid a' the weaker side.
King. We doubt it not, deliver them the foils.
Hamlet. First Leartes, here's my hand and love,
Protesting that I never wronged Leartes.
50 If Hamlet in his madness did amiss,
That was not Hamlet, but his madness did it,
And all the wrong I e'er did to Leartes,
I here proclaim was madness: therefore let's be at peace,
And think I have shot mine arrow o'er the house,
And hurt my brother.
Leartes. Sir I am satisfied in nature,
But in terms of honour I'll stand aloof,
And will no reconcilement,
Till by some elder masters of our time
60 I may be satisfied.
King. Give them the foils.
Hamlet. I'll be your foil Leartes, these foils,
Have all a length: come on sir.

32 *outward*: unclear, perhaps public or outdoor
42 *predestinate*: predestinated, preordained
63 *length*: Q laught

Here they play.
   A hit!
Leartes. No, none.
Hamlet. Judgement?
Gentleman. A hit, a most palpable hit.
Leartes. Well, come again.   *They play again.*
Hamlet. Another. Judgement?
Leartes. Ay, I grant, a touch, a touch.   70
King. Here Hamlet, the king doth drink a health to thee.
Queen. Here Hamlet, take my napkin, wipe thy face.
King. Give him the wine.
Hamlet. Set it by, I'll have another bout first,
   I'll drink anon.
Queen. Here Hamlet, thy mother drinks to thee.
      She drinks.
King. Do not drink Gertred! O 'tis the poisoned cup!
Hamlet. Leartes come, you dally with me,
   I pray you pass with your most cunning'st play.
Leartes. I! Say you so? have at you,   80
   I'll hit you now my lord:
   And yet it goes almost against my conscience.
Hamlet. Come on sir.
      They catch one another's rapiers, and both are wounded,
      Leartes falls down, the Queen falls down and dies.
King. Look to the queen!
Queen. O, the drink, the drink, Hamlet, the drink.
Hamlet. Treason, ho, keep the gates!
Lords. How is't my Lord Leartes?
Leartes. Even as a coxcomb should,
   Foolishly slain with my own weapon.
   Hamlet, thou hadst not in thee half an hour of life,   90
   The fatal instrument is in thy hand,
   Unbated and envenomed. Thy mother's poisoned:
   That drink was made for thee.
Hamlet. The poisoned instrument within my hand?

---

92 *Unbated*: Foil without its protective button and thus sharp

Then venom to thy venom, die, damned villain:
Come drink, here lies thy union here.   *The King dies.*
Leartes. O, he is justly served:
  Hamlet, before I die, here take my hand,
  And withal, my love: I do forgive thee.   *Leartes dies.*
100 *Hamlet.* And I thee, O I am dead, Horatio: fare thee well.
Horatio. No, I am more an antique Roman
  Than a Dane, here is some poison left.
Hamlet. Upon my love I charge thee let it go,
  O fie, Horatio, an if thou shouldst die,
  What a scandal wouldst thou leave behind?
  What tongue should tell the story of our deaths,
  If not from thee? O my heart sinks, Horatio,
  Mine eyes have lost their sight, my tongue his use:
  Farewell, Horatio, heaven receive my soul.   *Hamlet dies.*
    Enter Voltemar and the Ambassadors from England.
    Enter Fortenbrasse with his train.
110 *Fortenbrasse.* What is this bloody sight?
Horatio. If aught of woe or wonder you'd behold,
  Then look upon this tragic spectacle.
Fortenbrassse. O imperious death! how many princes
  Hast thou at one draught bloodily shot to death?
Ambassadors. Our embassy that we have brought from
    England,
  Where be these princes that should hear us speak?
  O most unlooked-for time! unhappy country.
Horatio. Content yourselves. I'll show to all, the ground,
  The first beginning of this tragedy.
120 Let there a scaffold be reared up in the marketplace,
  And let the state of the world be there:
  Where you shall hear such a sad story told,
  That never mortal man could more unfold.
Fortenbrasse. I have some rights of memory to this kingdom,
  Which now to claim my leisure doth invite me:
  Let four of our chiefest captains

101 *antique*: ancient

Bear Hamlet like a soldier to his grave:
For he was likely, had he lived.
To 'a proved most royal.
Take up the body, such a sight as this   130
Becomes the fields, but here doth much amiss.

FINIS

131 *fields*: battlefields

JOHN MARSTON

ANTONIO'S REVENGE

LIST OF CHARACTERS

GHOST OF ANDRUGIO *formerly duke of Genoa*
ANTONIO *his son*
MELLIDA *betrothed to Antonio*
PIERO SFORZA *duke of Venice, father of Mellida*
STROTZO *his accomplice*
JULIO *young son of Piero*
MARIA *widow of Andrugio, mother of Antonio*
LUCIO *her servant*
NUTRICHE *her nurse*
PANDULPHO FELICHE *stoic gentleman*
FELICHE *dead son of Pandulpho*
BALURDO *foolish gentleman*
ALBERTO
CASTILIO
FOROBOSCO
GALEATZO *prince of Florence*
MATZAGENTE
2 SENATORS
Pages, Attendants, Ladies, Herald, Mourners

List of Characters: the Italian names of the characters are drawn from, and thus illustrated from, John Florio's Italian/English dictionary, *A Worlde of Wordes* (1598)
4 SFORZA: 'force, power, strength'
5 STROTZO: 'to kill or crush to death, to strangle'
9 NUTRICHE: 'a nurse, a foster-mother'
11 FELICHE: 'happy, fortunate, lucky'
16 GALEATZO: 'a galleass' or ship
17 MATZAGENTE: 'a killer or queller of people'

The Prologue

The rawish dank of clumsy winter ramps
The fluent summer's vein; and drizzling sleet
Chilleth the wan bleak cheek of the numbed earth,
Whilst snarling gusts nibble the juiceless leaves
From the naked shuddering branch, and pills the skin
From off the soft and delicate aspects.
O now, methinks, a sullen tragic scene
Would suit the time with pleasing congruence.
May we be happy in our weak devoir,
And all part pleased in most wished content: 10
But sweat of Hercules can ne'er beget
So blest an issue. Therefore we proclaim:
If any spirit breathes within this round,
Incapable of weighty passion
(As from his birth, being hugged in the arms,
And nuzzled 'twixt the breasts of happiness),

Although *Antonio's Revenge* works, and was performed, as a stand-alone
play, it also makes reference to a contemporaneous play by Marston with
many of the same characters, *Antonio and Mellida*, which tells how Piero
Sforza, duke of Venice, tries to disrupt the love between his daughter Mellida
and Antonio, son of his enemy the Duke of Genoa Andrugio. The shipwrecked Antonio, disguised as an Amazon, arrives at the Venetian court and
persuades Mellida to escape with him, but she is captured and returned to
her father. Andrugio returns to Venice with his son's coffin to claim the
reward placed on their heads by Piero, who, moved by this act of valour,
wishes that Antonio were still alive to marry his daughter. Antonio, not truly
dead, rises from the coffin; Piero has to accept him as his son-in-law and end
his hatred of Andrugio, in a typical comic reconciliation. Piero's first bloody
acts are introduced at the beginning of *Antonio's Revenge* 1.1, and must be
thought to have happened between the comic ending of *Antonio and Mellida*
and the tragic begining of this play.

1 *clumsy*: 'benumbed or stiffened with cold' (*OED*)
1 *ramps*: snatches, tears; rises upon   5 *pills*: strips
6 *aspects*: appearances   9 *devoir*: business, appointed task
11 *Hercules*: Roman demigod renowned for strength and virility; see also
5.6.14–15 and note below, and *Hamlet*, scene 2.61
13 *round*: i.e. the semicircular form of Paul's theatre

Who winks, and shuts his apprehension up
From common sense of what men were, and are,
Who would not know what men must be – let such
20   Hurry amain from our black-visaged shows.
We shall affright their eyes. But if a breast
Nailed to the earth with grief, if any heart
Pierced through with anguish, pant within this ring,
If there be any blood, whose heat is choked
And stifled with true sense of misery;
If aught of these strains fill this consort up,
Th'arrive most welcome. O that our power
Could lackey, or keep wing with our desires;
That with unused peise of style and sense,
30   We might weigh massy in judicious scale.
Yet here's the prop that doth support our hopes:
When our scenes falter, or invention halts,
Your favour will give crutches to our faults.   *Exit.*

ACT 1

Scene 1

Enter Piero, unbraced, his arms bare, smeared in blood, a poniard in one hand bloody, and a torch in the other, Strotzo following him with a cord.

Piero. Ho, Gasper Strotzo, bind Feliche's trunk
     Unto the panting side of Mellida.   *Exit Strotzo.*

17 *winks*: shuts eyes   *apprehension*: perception, understanding
20 *amain*: at full speed
20 *black-visaged*: the stage was draped in black for tragedies
26 *aught*: 1602 ought: anything   *strains*: tunes
26 *consort*: musical harmony   28 *lackey*: dance attendance upon
29 *unused*: unusual   *peise*: 1602 paize: weight
OSD *unbraced*: with clothes unfastened
1 *trunk*: body

'Tis yet dead night, yet all the earth is clutched
In the dull leaden hand of snoring sleep:
No breath disturbs the quiet of the air,
No spirit moves upon the breast of earth
Save howling dogs, night-crows, and screeching owls,
Save meagre ghosts, Piero, and black thoughts.

                                        [*A clock strikes.*]

One, two. Lord, in two hours what a topless mount
Of unpeered mischief have these hands cast up!   10
   Enter Strotzo.
I can scarce coop triumphing vengeance up,
From bursting forth in braggart passion.
Strotzo. My lord, 'tis firmly said that –
Piero. Andrugio sleeps in peace: this brain hath choked
   The organ of his breast. Feliche hangs
   But as a bait upon the line of death,
   To 'tice on mischief. I am great in blood,
   Unequalled in revenge. You horrid scouts,
   That sentinel swart night, give loud applause
   From your large palms. First know, my heart was raised   20
   Unto Andrugio's life upon this ground.
Strotzo. Duke, 'tis reported –
Piero. We both were rivals in our May of blood,
   Unto Maria, fair Ferrara's heir.
   He won the lady, to my honour's death:
   And from her sweets cropped this Antonio;
   For which I burned in inward sweltering hate,
   And festered rankling malice in my breast,
   Till I might belk revenge upon his eyes.
   And now, O blessed now, 'tis done. Hell, night,   30
   Give loud applause to my hypocrisy!
   When his bright valour even dazzled sense,

---

3 *clutched*: 1602 cloucht
10 *unpeered*: without peer, unequalled   12 *braggart*: boasting
17 *'tice*: entice   18 *scouts*: spies (i.e. stars)   19 *swart*: dark
23 *May*: i.e. prime   26 *sweets*: pleasures
26 *cropped*: produced as a crop   28 *rankling*: festering
29 *belk*: belch, vent

In offering his own head, public reproach
Had blurred my name. Speak, Strotzo, had it not?
If then I had –
Strotzo. It had, so please –
Piero. What had so please? Unseasoned sycophant,
　　Piero Sforza is no numbed lord,
　　Senseless of all true touch. Stroke not the head
40　　Of infant speech, till it be fully born,
　　Go to.
Strotzo. How now? Fut, I'll not smother your speech.
Piero. Nay, right thine eyes; 'twas but a little spleen:
　　[*Aside*] Huge plunge!
　　Sin's grown a slave, and must observe slight evils.
　　Huge villains are enforced to claw all devils.
　　Pish, sweet thy thoughts, and give me –
Strotzo. Stroke not the head of infant speech? Go to!
Piero. Nay, calm this storm. I ever held thy breast
50　　More secret, and more firm in league of blood,
　　Then to be struck in heat with each slight puff.
　　Give me thy ears: huge infamy
　　Press down my honour, if even then, when
　　His fresh act of prowess bloomed out full,
　　I had ta'en vengeance on his hated head.
Strotzo. Why it had –
Piero. Could I avoid to give a seeming grant
　　Unto fruition of Antonio's love?
Strotzo. No.
60　*Piero.* And didst thou ever see a Judas kiss
　　With a more covert touch of fleering hate?
Strotzo. No.
Piero. And having clipped them with pretence of love,

---

37 *Unseasoned*: Not timely (because interrupting)
41 *Go to*: Expression of impatience　42 *Fut*: An expression of surprise
44 *plunge*: lurch; critical situation
45–6 *Sin's . . . devils*: set in italic in 1602 to mark as sententiae for extracting into a commonplace book
45–7 *Sin's . . . me*: 1602 puts in parenthesis　51 *puff*: expression of contempt
57 *grant*: agreement　61 *fleering*: laughing scornfully　63 *clipped*: hugged

Have I not crushed them with a cruel wring?
Strotzo. Yes.
Piero. Say, 'faith, didst thou e'er hear, or read, or see
    Such happy vengeance, unsuspected death?
    That I should drop strong poison in the bowl,
    Which I myself caroused unto his health
    And future fortune of our unity;   70
    That it should work even in the hush of night,
    And strangle him on sudden, that fair show
    Of death, for the excessive joy of his fate
    Might choke the murder? Ha, Strotzo, is't not rare?
    Nay, but weigh it: then Feliche stabbed,
    Whose sinking thought frighted my conscious heart,
    And laid by Mellida, to stop the match,
    And hale on mischief. This all in one night?
    Is't to be equalled thinkst thou? O, I could eat
    Thy fumbling throat, for thy lagged censure. Fut,   70
    Is't not rare?
Strotzo. Yes.
Piero. No? Yes? nothing but no, and yes, dull lump?
    Canst thou not honey me with fluent speech,
    And even adore my topless villainy?
    Will I not blast my own blood for revenge?
    Must not thou straight be perjured for revenge?
    And yet no creature dream 'tis my revenge?
    Will I not turn a glorious bridal morn
    Unto a Stygian night? Yet naught but no, and yes?   90
Strotzo. I would have told you, if the incubus
    That rides your bosom would have patience.
    It is reported, that in private state,
    Maria, Genoa's duchess, makes to Court,
    Longing to see him, whom she ne'er shall see,

---

64 *wring*: twist
76 *sinking*: deep, penetrating   78 *hale*: pull, haul   80 *lagged*: belated
80 *censure*: opinion   84 *honey*: flatter   85 *topless*: unending
86 *blast*: blight or ruin
90 *Stygian*: dark and foreboding as the underworld river Styx
91 *incubus*: nightmare demon

Her lord Andrugio. Belike she hath received
The news of reconciliation –
Reconciliation with a death!
Poor lady shall but find poor comfort in't.

100 *Piero.* O, let me swoon for joy. By heaven, I think
I ha' said my prayers within this month at least,
I am so boundless happy. Doth she come?
By this warm reeking gore, I'll marry her.
Look I not now like an inamorate?
Poison the father, butcher the son, and marry the mother, ha!
Strotzo, to bed: snort in securest sleep,
For see, the dapple-grey coursers of the morn
Beat up the light with their bright silver hooves,
And chase it through the sky. To bed, to bed.

110   This morn my vengeance shall be amply fed.   *Exit.*

ACT 1

Scene 2

Enter Lucio, Maria, and Nutriche.

Maria. Stay gentle Lucio, and vouchsafe thy hand.
Lucio. O, madam!
Maria. Nay, prithee give me leave to say, vouchsafe,
    Submiss entreats beseem my humble fate.
    Here let us sit. O, Lucio, fortune's gilt
    Is rubbed quite off from my slight tin-foiled state,
    And poor Maria must appear ungraced

96 *Belike*: Probably
104 *inamorate*: lover   107 *coursers*: horses (figuratively, clouds)
108 *Beat up*: 'to strike in order to rouse or drive game' (*OED*)
1 *vouchsafe*: 'grant, permit or allow, as an act of grace or condescension' (*OED*)
4 *Submiss*: Submissive   *entreats*: pleas   5 *gilt*: thin layer of gold

Of the bright fulgor of glossed majesty.
Lucio. Cheer up your spirits madam: fairer chance
    Than that which courts your presence instantly,   10
    Cannot be formed by the quick mould of thought.
Maria. Art thou assured the dukes are reconciled?
    Shall my womb's honour wed fair Mellida?
    Will heaven at length grant harbour to my head?
    Shall I once more clip my Andrugio,
    And wreathe my arms about Antonio's neck?
    Or is glib rumour grown a parasite,
    Holding a false glass to my sorrows' eyes,
    Making the wrinkled front of grief seem fair,
    Though 'tis much rivelled with abortive care?   20
Lucio. Most virtuous princess, banish straggling fear;
    Keep league with comfort. For these eyes beheld
    The dukes united: yon faint glimmering light
    Ne'er peeped through the crannies of the east,
    Since I beheld them drink a sound carouse
    In sparkling Bacchus
    Unto each other's health;
    Your son assured to beauteous Mellida,
    And all clouds cleared of threatening discontent.
Maria. What age is morning of?   30
Lucio. I think 'bout five.
Maria. Nutriche, Nutriche!
Nutriche. Beshrew your fingers! Marry, you have disturbed
    the pleasure of the finest dream. O God, I was even coming
    to it, la! O Jesu, 'twas coming of the sweetest. I'll tell you
    now, methought I was married, and methought I spent (O
    Lord, why did you wake me?) and methought I spent three

8 *fulgor*: dazzling brightness   *glossed*: glossy, bright
10 *courts*: invites you to court
14 *harbour*: shelter, lodging   16 *wreathe*: twist   17 *glib*: smooth
17 *parasite*: 'person who obtains the hospitality or patronage of the wealthy
by obsequiousness and flattery' (*OED*)
19 *front*: forehead   20 *rivelled*: wrinkled   *abortive*: useless
21 *straggling*: stray   26 *Bacchus*: god of wine (Greek Dionysus)
30 *age*: time   33 *Beshrew*: Curses on

spur-royals on the fiddlers for striking up a fresh hornpipe.
Saint Ursula, I was even going to bed, and you – methought,
40   my husband was even putting out the tapers – when you –
Lord, I shall never have such a dream come upon me, as long
as –
Maria. Peace, idle creature, peace.
     When will the Court rise?
Lucio. Madam, 'twere best you took some lodging up,
     And lay in private till the soil of grief
     Were cleared your cheek, and new burnished lustre
     Clothed your presence, 'fore you saw the dukes,
     And entered 'mong the proud Venetian states.
50 *Maria.* No Lucio, my dear lord's wise, and knows
     That tinsel glitter, or rich-purfled robes,
     Curled hairs, hung full of sparkling carcanets,
     Are not the true adornments of a wife.
     So long as wives are faithful, modest, chaste,
     Wise lords affect them. Virtue doth not waste,
     With each slight flame of crackling vanity.
     A modest eye forceth affection,
     Whilst outward gayness light looks but entice.
     Fairer than nature's fair is foulest vice.
60   She that loves art, to get her cheek more lovers,
     Much outward gauds, slight inward grace discovers.
     I care not to seem fair but to my lord.
     Those that strive most to please most strangers' sight,
     Follies may judge most fair, wisdom most light.
          Music sounds a short strain.
     But hark, soft music gently moves the air:
     I think the bridegroom's up. Lucio, stand close.
     O now Maria, challenge grief to stay
     Thy joy's encounter. Look Lucio, 'tis clear day.

38 *spur-royals*: gold coin worth 15 shillings
49 *states*: nobles   51 *rich-purfled*: richly trimmed and decorated
52 *carcanets*: jewels worn in the hair   55 *affect*: are affectionate to
56 *crackling*: 'trilling in singing (used in contempt)' (*OED*)
58 *light*: wanton, disrespectful   60 *art*: cosmetics
61 *gauds*: showy displays

ACT 1

Scene 3

[Maria, Lucio and Nutriche remain on stage.]
Enter Antonio, Galeatzo, Matzagente, Balurdo, Pandulpho
Feliche, Alberto, Castilio, and a Page.

Antonio. Darkness is fled: look, infant morn hath drawn
   Bright silver curtains 'bout the couch of night,
   And now Aurora's horse trots azure rings,
   Breathing fair light about the firmament.
   Stand, what's that?
Matzagente. And if a horned devil should burst forth,
   I would pass on him with a mortal stock.
Alberto. Oh, a horned devil would prove ominous
   Unto a bridegroom's eyes.
Matzagente. A horned devil? good, good; ha, ha, ha, very good.   10
Alberto. Good tanned prince, laugh not. By the joys of love,
   When thou dost girn, thy rusty face doth look
   Like the head of a roasted rabbit: fie upon't!
Balurdo. By my troth, methinks his nose is just colour-de-roy.
Matzagente. I tell thee fool, my nose will abide no jest.
Balurdo. No, in truth, I do not jest, I speak truth. Truth is the
   touchstone of all things: and if your nose will not abide the
   truth, your nose will not abide the touch: and if your nose
   will not abide the touch, your nose is a copper nose, and
   must be nailed up for a slip.   20
Matzagente. I scorn to retort the obtuse jest of a fool.
   Balurdo draws out his writing tables, and writes.

osD *Alberto*: 1602 Alberto, Forobosco   3 *Aurora*: goddess of the dawn
4 *firmament*: skies   6 *And if*: Even if
7 *stock*: in fencing, a thrust with a pointed weapon   12 *girn*: smile
12 *rusty*: sunburnt
14 *colour-de-roy*: 'king's colour', somewhere between purple and brown
17 *touchstone*: used to test the quality of gold and silver
19 *copper*: red   20 *slip*: counterfeit coin   21 *retort*: return
21SD *writing tables*: notebooks

Balurdo. Retort and obtuse, good words, very good words.

Galeatzo. Young prince, look sprightly; fie, a bridegroom sad!

Balurdo. In truth, if he were retort and obtuse, no question, he
would be merry, but and please my genius, I will be most
retort and obtuse ere night. I'll tell you, what I'll bear soon
at night in my shield, for my device.

Galeatzo. What, good Balurdo?

Balurdo. O, do me right: Sir Geoffrey Balurdo: sir, sir, as long
30   as ye live, sir.

Galeatzo. What, good Sir Geoffrey Balurdo?

Balurdo. Marry forsooth, I'll carry for my device my
grandfather's great stone-horse, flinging up his head, and
jerking out his left leg. The word: 'Wighy purt'. As I am a
true knight, will't not be most retort and obtuse, ha?

Antonio. Blow hence these hapless jests. I tell you bloods,
My spirit's heavy, and the juice of life
Creeps slowly through my stiffened arteries.
Last sleep, my sense was steeped in horrid dreams:
40   Three parts of night were swallowed in the gulf
Of ravenous time, when to my slumbering powers,
Two meagre ghosts made apparition:
The one's breast seemed fresh paunched with bleeding
      wounds,
Whose bubbling gore sprang in frighted eyes;
The other ghost assumed my father's shape.
Both cried 'Revenge!', at which my trembling joints,
Iced quite over with a frozed cold sweat,
Leaped forth the sheets. Three times I gasped at shades,
And thrice, deluded by erroneous sense
50   I forced my thoughts make stand, when lo, I oped
A large bay window, through which the night
Struck terror to my soul. The verge of heaven
Was ringed with flames, and all the upper vault

27 *device*: heraldic symbol   33 *stone-horse*: stallion   34 *word*: motto
34 *Wighy purt*: obscure: 'the neighing of a horse' (Gair)
43 *paunched*: punched, pierced
48 *shades*: shadows; 'the world of disembodied spirits' (*OED*)
50 *stand*: rest, halt

Thick-laced with flakes of fire; in midst whereof
A blazing comet shot his threatening train
Just on my face. Viewing these prodigies,
I bowed my naked knee, and pierced the star
With an outfacing eye; pronouncing thus:
Deus imperat astris. At which, my nose straight bled.
Then doubled I my word, so slunk to bed.   60

Balurdo. Verily, Sir Geoffrey had a monstrous strange dream
the last night. For methought I dreamt I was asleep, and
methought the ground yawned and belked up the abominable
ghost of a misshapen Simile, with two ugly pages – the one
called Master Even-as going before, and the other Monsieur
Even-so following after – whilst Signior Simile stalked most
prodigiously in the midst. At which I bewrayed the fearfulness
of my nature: and being ready to forsake the fortress of my
wit, start up, call for a clean shirt, eat a mess of broth, and
with that I awaked.   70

Antonio. I prithee peace. I tell you gentlemen,
The frightful shades of night yet shake my brain.
My jellied blood's not thawed; the sulphur damps
That flow in winged lightning 'bout my couch
Yet stick within my sense; my soul is great,
In expectation of dire prodigies.

Pandulpho. Tut, my young prince, let not thy fortunes see
Their lord a coward. He that's nobly born
Abhors to fear. Base fear's the brand of slaves:
He that observes, pursues, slinks back for fright,   80
Was never cast in mould of noble spright.

Galeatzo. Tush, there's a sun will straight exhale these damps
Of chilling fear. Come, shall's salute the bride?

Antonio. Castilio, I prithee mix thy breath with his.
Sing one of Signior Renaldo's airs,
To rouse the slumbering bride from gluttoning
In surfeit of superfluous sleep. Good signior, sing.

---

56 *prodigies*: portents   59 *Deus imperat astris*: 'God rules the stars'
60 *doubled*: repeated   67 *bewrayed*: revealed   69 *mess*: serving
71 *prithee*: I pray thee   75 *great*: expectant   81 *spright*: spirit
82 *Tush*: Expression of contempt or disapproval

[*They sing.*]
What means this silence and unmoved calm!
Boy, wind thy cornet: force the leaden gates
90   Of lazy sleep fly open, with thy breath,
My Mellida not up? not stirring yet? umh!
Maria. That voice should be my son's Antonio's.
Antonio?
Antonio. Here, who calls? Here stands Antonio.
Maria. Sweet son.
Antonio. Dear mother.
Maria. Fair honour of a chaste and loyal bed,
Thy father's beauty, thy sad mother's love:
Were I as powerful as the voice of fate,
100   Felicity complete should sweet thy state:
But all the blessings that a poor banished wretch
Can pour upon thy head, take, gentle son:
Live, gracious youth, to close thy mother's eyes,
Loved of thy parents, till their latest hour.
How cheers my lord, thy father? O sweet boy,
Part of him thus I clip, my dear, dear joy.
Antonio. Madam, last night I kissed his princely hand,
And took a treasured blessing from his lips.
O mother, you arrive in jubilee
110   And firm atonement of all boisterous rage.
Pleasure, united love, protested faith,
Guard my loved father, as sworn pensioners.
The dukes are leagued in firmest bond of love,
And you arrive even in the solsticy
And highest point of sunshine happiness.
        One winds a cornet within.
Hark, madam, how yon cornet jerketh up
His strained shrill accents in the capering air;
As proud to summon up my bright-cheeked love.
Now, mother, ope wide expectation:
120   Let loose your amplest sense, to entertain

89 *wind*: blow   104 *latest*: final   109 *jubilee*: celebration
111 *protested*: declared   112 *pensioners*: paid soldiers
114 *solsticy*: turning or culminating point

Th'impression of an object of such worth,
That life's too poor to –
Galeatzo. Nay, leave hyperboles.
Antonio. I tell thee prince, that presence straight appears,
    Of which thou canst not form hyperboles:
    The trophy of triumphing excellence,
    The heart of beauty. Mellida appears.
    See, look, the curtain stirs: shine nature's pride,
    Love's vital spirit, dear Antonio's bride.
       The curtain's drawn, and the body of Feliche, stabbed
       thick with wounds, appears hung up.
    What villain bloods the window of my love?   130
    What slave hath hung yon gory ensign up.
    In flat defiance of humanity?
    Awake thou fair unspotted purity.
    Death's at thy window, awake bright Mellida:
    Antonio calls.

ACT 1

Scene 4

Enter Piero as at first, with Forobosco.

Piero. Who gives these ill-befitting attributes
    Of chaste, unspotted, bright, to Mellida?
    He lies as loud as thunder: she's unchaste,
    Tainted, impure, black as the soul of hell.
       [Antonio] draws his rapier, offers to run at Piero, but
       Maria holds his arm and stays him.
Antonio. Dog, I will make thee eat thy vomit up,
    Which thou hast belked 'gainst taintless Mellida.
[Piero.] Ram't quickly down, that it may not rise up

---

131 *ensign*: flag OSD *at first*: as at his first entrance in 1.1

To imbraid my thoughts. Behold my stomach's –
Strike me quite through with the relentless edge
10   Of raging fury. Boy, I'll kill thy love.
Pandulph Feliche, I have stabbed thy son:
Look, yet his life-blood reeks upon this steel.
Albert, yon hangs thy friend. Have none of you
Courage of vengeance? Forget I am your duke.
Think Mellida is not Piero's blood.
Imagine on slight ground I'll blast his honour.
Suppose I saw not that incestuous slave
Clipping the strumpet with luxurious twines!
O, numb my sense of anguish, cast my life
20   In a dead sleep, whilst law cuts off yon main,
Yon putrid ulcer of my royal blood.
Forobosco. Keep league with reason, gracious sovereign.
Piero. There glow no sparks of reason in the world;
All are raked up in ashy beastliness.
The bulk of man's as dark as Erebus,
No branch of reason's light hangs in his trunk.
There lives no reason to keep league withal,
I ha' no reason to be reasonable.
Her wedding eve, linked to the noble blood
30   Of my most firmly-reconciled friend,
And found even clinged in sensuality!
O heaven! O heaven! were she as near my heart
As is my liver, I would rend her off.

---

8 *imbraid*: taunt   12 *reeks*: smokes   17 *slave*: villain
18 *strumpet*: 'a debauched or unchaste woman' (*OED*)
18 *luxurious*: lascivious   *twines*: embraces
20 *main*: power   25 *bulk*: majority   *Erebus*: Hell

ACT 1

Scene 5

Enter Strotzo.

Strotzo. Whither, O whither shall I hurl vast grief?
Piero. Here, into my breast: 'tis a place built wide
  By fate, to give receipt to boundless woes.
Strotzo. O no; here throb those hearts, which I must cleave
  With my keen piercing news: Andrugio's dead!
Piero. Dead?
Maria. O me, most miserable!
Piero. Dead, alas, how dead?
  [*Aside*] Fut: weep, act, feign.   *Give seeming passion.*
                               Dead, alas, how dead?
Strotzo. The vast delights of his large sudden joys   10
  Opened his powers so wide, that's native heat
  So prodigally flowed t'exterior parts,
  That th'inner citadel was left unmanned.
  And so surprised on sudden by cold death.
Maria. O fatal, disastrous, cursed, dismal!
  Choke breath and life – I breathe, I live too long.
  Andrugio my lord, I come, I come!
Piero. Be cheerful princess, help, Castilio:
  The lady's swooned, help to bear her in.
  Slow comfort to huge cares is swiftest sin.   20
Balurdo. Courage, courage sweet lady, 'tis Sir Geoffrey Balurdo
  bids you courage. Truly I am as nimble as an elephant about
  a lady.   [*Exeunt all but Antonio, Pandulpho and Alberto.*]
Pandulpho. Dead?
Antonio. Dead.
Alberto. Dead!
Antonio. Why now the womb of mischief is delivered,

4 *cleave*: split   9SD *seeming*: insincere

186   JOHN MARSTON

Of the prodigious issue of the night.
Pandulpho. Ha, ha, ha.
30 *Antonio.* My father dead, my love attaint of lust.
That's a large lie, as vast as spacious hell!
Poor guiltless lady, O, accursed lie.
What, whom, whether, which shall I first lament?
A dead father, a dishonoured wife. Stand:
Methinks I feel the frame of nature shake.
Cracks not the joints of earth to bear my woes?
Alberto. Sweet prince, be patient.
Antonio. 'Slid sir, I will not in despite of thee.
Patience is slave to fools: a chain that's fixed
40 Only to posts and senseless log-like dolts.
Alberto. 'Tis reason's glory to command affects.
Antonio. Lies thy cold father dead, his glossed eyes
New closed up by thy sad mother's hands?
Hast thou a love as spotless as the brow
Of clearest heaven, blurred with false defames?
Are thy moist entrails crumpled up with grief
Of parching mischiefs? Tell me, does thy heart
With punching anguish spur thy galled ribs?
Then come and let's sit and weep and wreathe our arms:
50 I'll hear thy counsel.
Alberto. Take comfort.
Antonio. Confusion to all comfort: I defy it!
Comfort's a parasite, a flattering Jack,
And melts resolved despair. O boundless woe,
If there be any black yet unknown grief,
If there be any horror yet unfelt,
Unthought of mischief in thy fiendlike power,
Dash it upon my miserable head.
Make me more wretch, more cursed if thou canst –
60 O, now my fate is more than I could fear:
My woes more weighty than my soul can bear.   *Exit.*
Pandulpho. Ha, ha, ha.

28 *prodigious*: monstrous, deformed   30 *attaint*: convicted
34 *Stand*: Pause   38 *'Slid*: God's eyelid (oath)   41 *affects*: emotions
45 *blurred*: stained   53 *Jack*: 'a low-bred or ill-mannered fellow' (*OED*)

Alberto. Why laugh you, uncle? That's my coz, your son,
　Whose breast hangs cased in his cluttered gore.
Pandulpho. True man, true: why, wherefore should I weep?
　Come sir, kind nephew: come on: thou and I
　Will talk as chorus to this tragedy.
　Entreat the music strain their instruments.
　With a slight touch whilst we – say on, fair coz.
Alberto. He was the very hope of Italy.　　*Music sounds softly.*　70
　The blooming honour of your drooping age.
Pandulpho. True, coz, true. They say that men of hope are
　　crushed,
　Good are suppressed by base desertless clods,
　That stifle gasping virtue. Look, sweet youth,
　How provident our quick Venetians are,
　Least hooves of jades should trample on my boy.
　Look how they lift him to eminence,
　Heave him, 'bove reach of flesh. Ha, ha, ha.
Alberto. Uncle, this laughter ill becomes your grief.
Pandulpho. Would'st have me cry, run raving up and down　80
　For my son's loss? Would'st have me turn rank mad,
　Or wring my face with mimic action,
　Stamp, curse, weep, rage, and then my bosom strike?
　Away, 'tis apish action, player-like.
　If he is guiltless, why should tears be spent?
　Thrice-blessed soul that dieth innocent.
　If he is lepered with so foul a guilt,
　Why should a sigh be lent, a tear be spilt?
　The grip of chance is weak to wring a tear
　From him that knows what fortitude should bear.　90
　Listen, young blood. 'Tis not true valour's pride,
　To swagger, quarrel, swear, stamp, rave, and chide,

63 *coz*: kinsman　64 *cluttered*: clotted　71 *drooping*: declining
73 *desertless*: undeserving　*clods*: fools, oafs
75 *provident*: prepared, careful
76 *jades*: a jade is an 'inferior or worn-out horse' (*OED*)
77 *eminence*: height　81 *rank*: excessively, completely
82 *mimic*: histrionic　87 *lepered*: infected　89 *chance*: luck
92 *chide*: quarrel

To stab in fume of blood, to keep loud coil,
To bandy factions in domestic broils,
To dare the act of sins, whose filth excels
The blackest customs of blind infidels.
No, my loved youth: he may of valour vaunt,
Whom fortune's loudest thunder cannot daunt,
Whom fretful gales of chance, stern fortune's siege,
100 Makes not his reason slink, the soul's fair liege,
Whose well-peised action ever rests upon
Not giddy humours, but discretion.
This heart in valour even Jove outgoes:
Jove is without, but this 'bove sense of woes:
And such a one eternity. Behold,
Good morrow, son: thou bid'st a fig for cold.
Sound louder music! Let my breath exact
You strike sad tones unto this dismal act.

ACT 2

Scene 1

The Cornets sound a sennet.
Enter two mourners with torches, two with streamers: Castilio
and Forobosco with torches: a Herald bearing Andrugio's helm
and sword, the coffin: Maria supported by Lucio and Alberto,
Antonio by himself: Piero and Strotzo talking: Galeatzo and
Matzagente, Balurdo and Pandulpho: the coffin set down:
helm, sword and streamers hung up, placed by the Herald:
whilst Antonio and Maria wet their handkerchers with their

93 *fume*: heat   *coil*: disturbance   94 *bandy*: toss from side to side
94 *factions*: parties, sides
96 *blind*: 'destitute of intellectual, moral or spiritual light' (*OED*)
97 *vaunt*: boast   98 *daunt*: overcome   100 *slink*: skulk or hide
101 *well-peised*: well-balanced, even   106 *bid'st a fig*: not care about
107 *exact*: require   o.1SD *sennet*: musical notes to signal a theatrical entrance
o.2SD *streamers*: long, pointed flags

tears, kiss them, and lay them on the hearse, kneeling: all go
out but Piero. Cornets cease, and he speaks.

Piero. Rot there, thou cerecloth that enfolds the flesh
　　Of my loathed foe; moulder to crumbling dust;
　　Oblivion choke the passage of thy fame.
　　Trophies of honoured birth drop quickly down:
　　Let naught of him, but what was vicious, live.
　　Though thou art dead, think not my hate is dead:
　　I have but newly twone my arm in the curled locks
　　Of snaky vengeance. Pale beetle-browed hate
　　But newly bustles up. Sweet wrong, I clap thy thoughts.
　　O, let me hug my bosom, rub my breast,   10
　　In hope of what may hap. Andrugio rots;
　　Antonio lives: umh, how long? ha, ha, how long?
　　Antonio packed hence, I'll his mother wed,
　　Then clear my daughter of supposed lust,
　　Wed her to Florence heir. O, excellent!
　　Venice, Genoa, Florence, at my beck,
　　At Piero's nod. Balurdo, O ho!
　　O, 'twill be rare, all unsuspected done.
　　I have been nursed in blood, and still have sucked
　　The steam of reeking gore. Balurdo, ho?   20
　　　　Enter Balurdo with a beard, half off, half on.
Balurdo. When my beard is on, most noble prince, when my
　　beard is on!
Piero. Why, what dost thou with a beard?
Balurdo. In truth, one told me that my wit was bald, and that
　　a mermaid was half fish, and half fish; and therefore to speak
　　wisely, like one of your council, as indeed it hath pleased you
　　to make me of your council, being a fool: if my wit be bald,
　　and a mermaid be half fish and half conger, then I must be
　　forced to conclude, the tiring man hath not glued on my

---

1 *cerecloth*: waxed cloth for wrapping dead bodies　7 *twone*: twined
8 *beetle-browed*: scowling　9 *bustles*: rouses itself　11 *hap*: occur
16 *beck*: command　28 *conger*: eel　29 *tiring man*: theatre-costume hand

30   beard half fast enough, God's bores, it will not stick to fall
       off.
   Piero. Dost thou know what thou hast spoken all this while?
   Balurdo. O, lord duke, I would be sorry of that. Many men can
       utter that which no man but themselves can conceive, but I
       thank a good wit, I have the gift to speak that which neither
       any man else, nor myself understands.
   Piero. Thou are wise. He that speaks he knows not what, shall
       never sin against his own conscience: go to, thou art wise.
   Balurdo. Wise? O no. I have a little natural discretion, or so:
       but or wise, I am somewhat prudent: but for wise, O lord –
40 *Piero.* Hold, take those keys, open the castle vault, and put in
       Mellida.
   Balurdo. And put in Mellida? Well, let me alone.
   Piero. Bid Forobosco and Castilio guard,
       Endear thyself Piero's intimate.
   Balurdo. Endear and intimate: good, I assure you. I will endear
       and intimate Mellida into the dungeon presently.
   Piero. Will Pandulpho Feliche wait on me?
   Balurdo. I will make him come, most retort and obtuse, to you
       presently. I think Sir Geoffrey talks like a councillor.
50   Go to, God's neaks: I think I tickle it.
   Piero. I'll seem to wind yon fool with kindest arm.
       He that's ambitious-minded, and but man,
       Must have his followers beasts, dubbed slavish sots
       Whose service is obedience, and whose wit
       Reacheth no further than to admire their lord,
       And stare in adoration of his worth.
       I love a slave raked out of common mud
       Should seem to sit in council with my heart –
       High honoured blood's too squeamish to assent,
60   And lend a hand to an ignoble act.
       Poison from roses who could e'er abstract?
       How now, Pandulpho, weeping for thy son?

   30 *God's bores*: God's wounds (oath)
   44 *Endear*: Render yourself dear to   50 *neaks*: obscure oath
   50 *tickle it*: '(?) to bring to an agreeable end' (*OED*)   51 *wind*: embrace
   53 *dubbed*: conferred with the rank of knight   61 *abstract*: extract, distil

ACT 2

Scene 2

Enter Pandulpho.

Pandulpho. No, no, Piero, weeping for my sins:
   Had I been a good father, he had been a gracious son.
Piero. Pollution must be purged.
Pandulpho. Why taint'st thou then the air with stench of flesh,
   And human putrefaction's noisome scent?
   I pray his body. Who less boon can crave,
   Than to bestow upon the dead his grave?
Piero. Grave? Why? Think'st thou he deserves a grave,
   That hath defiled the temple of –
Pandulpho. Peace, peace: 10
   Methinks I hear a humming murmur creep
   From out his jellied wounds. Look on those lips,
   Those now lawn pillows, on whose tender softness
   Chaste modest speech, stealing from out his breast,
   Had wont to rest itself, as loath to post
   From out so fair an inn: look, look, they seem to stir,
   And breathe defiance to black obloquy.
Piero. Think'st thou thy son could suffer wrongfully?
Pandulpho. A wise man wrongfully, but never wrong
   Can take: his breast's of such well-tempered proof,   20
   It may be raced, not pierced by savage tooth
   Of foaming malice. Showers of darts may dark
   Heaven's ample brow, but not strike out a spark,
   Much less pierce the sun's cheek. Such songs as these,

---

5 *noisome*: noxious   6 *boon*: request, prayer
11 *humming murmur*: it was widely believed the wounds of the dead would
bleed anew in the murderer's presence
12 *jellied*: coagulated   13 *lawn*: thin linen   15 *post*: make haste
17 *obloquy*: slander   18 *wrongfully*: unjustly (suffers)
20 *well-tempered*: like metal treated for hardness and strength
20 *proof*: tried or proven strength   21 *raced*: scratched

I often dittied till my boy did sleep.
But now I turn plain fool: alas, I weep.
Piero. [*Aside*] 'Fore heaven he makes me shrug: would 'a were
    dead:
He is a virtuous man. What has our court to do
With virtue, in the devil's name! Pandulpho, hark.
30 My lustful daughter dies. Start not, she dies.
I pursue justice, I love sanctity,
And an undefiled temple of pure thoughts.
Shall I speak freely? Good Andrugio's dead,
And I do fear a fetch – but, umh, would I durst speak –
I do mistrust – but, umh – death! [*Aside*] Is he all, all man:
Hath he no part of mother in him, ha?
No lickerish woman's inquisitiveness?
Pandulpho. Andrugio's dead!
Piero. Ay, and I fear his own unnatural blood,
40 To whom he gave life, hath given death for life.
[*Aside*] How could he come on, I see false suspect
Is viced, wrung hardly in a virtuous heart.
Well, I could give you reason for my doubts:
You are of honoured birth, my very friend.
You know how godlike 'tis to root out sin.
Antonio is a villain. Will you join
In oath with me, against the traitor's life,
And swear, you knew he sought his father's death?
I loved him well, yet I love justice more:
50 Our friends we should affect, justice adore.
Pandulpho. My lord, the clapper of my mouth's not glibbed
    With court oil: 'twill not strike on both sides yet.
Piero. 'Tis just that subjects act commands of kings.
Pandulpho. Command then just and honourable things.
Piero. Even so myself then will traduce his guilt.
Pandulpho. Beware, take heed, lest guiltless blood be spilt.
Piero. Where only honest deeds to kings are free,

25 *dittied*: sang 30 *Start*: Flinch 34 *fetch*: trick, plot
37 *lickerish*: greedy; lascivious 41 *suspect*: suspicion
42 *viced*: forced, pressed 50 *affect*: be affectionate to
51 *clapper*: tongue 51 *glibbed*: smoothed 55 *traduce*: defame, blame

It is no empire, but a beggary.
Pandulpho. Where more than noble deeds to kings are free.
    It is no empire, but a tyranny.   60
Piero. Tush, juiceless greybeard, 'tis immunity,
    Proper to princes, that our state exacts:
    Our subjects not alone to bear, but praise our acts.
Pandulpho. O, but that prince that worthful praise aspires,
    From hearts, and not from lips, applause desires.
Piero. Pish, true praise the brow of common men doth ring,
    False only girts the temple of a king.
    He that hath strength and's ignorant of power,
    He was not made to rule, but to be ruled.
Pandulpho. 'Tis praise to do not what we can but should.   70
Piero. Hence, doting Stoic! By my hope of bliss,
    I'll make thee wretched.
Pandulpho. Defiance to thy power, thou rifted chawn!
    Now, by the loved heaven, sooner thou shalt
    Rinse thy foul ribs from the black filth of sin,
    That soots thy heart, then make me wretched. Pish,
    Thou canst not coop me up! Hadst thou a jail
    With treble walls, like antique Babylon,
    Pandulpho can get out. I tell thee, duke,
    I have old Fortunatus' wishing cap,   80
    And can be where I list, even in a trice.
    I'll skip from earth into the arms of heaven:
    And from triumphal arch of blessedness,
    Spit on thy frothy breast. Thou canst not slave
    Or banish me: I will be free at home,
    Maugre the beard of greatness. The portholes
    Of sheathed spirits are ne'er corbed up:

61 *juiceless*: dried-up   67 *girts*: circles
67 *temple*: the side of the forehead   71 *doting*: stupid
71 *Stoic*: after the Greek philosophical school, a person who controls his
emotions to endure pain with patience
73 *rifted*: cleft   *chawn*: abyss
80 *old Fortunatus*: title character in Dekker's 1599 play, who has a magic
hat enabling him to travel where he wishes
81 *list*: want   84 *frothy*: vain, shallow   86 *Maugre*: Despite
87 *sheathed*: encased (in the body)   *corbed*: shut

But still stand open ready to discharge
Their precious shot into the shrouds of heaven.

90 *Piero*. O torture! Slave, I banish thee the town,
Thy native seat of birth –

Pandulpho. How proud thou speak'st! I tell thee, duke: the blasts
Of the swollen-cheeked winds, nor all the breath of kings
Can puff me out my native seat of birth.
The earth's my body's, and the heaven's my soul's
Most native place of birth, which they will keep,
Despite the menace of mortality.
Why duke:
That's not my native place, where I was rocked,
100 A wise man's home is wheresoe'er he is wise.
Now that from man, not from the place, doth rise.

Piero. Would I were deaf – O plague! – hence, dotard wretch:
Tread not in court. All that thou hast, I seize.
[*Aside*] His quiet's firmer than I can disease.

Pandulpho. Go, boast unto thy flattering sycophants:
Pandulpho's slave, Piero hath o'erthrown.
Loose fortune's rags are lost; my own's my own.
    Piero's going out, looks back.
'Tis true Piero, thy vexed heart shall see,
Thou hast but tripped my slave, not conquered me.
    Exeunt at several doors.

ACT 2

Scene 3

Enter Antonio with a book; Lucio, Alberto, Antonio in black.

Alberto. Nay, sweet, be comforted, take counsel and –
Antonio. Alberto, peace: that grief is wanton sick

102 *dotard*: imbecile   104 *quiet*: peace of mind   *disease*: disturb, infect
106 *slave*: body (as opposed to soul)
2 *peace*: shut up   *wanton*: extremely

Whose stomach can digest and brook the diet
Of stale ill-relished counsel. Pigmy cares
Can shelter under patience shield: but giant griefs
Will burst all covert.
Lucio. My lord, 'tis suppertime.
Antonio. Drink deep, Alberto; eat, good Lucio:
But my pined heart shall eat on naught but woe.
Alberto. My lord, we dare not leave you thus alone.   10
Antonio. You cannot leave Antonio alone.
The chamber of my breast is even thronged
With firm attendance that forswears to flinch.
I have a thing sits here: it is not grief,
'Tis not despair, nor the most plague
That the most wretched are infected with;
But the most grief-full, despairing, wretched,
Accursed, miserable – O, for heaven's sake
Forsake me now: you see how light I am,
And yet you force me to defame my patience.   20
Lucio. Fair gentle prince –
Antonio. Away, thy voice is hateful: thou dost buzz
And beat my ears with intimations
That Mellida, that Mellida is light,
And stained with adulterous luxury:
I cannot brook't. I tell thee, Lucio,
Sooner will I give faith, that virtue's cant
In princes' courts will be adorned with wreath
Of choice respect, and endeared intimate;
Sooner will I believe that friendship's rein   30
Will curb ambition from utility,
Than Mellida is light. Alas, poor soul!
Didst e'er see her, good heart, hast heard her speak?
Kind, kind soul, incredulity itself
Would not be so brass-hearted, as suspect so modest cheeks.
Lucio. My lord –
Antonio. Away, a self-one guilt doth only hatch distrust:

3 *brook*: tolerate   6 *covert*: shelter   9 *pined*: suffering
19 *light*: trivial; unchaste   27 *cant*: 1602 scant; niche or corner for a statue
37 *self-one*: '(?) Alone with itself' (*OED*)

But a chaste thought's as far from doubt as lust.
I intreat you leave me.
40 *Alberto.* Will you endeavour to forget your grief?
Antonio. I'faith I will, good friend, i'faith I will.
    I'll come and eat with you. Alberto, see,
    I am taking physic, here's philosophy.
    Good honest leave me, I'll drink wine anon.
Alberto. Since you enforce us, fair prince, we are gone.
        Exeunt Alberto and Lucio.
        Antonio reads.
*Antonio. Ferte fortiter: hoc est quo deum antecedatis. Ille enim
    extra patientiam malorum; vos supra. Contemnite dolorem:
    aut solvertur, aut solvet. Contemnite fortunam: nullum
    telum, quo feriret animum habet.*
50 Pish, thy mother was not lately widowed,
    Thy dear affied love, lately defamed
    With blemish of foul lust, when thou wrot'st thus.
    Thou wrapped in furs, beaking thy limbs 'fore fires,
    Forbid'st the frozen zone to shudder. Ha, ha! 'tis naught,
    But foamy bubbling of a fleamy brain,
    Naught else but smoke. O what dank marish spirit,
    But would be fired with impatience,
    At my – no more, no more: he that was never blest,
    With height of birth, fair expectation
60 Of mounted fortunes, knows not what it is
    To be the pitied object of the world.
    O, poor Antonio, thou mayest sigh –
        [*Mellida, Pandulpho Feliche, Maria and Alberto,
        speaking from offstage.*]
Mellida. Ay me!
Antonio. And curse –

46–9 *Ferte . . . habet*: from Seneca's *De Providentia*: 'Endure bravely. In this
you may surpass God. He is exempt from suffering, while you are superior to
it [. . .] scorn pain; either it will end or you [. . .] scorn fortune: it has no
weapon to strike your soul'
51 *affied*: betrothed
55 *fleamy*: consisting of phlegm, thought to be associated with inaction in
humoral theory
56 *marish*: marshy

Pandulpho. Black powers.
Antonio. And cry –
Maria. O heaven!
Antonio. And close laments with –
Alberto. O me most miserable!
Pandulpho. Woe for my dear, dear son!   70
Maria. Woe for my dear, dear husband!
Mellida. Woe for my dear, dear love!
Antonio. Woe for me all, close all your woes in me,
    In me, Antonio, ha? Where live these sounds?
    I can see nothing: grief's invisible,
    And lurks in secret angles of the heart –
    Come, sigh again, Antonio bears his part.
Mellida. [*Behind a grating.*] O here, here is a vent to pass my
        sighs.
    I have surcharged the dungeon with my plaints.
    Prison, and heart will burst, if void of vent.   80
    Ay, that is Phoebe, empress of the night,
    That 'gins to mount: O chastest deity,
    If I be false to my Antonio,
    If the least soil of lust smears my pure love,
    Make me more wretched, make me more accursed
    Than infamy, torture, death, hell and heaven
    Can bound with amplest power of thought. If not,
    Purge my poor heart from defamation's blot.
Antonio. Purge my poor heart from defamation's blot!
    Poor heart, how like her virtuous self she speaks.   90
    Mellida, dear Mellida, it is Antonio!
    Slink not away, 'tis thy Antonio.
Mellida. How found you out, my lord? Alas, I know
    'Tis easy in this age, to find out woe.
    I have a suit to you.
Antonio. What is't, dear soul?
Mellida. Kill me. I'faith I'll wink, not stir a jot –
    For God's sake kill me. In sooth, loved youth,

---

68 *close*: enclose; confide   79 *surcharged*: overburdened
81 *Phoebe*: goddess of the moon   88 *from*: 1602 with

I am much injured; look, see how I creep.
100   I cannot wreak my wrong, but sigh and weep.
Antonio. May I be cursed, but I credit thee.
Mellida. Tomorrow I must die.
Antonio. Alas, for what?
Mellida. For loving thee. 'Tis true, my sweetest breast,
       I must die falsely: so must thou, dear heart.
       Nets are a-knitting to entrap thy life.
       Thy father's death must make a paradise
       To my – I shame to call him – father. Tell me, sweet,
       Shall I die thine? dost love me still, and still?
110 *Antonio.* I do.
Mellida. Then welcome heaven's will.
Antonio. Madam, I will not swell like a tragedian,
       In forced passion of affected strains.
       If I had present power of aught but pitying you,
       I would be as ready to redress your wrongs,
       As to pursue your love. Throngs of thoughts
       Crowd for their passage, somewhat I will do.
       Reach me thy hand: think this is honour's bent.
       To live unslaved, to die innocent.
120 *Mellida.* Let me entreat a favour, gracious love –
       Be patient, see me die: good, do not weep:
       Go sup, sweet chuck; drink, and securely sleep.
Antonio. I'faith I cannot, but I'll force my face
       To palliate my sickness.
Mellida. Give me thy hand. Peace on thy bosom dwell;
       That's all my woe can breathe: kiss. Thus farewell.
Antonio. Farewell: my heart is great of thoughts,
       Stay dove:
       And therefore I must speak: but what? O love!
130 By this white hand, no more: read in these tears,
       What crushing anguish Antonio bears.
       Antonio kisseth Mellida's hand: then Mellida goes from
       the grate.

100 *wreak*: revenge   101 *credit*: believe
112–17 *Madam . . . do*: 1602 set as prose   122 *chuck*: term of endearment
123 *force my face*: pretend   125 *hand*: 1602 end

Mellida. Good night, good heart.
Antonio. Thus heat from blood, thus souls from bodies part.
    Enter Piero and Strotzo.
Piero. He grieves, laugh Strotzo; laugh, he weeps.
  Hath he tears? O pleasure! hath he tears?
  Now do I scourge Andrugio with steel whips
  Of knotty vengeance. Strotzo, cause me straight
  Some plaining ditty to augment despair.
  Triumph, Piero: hark he groans, o rare!
Antonio. Behold a prostrate wretch laid on his tomb.   140
  His epitaph, thus: *Ne plus ultra.* Ho!
  Let none outwoe me: mine's Herculean woe.
    [Song.] Exit Piero at the end of the song.

ACT 2

Scene 4

Enter Maria.

Antonio. May I be more cursed than heaven can make me.
  If I am not more wretched
  Than man can conceive me. Sore forlorn
  Orphan, what omnipotence can make thee happy?
Maria. How now, sweet son? good youth, what dost thou?
Antonio. Weep, weep.
Maria. Dost naught but weep, weep?
Antonio. Yes mother, I do sigh and wring my hands,
  Beat my poor breast, and wreathe my tender arms.
  Hark ye, I'll tell you wondrous strange, strange news.   10
Maria. What my good boy, stark mad?
Antonio. I am not.
Maria. Alas, is that strange news?
Antonio. Strange news? Why mother, is't not wondrous strange

138 *plaining*: lamenting, mournful   141 *Ne plus ultra*: 'Nothing more'

I am not mad? I run not frantic, ha?
Knowing my father's trunk scarce cold, your love
Is sought by him that doth pursue my life?
Seeing the beauty of creation,
Antonio's bride, pure heart, defamed and stowed
20   Under the hatches of obscuring earth.
        Heu quo labor, quo vota ceciderunt mea!
            Enter Piero.
Piero. Good evening to the fair Antonio.
    Most happy fortune, sweet succeeding time,
    Rich hope: think not thy fate a bankrupt though –
Antonio. Umh, the devil in his good time and tide forsake thee.
Piero. How now? hark ye, prince.
Antonio. God be with you.
Piero. Nay, noble blood, I hope ye not suspect –
Antonio. Suspect, I scorn't. Here's cap and leg; good night:
30   Thou that wants power, with dissemblance fight.
            Exit Antonio.
Piero. Madam, O that you could remember to forget –
Maria. I had a husband and a happy son.
Piero. Most powerful beauty, that enchanting grace –
Maria. Talk not of beauty, nor enchanting grace.
    My husband's dead, my son's distraught, accursed.
    Come, I must vent my griefs, or heart will burst.
            Exit Maria.
Piero. She's gone – and yet she's here: she hath left a print
    Of her sweet graces fixed within my heart,
    As fresh as is her face. I'll marry her.
40   She's most fair, true, most chaste, most false, because
    Most fair; 'tis firm, I'll marry her.

---

16 *trunk*: body
21 *Heu . . . mea*: Seneca's *Octavia*: 'Alas: to what end my labour and my prayers?'
29 *cap and leg*: courtly gestures of doffing hat and bowing

ACT 2

Scene 5

Enter Strotzo.

Strotzo. My lord.
Piero. Ha, Strotzo, my other soul; my life,
　　Dear, hast thou steeled the point of thy resolve?
　　Will't not turn edge in execution?
Strotzo. No.
Piero. Do it with rare passion, and present thy guilt,
　　As if 'twere wrung out with thy conscience grip.
　　Swear that my daughter's innocent of lust,
　　And that Antonio bribed thee to defame
　　Her maiden honour, on inveterate hate　　　　　　　　10
　　Unto my blood, and that thy hand was fee'd
　　By his large bounty, for his father's death.
　　Swear plainly that thou choked Andrugio,
　　By his son's only egging. Rush me in
　　Whilst Mellida prepares herself to die:
　　Halter about thy neck, and with such sighs,
　　Laments and acclamations lifen it,
　　As if impulsive power of remorse –
Strotzo. I'll weep.
Piero. Ay, ay, fall on thy face and cry: 'Why suffer you　　20
　　So lewd a slave as Strotzo is to breathe?'
Strotzo. I'll beg a strangling, grow importunate –
Piero. As if thy life were loathsome to thee: then I
　　Catch straight the cord's end; and, as much incensed
　　With thy damned mischiefs, offer a rude hand,
　　As ready to gird in thy pipe of breath.
　　But on the sudden straight, I'll stand amazed,
　　And fall in exclamations of thy virtues.

---

4 *turn edge*: be blunted   11 *fee'd*: paid   14 *egging*: urging
17 *lifen*: enliven, make lifelike   26 *pipe of breath*: windpipe

    Strotzo. Applaud my agonies and penitence –
30 *Piero.* Thy honest stomach, that could not digest
      The crudities of murder, but, surcharged,
      Vomited'st them up in Christian piety.
    Strotzo. Then clip me in your arms –
    Piero. And call thee brother, mount thee straight to state,
      Make thee of council; tut, tut, what not, what not?
      Think on't, be confident, pursue the plot.
    Strotzo. Look here's a trope: a true rogue's lips are mute.
      I do not use to speak, but execute.
        He lays a finger on his mouth and draws his dagger.
        [Exit.]
    Piero. So, so, run headlong to confusion.
40   Thou slight-brained mischief, thou art made as dirt,
      To plaster up the bracks of my defects.
      I'll wring what may be squeezed from out his use:
      And good night, Strotzo. Swell, plump bold heart.
      For now thy tide of vengeance rolleth in.
      O now *Tragedia cothurnata* mounts,
      Piero's thoughts are fixed on dire exploits.
      Pell mell! Confusion and black murder guides
      The organs of my spirit: shrink not, heart.
      Capienda rebus in malis praeceps via est.

ACT 3

Scene 1

A dumbshow. The cornets sounding for the Act.
Enter Castilio and Forobosco, Alberto and Balurdo, with

---

37 *trope*: 1602 troop   41 *bracks*: flaws, cracks
45 *Tragedia cothurnata*: see *Spanish Tragedy*, 4.1.159 note
47 *Pell mell*: Confusion, disorder
49 *Capienda ... est*: adapted from Seneca's *Agamemnon*: 'Amongst evil we must take the steepest path'

poleaxes; Strotzo talking with Piero, seemeth to send out Strot-
zo. Exit Strotzo. Enter Strotzo, Maria, Nutriche, and Lucio.
Piero passeth through his guard, and talks with her with seem-
ing amorousness: she seemeth to reject this suit, flies to the
tomb, kneels and kisseth it. Piero bribes Nutriche and Lucio;
they go to her, seeming to solicit his suit. She riseth, offers to
go out, Piero stayeth her, tears open his breast, embraceth and
kisseth her, and so they all go out in state.

Enter two pages, the one with two tapers, the other with a
chafing-dish: a perfume in it. Antonio in his nightgown and a
nightcap, unbraced, following after.

Antonio. The black jades of swart night trot foggy rings
    'Bout heaven's brow. [*Clock strikes twelve.*] 'Tis now stark
        dead night.
    Is this Saint Mark's Church?
Page. It is, my lord.
Antonio. Where stands my father's hearse?
2 Page. Those streamers bear his arms: ay, that is it.
Antonio. Set tapers to the tomb, and lamp the church.
    Give me the fire. Now depart and sleep.
        Exeunt Pages.
    I purify the air with odorous fume.
    Graves, vaults and tombs, groan not to bear my weight.   10
    Cold flesh, bleak trunks, wrapped in your half-rot shrouds,
    I press you softly, with a tender foot.
    Most honoured sepulchre, vouchsafe a wretch
    Leave to weep o'er thee. Tomb, I'll not be long
    Ere I creep in thee, and with bloodless lips
    Kiss my cold father's cheek. I prithee, grave,
    Provide soft mould to wrap my carcass in.
    Thou royal spirit of Andrugio, where'er thou hoverest,

0.3SD *poleaxes*: halberds, long-handled weapons with axe-heads
0.12SD *chafing-dish*: vessel holding burning charcoal
1 *jades*: a jade is an 'inferior or worn-out horse' (*OED*)
2SD *Clock strikes twelve*: 1602 (12.)   7 *lamp*: illuminate with lamps
17 *mould*: earth

Airy intellect, I heave up tapers to thee – view thy son –
20 In celebration of due obsequies.
Once every night, I'll dew thy funeral hearse
With my religious tears.
O, blessed father of a cursed son!
Thou diedst most happy, since thou livedst not
To see thy son most wretched, and thy wife
Pursued by him that seeks my guiltless blood.
O, in what orb thy mighty spirit soars,
Stoop and beat down this rising fog of shame
That strives to blur thy blood, and girt defame
30 About my innocent and spotless brows!
Non est mori miserum, sed misere mori.
     [*Enter Andrugio's ghost.*]
Andrugio. Thy pangs of anguish rip my cerecloth up:
And lo, the ghost of old Andrugio
Forsakes his coffin. Antonio, revenge!
I was empoisoned by Piero's hand.
Revenge my blood! Take spirit, gentle boy;
Revenge my blood. Thy Mellida is chaste:
Only to frustrate thy pursuit in love
Is blazed unchaste. Thy mother yields consent
40 To be his wife, and give his blood a son,
That made her husbandless and doth complot
To make her sonless. But before I touch
The banks of rest, my ghost shall visit her.
Thou vigour of my youth, juice of my love:
Seize on revenge, grasp the stern-bended front
Of frowning vengeance, with unpeised clutch.
Alarum Nemesis, rouse up thy blood,
Invent some stratagem of vengeance

19 *intellect*: spirit 20 *obsequies*: funeral rites
27 *orb*: astronomical sphere, heaven
31 *Non ... mori*: source unknown: 'It is not a wretched thing to die, but it is
to die wretchedly' (Gair)
39 *blazed*: proclaimed 41 *complot*: conspire
46 *unpeised*: obscure, unburdened

Which but to think on, may like lightning glide
With horror through thy breast! Remember this: 50
Scelera non ulcisceris, nisi vincis.
  Exit Andrugio's ghost.

ACT 3

Scene 2

*Enter Maria, her hair about her ears; Nutriche, and Lucio,
with pages, and torches.*

Maria. Where left you him? Show me, good boys. Away!
Nutriche. God's me, your hair!
Maria. Nurse, 'tis not yet proud day:
  The neat gay mistress of the light's not up,
  Her cheeks not yet slurred over with the paint
  Of borrowed crimson; the unpranked world
  Wears yet the night-clothes. Let flare my loosed hair:
  I scorn the presence of the night.
  Where's my boy? Run: I'll range about the church.
  Like frantic Bacchanal, or Jason's wife,   10
  Invoking all the spirits of the graves
  To tell me where. Hah? O my poor wretched blood,
  What dost thou up at midnight, my kind boy?
  Dear soul, to bed: O, thou hast struck a fright
  Unto thy mother's panting –

---

51 *Scelera . . . vincis*: Seneca's *Thyestes*: 'You do not avenge crimes unless
you surpass them'
OSD *hair about her ears*: symbol of grief or distraction
4 *mistress*: 1602 mistes 6 *unpranked*: undressed, not ready
8 *presence*: chamber
10 *Bacchanal, or Jason's wife*: Agave, a Bacchanal in Euripides' *Bacchae*;
Medea, Jason's wife: both were mad, bereaved mothers; see also *Tragedy of
Hoffman*, 1.3.21

Antonio. O quisquis nova
  Supplicia functis durus umbrarum arbiter
  Disponis, quisquis exeso iaces
  Pavidus sub antro, quisquis venturi times
20 *Montis ruinam, quisquis avidorum feros,*
  Rictus leonum, & dira furiarum agmina
  Implicitus horres, Antonii vocem excipe
  Properantis ad vos. Ulciscar.
Maria. Alas, my son's distraught! Sweet boy, appease
  Thy mutinying affections.
Antonio. By the astoning terror of swart night,
  By the infectious damps of clammy graves,
  And by the mould that presseth down
  My dead father's skull, I'll be revenged.
30 *Maria.* Wherefore? On whom? For what? Go, go to bed
  Good duteous son. Ho, but thy idle –
Antonio. So I may sleep, tombed in an honoured hearse
  So may my bones rest in that sepulchre.
Maria. Forget not duty, son: to bed, to bed.
Antonio. May I be cursed by my father's ghost,
  And blasted with incensed breath of heaven,
  If my heart beat on aught but vengeance.
  May I be numbed with horror, and my veins
  Pucker with a singeing torture, if my brain
40 Digest a thought but of dire vengeance.
  May I be fettered slave to coward chance,
  If blood, heart, brain, plot aught save vengeance.
Maria. Wilt thou to bed? I wonder when thou sleep'st,
  I'faith, thou look'st sunk-eyed. Go, couch thy head.
  Now 'faith, 'tis idle: sweet, sweet son, to bed.
Antonio. I have a prayer or two to offer up,
  For the good, good prince, my most dear, dear lord,

16–23 *O quisquis ... Ulciscar*: adapted from Seneca's *Thyestes*: 'O cruel
judge, whoever you are, that give new punishments to those already dead:
you who lie in fear beneath the hollow cavern, always frightened the mass
will fall upon you; you who shudder in the gaping jaws of the ravening lions,
and the awful Furies who tangle you in their nets. Listen to the words of
Antonio: "I shall revenge"'
26 *astoning*: paralysing

The Duke Piero, and your virtuous self.
And then when those prayers have obtained success,
In sooth I'll come (believe it now) and couch   50
My head in downy mould: but first I'll see
You safely laid. I'll bring ye all to bed.
Piero, Maria, Strotzo, Lucio,
I'll see you all laid. I'll bring ye all to bed,
And then i'faith, I'll come and couch my head,
And sleep in peace.
Maria. Look then, we'll go before.
    Exeunt all but Antonio.
Antonio. Ay, so you must, before we touch the shore
    Of wished revenge. O, you departed souls,
    That lodge in coffined trunks which my feet press –   60
    If Pythagorian axioms be true,
    Of spirits' transmigration – fleet no more
    To human's bodies. Rather live in swine,
    Inhabit wolves' flesh, scorpions, dogs and toads
    Rather than man. The curse of heaven rains
    In plagues unlimited through all his days;
    His mature age grows only mature vice,
    And ripens only to corrupt and rot
    The budding hopes of infant modesty.
    Still striving to be more than man, he proves   70
    More than a devil: devilish suspect, devilish cruelty,
    All hell-strained juice is poured to his veins,
    Making him drunk with fuming surquedries,
    Contempt of heaven, untamed arrogance,
    Lust, state, pride, murder.
    From above and beneath.
Andrugio. Murder!
Feliche. Murder!
Pandulpho. Murder!

---

51 *downy*: feathery
61 *Pythagorian*: the ancient Greek philosopher, Pythagoras, believed in the
transmigration of the soul across animal and human bodies
62 *transmigration*: theory that soul can pass at death into an animal's body
62 *fleet*: move 72 *hell-strained*: 1602 hell-straid
73 *surquedries*: arrogances, prides

Antonio. Ay, I will murder: graves and ghosts
80   Fright me no more, I'll suck red vengeance
        Out of Piero's wounds, Piero's wounds.   [*Hides himself.*]
            Enter two boys, with Piero in his nightgown and nightcap.
Piero. Maria, love, Maria! She took this aisle.
        Left you her here? On lights, away!
        I think we shall not warm our beds today.
            Enter Julio, Forobosco and Castilio.
Julio. Ho, father? Father?
Piero. How now, Julio, my little pretty son?
        Why suffer you the child to walk so late?
Forobosco. He will not sleep, but calls to follow you,
        Crying that bugbears and spirits haunted him.
            *Antonio offers to come near and stab Piero, presently
            withdraws.*
90 *Antonio.* [*Aside*] No, not so.
        This shall be sought for. I'll force him feed on life
        Till he shall loathe it. This shall be the close
        Of vengeance strain.
Piero. Away there! Pages, lead on fast with light.
        The church is full of damps: 'tis yet dead night.
            Exit all, saving Julio.

ACT 3

Scene 3

[*Antonio emerges.*]

Julio. Brother Antonio, are you here, i'faith?
        Why do you frown? Indeed my sister said
        That I should call you brother, that she did,
        When you were married to her. Buss me, good
        Truth, I love you better than my father, 'deed.
Antonio. Thy father? Gracious, O bounteous heaven!

4 *Buss*: Kiss

I do adore thy justice. *Venit in nostras manus*
Tandem vindicta, venit et tota quidem.
Julio. Truth, since my mother died, I loved you best.
   Something hath angered you; pray you, look merrily.   10
Antonio. I will laugh, and dimple my thin cheek
   With capering joy; chuck, my heart doth leap
   To grasp thy bosom! Time, place, and blood:
   How fit you close together. Heaven's tones
   Strike not such music to immortal souls,
   As your accordance sweets my breast withal.
   Methinks I pace upon the front of Jove,
   And kick corruption with a scornful heel,
   Gripping this flesh, disdain mortality.
   O, that I knew which joint, which side, which limb   20
   Were father all, and had no mother in't:
   That I might rip it vein by vein, and carve revenge
   In bleeding races: but since 'tis mixed together,
   Have at adventure, pell mell. No reverse.
   Come hither, boy. This is Andrugio's hearse.
Julio. O God, you'll hurt me! For my sister's sake,
   Pray you do not hurt me, and you kill me, 'deed,
   I'll tell my father.
Antonio. O, for thy sister's sake, I flag revenge.
    [*Enter Andrugio's ghost.*]
Andrugio. Revenge!   30
Antonio. Stay, stay, dear father, fright mine eyes no more!
                                    [*Exit Andrugio.*]
   Revenge as swift as lightning bursteth forth,
   And clears his heart. Come, pretty tender child,
   It is not thee I hate, not thee I kill.
   Thy father's blood that flows within thy veins,
   Is it I loathe, is that revenge must suck.
   I love thy soul: and were thy heart lapped up
   In any flesh, but in Piero's blood,

7–8 *Venit . . . quidem*: Seneca's *Thyestes*: 'At last revenge has come totally
into my hands' (Marston substituted 'revenge' for Seneca's 'Thyestes')
16 *accordance*: agreement, harmony 23 *races*: cuts
29 *flag*: delay, lose energy for 31 *Stay*: Stop

I would thus kiss it. But, being his: thus, thus,
40 And thus I'll punch it. [*Stabs Julio.*] Abandon fears,
      Whil'st thy wounds bleed, my brows shall gush out tears.
Julio. So you will love me, do even what you will.
Antonio. Now barks the wolf against the full-cheeked moon.
      Now lions' half-clammed entrails roar for food.
      Now croaks the toad, and night-crows screech aloud,
      Fluttering 'bout casements of departing souls.
      Now gapes the graves, and through their yawns let loose
      Imprisoned spirits to revisit earth.
      And now, swart night, so swell thy hour out,
50 Behold I spurt warm blood in thy black eyes.
      From under the stage a groan.
      Howl not, thy pury mould; groan not, ye graves:
      Be dumb all breath. Here stands Andrugio's son,
      Worthy his father. So. I feel no breath:
      His jaws are fallen, his dislodged soul is fled.
      And now there's nothing but Piero left.
      He is all Piero, father all. This blood,
      This breast, this heart, Piero all,
      Whom thus I mangle. Spirit of Julio,
      Forget this was thy trunk. I live thy friend.
60 May'st thou be twined with the softest embrace
      Of clear eternity: but thy father's blood,
      I thus make incense of, to vengeance.
      Ghost of my poisoned sire, suck this fume;
      To sweet revenge perfume thy circling air
      With smoke of blood. I sprinkle round his gore,
      And dew thy hearse with these fresh reeking drops.
      Lo, thus I heave my blood-dyed hands to heaven:
      Even like insatiate hell, still crying: more.
      My heart hath thirsting dropsies after gore.
70 Sound peace and rest to church, night ghosts, and graves;
      Blood cries for blood, and murder murder craves.

---

44 *half-clammed*: half-stuck together   51 *pury*: decomposed
67 *heave*: raise   69 *dropsies*: insatiable thirst

ACT 3

Scene 4

Enter two pages with torches. Maria, her hair loose, and Nutriche.

Nutriche. Fie, fie, tomorrow your wedding day, and weep!
God's my comfort. Andrugio could do well; Piero may do
better. I have had four husbands myself. The first I called
Sweet Duck; the second Dear Heart; the third, Pretty Pug;
but the fourth, most sweet, dear, pretty, all in all – he was the
very cockall of a husband. What lady? your skin is smooth,
your blood warm, your cheek fresh, your eye quick. Change
of pasture makes fat calves: choice of linen, clean bodies,
and – no question – variety of husbands perfect wives. I
would have you should know it, as few teeth as I have in my   10
head, I have read Aristotle's *Problems*, which sayeth, that
woman receiveth perfection by the man. What then be the
men? Go to, to bed; lie on your back; dream not on Piero. I
say no more: tomorrow is your wedding day: do, dream not
of Piero.
    Enter Balurdo with a bass viol.
Maria. What an idle prate thou keep'st! Good nurse, go sleep.
  I have a mighty task of tears to weep.
Balurdo. Lady, with a most retort and obtuse leg I kiss the
curled locks of your loose hair. The duke hath sent you the
most musical Sir Geoffrey, with his not base, but most
ennobled viol, to rock your baby thoughts in the cradle of   20
sleep.
Maria. I give the noble duke respective thanks.
Balurdo. Respective, truly a very pretty word indeed. Indeed,
  Madam, I have the most respective fiddle. Did you ever smell

6 *cockall*: ideal (with bawdy implications)
11 *Aristotle's Problems*: popular medical/science book: *The problems of
Aristotle with other philosophers and phisitions. Wherein are contayned
diuers questions, with their answers, touching the estate of mans bodie*, with
editions in 1595, 1597 and 1607

a more sweet sound? My ditty must go thus; very witty, I
assure you: I myself in an humorous passion made it, to the
tune of 'My mistress Nutriche's beauty'. Indeed, very pretty,
very retort and obtuse, I'll assure you. 'Tis this:

> My mistress' eye doth oil my joints,
30 > And makes my fingers nimble:
> O love, come on, untruss your points,
> My fiddlestick wants rosin.
> My lady's dugs are all so smooth,
> That no flesh must them handle.
> Her eyes do shine, for to say sooth
> Like a new-snuffed candle.

Maria. Truly, very pathetical and unvulgar.

Balurdo. Pathetical and unvulgar, words of worth, excellent
words. In sooth, Madam, I have taken a murr, which makes
40 my nose run most pathetically, and unvulgarly. Have you
any tobacco?

Maria. Good signior, your song.

Balurdo. Instantly, most unvulgarly, at your service
Truly, here's the most pathetical rosin. Umh.
[Song.]

Maria. In sooth, most knightly sung, and like Sir Geoffrey.

Balurdo. Why, look you lady, I was made a knight only for my
voice, and a councillor only for my wit.

Maria. I believe it. Good night, gentle sir, good night.

Balurdo. You will give me leave to take my leave of my mistress,
50 and I will do it most famously in rhyme.

> Farewell, adieu: sayeth thy love true,
> As to part loath,
> Time bids us part, mine own sweet heart,
> God bless us both.   *Exit Balurdo.*

Maria. Good night, Nutriche. Pages, leave the room,
The life of night grows short, 'tis almost dead.
Exeunt pages and Nutriche.

---

31 *untruss:* unfasten *points:* clothes' fastenings
39 *murr:* attack of catarrh
41 *tobacco:* considered a medicine for moist humours

O thou cold widow bed, sometime thrice blest
By the warm pressure of my sleeping lord,
Open thy leaves, and whilst on thee I tread,
Groan out: alas my dear Andrugio's dead.   60
   Maria draweth the curtains, and the ghost of Andrugio is
   displayed, sitting on the bed.
Amazing terror, what portent is this?

ACT 3

Scene 5

Andrugio. Disloyal to our hymeneal rites,
   What raging heat reigns in thy strumpet blood?
   Hast thou so soon forgot Andrugio?
   Are our love-bands so quickly cancelled?
   Where lives thy plighted faith unto this breast?
   O weak Maria! Go to, calm thy tears.
   I pardon thee, poor soul, O shed no tears.
   Thy sex is weak. That black incarnate fiend
   May trip thy faith, that hath o'erthrown my life.
   I was empoisoned by Piero's hand.   10
   Join with my son, to bend up strained revenge,
   Maintain a seeming favour to his suit.
   Till time may form our vengeance absolute.
   Enter Antonio, his arms bloody, [with] a torch and a poniard.
Antonio. See, unamazed, I will behold thy face,
   Outstare the terror of thy grim aspect,
   Daring the horridest object of the night.
   Look how I smoke in blood, reeking the steam
   Of foaming vengeance! O, my soul's enthroned
   In the triumphant chariot of revenge.
   Methinks I am all air, and feel no weight   20
   Of human dirt clog. This is Julio's blood.

57 *sometime*: formerly

Rich music, father: this is Julio's blood.
Why lives that mother?
Andrugio. Pardon ignorance. Fly dear Antonio:
Once more assume disguise, and dog the court
In feigned habit, till Piero's blood
May even o'erflow the brim of full revenge.
　　Exit Antonio.
Peace, and all blessed fortunes to you both.
Fly thou from court, be peerless in revenge:
30 Sleep thou in rest, lo, here I close thy couch.
　　Exit Maria to her bed, Andrugio drawing the curtains.
And now ye sooty coursers of the night,
Hurry your chariot into hell's black womb.
Darkness, make flight; graves, eat your dead again:
Let's repossess our shrouds. Why lags delay?
Mount sparking brightness, give the world his day.
　　Exit Andrugio.

ACT 4

Scene 1

Enter Antonio in a fool's habit, with a little toy of a walnut shell, and soap, to make bubbles; Maria and Alberto.

Maria. Away with this disguise in any hand!
Alberto. Fie, 'tis unsuiting to your elate spirit:
Rather put on some trans-shaped cavalier,
Some habit of a spitting critic, whose mouth
Voids nothing but gentle and unvulgar
Rheum of censure; rather, assume –
Antonio. Why then should I put on the very flesh

---

24 *ignorance*: Maria did not know of Piero's crimes 2 *elate*: lofty
3 *trans-shaped*: transformed (i.e. having lost his position)
4 *critic*: fault-finder or harsh judge 6 *Rheum*: Mucus

Of solid folly. No, this coxcomb is a crown
Which I affect, even with unbounded zeal.
Alberto. 'Twill thwart your plot, disgrace your high resolve.   10
Antonio. By wisdom's heart there is no essence mortal
  That I can envy, but a plump-cheeked fool:
  O, he hath a patent of immunities
  Confirmed by custom, sealed by policy,
  As large as spacious thought.
Alberto. You cannot press among the courtiers
  And have access to –
Antonio. What? not a fool? why friend, a golden ass,
  A babbled fool are sole canonical,
  Whilst pale-cheeked wisdom, and lean-ribb'd art   20
  Are kept in distance at the halberd's point.
  All held apocrypha, not worth survey.
  Why, by the genius of that Florentine,
  Deep, deep-observing, sound-brained Machiavel,
  He is not wise that strives not to seem fool.
  When will the duke hold fee'd intelligence,
  Keep wary observation in large pay,
  To dog a fool's act?
Maria. Ay, but such feigning, known, disgraceth much.
Antonio. Pish, most things that morally adhere to souls,   30
  Wholly exist in drunk opinion:
  Whose reeling censure, if I value not,
  It values naught.
Maria. You are transported with too slight a thought,
  If you but meditate of what is past.
  And what you plot to pass.
Antonio. Even in that, note a fool's beatitude:
  He is not capable of passion,
  Wanting the power of distinction;
  He bears an unturned sail with every wind: 40

8 *coxcomb*: fool's cap   19 *babbled*: talked foolishly or childishly
19 *canonical*: authoritative   22 *apocrypha*: spurious
24 *Machiavel*: Machiavelli's political philosophy for rulers was ruthless
pragmatism
26 *intelligence*: spies   31 *drunk*: unreliable

Blow east, blow west, he stirs his course alike.
I never saw a fool lean: the chub-faced fop
Shines sleek with full-crammed fat of happiness,
Whilst studious contemplation sucks the juice
From wizards' cheeks, who, making curious search
For nature's secrets, the first innating cause
Laughs them to scorn, as man doth busy apes
When they will zany men. Had heaven been kind,
Creating me an honest senseless dolt,
50 A good poor fool, I should want sense to feel
The stings of anguish shoot through every vein.
I should not know what 'twere to lose a father.
I should be dead of sense, to view defame
Blur my bright love. I could not thus run mad,
As one confounded in a maze of mischief,
Staggered, stark felled with bruising stroke of chance.
I should not shoot mine eyes into the earth,
Poring for mischief, that might counterpoise
        Enter Lucio.
Mischief, murder and – how now, Lucio?
60 *Lucio.* My lord, the duke, with the Venetian states,
        Approach the great hall to judge Mellida.
Antonio. Asked he for Julio yet?
Lucio. No motion of him. Dare you trust this habit?
Antonio. Alberto, see you straight rumour me dead.
        Leave me, good mother, leave me Lucio,
        Forsake me all. Now patience hoop my sides
        Exeunt omnes, saving Antonio.
        With steeled ribs, lest I do burst my breast
        With struggling passions. Now disguise, stand bold.
        Poor scorned habits, oft choice souls enfold.

42 *chub-faced*: chubby-faced   45 *wizards*: wise men
46 *innating*: that which endows   48 *zany*: mimic   58 *Poring*: Searching
63 *motion*: mention   *habit*: outfit, disguise   66 *hoop*: circle

ACT 4

Scene 2

The cornets sound a sennet.
Enter Castilio, Forobosco, Balurdo, and Alberto, with poleaxes;
Lucio bare; Piero and Maria talking together; two senators;
Galeatzo and Matzagente, Nutriche.

Piero. Entreat me not: there's not a beauty lives,
   Hath that imperial predominance
   O'er my affects, as your enchanting graces.
   Yet give me leave to be myself.
Antonio. [*Aside*] A villain.
Piero. Just.
Antonio. [*Aside*] Most just.
Piero. Most just and upright in our judgement seat.
   Were Mellida mine eye, with such a blemish
   Of most loathed looseness, I would scratch it out.   10
   Produce the strumpet in her bridal robes,
   That she may blush t'appear so white in show,
   And black in inward substance. Bring her in.
     Exeunt Forobosco and Castilio.
   I hold Antonio, for his father's sake,
   So very dearly, so entirely choice,
   That knew I but a thought of prejudice,
   Imagined 'gainst his high ennobled blood,
   I would maintain a mortal feud, undying hate
   'Gainst the conceiver's life. And shall justice sleep
   In fleshly lethargy, for mine own blood's favour,   20
   When the sweet prince hath so apparent scorn
   By my – I will not call her – daughter. Go,
   Conduct in the loved youth, Antonio.
     Exit Alberto to fetch Antonio.
   He shall behold me spurn my private good.

OSD *bare*: bareheaded   15 *choice*: excellent

Piero loves his honour more than's blood.

Antonio. [*Aside*] The devil he does more than both.

Balurdo. Stand back there, fool; I do hate a fool most, most
pathetically. O these that have no sap of retort and obtuse
wit in them, faugh!

30 *Antonio.* [*Blowing bubbles.*] Puff, hold world! puff, hold
bubble! puff, hold world! puff, break not behind! puff, thou
art full of wind! puff, keep up by wind! puff, 'tis broke; and
now I laugh like a good fool at the breath of mine own lips,
he, he, he, he, he!

Balurdo. You fool!

Antonio. You fool. Puff!

Balurdo. I cannot digest thee, the unvulgar fool. Go fool!

Piero. Forbear, Balurdo, let the fool along.
Come hither. (*Ficto*) Is he your fool?

40 *Maria.* Yes, my loved lord.

Piero. [*Aside*] Would all the states in Venice were like thee.
O then I were secured.
He that's a villain, or but meanly souled,
Must still converse, and cling to routs of fools,
That cannot search the leaks of his defects.
O, your unsalted fresh fool is your only man:
The vinegar tart spirits are too piercing,
Too searching in the unglued joints of shaken wits,
Find they a chink, they'll wriggle in and in,

50 And eat like salt sea in his siddow ribs,
Till they have opened all his rotten parts,
Unto the vaunting surge of base contempt,
And sunk the tossed galleass in depth
Of whirlpool scorn. Give me an honest fop –
Dud-a dud-a? Why lo, sir, this takes he,
As grateful now, as a monopoly.

---

37 *unvulgar*: unusual   39SD *Ficto*: In an artificial or feigned manner
44 *routs*: bands   45 *leaks*: weak points   46 *unsalted*: unseasoned
50 *siddow*: tender   53 *galleass*: heavy warship
55 *Dud-a*: Baby or nonsense talk
56 *monopoly*: topical allusion, since the royal granting of monopolies, or
economic rights over certain commodities, was a subject of controversy

ACT 4

Scene 3

The still flutes sound softly. Enter Forobosco, and Castilio:
Mellida supported by two waiting women.

Mellida. All honour to this royal confluence.
Piero. Forbear, impure, to blot bright honour's name
 With thy defiled lips. The flux of sin
 Flows from thy tainted body. Thou so foul,
 So all dishonoured, can'st no honour give,
 No wish of good, that can have good effect
 To this grave senate, and illustrate bloods.
 Why stays the doom of death?
1 Senator. Who riseth up to manifest her guilt?
2 Senator. You must produce apparent proof, my lord.   10
Piero. Why, where is Strotzo? he that swore he saw
 The very act, and vowed that Feliche fled
 Upon his sight, on which, I brake the breast
 Of the adulterous lecher with five stabs.
 Go fetch in Strotzo. Now thou impudent,
 If thou hast any drop of modest blood
 Shrouded within thy cheeks; blush, blush for shame,
 That rumour yet may say, thou felt'st defame.
Mellida. Produce the devil. Let your Strotzo come:
 I can defeat his strongest argument   20
Piero. With what?
Mellida. With tears, with blushes, sighs, and clasped hands,
 With innocent upreared arms to heaven:
 With my unnooked simplicity. These, these
 Must, will, can only quit my heart of guilt.
 Heaven permits not taintless blood be spilt.
 If no remorse live in your savage breast –

OSD *still*: soft 1 *confluence*: assembly 3 *flux*: discharge
7 *illustrate bloods*: illustrious families 18 *felt'st*: acknowledged
24 *unnooked*: ingenuous?

Piero. Then thou must die.

Mellida. Yet dying, I'll be blest.

30 *Piero.* Accursed by me.

Mellida. Yet blest, in that I strove,
    To live, and die –

Piero. My hate.

Mellida. Antonio's love.

Antonio. [*Aside*] Antonio's love!
        Enter Strotzo, a cord about his neck.

Strotzo. O what vast ocean of repentant tears
    Can cleanse my breast from the polluting filth
    Of ulcerous sin! Supreme efficient,
    Why cleav'st thou not my breast with thunderbolts
40 Of winged revenge?

Piero. What means this passion?

Antonio. [*Aside*] What villainy are they decocting now?
    Umh.

Strotzo. In me convertite ferrum, o proceres.
    Nihil iste, nec ista.

Piero. Lay hold on him. What strange portent is this?

Strotzo. I will not flinch. Death, hell, more grimly stare
    Within my heart, than in your threatening brows.
    Record, thou threefold guard of dreadest power;
    What I here speak is forced from my lips
50 By the pulsive strain of conscience.
    I have a mount of mischief clogs my soul,
    As weighty as the high-knolled Appennine,
    Which I must straight disgorge, or breast will burst.
    I have defamed this lady wrongfully,
    By instigation of Antonio,
    Whose reeling love, tossed on each fancy's surge,
    Began to loathe before it fully enjoyed.

---

38 *Supreme efficient*: Prime mover, God 42 *decocting*: devising
43–4 *In me . . . ista*: from Virgil's *Aeneid*: 'Turn the sword on me, o nobles.
Neither he nor she has done anything'
48 *threefold guard*: Cerberus, three-headed guard dog of the underworld
50 *pulsive*: propulsive 52 *high-knolled*: high-peaked
52 *Appennine*: Italian mountain range 56 *reeling*: changeable

Piero. Go, seize Antonio, guard him strongly in.
   Exit Forobosco.
Strotzo. By his ambition, being only bribed,
   Fee'd by his impious hand, I poisoned   60
   His aged father: that his thirsty hope
   Might quench their dropsy of aspiring drought,
   With full unbounded quaff.
Piero. Seize me Antonio!
Strotzo. O, why permit you now such scum of filth
   As Strotzo is, to live, and taint the air
   With his infectious breath?
Piero. Myself will be thy strangler, unmatched slave.
   *Piero comes from his chair, snatcheth the cord's end, and
   Castilio aideth him; both strangle Strotzo.*
Strotzo. Now change your –
Piero. Ay, pluck, Castilio! I change my humour: pluck, Castilio.   70
    Die, with thy death's entreats even in thy jaws. [*Strotzo
    dies.*]
   Now, now, now, now, now, my plot begins to work.
   Why, thus should statesmen do,
   That cleave through knots of craggy policies,
   Use men like wedges, one strike out another
   Till by degrees the tough and gnarly trunk
   Be rived in sunder. Where's Antonio?
    Enter Alberto, running.
Alberto. O black accursed fate! Antonio's drowned!
Piero. Speak, on thy faith! on thy allegiance speak.
Alberto. As I do love Piero, he is drowned.   80
Antonio. [*Aside*] In an inundation of amazement.
Mellida. Ay, is this the close of all my strains in love?
   O me, most wretched maid!
Piero. Antonio drowned? how? how? Antonio drowned?
Alberto. Distraught and raving, from a turret's top
   He threw his body into the high swollen sea,
   And as he headlong topsyturvy dinged down,

70 *pluck*: pull or jerk sharply   71 *entreats*: pleas
75 *wedges*: pieces of wood or metal hammered into a crack to force it open
77 *rived*: split   81 *inundation*: flood   87 *dinged*: dashed

He still cried Mellida.

Antonio. [*Aside*] My love's bright crown.

90 *Mellida.* He still cried Mellida?

Piero. Daughter, methinks your eyes should sparkle joy,
    Your bosom rise on tiptoe at this news.

Mellida. Ay me!

Piero. How now? Ay me? why, art not great of thanks
    To gracious heaven, for the just revenge
    Upon the author of thy obloquies?

Maria. [*Aside*] Sweet beauty, I could sigh as fast as you,
    But that I know that, which I weep to know:
    His fortunes should be such he dare not show

100 His open presence.

Mellida. I know he loved me dearly, dearly, ay.
    And since I cannot live with him, I die.

Piero. 'Fore heaven, her speech falters: look, she swoons!
    Convey her up into her private bed.

     Maria, Nutriche and the Ladies bear out Mellida, as
     being swooned.

    I hope she'll live. If not –

Antonio. [*Aside*] Antonio's dead, the fool will follow too, he,
    he, he!
    Now works the scene; quick observations scud
    To cote the plot, or else the path is lost;
    My very self am gone, my way is fled;

110 Ay, all is lost, if Mellida is dead.   *Exit Antonio.*

Piero. Alberto, I am kind, Alberto, kind.
    I am sorry for thy coz, i'faith I am.
    Go, take him down, and bear him to his father:
    Let him be buried, look ye, I'll pay the priest.

Alberto. Please you to admit his father to the court?

Piero. No.

Alberto. Please you to restore his lands and goods again?

Piero. No.

Alberto. Please you to vouchsafe him lodging in the city?

120 *Piero.* God's fut, no, thou odd uncivil fellow:

107 *scud*: move quickly   108 *cote*: pass by, outstrip
120 *God's fut*: God's foot (oath)

I think you do forget, sir, where you are.

Alberto. I think you do forget, sir, where you must be.

Forobosco. You are too malapert, i'faith you are.

Your honour might do well to –

Alberto. Peace, parasite, thou burr, that only sticks

Unto the nap of greatness.

Piero. Away with that same yelping cur, away!

Alberto. Ay, I am but gone: but mark, Piero, this.

There is a thing called scourging nemesis.   *Exit Alberto.*

Balurdo. God's neaks he has wrong, that he has: and s'fut, and   130
I were as he, I would bear no coals. La, I, – I begin to swell –
puff!

Piero. How now fool, fop, fool?

Balurdo. Fool, fop, fool? Marry muff! I pray you, how many
fools have you seen in a suit of satin? I hope yet, I do not
look a fool i'faith: a fool? God's bores, I scorn't with my
heel. 'Sneaks, and I were worth but three hundred pound a
year more, I could swear richly: nay, but as poor as I am, I
will swear the fellow hath wrong.

Piero. Young Galeatzo? Ay, a proper man.   140

Florence a goodly city: it shall be so.

I'll marry her to him instantly.

Then Genoa mine, by my Maria's match,

Which I'll solemnize ere next setting sun.

Thus Venice, Florence, Genoa, strongly leagued.

Excellent, excellent! I'll conquer Rome,

Pop out the light of bright religion;

And then, helter skelter, all cocksure!

Balurdo. Go to, 'tis just, the man hath wrong: go to.

Piero. Go to, thou shalt have right. Go to Castilio,   150

Clap him into the palace dungeon:

Lap him in rags, and let him feed on slime

That smears the dungeon's cheek. Away with him!

Balurdo. In very good truth now, I'll ne'er do so more; this one
time and –

Piero. Away with him, observe it strictly, go.

123 *malapert*: impudent   126 *nap*: pile on cloth
134 *Marry muff*: Expression of contempt

Balurdo. Why then, O wight,
   Alas poor knight.
   O, welladay, Sir Geoffrey.
160   Let poets roar
   And all deplore:
   For now I bid you good night.
     Exit Balurdo with Castilio. [Enter Maria.]
Maria. O, piteous end of love: O too, too rude hand
   Of unrespective death! Alas, sweet maid!
Piero. Forbear me, heaven. What intend these plaints?
Maria. The beauty of admired creation,
   The life of modest unmixed purity,
   Our sex's glory, Mellida is –
Piero. What, O heaven, what?
170 *Maria.* Dead.
Piero. May it not sad your thoughts, how?
Maria. Being laid upon her bed, she grasped my hand,
   And kissing it, spake thus: 'Thou very poor,
   Why dost not weep? The jewel of thy brow,
   The rich adornment that enlaced thy breast,
   Is lost: thy son, my love is lost, is dead.
   And do I live to say Antonio's dead?
   And have I lived to see his virtues blurred,
   With guiltless blots? O world, thou art too subtle,
180   For honest natures to converse withal.
   Therefore I'll leave thee. Farewell, mart of woe,
   I fly to clip my love Antonio.'
   With that her head sunk down upon her breast,
   Her cheek changed earth, her senses slept in rest:
   Until my fool, that pressed unto the bed,
   Screeched out so loud that he brought back her soul,
   Called her again, that her bright eyes 'gan ope.
   And stared upon him. He, audacious fool,
   Dared kiss her hand, wished her soft rest, loved bride;
190   She fumbled out, 'thanks good –', and so she died.

164 *unrespective*: unheeding   179 *guiltless*: that he is not guilty of
179 *subtle*: crafty   181 *mart*: centre of trade
187 *ope*: open

Piero. And so she died. I do not use to weep:
   But for thy love (out of whose fertile sweet,
   I hope for as fair fruit), I am deep sad.
   I will not stay my marriage for this.
   Castilio, Forobosco, all
   Strain your wits: wind up invention
   Unto his highest bent, to sweet this night.
   Make us drink Lethe by thy quaint conceits,
   That for two days oblivion smother grief.
   But when my daughter's exequies approach,   200
   Let's all turn sighers. Come, despite of fate,
   Sound loudest music, let's pass out in state.
     The cornets sound. Exeunt.

ACT 4

Scene 4

Enter Antonio solus, in fool's habit.

Antonio. Ay heaven, thou mayst; thou mayest, omnipotence.
   What vermin bred of putrefacted slime,
   Shall dare to expostulate with thy decrees?
   O heaven, thou mayst indeed: she was all thine,
   All heavenly. I did but humbly beg
   To borrow her of thee a little time.
   Thou gavest her me, as some weak-breasted dame
   Giveth her infant, puts it out to nurse;
   And when it once goes high-lone, takes it back.
   She was my vital blood, and yet and yet.   10
   I'll not blaspheme. Look here and behold.

192 *sweet*: embrace   194 *stay*: defer
198 *Lethe*: underworld river whose waters induced forgetfulness of the past
198 *quaint*: ingenious   *conceits*: fanciful tricks, entertainments
200 *exequies*: funeral ceremony   OSD *solus*: alone
9 *high-lone*: without support   11 *blaspheme*: challenge heaven

Antonio puts off his cap, and lieth just upon his back.
I turn my prostrate breast upon thy face.
And vent a heaving sigh. O hear but this.
I am a poor, poor orphan; a weak, weak child,
The wreck of splitted fortune, the very ooze,
The quicksand that devours all misery.
Behold the valiant'st creature that doth breathe!
For all this, I dare live, and I will live,
Only to numb some others' cursed blood
20   With the dead palsy of like misery.
Then death, like to a stifling incubus,
Lie on my bosom. Lo sir, I am sped.
My breast is Golgotha, grave for the dead.

ACT 4

Scene 5

*Enter Pandulpho, Alberto, and a page, carrying Feliche's trunk
in a winding-sheet, and lay it thwart Antonio's breast.*

Pandulpho. Antonio, kiss my foot: I honour thee
    In laying thwart my blood upon thy breast.
    I tell thee, boy: he was Pandulpho's son:
    And I do grace thee with supporting him,
    Young man.
    The domineering monarch of the earth,
    He who hath naught that fortune's grip can seize,
    He who is all impregnably his own,
    He whose great heart heaven cannot force with force
10   Vouchsafes his love. *Non servio Deo, sed assentio.*
Antonio. I ha' lost a good wife.

15 *ooze*: wet mud, slime
23 *Golgotha*: place of Christ's execution   OSD *thwart*: across
10 *Non . . . assentio*: Seneca's *De Providentia*: 'I am not a slave to God, but
assent to him'

Pandulpho. Did'st find her good, or did'st thou make her
    good?
  If found, thou mayst refind, because thou had'st her.
  If made, the work is lost, but thou that mad'st her
  Liv'st yet as cunning. Hast lost a good wife?
  Thrice-blessed man that lost her whilst she was good,
  Fair, young, unblemished, constant, loving, chaste.
  I tell thee, youth: age knows young loves seem graced
  Which with grey cares, rude jars, are oft defaced.
Antonio. But she was full of hope.   20
Pandulpho. May be, may be: but that which may be, stood,
  Stands now without all may; she died good.
  And dost thou grieve?
Alberto. I ha' lost a true friend.
Pandulpho. I live encompassed with two blessed souls.
  Thou lost a good wife, thou lost a true friend, ha?
  Two of the rarest lendings of the heavens,
  But lendings, which at the fixed rate of pay
  Set down by fate, thou must restore again.
  O what unconscionable souls are here?   30
  Are you all like the spokeshaves of the church?
  Have you no maw to restitution?
  Hast lost a true friend, coz? then thou had'st one.
  I tell thee, youth: 'tis all as difficult
  To find true friend in this apostate age
  That baulks all right alliance 'twixt two hearts,
  As 'tis to find a fixed modest heart,
  Under a painted breast. Lost a true friend?
  O happy soul that lost him whilst he was true.
  Believe me coz, I to my tears have found,   40
  Oft dirt's respect makes firmer friends unsound.
Alberto. You have lost a good son.
Pandulpho. Why there's the comfort on't, that he was good:
  Alas, poor innocent –

19 *jars*: discords   31 *spokeshaves*: carpenter's finishing tool
32 *maw*: stomach
35 *apostate*: characterized by moral or religious unfaithfulness
36 *baulks*: hinders   38 *painted*: coloured, feigned

Alberto. Why weeps mine uncle?
Pandulpho. Ha, dost ask me why? ha? hah?
   Good coz, look here.
     He shows him his son's breast.
   Man will break out, despite philosophy.
   Why, all this while I ha' but played a part,
50   Like to some boy, that acts a tragedy,
   Speaks burly words, and raves out passion,
   But, when he thinks upon his infant weakness,
   He droops his eye. I spake more than a god;
   Yet am less than a man.
   I am the miserablest soul that breathes.
     Antonio starts up.
Antonio. 'Slid sir, ye lie: by th'heart of grief, thou liest!
   I scorn't that any wretched should survive,
   Outmounting me in that superlative,
   Most miserable, most unmatched in woe.
60   Who dare assume that, but Antonio?
Pandulpho. Will't still be so? and shall yon bloodhound live?
Antonio. Have I an arm, a heart, a sword, a soul?
Alberto. Were you but private unto what we know –
Pandulpho. I'll know it all; first let's inter the dead.
   Let's dig his grave, with that shall dig the heart,
   Liver, and entrails of the murderer.
     They strike the stage with their daggers, and the grave
     openeth.
Antonio. Will't sing a dirge, boy?
Pandulpho. No, no song; 'twill be vile out of tune.
Alberto. Indeed he's hoarse: the poor boy's voice is cracked.
70 *Pandulpho.* Why coz, should it not be hoarse and cracked,
   When all the strings of nature's symphony
   Are cracked, and jar? Why should his voice keep tune,
   When there's no music in the breast of man?
   I'll say an honest antique rhyme I have.
   Help me, good sorrow-mates, to give him grave.

---

48 *philosophy*: i.e. the stoicism previously expressed

They all help to carry Feliche to his grave.
Death, exile, plaints, and woe,
Are but men's lackeys, not his foe.
No mortal 'scapes from fortune's war,
Without a wound, at least a scar.
Many have led these to the grave: 80
But all shall follow, none shall save.
Blood of my youth, rot and consume;
Virtue, in dirt, doth life assume.
With this old saw, close up this dust;
Thrice-blessed man that dieth just.
Antonio. The gloomy wing of night begins to stretch
    His lazy pinion over all the air.
    We must be stiff and steady in resolve:
    Let's thus our hands, our hearts, our arms involve.
        They wreathe their arms.
Pandulpho. Now, swear we by this Gordian knot of love,   90
    By the fresh turned-up mould that wraps my son,
    By the dead brow of triple Hecate:
    Ere night shall close the lids of yon bright stars,
    We'll sit as heavy on Piero's heart.
    As Etna doth on groaning Pelorus.
Antonio. Thanks, good old man.
    We'll cast at royal chance.
    Let's think a plot; then pellmell vengeance!
        Exeunt, their arms wreathed.

84 *saw*: saying   87 *pinion*: bird's wing   89 *involve*: join together
90 *Gordian knot*: legendary knot sliced through by Alexander the Great –
hence, a difficult problem requiring a decisive solution
92 *Hecate*: goddess of magic   95 *Etna*: volcano in Sicily
95 *Pelorus*: Sicilian promontory

ACT 5

Scene 1

The cornets sound for the Act.
The dumbshow.
Enter as at one door, Castilio and Forobosco, with halberds:
four pages with torches: Lucio bare: Piero, Maria and Alberto
talking: Alberto draws out his dagger, Maria her knife, aim-
ing to menace the duke. Then Galeatzo betwixt two Senators,
reading a paper to them: at which, they all make semblence of
loathing Piero, and knit their fists at him; two ladies and Nutri-
che: all these go softly over the stage, whilst at the other door
enters the ghost of Andrugio, who passeth by them, tossing his
torch about his head in triumph.
All forsake the stage, saving Andrugio, who speaking, begins
the Act.

Andrugio. *Venit dies, tempusque, quo reddat suis*
  Animam squallentum sceleribus.
  The first of strenuous vengeance is clutched,
  And stern Vindicta towereth up aloft,
  That she may fall with a more weighty peise,
  And crush life's sap from out Piero's veins.
  Now 'gins the leprous cores of ulcered sins
  Wheal to a head; now is his fate grown mellow,
  Instant to fall into the rotten jaws
10 Of chap-fallen death. Now down looks providence
  T'attend the last act of my son's revenge.
  Be gracious, observation, to our scene.
  For now the plot unites his scattered limbs
  Close in contracted bands. The Florence prince,
  Drawn by firm notice of the duke's black deeds,

1–2 *Venit . . . sceleribus*: Seneca's *Octavia*: 'The day has come, that time
when he pays back the foul mind for its crimes'
4 *Vindicta*: personification of revenge   8 *Wheal*: Suppurates, gathers
8 *mellow*: ripe   10 *chap-fallen*: with the jaw sagging, as in death

Is made a partner in conspiracy.
The states of Venice are so swollen in hate
Against the duke, for his accursed deeds –
Of which they are confirmed by some odd letters
Found in dead Strotzo's study, which had passed   20
Betwixt Piero and the murdering slave –
That they can scarce retain from bursting forth
In plain revolt. O, now triumphs my ghost;
Exclaiming, heaven's just! For I shall see
The scourge of murder and impiety.   *Exit.*

ACT 5

Scene 2

Balurdo from under the stage.

Balurdo. Ho, who's there above, ho? A murrain on all proverbs.
They say, hunger breaks through stone walls; but I am as
gaunt as lean-ribbed famine, yet I can burst through no stone
walls. O, now, Sir Geoffrey, show thy valour: break prison,
and be hanged. Nor shall the darkest nook of hell contain the
discontented Sir Balurdo's ghost. Well, I am out well, I have
put off the prison to put on the rope. O poor shotten herring,
what a pickle art thou in! O hunger, how thou domineer'st in
my guts! O, for a fat leg of ewe mutton in stewed broth; or
drunken song to feed on – I could belch rarely, for I am all   10
wind. O cold, cold, cold, cold, cold! O poor knight, O poor
Sir Geoffrey; sing like an unicorn, before thou dost dip thy
horn in the water of death; O cold, O sing, O cold, O poor Sir
Geoffrey, sing, sing.
    [*Song.*]

1 *murrain*: plague
7 *shotten herring*: a fish that has spawned, i.e. a person exhausted and
depleted
10 *rarely*: splendidly

ACT 5

Scene 3

Enter Antonio and Alberto, at several doors, their rapiers drawn, in their masquing attire.

Antonio. Vindicta.
Alberto. Mellida.
Antonio. Alberto.
Alberto. Antonio.
Antonio. Hath the duke supped?
Alberto. Yes, and triumphant revels mount aloft.
  The duke drinks deep to overflow his grief.
  The court is racked to pleasure; each man strains
  To feign a jocund eye. The Florentine –
10 *Antonio.* Young Galeatzo?
Alberto. Even he is mighty on our part. The states of Venice –
      Enter Pandulpho, running, in masquing attire.
Pandulpho. Like high-swollen floods, drive down the muddy dams
  Of pent allegiance. O my lusty bloods,
  Heaven sits clapping of our enterprise.
  I have been labouring general favour firm.
  And I do find the citizens grown sick
  With swallowing the bloody crudities
  Of black Piero's acts, they fain would cast
  And vomit him from off their government.
20 Now is the plot of mischief ripped wide ope.
  Letters are found 'twixt Strotzo and the duke,
  So clear apparent, yet more firmly strong
  By suiting circumstance, that as I walked
  Muffled, to eavesdrop speech, I might observe
  The graver statesmen whispering fearfully.
  Here one gives nods and hums, what he would speak:
  The rumour's got 'mong troop of citizens,

8 *racked*: strained, tortured   17 *crudities*: indigestible food

Making loud murmur, with confused din:
One shakes his head, and sighs: 'O ill-used power!'
Another frets and sets his grinding teeth,   30
Foaming with rage, and swears this must not be.
Here one complots, and on a sudden starts,
And cries: 'O monstrous, o deep villainy!'
All knit their nerves, and from beneath swollen brows
Appears a gloating eye of much mislike:
Whilst swart Piero's lips reek steam of wine,
Swallows lust-thoughts, devours all pleasing hopes,
With strong imagination of, what not?
O, now Vindicta; that's the word we have:
A royal vengeance or a royal grave.   40
Antonio. Vindicta!
Balurdo. [*Under the stage.*] I am a-cold.
Pandulpho. Who's there? Sir Geoffrey?
Balurdo. A poor knight, God wot: the nose of thy knighthood
   is bitten off with cold. O poor Sir Geoffrey, cold, cold.
Pandulpho. What chance of fortune hath tripped up his heels,
   And laid him in the kennel? ha?
Alberto. I will discourse it all. Poor honest soul,
   Hadst thou a beaver to clasp up thy face.
   Thou shouldst associate us in masquery,   50
   And see revenge.
Balurdo. Nay, and you talk of revenge, my stomach's up, for I
   am most tyrannically hungry. A beaver? I have a headpiece,
   a skull, a brain of proof, I warrant ye.
Alberto. Slink to my chamber then, and tire thee.
Balurdo. Is there a fire?
Alberto. Yes.
Balurdo. Is there a fat leg of ewe mutton?
Alberto. Yes.
Balurdo. And a clean shirt?   60
Alberto. Yes.

49 *beaver*: helmet face-guard   55 *tire*: dress

Balurdo. Then am I for you, most pathetically and unvulgarly, la!
Exit.

Antonio. Resolved hearts, time curtails night, opportunity
shakes his foretop. Steep your thoughts, sharp your resolve,
embolden your spirit, grasp your swords, alarum mischief,
and with an undaunted brow, out scout the grim opposition
of most menacing peril.

Hark here, proud pomp shoots mounting triumph up
Born in loud accents to the front of Jove.

70 *Pandulpho.* O now, he that wants soul to kill a slave,
Let him die slave, and rot in peasant's grave.

Antonio. Give me thy hand and thine, most noble heart,
Thus will we live, and, but thus, never part.

Exeunt twin'd together.

ACT 5

Scene 4

Cornets sound a sennet.
Enter Castilio and Forobosco, two pages with torches, Lucio
bare, Piero and Maria, Galeatzo, two senators and Nutriche.
Piero to Maria.

Piero. Sit close unto my breast, heart of my love,
Advance thy drooping eyes: Thy son is drowned.
Rich happiness that such a son is drowned.
Thy husband's dead: life of my joys, most blest,
In that the sapless log that pressed thy bed
With an unpleasing weight, being lifted hence.
Even I Piero live to warm his place.
I tell you, lady, had you viewed us both
With an unpartial eye, when first we wooed
10 Your maiden beauties, I had borne the prize,

2 *drooping*: miserable   9 *unpartial*: unbiased

'Tis firm I had: for, fain, I ha' done that.
Maria. [*Aside*] Murder!
Piero. Which he would quake to have adventured;
    Thou know'st I have –
Maria. [*Aside*] Murdered my husband.
Piero. Borne out the shock of war, and done what not
    That valour durst. Dost love me fairest? say.
Maria. As I do hate my son, I love thy soul.
Piero. Why then Io to Hymen, mount a lofty note:
    Fill red-cheeked Bacchus, let Lyaeus float   20
    In burnished goblets. Force the plump-lipped god
    Skip light lavoltas in your full-sapped veins.
    'Tis well brimful. Even I have glut of blood.
    Let quaff carouse; I drink this Bordeaux wine
    Unto the health of dead Andrugio,
    Feliche, Strotzo, and Antonio's ghosts.
[*Aside*] Would I had some poison to infuse it with,
    That having done honour to the dead,
    I might send one to give them notice on't.
    I would endear my favour to the full.   30
    Boy, sing aloud, make heaven's vault to ring
    With thy breath's strength. I drink. Now loudly sing.
        [*Song.*] *The song ended, the cornets sound a sennet.*

ACT 5

Scene 5

*Enter Antonio, Pandulpho, and Alberto, in masquery; Balurdo
and a torchbearer.*

Piero. Call Julio hither; where's the little soul?
    I saw him not today. Here's sport alone

11 *fain*: gladly   19 *Io*: joyful song   19 *Hymen*: goddess of marriage
20 *Lyaeus*: in Greek mythology, Bacchus, hence soothing through wine
22 *lavoltas*: lively dances

For him, i'faith; for babes and fools, I know,
Relish not substance, but applaud the show.
   [Enter Galeatzo, speaks aside] to the conspirators as they
   stand in rank for the measure.
Galeatzo. To Antonio. All blessed fortune crown your brave
   attempt.
To Pandulpho. I have a troop to second your attempt.
To Alberto. The Venice states join hearts unto your hands.
Piero. By the delights in contemplation
   Of coming joys, 'tis magnificent.
10   You grace my marriage eve with sumptuous pomp.
   Sound still, loud music. O your breath gives grace
   To curious feet, that in proud measure pace.
Antonio. [*Aside*] Mother, is Julio's body –
Maria. [*Aside*] Speak it not, doubt not; all is above all hope.
Antonio. [*Aside*] Then will I dance and whirl about the air.
   Methinks I am all soul, all heart, all spirit.
   Now murder shall receive his ample merit.
   The measure. While the measure is dancing, Andrugio's
   ghost is placed betwixt the music houses.
Piero. Bring hither suckets, candied delicates.
   We'll taste some sweetmeats, gallants, ere we sleep.
20 *Antonio.* We'll cook your sweetmeats, gallants, with tart sour
   sauce.
Andrugio. Here will I sit, spectator of revenge,
   And glad my ghost in anguish of my foe.
   The masquers whisper with Piero.
Piero. Marry and shall; i'faith I were too rude,
   If I gainsaid so civil fashion:
   The masquers pray you to forbear the room,
   Till they have banqueted. Let it be so:
   No man presume to visit them, on death.
                      [Exit attendants.]

4SD *measure*: stately dance
17SD *music houses*: part of the Paul's theatre building
18 *suckets*: sweetmeats   23 *Marry*: Expression of surprise or outrage
24 *gainsaid*: denied   25 *forbear*: leave

The masquers whisper again.
Only myself? O, why with all my heart.
I'll fill your consort: here Piero sits:
Come on, unmask, let's fall to.   30
   The conspirators bind Piero, pluck out his tongue, and
   triumph over him.
Antonio. Murder and torture: no prayers, no entreats!
Pandulpho. We'll spoil your oratory. Out with his tongue!
Antonio. I have't Pandulpho: the veins panting bleed,
   Trickling fresh gore about my fist. Bind fast, so, so.
Andrugio. Blest be thy hand. I taste the joys of heaven,
   Viewing my son triumph in his black blood.
Balurdo. Down to the dungeon with him, I'll dungeon with
   him; I'll fool you; Sir Geoffrey will be Sir Geoffrey. I'll tickle
   you.
Antonio. Behold, black dog.   40
Pandulpho. Grin'st thou, thou snarling cur?
Alberto. Eat thy black liver.
Antonio. To thine anguish see
   A fool triumphant in thy misery.
   Vex him, Balurdo.
Pandulpho. He weeps: now do I glorify my hands.
   I had no vengeance, if I had no tears.
Antonio. Fall to, good duke, O these are worthless cates,
   You have no stomach to them; look, look here
   Here lies a dish to feast thy father's gorge.   50
                              [*Shows him Julio's body.*]
   Here's flesh and blood, which I am sure thou lovest.
   Piero seems to condole his son.
Pandulpho. Was he thy flesh, thy son, thy dearest son?
Antonio. So was Andrugio my dearest father.
Pandulpho. So was Feliche my dearest son.
   Enter Maria.
Maria. So was Andrugio my dearest husband.
Antonio. My father found no pity in thy blood.

30 *fall to*: eat   48 *cates*: dainty food   51SD *condole*: lament

Pandulpho. Remorse was banished, when thou slew'st my son.
Maria. When thou empoisoned'st my loving lord,
  Exiled was piety.
60 *Antonio.* Now, therefore, pity, piety, remorse
  Be aliens to our thoughts: grim fiery-eyed rage
  Possess us wholly.
Pandulpho. Thy son? true: and which is my most joy.
  I hope no bastard, but thy very blood
  Thy true-begotten most legitimate
  And loved issue: there's the comfort on't.
Antonio. Scum of the mud of hell!
Alberto. Slime of all filth!
Maria. Thou most detested toad!
70 *Balurdo.* Thou most retort and obtuse rascal!
Antonio. Thus charge we death at thee: remember hell,
  And let the howling murmurs of black spirits,
  The horrid torments of the damned ghosts
  Affright thy soul, as it descendeth down
  Into the entrails of the ugly deep.
Pandulpho. Sa, sa; no, let him die, die, and still be dying.
    They offer to run all at Piero, and on a sudden stop.
  And yet not die, till he hath died and died
  Ten thousand deaths in agony of heart.
Antonio. Now pellmell! This the hand of heaven chokes
80   The throat of murder. This for my father's blood.
    He stabs Piero.
Pandulpho. This for my son.
Alberto. This for them all.
  And this, and this; sink to the heart of hell.
    They run all at Piero with their rapiers.
Pandulpho. Murder for murder, blood for blood doth yell.
Andrugio. 'Tis done, and now my soul shall sleep in rest.
  Sons that revenge their father's blood are blest.
    The curtains being drawn, exit Andrugio.

ACT 5

Scene 6

Enter Galeatzo, two senators, Lucio, Forobosco, Castilio, and Ladies.

1 Senator. Whose hand presents this gory spectacle?
Antonio. Mine.
Pandulpho. No: mine.
Alberto. No: mine.
Antonio. I will not lose the glory of the deed,
　　Were all the tortures of the deepest hell
　　Fixed to my limbs. I pierced the monster's heart
　　With an undaunted hand.
Pandulpho. By yon bright spangled front of heaven, 'twas I:
　　'Twas I sluiced out his lifeblood.   10
Alberto. Tush, to say troth, 'twas all.
2 Senator. Blessed be you all, and may your honours live
　　Religiously held sacred, even for ever and ever.
Galeatzo. *To Antonio.* Thou art another Hercules to us.
　　In ridding huge pollution from our state.
1 Senator. Antonio, belief is fortified,
　　With most invincible approvements of much wrong,
　　By this Piero to thee. We have found
　　Beadrolls of mischief, plots of villainy,
　　Laid 'twixt the duke and Strotzo, which we found   20
　　Too firmly acted.
2 Senator. Alas, poor orphan.
Antonio. Poor? Standing triumphant over Beelzebub?
　　Having large interest for blood, and yet deemed poor?
1 Senator. What satisfaction outward pomp can yield,
　　Of chiefest fortunes of the Venice state,

8 *undaunted*: fearless
14–15 *Hercules . . . pollution*: one of his labours was cleaning the Augean stables   17 *approvements*: actions of proving guilty
19 *Beadrolls*: Catalogues

Claim freely. You are well-seasoned props
And will not warp or lean to either part.
Calamity gives man a steady heart.

30 *Antonio.* We are amazed at your benignity:
But other vows constrain another course.

Pandulpho. We know the world, and did we know no more,
We would not live to know: but since constraint
Of holy bands forceth us keep this lodge
Of dirt's corruption, till dread power calls
Our souls' appearance, we will live enclosed
In holy verge of some religious order,
Most constant votaries.

    The curtains are drawn. Pandulpho departeth.

Antonio. First let's cleanse our hands,
40 Purge hearts of hatred, and entomb my love,
Over whose hearse, I'll weep away my brain
In true affection's tears.
For her sake, here I vow a virgin bed.
She lives in me, with her my love is dead.

2 Senator. We will attend her mournful exequies.
Conduct you to your calm sequestered life,
And then –

Maria. Leave us to meditate on misery;
To sad our thought with contemplation
50 Of past calamities. If any ask
Where lives the widow of the poisoned lord?
Where lies the orphan of a murdered father?
Where lies the father of a butchered son?
Where lives all woe? conduct him to us three;
The downcast ruins of calamity.

Antonio. Sound, doleful tunes; a solemn hymn advance
To close the last act of my vengeance.
And when the subject of your passion's spent,
Sing Mellida is dead: all hearts will relent
60 In sad condolement, at that heavy sound.

---

34 *lodge*: the physical body   37 *verge*: within the boundaries
39 *Antonio*: 1602 *And.*   60 *condolement*: sorrow

Never more woe in lesser plot was found
And O, if ever time create a muse,
That to th'immortal fame of virgin faith
Dares once engage his pen to write her death,
Presenting it in some black tragedy,
May it prove gracious, may his style be decked
With freshest blooms of purest elegance.
May it have gentle presence, and the scenes sucked up
By calm attention of choice audience:
And when the closing epilogue appears,   70
Instead of claps, may it obtain but tears.
   [*Song.*]
   Exeunt omnes, Antonij vindictae finis.

71SD *Antonij vindictae finis*: The end of Antonio's revenge

HENRY CHETTLE

THE TRAGEDY OF
HOFFMAN OR A REVENGE
FOR A FATHER

LIST OF CHARACTERS

Clois HOFFMAN
LORRIQUE
OTHO *prince of Luningberg*
MARTHA *duchess of Luningberg, mother of Otho*
FERDINAND *duke of Prussia*
JEROME *son of Ferdinand*
STILT *servant of Jerome*
DUKE OF SAXONY
RODORICK *a hermit, brother to Saxony*
LODOWICK *son of Saxony*
MATHIAS *son of Saxony*
DUKE OF AUSTRIA
LUCIBELLA *daughter of Austria*
OLD STILT *soldier*
FIBS *soldier*
LORD *Martha's attendant*
Attendants, Herald, Soldiers

Chettle uses Lucibel, Lucibell and Lucibella; 'Lucibell' (2.2.18–5.3.40) has
been standardized to 'Lucibel' (as 5.3.9)

[ACT 1

Scene 1]

Enter Hoffman.

Hoffman. Hence clouds of melancholy!
  I'll be no longer subject to your schisms.
  But thou dear soul, whose nerves and arteries
  In dead resoundings summon up revenge,
  And thou shalt ha't; be but appeased, sweet hearse,
  The dead remembrance of my living father.
    Strikes ope a curtain where appears a body.
  And with a heart as air, swift as thought
  I'll execute justly in such a cause.
  Where truth leadeth, what coward would not fight?
  Ill acts move some, but mine's a cause is right.   10
    Thunder and lightning.
  See the powers of heaven in apparitions
  And fight-full aspects, as incensed
  That I thus tardy am to do an act
  Which justice and a father's death excites.
  Like threatening meteors antedates destruction.   *Thunder.*
  Again! I come, I come, I come,
  Be silent, thou effigies of fair virtue;
  That like a goodly scion wert plucked up
  By murderous winds, infectious blasts and gusts,
  I will not leave thee, until like thyself   20
  I've made thy enemies; then hand in hand
  We'll walk to paradise. [*Thunder.*] Again more blast,
  I'll to yon promont's top, and there survey
  What shipwrecked passengers the Belgic sea
  Casts from her foamy entrails by mischance.

---

2 *schisms*: divisions   4 *resoundings*: ringing, echoing
5 *ha't*: Q hate   *hearse*: dead body   6SD *ope*: open
8 *execute*: Q excuse   15 *antedates*: precedes   18 *scion*: shoot, twig
22 *blast*: Q blest   23 *promont*: cliff, headland

Roar sea and winds, and with celestial fires,
Quicken high projects with your highest desires.
    Enter Lorrique.
Lorrique. Yet this is somewhat like, but brambles, you are too
    busy: were I at Luningberg, and you catch me thus, I should
30 go near to ask you at whose suit – but now I am out of scent
    and fear no sergeants, for I think these woods and waters are
    commonwealths that need no such subjects; nay they keep
    not a constable at sea, but a man's overwhelmed without
    order. Well, dry land I love thee, though thou swarm with
    millions of devourers, yet hast thou no such swallow as the
    sea.
Hoffman. Thou liest: there lives upon the earth more beasts
    With wide-devouring throats than can be found
    Of ravenous fishes in the ocean.
40 The huge leviathan is but a shrimp
    Compared with our balena on the land.
Lorrique. I am of your mind, but the whale has a wide mouth
    To swallow fleeting waters and poor fish.
[Hoffman.] But we have epicures and cormorants
    Whom neither sea, nor land can hardly serve.
    They feed them fat, while arms and honour starve.
    Desert looks pale as death, like those bare bones.
Lorrique. Ha —— amazed!
Hoffman. Seest thou them, trembling slave? Here were arms
50 That served the trothless state of Luningberg.
Lorrique. So do I sir, serve the duke's son of the state.
Hoffman. Ha, ha! I laugh to see how dastard fear
    Hasten the death-doomed wretch to his distress –
    Say, didst thou serve the duke of Luningberg?
Lorrique. His son Otho, sir: I'm a poor follower of his,
    And my master is airing of himself at your cell.
Hoffman. Is he that 'scaped the wreck young Luningberg?

26 *celestial fires*: lightning   31 *sergeants*: officers   35 *swallow*: throat
40 *leviathan*: sea-monster   41 *balena*: whales   43 *fleeting*: drifting
44 *cormorants*: seabirds; also greedy, rapacious persons
48 *amazed*: perhaps a stage direction   50 *trothless*: faithless
56 *cell*: room or dwelling

Lorrique. Ay, sir, the same sir; you are in the right, sir.

Hoffman. Revenge I kiss thee, vengeance y'are at liberty!
  Wouldst thou having lost a father as I have,   60
  Whose very name dissolves my eyes to tears;
  Could duty and thy love so different prove,
  Not to avenge his death whose better part
  Was thine, thou his; when he fell, part of thee
  Fell with him, each drop being part thine own,
  And wouldst not be revenged?

Lorrique. Yes, on the murderer.

Hoffman. On him, or any man that is allied;
  Has but one ounce of blood, of which he's part.
  He was my father: my heart still bleeds,   70
  Nor can my wounds be stopped till an incision
  I've made to bury my dead father in.
  Therefore without protraction, sighing, or excuses:
  Swear to be true, to aid, assist me, not to stir
  Or contradict me in my enterprise
  I shall now undertake, or hereafter.

Lorrique. I swear.

Hoffman. Were I persuaded that thou couldst shed tears,
  As doth the Egyptian serpents near the Nile,
  If thou wouldst kiss and kill, embrace and stab,   80
  Then thou shouldst live: for my invictive brain
  Hath cast a glorious project of revenge.
  Even as thou kneel'st, wilt thou turn villain, speak?

Lorrique. Oh sir, when was I otherwise? From my creation, nothing else; I was made of no other stuff. Villainy is my only patrimony: though I be an irreligious slave, yet I bear a religious name; though I want courage, yet in talk I'll put them all down, though I have nothing in me that is good. Yet I'll ——

Hoffman. Forbear, thy lord is coming: I'll go in   90
  And royally provide for such a prince.
  Say thou hast met the kindest host alive,

---

61 *name*: reputation   74 *stir*: disturb
79 *serpents*: crocodiles   81 *invictive*: invincible; vindictive

One that adores him, with no less zeal
Then rich men gold, or true religious heaven.
Dissemble cunningly, and thou shalt prove
The minion of my thoughts, friend to my love.   *Exit.*

Lorrique. Well sir, ne'er fear me. This is an excellent fellow, a
true villain fitter for me than better company: this is Hans
Hoffman's son that stole down his father's anatomy from the
gallows at Luningberg. Ay, 'tis the same! Upon the dead skull
there's the iron crown that burnt his brains out. What will
come of this I neither know nor care; but here comes my
lord.

    Enter Otho.

How cheers my most noble, most honourable, my most gracious: yea, my most grieved prince?

Otho. A fearful storm.

Lorrique. And full of horror.

Otho. Trust me Lorrique; besides the inly grief
That swallows my content when I perceive
How greedily the fierce, unpitying sea and waves
Devoured our friends, another trouble grieves my vexed
    eyes:
With ghastly apparitions, strange aspects,
Which either I do certainly behold,
Or else my soul, divining some sad fate,
Fills my imaginary powers with shapes
Hideous and horrid.

Lorrique. My lord, let your heart have no commerce with that
mart of idle imaginations, rouse up your nobleness to
apprehend comfort, kindness, ease and what otherwise
entertained in so solitary a place as this, can the ancient
subject of the state of Luningberg collect – 'tis, I take it, the
son to that vice-admiral that turned a terrible pirate!

Otho. Let us turn back into the sea again
Yielding our bodies to the ruthless sound
That hath divided us and our late friends,

---

99 *anatomy*: skeleton   108 *inly*: internal   113 *certainly*: actually

Rather than see choice Hoffman.
Lorrique. Courage, brave Otho, he'll use thee kindly.
   Enter Hoffman.
   Here he comes: sweet host, here is the duke's heir of Luning-
      berg. Do homage, and after entertain him and me his
      follower with the most conspictious pleasures that lies in   130
      thy poor hability.
Hoffman. Before I speak to my most sacred lord,
   I join my soft lips to the solid earth,
   And with an honoured benison I bless
   The hour, the place, the time of your arrive.
   For now my savage life, led amongst beasts,
   Shall be turned civil by your gracious help.
Otho. I see thy true heart's love drop down in tears
   And this embrace shows I am free from fears.
   My disturbed blood runs smoothly through my veins   140
   And I am bold to call thee friend, bold to entreat
   Food – for by wreck I have lost ship, friends and meat.
Hoffman. You that attend my lord, enter the cave:
   Bring forth the homely cakes these hands prepared,
   While I entreat his excellence sit down.
   Villain, bring nothing but a burning crown.
                                          Exit [Lorrique].
Otho. What's that thou bidst him bring, a burning crown?
Hoffman. Still you suspect my harmless innocence.
   What, though your father with the Pomer state
   And your just uncle, duke of Prussia,   150
   After my father had in thirty fights
   Filled all their treasures with foemen's spoils,
   And paid poor soldiers from his treasury;
   What though for this his merits he was named

126 *choice*: excellent
130 *conspictious*: Lorrique's nonsense word – perhaps combining 'conspicu-
ous' and 'auspicious'
131 *hability*: ability   134 *benison*: blessing
149 *Pomer*: Pomeranian region of the south coast of the Baltic sea; Q power
(emendation Jowett)
152 *foemen*: enemies

      A proscript outlaw for a little debt,
      Compelled to fly into the Belgic sound
      And live a pirate?
Otho. Prithee speak no more:
      Thou raisest new doubts in my troubled heart,
160   By repetition of thy father's wrongs.
Hoffman. Then he was wronged, you grant, but not by you:
      You, virtuous gentleman,
      Sat like a just judge of the under-shades,
      And with an unchanged Rhadamantine look,
      Beheld the flesh, mangled with many scars,
      Pared from the bones of my offended father.
      And when he was a bare anatomy,
      You saw him chained unto the common gallows.
Otho. Hoffman –
170 *Hoffman.* Nay hear me patiently, kind lord.
      My innocent youth, as guilty of his sin,
      Was in a dungeon hidden from the sun,
      And there I was condemned to endless night
      Except I passed my vow never to steal
      My father's fleshless bones from that base tree.
      I know not who it was, I guess your mother,
      She kneeled and wept for me, but you did not,
      Beseeching from that vow I might be freed;
      Then did I swear if nation's sovereign power
180   Compelled me to take down those chains,
      Never entomb them, but immediately
      Remove them from that gallows to a tree.
      I kept mine oath: look Luningberg, 'tis done
      Behold a father hanged up by his son!
Otho. O, horrible aspect: murderer stand off!
      I know thou mean'st me wrong.
Hoffman. My lord, behold these precious twins of light

158 *Prithee*: I pray thee   163 *under-shades*: underworld
164 *Rhadamantine*: of Rhadamanth, one of the underworld's judges; cf.
Spanish Tragedy, 1.1.33
174 *Except*: Unless   179 *sovereign*: Q forraigne
187 *twins of light*: eyesockets

Burnt out by day, eclipsed when as the sun
For shame obscured himself this deed was done;
Where none but screech owls sing, thou receptacle,   190
Thou   organ of the soul.
Rest, go rest, and you most lovely couplets,
Legs and arms reside, for ever here.
This is my last farewell. What, do you weep?
Otho. Oh Lorrique, I am betrayed! Slave, touch me not.
Hoffman. Not touch thee? yes, and thus trip down thy pride:
You placed my father in a chair of state.
This earth shall be your throne. Villain, come forth.
    Enter Lorrique [with burning crown].
And as thou mean'st to save thy forfeit life,
Fix on thy master's head my burning crown,   200
While in these cords I in eternal bands
Bind fast his base and coward trembling hands.
Otho. Lorrique, art thou turned villain to my life?
Lorrique. I'll turn anything sir, rather than nothing, I was
taken; life promised to betray you, and I love life so well,
that I would not lose it for a kingdom, for a king's crown, an
empire.
Hoffman. On with the crown.
Otho. O torture above measure!
Hoffman. My father felt this pain, when thou hadst pleasure.   210
Otho. Thy father died for piracy.
Hoffman. Oh peace, had he been judge himself, he would have
        showed
He had been clearer than the crystal morn!
But wretches sentenced never find defence,
How ever guiltless be their innocence.
No more did he, no more shalt thou, no ruth
Pitied his winter age, none helps thy youth.
Otho. O, Lorrique torture! I feel an Etna burn
Within my brains, and all my body else
Is like a hall of ice; all these Belgic seas   220

191 *Thou*: followed by a long space, perhaps indicating the setting-copy was
damaged or illegible
216 *ruth*: pity 218 *Etna*: volcano in Sicily

That now surround us cannot quench this flame.
Death like a tyrant seizeth me unawares;
My sinews shrink like leaves parched with the sun;
My blood dissolves, veins and tendons fail;
Each part's disjointed, and my breath expires!
Mount soul to heaven, my body burns in fire.   [*He dies.*]
Lorrique. He's gone.
Hoffman. Go, let him. Come, Lorrique:
    This but the prologue to the ensuing play,
230   The first step to revenge. This scene is done
    Father, I offer thee thy murderer's son.   *Exeunt.*

[ACT 1

Scene 2]

*Flourish. Enter Ferdinand, Rodorick, Lodowick, Mathias,
Lucibel, Jerome, Stilt, attendants.*

Ferdinand. Princes of Saxony and Austria,
    Though your own words are of sufficient weight
    To justify the honourable love borne by Lodowick to bright
        Lucibel,
    Yet since your parents live and as I hear
    There is between them some dissension,
    Blame us not for detaining you thus long
    Till we had notice how the business stood.
Lodowick. Your royal entertain, great Ferdinand,
    Exceeding expectation in our stay,
10   Bind us to thanks, and if my brother please
    To hold his challenge for a tournament
    In praise of Lucibella's excellence,
    No doubt our father and the Austrian duke
    Will be in person at so royal sport.

8 *entertain*: entertainment

Ferdinand. We trust they will.
Rodorick. I do assure your grace,
   The Austrian and the duke of Saxony –
   By true report of pilgrims at my cell –
   From either of their courts set hitherward
   Some six days hence.   20
Ferdinand. Thanks Rodorick, for this news.
   They are more welcome than the sad discourse
   Of Luningberg our nephew's timeless wreck,
   Which addeth sorrow to the mourning griefs
   Abound in us for our duchess' death.
Jerome. Ay truly, princes: my father has had but hard luck since
   your coming to his court. For aught I know you are bred of
   ill weather, come before you are sent for. Yet, if my most
   gracious father say you are welcome, I his more gracious son
   take you by the hands; though I can tell you my mother's   30
   death comes somewhat near my heart; but I am a prince, and
   princes have power more than common people to subdue
   their passions.
Mathias. We know your worthiness is experienced in all true
   wisdom.
Jerome. True, I am no fool, I have been at Wittenberg, where
   wit grows.
Ferdinand. Peace, thou unshapen honour, my state's shame
   My age's corsive, and my black sins' curse!
   Oh hadst thou never been, I had been then   40
   A happy childless man; now among men
   I am the most unhappy, one that knows
   No end of mine and of my people's woes.
   I tell you, princess, and most gracious maid:
   I do not wear these sable ornaments
   For Isabella's death, though she were dear,
   Nor are my eyelids overflown with tears,
   For Otho at Luningberg, wrecked in the sound,
   Though he were all my hope; but here's my care:

---

23 *timeless*: untimely   36 *Wittenberg*: famous German university
39 *corsive*: corrosive   45 *sable*: black   48 *sound*: Q soun; straits

50   A witless fool must needs be Prussia's heir.

     Jerome. Well, and you were not my father, – 'snails, and I would
not draw rather than put up the fool, would I might never
win this lady at tilt and tournament. As knights, I defy you
both, for her; even you, Lodowick, that loves her, and your
brother that loves you. Look to me: Stilt and I have practised
these two days: 'snails – God forgive me to swear, she shall
not be carried away so.

     Mathias. We are glad to hear your grace so resolute.

     Jerome. As I am a prince, and a duke's heir, though I say it
60   myself, I am as full of resolution as the proudest of you all.

     Lucibella. I thank Prince Lodowick, he has bound my youth
       To be the conqueror's prize, and if my stars
       Allot me to be yours, I will be proud:
       For howsoe'er you seem not fashioned
       Like many cunning courtiers, I protest,
       By some small love I bear thee in mine eye,
       You're worthy beauty, wealth and dignity.

     Jerome. Heart, you would not unhorse Hercules for her, father?
       I'll practise again at Dantzig, you say in the duke's mead? I'll
70   meet thee, Mathias: there's my glove for a gauntlet. Though
my father count me a fool, you shall find me none.

                                Exit.

       Enter Lorrique.

     Lorrique. Health to the right gracious, generous, virtuous, and
valorous Ferdinand, duke of Prussia.

     Ferdinand. Hermit, dost thou not know this young man's face?
       Is't not Lorrique, that met us at thy cell
       With letters from our brother Luningberg?

     Rodorick. It is that gentleman.

     Lorrique. I am no less.

     Ferdinand. Thou said'st thou wast my nephew's playfellow,
80   Appointed to await his virtuous person.
       How is it then thou wert so ill advised

---

51 *'snails*: God's nails (oath)   65 *many*: Q mee, and   69 *mead*: meadow
79 *playfellow*: companion

To take the land-way, and forsake thy lord?
Whom I have never seen, nor never may,
Though in his life my hope and comfort lay.

Lorrique. Be it known, right gracious: Lorrique had never so
little grace, as to leave his loved lord for weather or water,
for torture or fire, for death or for life since I first came to
move in a pilgrim's proportion – much disguised, being so
proper a man – but only for these six words: that I was sent
wholly to give notice of his coming.   90

Ferdinand. But thou hast left him now sunk in the sea.

Lorrique. I left the ship sunk, and his highness saved. For when
all hope had left, master and pilot, sailor and swabber, I
caused my lord to leap into the cock. And for fear she should
be sunk with too much company, I capered out, and cut the
cable. 'Rouse!' quoth the ship against the rocks; 'Roomer!'
cry I in the cock: my lord wept for the company; I laughed to
comfort him. Last, by the power of heaven, goodness of
stars, kindness of winds, mercy of the waves, our cock and
we were cast ashore under Resshopscur, we clambered up.   100
But, having 'scaped drowning, were in danger of killing –

Ferdinand. What there betided you?

Lorrique. Marry, my lord: a young villain, son of a damned
pirate, a maid ravisher.

Ferdinand. Be brief: what was he?

Lorrique. Clois Hoffman.

Ferdinand. Oh my heart! Did the false rebel hurt his sovereign's
son?

Lorrique. No my lord, the prince so houghed and hoffed him,
that he had no other help but to his heels; then I, my good   110
lord, being roe-footed, outstripped him in running, tripped
him by strength, and in fine, finely cut's throat.

---

82 *land-way*: Q land away   88 *proportion*: form, shape
93 *swabber*: sailors of low rank   94 *cock*: 'a small ship's boat' (*OED*)
96 *Roomer*: avoid, steer clear
103 *Marry*: Expression of surprise or outrage
109 *houghed*: disabled by cutting calf tendons; hamstrung
109 *hoffed*: drove or ran off

Ferdinand. Where is the villain's body?

Lorrique. Marry, even heaved over the scar, and sent a-swimming
toward Burtholme, his old habitation; if it be not intercepted
by some seal, shark, sturgeon or suchlike.

Ferdinand. Where is our nephew?

Lorrique. He intends to stay at the same hermitage where I
saluted your excellence, with news of my lord's excellency's
120   intent, to visit you: for that his apparel is somewhat seasick,
and he wants shift.

Ferdinand. A chariot, and rich robes attend Lorrique.
And for his reward be thirteen hundred dollars,
For he hath driven dolour from our heart.
Princes and princess, in your kindest love,
Attend our person to the hermitage,
Where we shall meet the heir of two great states:
Rich Luningberg and warlike Prussia.
Otho living, we'll disinherit our fond son,
130   And bless all Dantzig, by our son elect.
Hermit, you have at home a guest of ours,
Your little cell is a great prince's court:
Had you been there to entertain young Otho,
He would have took your welcome thankfully,
Where now he mourns, for want of company.

Rodorick. I will go on before my gracious lord.

Ferdinand. Nay, I am jealous of my approaching joy,
And fearful any eye but mine should gain
The pleasure of my glad divining soul.
140   Forward come all, in my delight take part;
He that's now glad, adds joy to gladness' heart.   *Exeunt.*

121 *shift*: change of clothing   137 *jealous*: protective

[ACT 1

Scene 3]

Enter Clois Hoffman [and reveals the skeleton].

Hoffman. If there live e'er a surgeon that dare say
  He could do better, I'll play Mercury,
  And like fond Marsyas flay the quacksalver.
  There were a sort of filthy mountebanks,
  Expert in nothing but in idle words,
  Made a day's work with their incision knives
  On my oppressed poor father, silly man;
  Thrusting their dastard fingers in his flesh,
  That durst not while he lived behold his face.
  I have fitted my anatomy   10
  In a fair chain too: father, this youth scorned
  When he was set in an ascending throne,
  To have you stand by him; would he could see
  How the case alters! You shall hang by him,
  And hang afore him too, for all his pride.
                     [Hangs up Otho's skeleton.]
  Come, image of bare death, join side to side
  With my long-injured father's naked bones.
  He was the prologue to a tragedy,
  That, if my destinies deny me not,
  Shall pass those of Thyestes, Tereus,   20

2–3 *Mercury . . . Marsyas*: Marsyas was flayed by Apollo (not Mercury) after beating him in a flute-playing contest; see also *Spanish Tragedy*, 2.1.16 and note
3 *quacksalver*: fraudulent doctor
4 *mountebanks*: charlatans who sold supposed remedies
7 *silly*: deserving of pity   20 *pass*: surpass
20 *Thyestes*: Seneca's play in which Thyestes is served a dish of his own children's flesh
20 *Tereus*: punished for raping Philomela by being served a meal of his own son, in Ovid's *Metamorphoses*

Jocasta, or duke Jason's jealous wife.
So shut our stage up: there is one act done,
Ended in Otho's death; 'twas somewhat single.
I'll fill the other fuller, if Lorrique
That I have late sworn to be murder's slave,
Swears he will protest me to be Otho,
Whom Prussia his uncle unknown loves;
If I be taken for him, well: oh then!
Sweet vengeance make me happiest of all men.
Prussia, I come, as comets against change:
As apparitions before mortal ends.
If thou accept me for thy nephew, so:
Uncle, I'll uncle thee of thy proud life.
Father farewell, I'll to the hermitage,
Where if I be received for Luningberg,
I will have thy dry bones, sanguined all o'er
With thy foe's blood. Rhamnusia, help thy priest:
My wrong thou know'st, my willingness thou seest.

ACT 2

Scene 1

Enter Jerome and Stilt.

Jerome. Come Stilt: bestir your stumps. You know I must be a tilter.

Stilt. Ay, my lord, I know you should be one, but I hope you are not so mad.

21 *Jocasta*: Oedipus's mother killed herself on discovering she had married her own son

21 *Jason's jealous wife*: Medea killed her children in revenge for Jason's abandoning her; see also *Antonio's Revenge*, 3.2.10

36 *sanguined*: bloodied 37 *Rhamnusia*: Nemesis

1 *bestir your stumps*: get moving

2 *tilter*: combatant in a tilt: a fight on horseback with lances with the aim of unseating the opponent

Jerome. What, dost thou count it madness to run a tilt?

Stilt. Ay, my lord, for you that cannot fit a hobby, you'll hardly manage your tilt-horse.

Jerome. Why, they say, Stilt, that stone-mares are gentler, see if thou canst get me one of them.

Stilt. Not afore next grass. I could help you now to a stone-mule, a stone-ass.

Jerome. Well, I'll try one course with thee at the half-pike, and then go: come, draw thy pike.

Stilt. That's not your fit word; you must say, 'advance your pike', and you must be here sir, and here. You'll never learn, for all my teaching.

Jerome. I have answered you, Stilt, that princes have no need to be taught, and I have e'en determined with myself, not to run at tilt, lest I hazard my horse and harness. Therefore I'll to the court, and only see my new cousin that they said was drowned, and then retire to my castle at Helsen, and there write a new poem that I have taken pains in, almost these ten years. It is in praise of picktooths.

Stilt. That will be excellent, my lord: the barbers will buy those poems abominably.

Jerome. Nay, sirrah, I'll get a patent from the duke my father, for the *cum privilegio* for that poem *Ad imprimendum solum*; besides thou shalt have a privilege, that no man shall sell toothpicks without thy seal. My father says I am a fool, but I think I bestow my time to look out for setting a new nap upon his threadbare commonwealth. Who's that knocks? who dares disturb our honourable meditation? hark, Stilt, dost thou see no noise?

Stilt. No, but I hear a noise.

---

6 *hobby*: pony; hobby-horse
8 *stone-mares*: presumably Jerome's ignorance: an impossibility, derived from stone-horse = uncastrated stallion
10 *grass*: spring   12 *half-pike*: small weapon   19 *hazard*: endanger
23 *picktooths*: toothpicks   24 *barbers*: served as dentists
26 *patent*: exclusive right
27–8 *cum privilegio . . . solum*: 'with exclusive right to print'
31 *nap*: pile on fabric

Jerome. A hall then: my father and my new cousin. Stand aside,
that I may set my countenance. My beard-brush and mirror,
Stilt, that set my countenance right to the *Mirror of
Knighthood*, for your *Mirror of Magistrates* is somewhat too
sober. How lik'st me?

40   *Stilt.* Oh excellent! here's your casting-bottle.

Jerome. Sprinkle, good Stilt, sprinkle, for my late practice
had brought me into strange favour. Ha, mother of me, thou
hadst almost blinded the eyes of excellence; but *omnia bene*,
let them approach now, and I appear not like a prince, let my
father cashier me, as some say he will.

Stilt. Cashier you? no, do but manage your body, and have here
and here your congés, and then *quid sequitur*, Stilt knows,
and all the court shall see.

    *Hautboys. Enter Ferdinand leading Clois Hoffman;
Mathias and Lodowick leading Lucibella; Lorrique, with
other lords attending. Coming near the chair of state,
Ferdinand ascends, places Hoffman at his feet, sets a
coronet on his head. A Herald proclaims.*

Herald. Ferdinand, by the divine grace Prince of Heidelberg,
50   Lord of Pomer, and Duke of Prussia, for sundry reasons him
moving, the quiet state of his people especially, which, as a
witless and insufficient prince, disinherits Jerome Heidelberg
his known son, and adopteth Otho of Luningberg his sister's
son as heir, immediately to succeed after his death in all his
provinces. God save Duke Ferdinand and Otho his heir.

    Flourish.

Ferdinand. Amen. Heaven witness how my heart is pleased,
  With the conceit of Prussia's after-peace,
  By this election.

Jerome.   Why? but hear you father –

37–8 *Mirror of Knighthood*: popular chivalric romance translated from
Spanish
38 *Mirror of Magistrates*: popular work of didactic history
40 *casting-bottle*: bottle for sprinkling perfumed waters
43 *omnia bene*: 'all is well'   45 *cashier*: dismiss   47 *congés*: farewells
47 *quid sequitur*: 'what will follow'   48sd *Hautboys*: Oboes

Ferdinand. Away, disturb us not: let's in and feast,
  For all our country in our choice is blessed.   60
      Flourish. Exeunt [all except Jerome and Stilt].
Jerome. Why, but Stilt: what's now to be done, Stilt?
Stilt. Nay that's more than I know: this matter will trouble us
  more than all your poem of picktooths. 'Snails, you were
  better be unknighted than unprinced. I have lost all my hope
  of preferment if this hold.
Jerome. No more, Stilt, I have it here: 'tis in my head, and out
  it shall not come, till red revenge in robes of fire and madding
  mischief run and rave. They say I am a fool, Stilt, but follow
  me. I'll seek out my notes of Machiavel; they say he's an odd
  politician.   70
Stilt. I'faith he's so odd, that he hath driven even honesty from
  all men's hearts.
Jerome. Well, sword come forth, and courage enter in;
  Breast break with grief, yet hold to be revenged;
  Follow me, Stilt: widows unborn shall weep,
  And beardless boys with armour on their backs
  Shall bear us out. Stilt, we will tread on stilts
  Through the purple pavement of the court,
  Which shall be – let me see, what shall it be?
  No court, but even a cave of misery.   80
  There's an excellent speech Stilt, follow me, pursue me: we'll
    acquire
  And either die or compass my desire.
Stilt. Oh brave master, not a lord? O, Stilt will stalk, and make
    the earth a stage,
  But he will have thee lord in spite of rage.
      Exeunt.

64 *unknighted*: i.e. in the tilt
69 *Machiavel*: Machiavelli's political philosophy for rulers was ruthless
pragmatism

[ACT 2

Scene 2]

Enter [Rodorick] and Austria's Duke; some followers.

Rodorick. Sir, since you are content, you here shall find,
  A sparing supper, but a bounteous mind:
  Bad lodging, but a heart as free and generous,
  As that which is fed with generous blood.
Austria. Your hermitage is furnished for a prince.
Rodorick. Last night this roof covered the sacred heads
  Of five most noble, fair and gracious princes:
  Duke Ferdinand himself, and Otho his nephew,
  The sons of Saxon, and the Austrian princess.
10 *Austria.* Oh God! that girl which fled my court and love,
  Making love colour for her heedless flight.
Rodorick. Pardon, great prince: are you the Austrian duke?
Austria. Hermit, I am: Saxon's proud wanton sons
  Were entertained like Priam's firebrand
  At Sparta: all our state gladly appeared
  Like cheerful Lacademons, to receive
  Those demons that with magic of their tongues
  Bewitched my Lucibel, my Helen's ears.
    Knocking and calling within.
Rodorick. Who travelleth so late? Who knocks so hard?
20   Turn to the east end of the chapel, pray;
  We are ready to attend you.
    Enter the Duke of Saxony.
Saxony. Which is the way to Dantzig?
Rodorick. There is no way to Dantzig you can find
  Without a guide thus late: come near, I pray.
Saxony. Look to our horses. By your leave, master hermit,

OSD *[Rodorick]*: Qz Rodorigo   11 *colour*: excuse
14–15 *Priam's firebrand/At Sparta*: Hecuba, wife of Priam of Troy, dreamt she would give birth to a firebrand, predicting the destruction of Troy. Paris, their son, abducted Helen from Sparta, precipitating the Trojan War
16 *Lacademons*: Spartans   17 *tongues*: languages

We are soon bidden, and will prove bold guests.
God save you, sir.
Austria. That should be Saxon's tongue.
Saxony. Indeed, I am the duke of Saxony.
Austria. Then art thou father to lascivious sons,   30
    That have made Austria childless.
Saxony. O subtle duke, thy craft appears in framing thy excuse,
    Thou dost accuse my young sons' innocence.
    I sent them to get knowledge, learn the tongues,
    Not to be metamorphized with the view
    Of flattering beauty, peradventure painted.
Austria. No! I defy thee, John of Saxony:
    My Lucibel for beauty needs no art,
    Nor do I think the virtues of her mind
    Ever inclined to this ignoble course   40
    But by the charms and forcings of thy sons.
Saxony. Oh, would thou dur'st maintain thy words proud duke.
                 [They draw their swords.]
Rodorick. I hope, great princes, neither of you dare
    Commit a deed so sacrilegious. This holy cell
    Is dedicated to the son of peace:
    The foot of war never profaned this floor,
    Nor doth wrath here with his consuming voice
    Affright these buildings; charity with prayer,
    Humility with abstinence combined,
    And here the guardians of a grieved mind.   50
Austria. Father, we obey thy holy voice.
    Duke John of Saxony, receive thy faith;
    Till our ears hear the true course thy sons
    Have taken with my fond and misled child.
    I proclaim truce. Why dost thou sullen stand?
    If thou mean peace, give me thy princely hand.
Saxony. Thus do I plight thee troth, and promise peace.
Austria. Nay, but thy eyes agree not with thy heart.
    In vows of combination, there's a grace
    That shows the intention in the outward face   60

38 *art*: cosmetics

Look cheerfully, or I expect no league.

Saxony. First give me leave to view a while the person
  Of this hermit. Austria, note him well.
  Is he not like my brother Rodorick?

Austria. He's like him, but I heard he lost his life
  Long since in Persia, by the Sophy's wars.

Rodorick. I heard so much, my lords, but that report
  Was purely feigned, spread by my erring tongue,
  As double as my heart, when I was young.

70   I am that Rodorick that aspired your throne;
  That vile false brother who with rebel breath,
  Drawn sword, and treacherous heart, threatened your death.

Saxony. My brother! nay, then i'faith, old John, lay by
  Thy sorrowing thoughts, turn to thy wonted vein,
  And be mad John of Saxony again.
  Mad Rodorick, art alive? My mother's son,
  Her joy and her last birth; oh, she conjured me
  To use thee thus, and yet I banished thee.
  Body of me, I was unkind, I know,

80   But thou deserv'st it then. But let it go.
  Say thou wilt leave this life thus truly idle,
  And live a statesman: thou shalt share in reign,
  Commanding all but me, thy sovereign,

Rodorick. I thank your highness: I will think on it,
  But for my sins this sufferance is more fit.

Saxony. Tut, tittle-tattle: tell not me of sin.
  Now, Austria: once again, thy princely hand.
  I'll look thee in the face, and smile and swear:
  If any of my sons have wronged thy child,

90   I'll help thee in revenging it myself;
  But if, as I believe, they mean but honour,
  As it appeareth by these jousts proclaimed,
  Then thou shalt be content to name him thine,
  And thy fair daughter I'll account as mine.

Austria. Agreed.

64 *my*: Q your   66 *Sophy*: Persian ruler   75 *mad*: merry
92 *jousts*: Q iusts

Saxony. Ah Austria! 'Twas a world when you and I
  Ran these careers, but now we are stiff and dry.
Austria. I am glad you are so pleasant, my good lord.
Saxony. 'Twas my old mood, but I was soon turned sad
  With over-grieving for this long-lost lad.   100
  And now the boy is grown as old as I,
  His very face as full of gravity.
Rodorick. Please your graces enter.
  I know the servants that attend on me
  By the appointment of Duke Ferdinand
  By this have covered.
Saxony. Why then let's in: brother, I trust, and brother,
  Hold you this hand; Rodorick, hold thou the other.
  By heaven my heart with happiness is crowned,
  In that my long-lost brother now is found.   *Exeunt.*   110

[ACT 2

Scene 3]

Enter Clois Hoffman solus.

Hoffman. So run on fate, my destinies are good.
  Revenge hath made me great by shedding blood.
  I am supposed the heir of Luningberg,
  By which I am of Prussia prince-elect.
  Good: who is wronged by this? only a fool:
  And 'tis not fit that idiots should bear rule.
    Enter Lorrique.
Lorrique. My lord, I have as you enjoined, enticed Saxon's
  elder son to talk with you, and here he comes with his most
  excellent, amorous, and admirable lady.
Hoffman. Hast thou the hermit's weeds for my disguise?   10

---

97 *careers*: races, gallops in tournaments 106 *covered*: prepared the table
OSD *solus*: alone

Lorrique. All ready, fit; fit in the next chamber. Your beard is
   point-vice, not a hair amiss.
Hoffman. Faithful Lorrique in thy unfaithfulness:
   I kiss thy cheek, and give thee in that kiss
   The moiety of an earthly bliss. *Exit.*
Lorrique. Good: I am half a monarch, half a fiend.
   Blood I begun in and in blood must end.
   Yet this Clois is an honest villain, has conscience in his killing
20   of men; he kills none but his father's enemies, and their issue.
   'Tis admirable, 'tis excellent, 'tis well, 'tis meritorious: where?
   in heaven? no, hell.
      Enter Lodowick and Lucibella.
Lodowick. Now friend, where is Prince Otho?
Lorrique. Sad, sir, and grieved.
Lucibella. Why? prithee why?
Lorrique. Alas, I know not why.
   The hermit Rodorick talked with him
   Somewhat of you, and somewhat of the duke,
   About surprising you and murdering Lodowick:
   Or such a thing, nay sure 'twas such a thing.
30 *Lucibella.* Surprising me and murdering Lodowick?
Lodowick. By whom? by what complot?
Lorrique. Sure, by the duke; the duke's an odd old lad.
   I know this night there's set a double guard,
   And there's some trick in that: but patience –
   Here comes the hermit, holy reverent man.
      Enter Clois Hoffman like a hermit.
   Somewhat important wings his aged feet
   With speedy nimbleness: heaven grant that all be well.
Hoffman. Princes, in pity of your youth, your love,
   Your virtues, and what not that may move ruth,
40   I offer you the tender of our lives,
   Which yet you may preserve; but if you stay,
   Death and destruction waiteth your delay.
Lodowick. Who had conspired our deaths? speak, reverent
   man.

12 *point-vice*: exact   15 *moiety*: reward   31 *complot*: conspiracy

Hoffman. The duke of Prussia, doting on this face –
    Worthy indeed of wonder, being so fair –
    This night hath plotted, first to murder you.
    The guard are set that you may not escape,
    Within, without, and round about the court;
    Only one way, through Prince Otho his lodging
    Is left: here is the key, and for more proof   50
    Of my great zeal and care, on with these robes.
    Within are Grecian habits for your heads.
    Nay, if you love life do not stand amazed,
    But take the path towards my hermitage.
    Yet I advise you, that you go not in;
    There may be plots too, for aught I know;
    But turn down by the river; there's a way
    Leads to a little chapel. In that porch
    Stay, till I visit you with better news.
Lodowick. I will but call my brother, and then go.   60
Hoffman. That were a going never to return:
    I'll send him after you, be well assured.
Lucibella. Oh God! the duke of Prussia grown thus false,
    Such shows of friendship and so little faith!
Lodowick. Come, Lucibella: let's embrace this mean.
    Duke Ferdinand shall with a sorrowing heart
    Repent this base dishonourable plot.
    Father, our fortunes if they sort aright,
    Shall with continual thankfulness requite
    This virtuous and this charitable care.   70
    Farewell: we'll wait thee in the chapel porch.
    Bring Prince Mathias, our kind brother, thither.
    And thou shalt add good works to charity.
    Once more farewell, Lorrique; that's for thee,
    Commend me to thy lord, tell him this wrong
    Of his false uncle, shall meet full revenge,
    But do to him our duties. Come chaste, fair:
    We must not now by tilt and tournament
    Maintain thy honour, for thy champion knight
    Is forced by treason to unwilling flight.   80
        Exit [Lucibella and Lodowick].

Hoffman. So run to mischief. Oh my dear Lorrique!
   When I have summed up my account of death,
   And robbed those fathers of their lives and joy
   That robbed me of my joy, my father's life,
   Thus thy hand clasped in mine, we'll walk and meditate,
   And boast in the revenges I have wrought.
   That done, I'll seat thee by my throne of state,
   And make thee rival in those governments,
   That by thy secrecy thou lift'st me to.
90   Shalt be a duke at least.
Lorrique. I thank your grace, but pray resolve me
   What you now intend
   To these three Princes Lodowick and Mathias,
   And the thrice beauteous Princess Lucibel?
Hoffman. Death, certain. Call in Mathias: if my plot prove good,
   I'll make one brother shed the other's blood.
Lorrique. I am nimble as your thought, devise, I'll execute what
   you command.
     Exit.
Hoffman. A precious villain, a good villain too.
100   Well if he be no worse – that is, do worse,
   And honey me in my death-stinging thoughts –
   I will prefer him: he shall be preferred
   To hanging, peradventure. Why not? 'tis well
     Enter Lorrique.
   His sufferance here may save his soul from hell.
   He comes. What news my faithful servant? Where's the
   prince?
Lorrique. He's talking with the Lady Lucibel,
   And when I said your highness sent for him,
   He 'gan with courtly salutations,
   To take his leave and to attend your grace.
110 *Hoffman.* Well God-a-mercy friend, thou got'st me grace:
   But more of that at leisure. Take this gown:

---

88 *rival*: partner 89 *secrecy*: plotting 101 *honey*: flatter
102 *prefer*: promote

My cloak, a chair. I must turn melancholy.
> *[Takes off hermit disguise.]*
    Enter Mathias.
Second whate'er I say: approve my words,
That we may move Mathias to mad rage.
Mathias. God save your excellence. What, sad, dull, heavy?
    Or are you now in meditation
    Which part to take tomorrow at the tilt?
    The mead is ringed with tents of stranger knights,
    Whose rich devices and caparisons
    Exceed the Persian monarch's, when he met   120
    Destruction and pale death sent from the sword
    Of Philip's son, and his stout Macedons.
    Cheerly Prince Otho, there's such a warlike sight
    That would stir up a leaden heart to fight.
Hoffman. For what?
Mathias. For honour and fair Lucibel.
Hoffman. Oh Prince Mathias! It is ill-combined
    When honour is with fickle beauty joined.
    Where is your most princely brother?
Mathias. I cannot tell: I left him with his loved Lucibel.   130
Hoffman. But she has got another love,
    Dishonoured all this rich assembly,
    Left the memorial of such infamy,
    As cannot die while men have memory.
Mathias. How? pray you how? what hath the princess done?
Hoffman. She with a Grecian is but new-fled hence,
    Belike some other love of hers before.
    Our tilt and tournament is spoiled and crossed,
    The fair we should defend, her faith hath lost.
Mathias. Fled with a Grecian? saw you them go, Prince Otho?   140
Hoffman. Ay, ay, I saw them go.
Mathias. And would not stay them?

118 *stranger*: foreign   119 *devices*: heraldic insignia
119 *caparisons*: ornamented horse-cloths
122 *Philip's son*: Alexander the Great, referring to the defeat of Darius at
Marathon
137 *Belike*: Probably   138 *crossed*: thwarted

Hoffman. My true servant knows
  How at the sight of such inconstancy,
  My gentle heart was smit with inward grief
  And I sunk down with sorrow.
Mathias. 'Sdeath, what path? which way? that I may track her
  harlot-steps.
  Fled now? gone now? I'll go seek Lodowick.
Hoffman. Nay, then you add an irreligious work,
150 To their lascivious act; follow yourself.
  I and my man will bear you company.
  Lorrique, as I think, thou named'st a chapel?
  A hermit, some such thing; I have lost the form.
Lorrique. I heard her say she could not travel far;
  He told her, they would rest the dead of night
  Near to a chapel, by a hermitage.
Mathias. Where is that chapel? where's that hermitage?
  If you love honour, princely Luningberg,
  Let's to that chapel, if you know the way,
160 That I may kill our shame ere it see day.
Hoffman. I'll guide you to the chapel, aid your arm
  In your revenge against that Grecian.
  But for the lady, spare her: she is fair.
Mathias. I will do what I can; oh hell of life!
  Who but a fool would strive to win a wife?
  Shall we call Lodowick?
Hoffman. Not, 'twould smite his soul in sunder, split his heart,
  If he should hear of such adulterate wrong.
  Cover the fault or punish as you please:
170 Yet I would save her fain, for she deserves pity for beauty.
Mathias. Nothing, no for nothing.
  She is as harlots: fair, like gilded tombs;
  Goodly without, within all rottenness.
  She's like a painted fire upon a hill,
  Set to allure the frost-nipped passengers,
  And starve them after hope. She is indeed

145 *smit*: struck   170 *fain*: gladly

As all such strumpets are, angel in show,
  Devil in heart. Come, come if you love me, go.   *Exit.*
Hoffman. Follow Lorrique; we are in the right way.   *Exit.*
Lorrique. To hell I fear: tush, let all fear go by: 180
  Who'll shun a bad way with good company?   *Exit.*

[ACT 3

Scene 1]

Enter Lodowick and Lucibella.

Lodowick. Are you not faint, divinest Lucibel?
Lucibella. No, the clear moon strews silver in our path,
  And with her moist eyes weeps a gentle dew
  Upon the spotted pavement of the earth,
  Which softens every flower whereon I tread.
  Besides, all travel in your company
  Seems but a walk made in some goodly bower,
  Where love's fair mother strips her paramour.
Lodowick. This is the chapel, and behold a bank
  Covered with sleeping flowers that miss the sun.   10
  Shall we repose us till Mathias come?
Lucibella. The hermit will soon bring him: let's sit down.
  Nature, or art, hath taught these boughs to spread,
  In manner of an arbour o'er the bank.
Lodowick. No, they bow down as veils to shadow you,
  And the fresh flowers beguiled by the light
  Of your celestial eyes, open their leaves,
  And when they entertain the lord of day
  You bring them comfort like the sun in May.
Lucibella. Come, come, you men will flatter beyond mean.   20
  Will you sit down and talk of the late wrongs

177 *strumpets*: a strumpet is 'a debauched or unchaste woman' (*OED*)
180 *tush*: expression of contempt or disapproval
8 *love's . . . mother*: i.e. Venus

Intended by the duke of Prussia?
Lodowick. Fairest, forget it: leave till we are clear freed hence,
   I will defy him, and cause all the knights
   Assembled for our purposed tournament
   To turn their keen swords 'gainst his caitiff head.
Lucibella. Prithee no more. I feel thy blood turn hot,
   And wrath inflames thy spirit: let it cease.
   Forgive this fault, convert this war to peace.
30 *Lodowick*. O breath-sweet touch: with what a heavenly charm
   Do your soft fingers my war-thoughts disarm.
   Prussia had reason to attempt my life,
   Enchanted by the magic of these looks,
   That cast a lustre on the blushing stars.
   Pardon, chaste queen of beauty, make me proud
   To rest my toiled head on your tender knee;
   My chin with sleep is to my bosom bowed;
   Fair, if you please a little rest with me.
Lucibella. No, I'll be sentinel; I'll watch for fear
40   Of venomous worms, or wolves, or wolvish thieves:
   My hand shall fan your eyes, like the filmed wing
   Of drowsy Morpheus; and my voice shall sing
   In a low compass for a Lucibel.
   Sleep, sweet, perhaps I'll sleep for company.
Lodowick. I thank you: I am drowsy, sing I pray;
   Or sleep; do what you please, I am heavy, ay.
   Good night to all our care. Oh, I am blest
   By this soft pillow where my head doth rest.
     He sleeps.
Lucibella. By my troth I am sleepy too: I cannot sing.
50   My heart is troubled with some heavy thing.
   Rest on these violets, whilst I prepare,
   In thy soft slumber to receive a share.
   Blush not chaste moon to see a virgin lie
   So near a prince, 'tis no immodesty.
   For when the thoughts are pure, no time, no place,

26 *caitiff*: captive   40 *worms*: snakes
42 *Morpheus*: god of dreams and sleep

Hath power to work fair chastity's disgrace;
Lodowick, I clasp thee thus, so arm clip arm,
So sorrow fold them that wish true love harm.
   Sleeps.
   Enter Lorrique, Mathias, Clois Hoffman.
Mathias. Art sure tha'st found them?
Lorrique. Look, are these they?   60
Mathias. Adulterer! strumpet!
                 [Stabs Lodowick and Lucibella.]
Lodowick. Oh!
Lucibella. Oh!
Hoffman. Inhuman deed to kill both.
Mathias. Both have abused our glory, both shall bleed.
Lucibella. How now! what have ye done? my Lodowick bleeds.
  Some savage beast hath fixed his ruthless fang
  In my soft body: Lodowick, I faint,
  Dear, wake: my Lodowick – alas what means
  Your breast to be thus wet? Is't blood or sweat?   70
Lodowick. Who troubles me?
Mathias. Brother!
Lodowick. Who is that? Mathias?
Mathias. Ay, accursed I!
Lodowick. Where's the good hermit? thank him for his love,
  Yet tell him, Ferdinand of Prussia
  Hath a long arm: some murderer of his
  Hath killed us sleeping.
Lucibella. Killed thee? no! I trust the careful destinies deny
  So hard a fate: 'tis I alone am killed.   80
  Come Lodowick, and close up my night-veiled eyes
  That never may again behold the day.
Hoffman. What means Mathias?
                 [Mathias] offers to kill himself.
Mathias. Hold me not, Prince Otho.
  I will revenge myself upon myself,
  For parricide, for damned parricide.
  I have killed my brother sleeping in the arms

57 *clip*: embrace

Of the divinest form that e'er held breath.
I have killed love's queen; defaced with my foul hand
90   The goodliest frame that ever nature built;
And driven the graces from the mansion
Wherein they have continued from their birth.
She now being dead, she'll dwell no more on earth.
Lodowick. What moved you to it, brother?
Mathias. Jealous rage, suspicion by Prince Otho,
That Lucibel had fled with a base Greek.
Oh me accursed! I am born to shame.
Hoffman. But I am wretcheder, that from the love
Devoted to the house of Saxony,
100 Have thus begot this monster cruelty.
I lay within an arbour, whence I saw
The princess, and yourself in this disguise
Departing secretly my uncle's court.
I judged you for a Greek as you appeared,
Told Prince Mathias of your secret flight,
And he led on by fury followed you,
Where thus deceived by night and your attire,
Hath robbed your heart of life, his own of joy.
Mathias. Forgive me brother, pardon, fairest maid,
110 And ere the icy hand of ashy death
Fold your fair bodies in this sable veil,
Discover why you put on this disguise.
Lodowick. To 'scape the lustful duke of Prussia,
Who purposed this night to murder me,
And ravish her whom death hath made his prey:
My Lucibel, whose lights are masked with clouds
That never will be cleared.
Hoffman. My uncle? fie, who buzzed into your head
This damned lie?
120 *Lodowick.* It's no lie.
Lucibella. No lie: 'tis true, 'tis true,
The reverent hermit Rodorick told it us.

107 *deceived*: Q deceased

Hoffman. The hermit is a villain damned in hell
    Before the world's creation, if he say't
    My princely uncle purposed such a thought.
    Look to the princess, there's life in her!
    Cheer up your heart, Prince Lodowick, courage, man.
    Your being of comfort may recover her;
        Enter Rodorick, Saxony and Austria [unseen].
    While I bring forth the hermit and disprove
    This false assertion. Rodorick is a slave,   130
    A vile and irreligious hypocrite:
    No hermit but a devil if he dare
    Affirm such falsehood of Duke Ferdinand.
Rodorick. Rodorick is not as you report him sir,
    Nor did he e'er belie Duke Ferdinand.
Hoffman. No did? why then did you maliciously
    Advise Prince Lodowick and fair Lucibel
    To fly the Prussian court this dismal night?
Rodorick. Who I? I spake not with them.
Lodowick. Yes ye did.   140
Saxony. Where was it that he spake with you? tell us where?
Lodowick. At Dantzig, in the duke of Prussia's court.
Saxony. Who heard him besides you?
Lodowick. The Princess Lucibel.
Lucibella. As heaven shall help my fleeting soul, I did.
Austria. Why speaks my dukedom's hope in hollow sounds?
    Look up fair child, here's Saxony and I,
    Thy father: Lucibella, look on me.
    I am not angry that thou fledst away,
    But come to grace thy nuptials: prithee speak.   150
Lucibella. Father, I thank you: Lodowick, reach me thy hand.
    How cold thou art! Death now assails our hearts,
    Having triumphed over the outward parts.
    Farewell awhile: we die but part, to meet
    Where joys are certain, pleasures endless, sweet.
    Father, this latest boon of yours I crave,
    Let him and me lie in one bed and grace.

Moritur.

Austria. Oh me! Oh miserable wretched me!

Lodowick. Hover a little longer, blessed soul.

160   Glide not away too fast: mine now forsakes his earthly
mansion, and on hope's gilt wings will gladly mount with
thine, where angels sing celestial ditties to the King of Kings.
Brother, adieu: your rashness I forgive; pardon me, father,
pardon Austria: your daughter is become a bride for death,
the dismal even before her wedding day. Hermit, God pardon thee: thy double tongue hath caused this error: but
in peace farewell. He that lifts us to heaven keep thee from
hell.

     Moritur.

Rodorick. Oh strange conjecture! what should move this prince

170 To charge me with such horrid cruelty?

Mathias. I'll tell thee, hypocrite.

Saxony. Stay, Mathias, stay,

It is thy uncle Rodorick, and besides,

My honour and Duke Austria's shall be 'gaged:

He never parted from our company in his own hermitage

Since day declined, and glimmering twilight ushered in the
night.

Hoffman. Not from his hermitage?

Austria. No not he.

Hoffman. Is't possible?

180 *Austria.* By heaven he did not.

Hoffman. Then there is villainy, practice and villainy.

Mathias hath been wronged and drawn to kill

His natural brother; with him to destroy

The rarest piece of nature's workmanship,

No doubt by practice and base villainy.

The hermit not at court? strange: wondrous!

Saxony. Oh, for my son, and Austria's worthy child!

Austria. Thou weep'st in scorn, and every tear of thine

Covers a smile: Saxony, I defy

190 All truce, all league of love, guard thee proud duke.

162 *King of Kings*: God (e.g. Revelation 17:14) 168sᴅ *Moritur*: Dies

Thy sons have made me childless! I'll have thee
Consort in death with my wronged girl and me.
　　[*Austria and Saxony fight. Hoffman, unseen, stabs
　　Austria.*]
Hoffman. Help, Prince Mathias, hermit: oh, the heavens!
　　The Austrian duke sinks down upon the earth.
Austria. Proud John of Saxony: hast thou no wound?
Saxony. Not any, Austria: neither touched I thee.
Austria. Somebody touched me home: vain world, farewell,
　　Dying I fall on my dead Lucibel.　　[*Dies.*]
Saxony. Sir, what are you that take on you to part?
　　It's by your weapon that the duke is fallen.　　　　　　　　　200
Hoffman. If I thought so, I'd fall upon the point,
　　But I am innocent of such an ill:
　　Kill my good kinsman, duke of Austria?
　　Then were Prince Otho of Luningberg set down
　　In sad despair's black book to rave and die:
　　But I am free from such impiety.
Saxony. Are you Prince Otho of Luningberg?
Rodorick. He is, and heir apparent to Duke Ferdinand.
Saxony. Maybe the moon deceives me, and my grief
　　As well in the distinguishing of sounds　　　　　　　　　　210
　　As sight: I have heard of young Luningberg,
　　And seen him too at Hoffman's overthrow.
　　He looked not like you, neither spake like you.
Mathias. Father, 'tis he: Lorrique, his man, attends him,
　　That fellow which is all composed of mirth.
　　Of mirth? of death. Why should I think of mirth
　　After so foul a murder? Come, lend hands
　　To give this princely body funeral rites,
　　That I may sacrifice this hand and heart
　　For my peace-offerings on their sepulchres.　　　　　　　220
Saxony. Nay boy, thou shall not leave old Saxony
　　Childless for all this sorrow: prince, and if Otho,
　　Help in my son with noble Austria,
　　Lodowick shall be my burden: brother, yours

197 *home*: the grave

The lovely but the luckless Lucibel.
So tread a heavy measure. Now let's go
To inter the dead, our hearts being dead with woe.
  *Exeunt carrying the dead bodies (Rodorick last with
  Lucibel).*
Rodorick. There's life in Lucibel, for I feel
A breath, more odoriferous than balm
230 Thirl through the coral portals of her lips.
Apparent signs of life: her pulses beat;
Oh if I could but yet recover her,
'Twould satisfy the state of Austria,
That else would be disturbed for want of heirs.
Heaven be propitious: guide my artless hand
To preserve fainting life in this clear form.
Grant this thou soul of all divinity.
And I will strive whatever mortal may
  Enter Hoffman and Saxony.
To serve thee on my knees both night and day.
240 Tarry, Prince Otho, and see their bodies balmed.
Hoffman. I pray you think me not in passion dull.
I must withdraw, and weep: my heart is full.
Oh reverent man, thou bear'st the richest fruit
That ever fell in the unripened spring.
Go lay her soft, she had ill fate to fall:
But rich or fair or strong, death swallows all.
                    [*Exit Rodorick with Lucibella, Saxony.*]
Hola! Lorrique, leave our horse; draw near.
  Enter Lorrique.
Help me to sing a hymn unto the fates
Composed of laughing interjections.
250 *Lorrique.* Why, my good lord? what accidents
Have chanced that tickle so your spleen?
Hoffman. Oh my dear self, thou trusty treasurer of my revenge:
Kneel down, and at my bidding kiss the earth,
And on her cold ear whisper this strict charge.

226 *measure*: stately dance   230 *Thirl*: Pierce   240 *balmed*: embalmed

That she provide the best of her perfumes,
The fat of lambs raped from the bleating ewes,
The sweetest-smelling wood she can devise;
For I must offer up a sacrifice
To blest occasion that hath seconded
With opportune means my desire of wreak.   260
Lorrique. Now I have kissed the earth, let me partake
  In your great joy, that seems to exceed.
  Are Lodowick and the princess murdered?
Hoffman. 'Tis done. Go, hie thee to Prince Ferdinand.
  Tell him how misadventure and mistrust
  Hath killed Prince Lodowick and bright Lucibel,
  By Prince Mathias' hand; add to that chance
  Another unexpected accident.
  Say that the dukes of Austria and Saxony,
  Being by the hermit Rodorick entertained,   270
  And hearing outcries in the dead of night,
  Came and beheld the tragic spectacle
  Which sight did so enrage the Austrian duke,
  That he assailed the Saxon, but fell slain
  On his pale daughter, new-deflowered by death.
Lorrique. Is Austria then slain by Saxony?
Hoffman. Come, come, he's dead; either by him or me,
  No matter, he's gone. There's more to go.
  Run with the news; away.
      Exit [Lorrique and Hoffman].

256 *raped*: plundered   260 *wreak*: revenge

[ACT 3

Scene 2]

*Enter Stilt, and a rabble of poor soldiers; Old Stilt his father,
with his scarf like a Captain. A scurvy march.*

Stilt. Father, set you the army in beray, while I invoke the
general folks: Fibs, foreman, and friends all, officers all, help
to marshal; Prince Jerome my lord shall remunerate, that is,
shall be full of thanksgiving, while nature is able to nourish
or sustain. Father, you have order to say the rest: be
sententious, and full of circumstance I advise you, and
remember this, that more than mortality fights on our side;
for we have treason and iniquity to maintain our quarrel.

Old Stilt. Hah! what sayest my son? treason and iniquity?

10 *Stilt.* Reason, and equity I meant, father; there's little
controversity in the words. But, like a captain courageous, I
pray, go forward. Remember the place you are in no more
but this; the days of old, no more, but that; and the glory,
father. Knighthood at least, to the utter defacing of you and
your posterity, no more but so.
     Exit.

Old Stilt. Well, go thy ways: thou are able to put fire into a
flintstone. Thou hast as rheumatic a tongue to persuade as
any is between Pole and Pomer, but thou are even kit after
kind. I am thy father, and was infamous for my exprobations,

20 to discourage a dissembly of tall soldiers afore thou wert
born; and I have made them stand to it tooth and nail. How

OSD *scarf*: sash   *scurvy*: shabby, contemptible
1 *beray*: sullied or dirtied, apparently Stilt's mistake for 'array'
1 *invocate*: call upon   2 *folks*: Q Foulks   7 *mortality*: 'morality'?
11 *controversity*: controversy (Stilt and Old Stilt glossed in quotation marks
below)
14 *defacing*: 'gracing'?   17 *rheumatic*: stiff
18 *kit after kind*: like your father (proverbial)
19 *exprobations*: rhetorical expressions of reproach
20 *dissembly*: 'assembly'

say you, most valiant and reprobate countrymen? Have ye
not heard I have been a stinger, a tickler, a wormer?

Fibs. Yes: noble, ancient captain Stilt. Ye have removed men's
hearts, I have heard that of my father – God rest his soul –
when ye were but one of the common all soldiers that served
old Hoffman in Norway.

Old Stilt. I then was, and Hoffman was a gentleman would not
have given his head for the washing, but he is cut off, as all
valiant cavalieros shall, and they be no more negligent of   30
themselves. But to the purpose: we are dissembled together,
and fallen into a battle beray in the behalf Prince Jerome, a
virtuous prince, a wise prince, and a most respectless prince,
my son Timothy's master, and the unlawful heir of this land.
Now sir, the old duke has put out a declamation, and says
our rising is no other than a resurrection; for the prince
inspires not against his father, but the duke inspires against
his son, using him most naturally, charitably, and abominably,
to put him from intercession of the crown. Wherefore as ye
be true men, and obstinate subjects, to the state uncover   40
your heads, and cast up your caps, and cry 'a Jerome, a
Jerome!'

All. A Jerome, a Jerome, a Jerome!

    Enter Jerome and Stilt.

Jerome. Most noble countrymen, I cannot but condole in joy,
and smile in tears to see you all assembled in my right, but
this is the lamentation that I, poor prince, must make, who
for my father's proclamation am like for to lose my head,

---

23 *stinger*: one who goads or stabs   *tickler*: one who provokes
23 *wormer*: one who pries into secrets
27 *Hoffman*: Q Sarloys: there is confusion with this name elsewhere in the
scene, but Jowett's emendation must be right
28 *Hoffman*: Q Sarloys (see preceding note)
30 *cavalieros*: knights (may be an allusion to the Earl of Essex, executed in
1601)
33 *respectless*: 'respected'   34 *unlawful*: 'lawful'
35 *declamation*: 'proclamation'   36 *resurrection*: 'insurrection'
37 *inspires*: 'conspires'   38 *naturally*: 'unnaturally'
38 *charitably*: 'uncharitably'   40 *obstinate*: 'loyal'?

except you stand to me, for they are coming on with bows,
bills, and guns against us. But if you be valiant, and stand to
50   me lustily, all th'earth shall roar, but we'll have victory.
  Enter with Drum and Colours, Duke Ferdinand,
  Hoffman, Lorrique, Captains to lead the drum, the
  soldiers march and make a stand. All on Jerome's side
  cast up their caps and cry 'a Jerome'.
Ferdinand. Upon those traitors, valiant gentlemen!
  Let not that beast the multitude confront
  With garlic-breath and their confused cries
  The majesty of me their awful duke.
  Strike their Typhoean body down to fire,
  That dare 'gainst us, their sovereign, conspire.
Jerome. Come, come, you shall have your hands full, and you
  Come where we have to do: stand to it, Stilt.
Stilt. Stand to't? Here's the father and the son will stand, though
60   all the rest fly away.
Old Stilt. I warrant you, prince, when the battle comes to
  joining, my son and I will be invisible; and they overcome us,
  I'll give you leave to say I have no pith in me; upon 'em, true
  prince, upon 'em.
  An Alarum. Hoffman kneels between the armies.
Stilt. I thought 'twould come to that.
  I thought we should bring
  The false prince on his knees.
Ferdinand. What means my dukedom's hope to turn thus base?
  Arise, and smite thy foes.
70 *Hoffman.* I see them not, my most honoured uncle. Pity,
    I beseech
  These silly people, that offend as babes:
  Not understanding how they do offend.
  And suffer me, chief agent in this wrong,
  To plead their pardons with a peaceful tongue.

48 *stand*: hold a military position   54 *awful*: awe-inspiring
55 *Typhoean*: Typhoeus was a monster in Greek mythology, eventually
defeated by Zeus and imprisoned under Etna
62 *invisible*: 'invincible'

Stilt. We scorn pardons, peace and pity: we'll have a prince of
our own choosing: Prince Jerome!

Old Stilt. Ay, ay, Prince Jerome or nobody! Be not obstacle, old
duke: let not your own flesh and blood be inherited of your
dukedom, and a stranger displaced in his retority, for and
you do, we will take no comparison of you and your army,   80
but fall upon you like temperance and lightning.

Ferdinand. Upon your peril: gentlemen, assail!

Hoffman. If any bosom meet the brunt of war,
Mine shall be first opposed. These honest men
That rise in arms for my young cousin's right
Shall be protected whilst Prince Otho can stand.

Jerome. Why, see now what a thing majesty is!
Stilt and the rest of my good people, my cousin
Otho looking but in the face of our excellence,
Cannot choose but take our part.   90

Stilt. Nay, but trust him not, my lord: take heed of him,
Aware your enemies at any hand.

Ferdinand. Why should you make this intercession
For these base abjects, whose presumptuous hearts
Have drawn their rebel bodies 'gainst their head?
Entreat not for them, they are all but dead.

Hoffman. Forbear a little, worthy countrymen.

Stilt. Nay, we deny that, we are none of your countrymen. You
are an arrant, arrant alien!

Old Stilt. True, son: a mere peregrination, and one that was not   100
born within our duke's damnation, and therefore not to be
remitted to any upstantial degree of office amongst us. That's
the fine; that's the fine; that's the confusion of all.

Hoffman. But hear me.

Jerome. Ay, ay: pray hear him. Nay, I charge you all upon pain
of death that you hear my cousin.

78–9 *inherited . . . displaced*: Stilt has these the wrong way round
79 *retority*: 'territory'   81 *temperance*: 'tempest' or 'thunder'
86 *Otho*: Q *Charles*: both names are used in the play, but Otho is the more
frequent
89 *Otho*: Q *Charles* (see preceding note)   92 *Aware*: 'Beware'
95 *head*: ruler   101 *damnation*: 'dominion'   103 *fine*: conclusion

Stilt. Well, we will hear him: come on, speak. What will ye say?

Hoffman. O, I beseech you, save your lives and goods,
For the duke's squadrons, armed with wrath and death,
110   Watch but the signal when to seize on you,
That can no more withstand their approved strengths
Than sparrows can contend with towering hawks:
Or 'gainst the eagle's eyrie.
This act of yours, by gathering to a head,
Is treason capital, and, without grace,
Your lives are forfeit to extremest law.

Old Stilt. Mass, he says true so. But what's the remedy?

Stilt. None at all father, now we are in, we must go through-
stitch.

120   *Hoffman.* Yes, there is remedy. Cast your weapons down,
And arm yourselves with mercy of your prince;
Who, like a gracious shepherd ready stands,
To take his lost sheep home in gentle hands.
As for your prince, I will for him entreat
That he may be restored again in love,
And unto offices of dignity, as either taster,
Sewer, cup-bearer – the place himself thinks
Fittest for his state. And for my part, when
That unhappy time of Prince Ferdinand's
130   Sad death shall come –
Which moment –
But should I as I say behold that hour,
Although I am elected for your prince,
Yet would I not remove this gentleman,
But rather serve him as his counsellor.

Jerome. Give me your hand of that, cousin. Well said: now get
a pardon for me, and my merry men all; and then let me be
my father's taster – being the office belonging to his eldest
son; I being the same – and then you shall see me behave
140   myself not as a rebel or a reprobate, but as a most reasonable
prince and sufficient subject.

112 *towering*: mounting high in the sky   117 *Mass*: Used in oaths
127 *Sewer*: Butler supervising meals
127 *cup-bearer*: household officer serving wine

Stilt. Well, since my lord has said the word, bring that of spake
he to pass and ye shall have my word too, and old Stilt my
father's, being a man of good reproach I tell you, and
condemnation in his country.

Old Stilt. Ay, that I am, my lord. I have lived in name and
shame these threescore and seven winters. All my neighbours
can bear me testament and accord.

Hoffman. Well, rest ye quiet. Sovereign, on my knees
I beg your highness grant to their request: 150
Suppose them silly, simple, and your own;
To shed their blood were just, yet rigorous.
The praise of kings is to prove gracious.

Ferdinand. True soul of honour, substance of myself,
Thy merit wins them mercy. Go in peace:
Lay by your unjust arms; live by your sweat;
And in content the bread of quiet eat.

All. God save Duke Ferdinand!
    Exeunt.

Jerome. Pray father, forgive me, and my man,
And my man's father by our single selves;   160
For we have been the capital offenders.

Old Stilt. Ay truly, my lord, we raised the resurrection.

Ferdinand. I pardon all, give thee my taster's place;
Honour this prince that hath thus won you grace.

Old Stilt and Young Stilt. God save Duke Ferdinand and Prince
    Otho!

Jerome. Ay, and me too.

Old Stilt. And Prince Jerome too. Well son, I'll leave thee a
courtier still, and get me home to my own desolation, where
I'll labour to compel away excessity, and so, fare ye well.
    Exit.

Ferdinand. This business over, worthy nephew Otho,   170
Let us go visit the sad Saxon duke,
The mourning hermit,
That through affection wrought his brother's fall.

144 *reproach*: 'repute'   145 *condemnation*: 'reputation'
152 *rigorous*: harsh   155 *them*: Q thee

Hoffman. I'll wait your highness to that house of woe,
　　Where sad mischance sits in a purple chair,
　　And underneath her beetle cloudy brows
　　Smiles at unlooked-for mischiefs; oh, there
　　Doth grief unpainted in true shape appear.
Ferdinand. Shrill trumpets sound a flourish
180　For the cries of war are drowned!
　　　Exit.
Jerome. Nay but cousin, cousin: is't not necessary I wait
　　Upon mine own father? and Stilt upon me?
Hoffman. It's most expedient; be obsequious.
　　No doubt his excellence will like that well.
　　　Enter Lorrique like a French Doctor.
Lorrique. Dieu vous garde, monsieur.
Hoffman. Welcome my friend, hast any suit to me?
Lorrique. Away monsieur, if you be the grand prince
　　Legitimate of Prussia. I have for tendre
　　To your excellence de service of one poor
190　Gentle homme of Champagne.
Hoffman. I am not he you look for, gentleman:
　　My cousin is the true and lawful prince.
Jerome. Ay sir, I am the legitimate, and am able to entertain
　　A gentleman though I say't, and he be of any quality.
Hoffman. [*Aside*] Lorrique, now or never play thy part:
　　This act is even our tragedy's best heart.
Lorrique. [*Aside*] Let me alone for plots and villainy,
　　Only commend me to this fool the prince.
Jerome. I tell thee, I am the prince: my cousin knows it.
200　That's my cousin, this is Stilt my man.
Lorrique. A vôtre service, monsieur most généreux.
Hoffman. No doubt he is some cunning gentleman.

---

174 *wait*: attend   176 *cloudy*: sullen
184SD *French Doctor*: this stage type had already appeared in a number of
plays, including Shakespeare's *Merry Wives of Windsor* and the anonymous
The Wisdom of Dr Dodypoll   185 *Dieu vous garde*: 'God save you' (French)
190 *homme*: 'man' (French)   191 *gentleman*: Q gentlemen
201 *A vôtre … généreux*: 'At your service, most generous sir' (French)
202 *cunning*: clever

Your grace may do a deed befitting you
To entertain this stranger.

Jerome. It shall be done, cousin: I'll talk with him a little and
follow you, go commend me to my father. Tell him I am
coming, and Stilt, and this stranger; be mindful cousin, as
you shall answer to my princely indignation.

Hoffman. Well sir, I will be careful, never doubt.

    [*Aside*] Now scarlet mistress from thick sable clouds   210
Thrust forth thy blood-stained hands, applaud my plot,
That giddy wonderers may amazed stand,
While death smites down suspectless Ferdinand.
    Exit.

Stilt. Sweet prince, I scarce understand this fellow well, but I
like his conceit in not trusting Prince Otho. You must give
him the remove, that's flat.

Lorrique. Ay, be gar, he be chosen agen' you, he give you good
word, so be dat, but he will have one fisgig or dra', be gar, for
companion, in principality no be possible.

Jerome. Well, I apprehend thee, I have a certain princely feeling   220
in myself that he loves me not.

Stilt. Hold ye there, my lord: I am but a poor fellow and have
but a simple living left me; yet my brother, were he a very
natural brother of my own, should he be 'dopted, I would
'dopt him and 'herit him: I'll fit him.

Jerome. But how, Stilt, but how?

Lorrique. Be gar, my Lord, I will tell you fine knacks for make
him kick up his heels, and cry 'wee!', or be gar I be hang, and
so shall I be too, and for de grand love I bear you, for de Lady
Isabella's sake, your most très-excellent lady moder.   230

Jerome. Didst thou know her, French doctor? didst thou?

---

210 *scarlet mistress*: Nemesis
216 *remove*: dismissal   217 *be gar*: 'by god', a kind of stage-French
217 *agen'*: 'against'   218 *fisgig*: 'a light, frivolous woman' (*OED*)
218 *dra'*: drab: prostitute   219 *companion*: Q company on
219 *principality*: the quality of prince-ship   224 *natural*: illegitimate
224 *'dopted*: adopted (as heir)
225 *fit*: treat you appropriately (with a sense of threat)   227 *knacks*: tricks
230 *très-excellent . . . moder*: Lorrique's 'French': 'very excellent lady
mother'

Stilt. Ay, as beggars do the ladies that are their almsgivers.

Lorrique. Be gar you, lie, like jackanape: I love de lady
    With a bonne coeur, and for her sake here take dis same, and
    dis same. [*Gives him two potions.*] Put dis in de cup where
    de competitor Prince Otho shall drink; be gar it will poison
    him bravely.

Stilt. That were excellent, my lord, and it could be done, and
    nobody know on't.

240 *Jerome.* Ay, but he always drinks in my father's cup.

Lorrique. Ay so let be, let de duke drink de same.

Jerome. What, poison my father? no, I like not that so well.

Lorrique. You shall drink too, and I too, and when we sick, as
    we shall have a petit rumble in da belly; dan take a dis same,
    and give your fadra dis, but your cousin none of it, and be
    gar nobody shall be dead, and kicka, and cry 'oh!' – but
    Otho.

Stilt. That's excellent, master.

Jerome. This is the poison then, and this is the medicine?

250 *Lorrique.* Ay, dat be true.

Jerome. Well physician, attend in my chamber here, till Stilt
    and I return; and if I pepper him not, say I am not worthy to
    be called a duke, but a draw-latch.

Stilt. Farewell a oui, and je bit a vous; and we speed by thy
    practice, we'll crush a cup of thine own country wine.
    [*Exeunt.*]

Lorrique. Go speed to spoil yourselves: [*Takes off disguise.*]
    Doctor, lie there; Lorrique, like thyself appear.
    So now I'll post unto the hermitage, and smile
    While silly fools act treason through my guile.   *Exit.*

---

232 *almsgivers*: charitable patrons
233 *jackanape*: monkey; impudent fellow
234 *bonne coeur*: 'good heart' (French)   244 *petit*: 'little' (French)
249 *medicine*: antidote   252 *pepper*: destroy   253 *draw-latch*: lazy fellow
254 *oui*: Q awe; 'yes' (French)
254 *je bit a vous*: Q iebbet a vow; Lorrique's 'French' is untranslatable
258 *post*: hurry

ACT 4

Scene 1

Enter Ferdinand and Hoffman, open a curtain; kneel Saxony, the hermit and Mathias; tapers burning.

Hoffman. See princely uncle, the black dormitory
    Where Austria and Prince Lodowick are laid
    On the cold bed of earth, where they must sleep
    Till earth and air and sea consume by fire.
Ferdinand. Their rest be peace, their rising glorious.
    Sad mourners, give your partners leave to kneel,
    And make their offertory on this tomb
    That does contain the honourablest earth
    That ever went upright in Germany.
Saxony. Welcome Duke Ferdinand: come, come; kneel, kneel,   10
    Thus should each friend another's sorrow feel.
Hoffman. Is Lucibella in this monument?
Rodorick. No, she's recovered from death's violence;
    But through her wounds and grief distract of sense.
Hoffman. Heaven help her, here she comes:
       Enter Lucibella, mad.
Rodorick. Kneel still, I pray.
Mathias. Oh me accursed! why live I this black day?
                          [Draws his sword to kill himself.]
Lucibella. Oh a sword! I pray you kill me not,
    For I am going to the river's side
    To fetch white lilies and blue daffodils   20
    To stick in Lodowick's bosom, where it bled;
    And in mine own. My true love is not dead,
    No: y'are deceived in him. My father is;
    Reason he should, he made me run away,
    And Lodowick too, and you Mathias too.
    Alack, for woe; yet what's the remedy?
    We all must run away: yet all must die.

1 *dormitory*: vault, grave

'Tis so, I wrought it in a sampler.
'Twas heart in hand, and true love's knots and words,
30   All true-stitched by my troth. The poesie thus:
No flight, dear love, but death shall sever us.
Nor that did not neither; he lies here does he not?
Rodorick. Yes, lovely madam. Pray be patient.
Lucibella. Ay, so I am, but pray tell me true,
Could you be patient, or you, or you, or you,
To lose a father and a husband too?
Ye could, I cannot; open door, here, ho!
Tell Lodowick, Lucibel would speak with him.
I have news from heaven for him: he must not die,
40   I have robbed Prometheus of his moving fire.
Open the door, I must come in, and will,
I'll beat myself to air, but I'll come in!
Hoffman. Alas, her tender hands smiting the stone
Beweep their mistress' rage in tears of blood.
Ferdinand. Fair lady, be of comfort: 'tis in vain
To invocate the dead to life again.
Hoffman. Ay, gentle daughter: be content, I pray.
Their fate is come, and ours is not far off.
Mathias. Here is a hand over my fate hath power,
50   And I now sink under the stroke of death,
But that a purer spirit fills my breast
And guides me from the footsteps of despair.
Hoffman. A heavenly motion, full of charity!
Yourself to kill yourself were such a sin
As most divines hold deadly.
Lucibella. Ay, but a knave may kill one by a trick,
Or lay a plot, or foe, or cog, or prate,
Make strife, make a man's father hang him
Or his brother: how think you, godly prince?

28 *wrought*: worked
30 *true-stitched*: worked with an embroidery identical on both sides
30 *poesie*: motto
40 *robbed Prometheus . . . fire*: in Greek mythology, Prometheus stole fire
from Zeus
40 *moving*: life-giving   57 *cog*: trick

God give you joy of your adoption!   60
May not tricks be used?
Hoffman. Alas, poor lady –
Lucibella. Ay, that's true, I am poor, and yet have things,
    And gold rings, and amidst the leaves green a –
    Lord, how d'ye; well, I thank god, why that's well;
    And you, my lord, and you too. Never a one weep;
    Must I shed all the tears? Well, he is gone,
    And he dwells here, ye said; ho, I'll dwell with him.
    Death: dastard, devil, robber of my life,
    Thou base adulterer, that part'st man and wife,   70
    Come I defy thy darts.
Ferdinand. O sweet, forbear!
    For pity's sake awhile her rage restrain
    Lest she do violence upon herself.
Lucibella. O, never fear me, there is somewhat cries
    Within me 'no': tells me there's knaves abroad,
    Bids me be quiet, lay me down and sleep.
    Good night good gentlefolks; brother, your hand,
    And yours, good father – you are my father now.
    Do but stand here: I'll run a little course   80
    At base, or barley-break, or some such toy,
    To catch the fellow, and come back again.
    Nay, look thee now: let go, or by my troth
    I'll tell my Lodowick how ye use his love.
    So now goodbye, now good night indeed:
    Lie further, Lodowick, take not all the room;
    Be not a churl, thy Lucibel doth come.
        Exit.
Saxony. Follow her, brother; follow, son Mathias.
    Be careful guardians of the troubled maid
    While I confer with princely Ferdinand   90
    About an embassy to Austria,
    With true reports of their disastrous haps.
Mathias. Well, I will be her guardian and her guide.
    By me her senses have been weakened,

---

81 *barley-break*: traditional rural game of chase played by three couples

But I'll contend with charitable pain
To serve her, till they be restored again.
    Exit.
Hoffman. A virtuous, noble resolution.
Ferdinand. Worthy Prince Rodorick, when tempestuous woe
    Abates her violent storm, I shall have time
100 To chide you for unkindness, that have lived
    In solitary life with us so long.
    Believe me, Saxon prince, you did us wrong.
Rodorick. Would I might never live in no worse state:
    For contemplation is the path to heaven.
    My new conversing in the world is proved
    Luckless and full of sorrow. Fare ye well
    My heaven's alone; all company seems hell.
        Exit.
Ferdinand. My nephew, call for wine: my soul is dry.
    I am sad at sight of so much misery.
            Enter Jerome and Stilt, with cup, towel and wine.
110 *Hoffman.* Is the duke's taster there?
Jerome. I am at hand with my office.
Hoffman. Fill for the duke, good cousin: taste it first.
Jerome. [*Aside*] I have no mind to it, Stilt, for all my antidote.
Stilt. I warrant you, master, let Prince Otho drink.
Jerome. Here cousin, will you begin to my father?
Hoffman. I thank you kindly. I'll not be so bold;
    It is your office. Fill unto my lord.   [*Jerome drinks.*]
Jerome. Well, God be with it, it's gone down, and now I'll send
    the medicine after. [*Drinks.*] Father, pray drink to my cousin,
120 for he is so mannerly that he'll not drink before you.
Stilt. Pray ye do, my lord; for Prince Otho is best worthy of all
    this company to drink of that cup. [*Aside*] Which and he do,
    I hope he shall ne'er drink more.
Ferdinand. Good fortune after all this sorrow, Saxony.
Saxony. O worthy Ferdinand, Fortune and I are parted: she
    has played the minion with me, turned all her favours into

105 *conversing*: dealing
115 *begin to*: pledge a toast to
126 *minion*: mistress

frowns; and in scorn robbed me of all my hopes; and in one
hour o'erturned me from the top of her proud wheel.

Ferdinand. Build not on Fortune, she's a fickle dame
And those that trust unto her sphere are fools.   130
Fill for his excellence.

Jerome. Here, cousin for your excellence: pray, drink you to the
duke of Saxony.

Hoffman. Not I, kind cousin, I list not to drink.

Jerome. God's lady! I think Stilt, we are all undone, for I feel a
jumbling worse and worse.

Stilt. O, give the duke some of the medicine!

Ferdinand. What medicine talk'st thou of? what ails my son?

Jerome. O lord, father, and ye mean to be a live man, take some
of this.   140

Ferdinand. Why, this is deadly poison unprepared!

Jerome. True, but it was prepared for you and me by an
excellent fellow, a French doctor.

Stilt. Ay, he is one that had great care of you.

Ferdinand. Villain what was he? drink not, Saxony:
I doubt I am by treason poisoned.

Hoffman. Heaven keep that fortune from my dread lord.
      Enter Lorrique hastily.

Lorrique. Treason ye princes, treason to the life
Of Ferdinand the duke of Prussia!
My princely master Otho of Luningberg!   150

Hoffman. Who should intend us treason?

Lorrique. This fond prince.

Jerome. Never to you, father, but to my cousin Otho; indeed I
meant to poison him, but I have peppered myself.

Hoffman. I never gave thee cause.

Stilt. That's nothing to the purpose; but my lord took occasion
by the counsel of a French doctor.

Hoffman. Physicians for the duke, my uncle faints.

Stilt. Surgeons for the prince, my master falls.

Ferdinand. Call no physicians, for I feel't too late.   160

134 *list*: like
136 *jumbling*: stirring, agitation

The subtle poison mingled with my blood
Numbs all the passages, and nimble death
Fleets on his purple currents to my heart.

Jerome. Father, I am dying too: oh, now I depart;
Be good to Stilt my man; he was accessary to all this.

Stilt. Ay truly was I sir, therefore I hope you'll be good to me. I
helped to mingle the poison as the French doctor and my
master charged me.

Ferdinand. What's that French doctor?

170 *Hoffman.* What's become of him?

Stilt. We left him in the court in my master's chamber.

Jerome. Ay sir, woe worth him. Farewell Stilt; farewell father.
I ask you pardon with repentant eyes.
Fall stars, O Stilt, for thus thy master dies.
        Moritur.

Ferdinand. Take hence that traitor for the fool, his man.

Stilt. I pray provide for me, sir.

Ferdinand. Let him be tortured, then upon a wheel broke like a
traitor and a murderer.

Stilt. O lord sir, I meant you no hurt, but to Prince Otho.

180 *Hoffman.* Away, disturb us not with idle talk.

Stilt. 'Provide,' quoth 'a, and you call this providing; pray let
me provide for myself. Alas my poor father, he'll creep upon
crutches into his grave when he hears his proper'st Stilt is cut
off by the stumps.

Ferdinand. Hence with that fellow.

Stilt. Pray, not so hasty: you would scarce be so forward, and
you were going as I am, to the gallows.
        Exeunt guard with Stilt.

Hoffman. How cheers my royal uncle?

Ferdinand. Like a ship that having long contended with

190 The waves, is at last with one proud billow
Smit into the ruthless swallow of the sea.
For thee, alas, I perceive this plot was laid:

---

163 *Fleets*: Rushes   165 *accessary*: privy to a crime
172 *woe worth him*: evil betide him

But heaven had greater mercy on thy youth,
And on my people, that shall find true rest
Being with a prince so wise and virtuous blest.
Farewell most noble John of Saxony,
Bear thy unmatched grief with a mind bent
Against the force of all temptations;
By my example, princely brother, see,
How vain our lives and all our glories be.   [*Dies.*]   200

Saxony. God for thy mercy! treason upon treason,
How now young Otho; what art thou poisoned too?

Hoffman. Would God I were, but my sad stars reserve
This simple building for extremer ruin:
Oh, that French doctor!

Lorrique. Ay, that worst of hell!
No torment shall content us in his death.

Saxony. Nay soft and fair, let him be taken first.
     Enter Rodorick.
How now, sad brother, are you come to see
This tragic end of worthy Ferdinand?   210

Rodorick. I heard of it too soon, and come too late.

Saxony. Well brother, leave the duke and wait on me:
Mathias and the heart-grieved Lucibel
Shall go with us to Wittenberg, and shun
That fatal land filled with destruction.

Rodorick. But Lucibella, like a chased hind
Flies through the thickets, and neglects the briars.
After her runs your princely son Mathias,
As much disturbed, though not so much distract,
Vowing to follow her, and if he can,   220
Defend her from despairing actions.

Saxony. And we will follow them. Prince Otho, adieu:
Care goes with us, and yet we leave grief with you.
Inter your uncle, punish traitors' crimes,
Look to your person, these are dangerous times.
     Exit Saxony and Rodorick.

---

204 *extremer*: the utmost   217 *neglects*: ignores

Hoffman. Lords, take this body, bear it to the court,
And all the way sound a sad heavy march,
Which you may truly keep, then people tread
A mournful march indeed.

230 Go on afore; I'll stay awhile, and weep
My tributary tears paid on the ground
Where my true joy, your prince my uncle fell.
I'll follow, to drive you from all distress
And comfort you, though I be comfortless.
        Exeunt with the body [except Lorrique and Hoffman].
        A march.
Are not thou plumped with laughter, my Lorrique?
Lorrique. All this, excellent but worthy lord,
There is an accident in this instance chanced
Able to overthrow in one poor hour
As well your hopes as these assurances.

240 *Hoffman.* What's that Lorrique? What can fortune do
That may divert my strain of policy?
Lorrique. You know all Prussia take you for the son
Of beauteous Martha.
Hoffman. Ay, they suppose me to be Otho her son,
And son to that false duke, whom I will kill
Or curse my stars.
Lorrique. His star is sunk already: death and he
Have vowed an endless league of amity.
Hoffman. Had I Briareus' hands, I'd strive with heaven

250 For executing wrath before the hour.
But wishes are in vain, he's gone.   [*Exeunt.*]

231 *tributary*: tribute
249 *Briareus*: a hundred-handed giant in Greek mythology
251 *gone*: Jowett conjectures that this abrupt ending indicates missing text,
in which, perhaps, Hoffman vows revenge on Martha instead of her
husband, and he and Lorrique agree the plan carried out in 4.2

[ACT 4

Scene 2]

Flourish.
Enter as many as may be spared, with lights, and make a lane
kneeling, while Martha the duchess like a mourner with her
train passeth through.

Martha. Our son is somewhat slack, as we conceive
   By this delaying, while our heart is feared,
   And our eyes dimmed with expectation –
   As are the lights of such as on the beach
   With many a longing, yet a little proof
   Stand waiting the return of those they love.
     Enter Lorrique, falls on's knees.
Lord. His excellence no doubt hath great affairs,
   But his familiar friend Lorrique is come.
Martha. Kneel not Lorrique, I prithee. Glad my heart
   With thy tongue's true report of my son Otho   10
   Whom since his princely father is deceased
   I am come from [Luningberg], oppressed with grief,
   In person to salute him for our duke.
Lorrique. Your mother-like affection and high care,
   His highness doth return with courteous thanks
   Desiring pardon of your excellence,
   In that he did not first salute your grace;
   But dismal accidents and bloody deeds,
   Poisonings, treasons so disturb this state,
   Chiefly this gentle mind, since the late death   20
   Of your right princely brother Ferdinand,
   That like the careful captain of a band
   He is compelled to be the last in field.

1 *slack*: negligent
12 *[Luningberg]*: a gap in the text here may indicate that the name was
illegible; the plot suggests Martha has come from Luningberg
13 *salute*: acknowledge

Yet he protests by me, and I for him,
That no soft rest shall enter his grieved eyes
Till he behold your presence, more desired
Than the large empire of the wide earth;
Only he prays that you would take your rest
For in your soft content his heart is blest.
30 *Martha.* Spread me a carpet on the humble earth:
My hand shall be the pillow to my head
This step my bolster, and this place my bed.
Lorrique. Your highness will take harm.
Martha. Nay, never fear.
A heart with sorrow filled sleeps anywhere.
Will our son come tonight?
Lorrique. Madam, he will.
Martha. See our train lodged, and then, Lorrique, attend.
For captain of the guard that wait on us,
40 Go all away, nobody stay with me
Except our son come. If we chance to call,
Trouble us not: good night unto you all.
   All with doing duty depart, and she sits down having a
   candle by her, and reads.
   Quo fugiat mortale genus? Nil denique tutum est;
   Crudelis nam mors omnia falce secat.
   Nil durum, nil non mortis penetrabile telis;
   Omnia vi demit mors violenta sua.
'Tis true: the wise, the fool, the rich, the poor,
The fair, and the deformed fall; their life turns
Air. The king and captain are in this alike
50 None hath freehold of life, but they are still,
When death, heaven's steward comes, tenants at will.
I lay me down, and rest in thee my trust:
If I wake never more, till all flesh rise,
I sleep a happy sleep, sin in me dies.

43–6 *Quo . . . sua*: 'Where may our mortal race flee? In the end, nothing is
safe; for cruel death scythes everything. For the weapons of death nothing is
difficult, nothing is impenetrable; violent death carries off everything in his
power' (source unknown)
50 *freehold*: permanent possession

Enter Hoffman and Lorrique.

Hoffman. Art sure she is asleep?

Lorrique. I cannot tell, be not too hasty.

Hoffman. She stirs not, she is fast.

   Sleep sweet fair duchess, for thou sleep'st thy last.

   Endymion's love, muffle in clouds thy face,

   And all ye yellow tapers of the heaven   60

   Veil your clear brightness in Cimmerian mists.

   Let not one light my black deed beautify;

   For with one stroke, virtue and honour dies.

   And yet we must not kill her in this kind.

   Weapons draw blood, bloodshed will plainly prove

   The worthy duchess, worthless of this death

   Was murdered, and the guard are witnesses

   None entered but ourselves.

Lorrique. Then strangle her: here is a towel fit.

Hoffman. Good! Kneel and help, compass her neck about.   70

   Alas, poor lady! Thou sleep'st here secure,

   And never dream'st of what thou shalt endure.

Lorrique. Nay good my lord, dispatch.

Hoffman. What, ruthless hind,

   Shall I wrong nature that did ne'er compose

   One of her sex so perfect? Prithee stay:

   Suppose we kill her thus about her neck,

   Circles of purple blood will change the hue

   Of this white porphyry; and the red lines

   Mixed with a deadly black will tell the world   80

   She died by violence. Then 'twill be inquired,

   And we held ever hateful for the act.

Lorrique. Then place beneath her nostrils this small box,

   Containing such a powder that hath power,

   Being set on fire, to suffocate each sense

   Without the sight of wound, or show of wrong.

---

59 *Endymion's love*: in Greek mythology, the moon fell in love with
Endymion

61 *Cimmerian*: of a race of people fabled to live in perpetual darkness

61 *mists*: Q mistmis   79 *porphyry*: ornamental stone like marble

81 *inquired*: investigated

Hoffman. That's excellent! Fetch fire; or do not, stay:
    The candle shall suffice. Yet that burns dim,
    And drops his waxen tears as if it mourned
90   To be an agent in a deed so dark.
Lorrique. Will you confound yourself by dotage? Speak.
    'Swounds, I'll confound her, and she linger thus.
Hoffman. Thou wert as good, and better – note my words:
    Run unto the top of dreadful scar,
    And thence fall headlong on the under-rocks;
    Or set thy breast against a cannon fired,
    When iron death flies thence on flaming wings;
    Or with thy shoulders, Atlas-like attempt
    To bear the ruins of a falling tower;
100   Or swim the ocean; or run quick to hell –
    As dead assure thyself no better place –
    Then once look frowning on this angel's face.
    Confound her? Black confusion be my grave!
    Whisper one such word more, thou diest, base slave.
Lorrique. I have done: I'll honour her if you command.
Hoffman. She stirs, and when she wakes, observe me well,
    Soothe up whate'er I say touching Prince Otho.
Martha. Prince Otho, is our son come? Who's there, Lorrique?
Lorrique. What shall I answer her?
110 *Martha.* Who's that thou talk'st with?
Hoffman. The most indebted servant to your grace
    Of any creature underneath the moon.
Martha. I prithee, friend, be brief: what is thy name?
    I know thee not; what business hast thou here?
    Art thou a messenger come from our son?
    If so acquaint us with the news thou bring'st.
Hoffman. I saw your highness' son, Lorrique here knows, the
    last of any living.
Martha. Living? Heaven help!
    I trust my son has no commerce with death.

91 *confound*: ruin *dotage*: infatuation
92 *linger*: continues to live
94 *scar*: cliff, ridge
98 *Atlas*: bore the world on his shoulders, according to Greek mythology

Hoffman. Your son no doubt is well, in blessed state. 120

Martha. My heart is smitten through thy answer,
  Lorrique, where is thy gracious lord?

Lorrique. In heaven, I hope.

Hoffman. True madam, he did perish in the wreck
  When he came first by sea from Lubeck haven.

Martha. What false imposter then hath mocked my care?
  Abused my princely brother Ferdinand?
  Gotten his dukedom in my dead son's name?

Hoffman. I grant him an imposter, therein false,
  But when your highness hears the circumstance, 130
  I know your wisdom and meek piety
  Will judge him well-deserving in your eyes.

Martha. What can be said now I have lost my son?
  Or how can this base, two-tongued hypocrite
  Excuse concealing of his master's death?
  Unhappy Martha, in thy age undone:
  Robbed of a husband, cheated of a son.

Hoffman. Hear me with patience, for that pity's sake
  You showed my captive body, by the tears
  You shed when my poor father, dragged to death, 140
  Endured all violence at their hands;
  By all the mercies poured on him and me
  That like cool rain somewhat allayed the heat
  Of our sad torment, and red sufferings:
  Hear me but speak a little, to repay
  With gratitude the favours I received.

Martha. Art thou the luckless son of that sad man,
  Lord of Burtholme, sometime admiral?

Hoffman. I was his only son, whom you set free,
  Therefore submissively I kneel, and crave 150
  You would with patience hear your servant speak.

Martha. Be brief, my swollen heart is at point to break.

Hoffman. I stood upon the top of the high scar,
  Where I beheld the splitted ship let in
  Devouring ruin in the shape of waves.
  Some got on rafts, but were as soon cast off

As they were seated; many strid the mast,
But the sea's working was so violent
That nothing could preserve them from their fury.
160   They died and were entombed in the deep,
Except some two the surges washed ashore
Prince Otho being one, who on Lorrique's back,
Hang with clasped hands, that never could unfold.
Martha. Why not as well as he, Lorrique doth live?
Or how was he found clasped upon his back,
Except he had had life to fold his hands?
Hoffman. Madam, your highness errs in that conceit,
For men that die by drowning, in their death
Hold surely what they clasp, while they have breath.
170   *Lorrique.* Well he held me, and sunk me too.
Hoffman. I'll witness, when I had recovered him,
The prince's head being split against a rock
Past all recover, Lorrique in desperate rage
Sought sundry means to spoil his new-gained life,
Exclaiming for his master, cursing heaven
For being unjust to you, though not to him,
For robbing you of comfort in your son.
'Oh gracious lady,' said this grieved man
'Could I but work a means to calm her grief,
180   Some reasonable course to keep black care
From her white bosom; I were happy then.
But knowing this, her heart will sink with woe
And I am ranked with miserablest men.'
Lorrique. Ay, God's my witness, these were my laments,
Till Hoffman being as willing as myself;
Did, for his love to you that pitied him,
Take on him to be called by your son's name,
Which now he must refuse, except your grace
Accept his service in Prince Otho's place.
190   *Martha.* If this that you protest be true, your care
Was like a long reprieve: the date worn out,
The execution of my woe is come,

160 *died*: Q did   179 *calm*: Q cald me

And I must suffer it with patience.
Where have you laid the body of my son?
Hoffman. Within the chapel of an hermitage,
Some half a mile hence.
Martha. I'll build me there a cell,
Made like a tomb; till death therein I'll dwell.
Yet for thy wrongs, young man, attend my words:
Since neither Ferdinand nor Saxony   200
Have an heir to sway their several states,
I'll work what lies in me to make thee duke;
And since thou art accepted for my son,
Attempting it only to do me good
I here adopt thee mine; christen thee Otho.
Mine eyes are now the font, the water tears,
That do baptize thee in thy borrowed name.
Hoffman. I thank your highness, and of just heaven crave
The ground I wrong you in may turn my grave.
Martha. Lights to our chamber. Now our fears are past: 210
What we long doubted is proved true at last.
Attend us, son.
    Exeunt Martha and Lorrique.
Hoffman. We'll wait upon your grace.
Son! This is somewhat; this will bear the eyes
Of the rude vulgar, but this serves not me.
Dukedoms, I will have them. My sword shall win
If any interposer cross my will.
But, new-made mother, there's another fire
Burns in this liver: lust and hot desire
Which you must quench. Must? ay, and shall: I know   220
Women will like however they say no;
And since my heart is knit unto her eyes
If she, being sanctimonious, hate my suit
In love, this course I'll take: if she deny,
Force her. True, so: *si non blanditus, vi.*   *Exit.*

215 *rude vulgar:* common people   219 *liver:* regarded as the seat of love
225 *si . . . vi:* 'if not by flattery, by force'

ACT 5

Scene 1

Enter Saxony, Rodorick, Mathias, severally.

Mathias. Have you not found her yet?
Saxony. Not I.
Rodorick. Nor I.
Mathias. Then I believe, borne by her fits of rage,
    She has done violence to her bright fame,
    And fallen upon the bosom of the Balt.
Saxony. What reason leads ye to believe it, son?
Mathias. I did perceive her some half hour since
    Clambering upon the steepness of the rock;
10   But whether up or down I could not guess
    By reason of the distance.
       Enter Lucibella with rich clothes.
Rodorick. Stand aside, she comes: let her not 'scape us now.
Saxony. What has she got, apparel? Ay, and rich.
    Poor soul, she in her idle lunacy
    Hath took it from some house where 'twill be missed.
Mathias. Let's circle her about, lest spying us
    She run away with wonted nimbleness.
    Fairest, well met.
Lucibella. Well overtaken, sir.
20 *Saxony.* What have ye here?
Lucibella. And you too, heartily.
Rodorick. I am sure you know.
Lucibella. Why that's well, I like that; that you are well and
    you, and you: goodbye.
Saxony. Nay, nay, you must not go, we'll hold you now.
Lucibella. Why that's well done. Pray come, see my house,
    I have a fine house now, and goodly knacks
    And gay apparel. Look ye here, this is brave:

OSD *severally*: from separate directions or doors   6 *Balt*: Baltic Sea
17 *wonted*: usual   27 *knacks*: trinkets

And two lean porters starved for lack of meat,
Pray let go mine arms, look here they be.   30
                           [Reveals the skeletons.]
All. Oh, horrid sight!
Lucibella. Nay, never start, I pray; is it not like I keep
  A princely house, when I have such fat porters at my gate?
Saxony. What should this mean? Why in this wood,
  So thick, so solitary, and remote
  From common road of men, should these hang thus?
  Brother, your hermitage is not far hence,
  When knew you any execution here?
Rodorick. I never knew any, and these bones are green;
  This less anatomy has not hung long.   40
  The bigger, by the moss and dryness seems
  Of more continuance.
Mathias. What's on their heads?
Lucibella. Why golden crowns: my porters shall be kings,
  And hide these bare bones with these gay weeds.
Saxony. I do remember: the admiral
  Hoffman, that kept the island of Burtholme,
  Was by the duke of Prussia adjudged
  To have his head seared with a burning crown,
  And after made a bare anatomy,   50
  Which by his son was from the gallows stolen.
Lucibella. Ay, that same son of his, but where lives he?
Saxony. No doubt, he doth possess some cave hard by.
Lucibella. Come, go with me: I'll show you where he dwells,
  Or somebody; I know not who it is.
  Here, look, look here, here is a way goes down,
  Down, down a down, hey down, down.
  I sung that song, while Lodowick slept with me.
Rodorick. This is some cave, let's boldly enter in,
  And learn the mystery of that sad sight.   60
  Come lady, guide us in, you know the way.
Lucibella. True, that's the way, you cannot miss the path;

---

39 *green*: fresh   42 *continuance*: age
62–4 *that's the way ... wide way*: cf. 'for wide is the gate, and broad is the
way, that leadeth to destruction' (Matthew 7:13)

The way to death and black destruction
Is the wide way. Nobody is now at home –
Or tarry, peradventure, here comes some will tell you more.
   Enter Martha and Lorrique.
Mathias. Stand close: this is Lorrique. I do not know the lady
   comes with him.
Saxony. I ha' seen that countenance.
Rodorick. Stand close, I pray: my heart divines
70   Some strange and horrid act will be revealed.
Lucibella. Nay that's most true, a fellow with a red cap told me
    so,
   And bade me keep these clothes, and give them
   To a fair lady in a mourning gown.
   Let go my arms: I will not run away.
   I thank you now, now you shall see me stay;
   By my troth I will, by my maidenhead I will.
Martha. Lorrique, return into the beaten path,
   I ask'st thee for a solitary plot,
   And thou hast brought me to the dismal'st grove
80   That ever eye beheld; no wood-nymphs here
   Seek with their agile steps to outstrip the roe,
   Nor doth the sun suck from the queachy plot
   The rankness and venom of the earth.
   It seems frequentless for the use of men:
   Some basilisks', or poisonous serpents', den!
Lorrique. It is indeed an undelightful walk,
   But if I do not err in my belief,
   I think the ground, the trees, the rocks, the springs,
   Have, since my princely master Otho his wreck,
90   Appeared more dismal, than they did before,
   In memory of his untimeless fall.
   For hereabouts, hereabouts the place
   Where his fair body lay deformed by death;
   Here Hoffman's son and I embalmed him,

69 *divines*: predicts 81 *roe*: deer 82 *queachy*: boggy
84 *frequentless*: unfrequented 85 *basilisks*: a basilisk is a fabled reptile
91 *untimeless*: untimely

After we had concluded to deceive
Your sacred person and Duke Ferdinand
By causing Hoffman to assume his name.
Saxony. This is very strange.
Lucibella. Nay tarry, you shall hear all the knavery anon.
Martha. And where's the chapel that you laid him in?   100
Lorrique. It's an old chapel near the hermitage.
Martha. But was the hermit at his burial?
Lorrique. No, Hoffman and I only digged the grave;
    Played priest and clerk, to keep his burial close.
Rodorick. Most admirable!
Saxony. Nay, pray you peace!
Martha. Alas! poor son, the soul of my delights.
    Thou in thy end were robbed of funeral rites;
    None sung thy requiem, no friend closed thine eyes,
    Nor laid the hallowed earth upon thy lips.   110
    Thou wert not houseled, neither did the bells ring –
    Blessed peals – nor toll thy funeral knell.
    Thou went'st to death as those that sink to hell.
    Where is the apparel that I bade him wear
    Against the force of witches and their spells?
Lorrique. We buried it with him: it was his shroud;
    The desert woods no fitter means allowed.
Lucibella. I think he lies.
    Now by my troth, that gentleman smells knave.
Martha. Swear one thing to me, ere we leave this place: 120
    Whether young Hoffman did the most he might
    To save my son.
Lorrique. By heaven, it seems he did, but all was vain.
    The flinty rocks had cut his tender skull,
    And the rough water washed away his brain.
Lucibella. Liar, liar lick-dish.
Martha. How now, what woman's this? what men are these?
Lucibella. A poor maiden, mistress, has a suit to you,
    And 'tis a good suit: very good apparel.

104 *close*: private   111 *houseled*: purified by being given Holy Communion
126 *lick-dish*: parasite

130   *Lo, here I come a-wooing my ding-ding,*
         Lo, here we come a-suing, my darling,
         Lo, here I come a-praying, so bide-a, bide-a.
         How do you lady? well, I thank God; will you buy
         A bargain, pray? it's fine apparel.
Martha. Run my life's blood; comfort my troubled heart,
         That trembles at the sight of this attire.
         Lorrique, look on them: knowest thou not these clothes?
         Nor the distracted bringer? prithee, speak.
Lorrique. Ay me, accursed and damned: I know them both;
140   The bringer is the Austrian Lucibel.
Lucibella. Ay, you say true, I am the very same.
Lorrique. The apparel was my lord's, your princely son's.
Martha. This is not sea-wet: if my son were drowned
         Then why thus dry is his apparel found?
Lorrique. O me accursed, o miserable me?
         Fall heaven, and hide my shame; gape earth, rise sea,
         Swallow, o'erwhelm me. Wherefore should I live,
         The most perfidious wretch that ever breathed,
         And base consenter to my dear lord's death?
150 *Lucibella.* Nay, look you here, do you see these poor starved
         ghosts? Can you tell whose they be?
Martha. Alas! what are they? What are you that seem
         In civil habits to hide ruthless hearts?
         Lorrique, what are they? what wilt thou attempt?
            [*Lorrique makes to kill himself.*]
         Help gentlemen, if ye be gentlemen,
         And stay this fellow from despairing ill.
Lorrique. I was ordained unto perdition, stay me not;
         For when ye know the mischiefs I have done –
         At least, consented to, through coward fear –
160   You would not stop me, if I skipped in quick
         To that black, bottomless and ruthless gulf,
         Where everlasting sorrows like linked chains
         Fetter the wretched in eternal night.
Martha. What hast thou done?

158 *ordained*: planned

Lucibella. Knavery I warrant you: tell truth and shame the devil,
  my boy; do, and thou shalt have a fine thing by and by.
Saxony. I take your highness for that reverend duchess
  Late wife unto the duke of Prussia.
Martha. I am the wretched, childless widow, sir.
Lorrique. Princess, hear me, and I will briefly tell   170
  How you became childless, you brotherless,
  You husbandless, and fatherless; all, all,
  I'll tell you. Having ended, act my fall.
Mathias. Well, forward.
Lorrique. Be it so; I have deserved a greater cruelty,
  To be kept living when I long to die.
Martha. I charge thee, setting by all circumstance,
  Thou utter what thou knowest: my heart is steel,
  Nor can it suffer more than it doth feel.
Lorrique. Then thus: Prince Otho and I escaped the wreck,   180
  Came safe ashore to this accursed plot,
  Where we met Hoffman, who upon yon tree
  Preserved his father's bare anatomy –
  The biggest of them two were those strong bones
  That acted mighty deeds.
  Hoffman the son, full of revenge and hate
  'Gainst every hand that wrought his father's hurt,
  Yet gilded o'er his envy with fair shows,
  And entertained us with as friendly terms
  As falsehood could invent; and 'tis well known,   190
  Bitter deceit useth the sweetest speech.
  At length he took advantage: bound my lord,
  And in a chain tied him to yonder rock;
  While with a burning crown he seared in twain
  The purple veins, strong sinews, arteries, nerves,
  And every cartilage about the head;
  In which sad torment, the mild prince fell dead.
Martha. Did Hoffman this? and thou conceal'st the deed?
Lorrique. Pardon my fear, dread madam.
Martha. Well, go on, I am confident to hear all cruelty;   200
  And I am resolved to act some, if no hand

Will else attempt the murderer's end but mine.
Lorrique. Be patient, you will find associates,
    For there are many murderers more behind.
Martha. What did he with the body of my son?
Lorrique. Buried the flesh; the bones are they that hang
    Close by his father's.
Martha. Let them hang awhile,
    Hope of revenge in wrath doth make me smile.
210 *Lucibella.* Pray let him tell the rest.
Lorrique. This acted, Hoffman forced me to conceal
    The murder of my lord, and threatened more
    Than death by many torments, till I swore
    To call him Otho, and say he was your son.
    I swore and kept my oath.
Rodorick. O heaven!
Saxony. O devil!
Lucibella. Nay, I pray you, peace.
Lorrique. Then sent he me for you, and you he sent,
220   Or as I best remember, led you on
    Unto the chapel porch, where he himself
    Appointed them to stay, and there you know
    What happened in your wrath.
Lucibella. To me asleep,
    And to my harmless Lodowick in my arms.
Mathias. On, on: that deed is writ among the acts of guilt;
    A brother's sword a brother's lifeblood spilt.
Saxony. Proceed, what's next? Killed he not Austria?
Lorrique. He did.
230 *Lucibella.* O villain, did he kill my father?
    And make my brother kill my husband too?
Saxony. Go forward.
Lorrique. After all those hated murders,
    He taught the foolish prince, in the disguise
    Of a French doctor, to prepare a poison,
    Which was the death of princely Ferdinand.
    Next plot, he purposed your grace's death,

And had he opposed my strength of my tears,
You had been murdered as you lay asleep.
Saxony. Let's hear no more. Seek out the hated wretch,   240
    And with due torture let his life be forced
    From his despised body.
Rodorick. Do, I pray.
Saxony. All the land will help,
    And each man be a justice in this act.
Martha. Well, I that never knew revenge's power,
    Have entertained her newly in my breast:
    Determine what's to do.
Lucibella. Even what you will; would I were with my
        Lodowick asleep
    In the Elysian fields, where no fears dwell,   250
    For earth appears as vile to me as hell.
Lorrique. Let me be prologue to your scene of wrath,
    And as the Roman Catiline resolved
    His doubtful followers by exhausting blood
    From the live body, so draw mine, cast mine
    Upon the troubled and offended earth.
    Offer blood fit for an infernal sacrifice;
    Wine is not poured but on celestial offerings,
    Therefore I advise you,
    As you hope to thrive in your revenge, smite me,   260
    That have been pander to this injury.
Martha. Thou merit'st death indeed.
Mathias. Stay: judge him not; let me a little plead in his excuse,
    And this one sentence serves. A man compelled
    To evil acts, cannot be justly held
    A wilful malefactor. The law still
    Looks upon the deed, ne'er on the will.
    Besides, although I grant the matter small
    And very safe to raise a multitude,

238 *had he*: Q had
253 *Catiline*: Roman conspirator who apparently shared the blood of a slave
with his fellows to strengthen their bond
253 *resolved*: made resolute   261 *pander*: go-between, pimp

270   That by their power might seize the murderer,
        Yet two especial reasons cross that course.
        First: many having notice of our plot,
        One babbling tongue may utter out intent,
        And Hoffman being warned is surely armed,
        Having the fort and treasure in his power;
        And be his cause more than notorious ill,
        He may with gold maintain it at his will;
        'Scape us, for no doubt he's full of sleights.
        Besides, revenge should have proportion:
280   By sly deceit he acted every wrong,
        And by deceit I would have him entrapped;
        Then the revenge were fit, just, and square,
        And 'twould more vex him that is all composed
        Of craft and subtlety to be outstripped
        In his own fashion, than a hundred deaths.
        Therefore by my advice, pardon Lorrique
        Upon condition that he lay some plot
        To intercept the other.
     All. We are agreed.
290 *Lorrique.* Your mercy doth all bounds of hope exceed,
        And if you will repose that trust in me,
        By all the protestations truth can make,
        Before the sun have run his midday's course,
        I will tomorrow yield him to your hands.
     Saxony. Show us the means.
     Lorrique. The means is in the duchess' policy,
        If she can smooth the murder but a while.
     Martha. I'll turn deceit to overthrow his fraud.
     Lorrique. Then, with fair words his flatteries entertain,
300   And when he doth importune you for love,
        Desire him first to show you the first place,
        Where he beheld Prince Otho after the wreck.
        Say you have earnestly entreated me,
        But I have led you in a labyrinth

    275 *fort*: strength   296 *policy*: political acumen

Of no effect; he full of heat and lust,
Glad of occasion, will no doubt alone
Conduct you to this fatal horrid cave,
Thinking by force, or fair means, to attain
His false heart's longing, and your honour's stain;
But being in the height of his base pride,   310
The duke, the hermit, Mathias and myself
Will change his pleasures into wretched
And redeemless misery.
Saxony. The plot is good: madam, are you agreed?
Martha. To anything, however desperate.
Lucibella. Ay, but by your leave, lady and lords all, what if
    This knave that has been, play the knave still,
    And tells tales out of school, how then?
Lorrique. I know not what to swear by; but no soul
    Longs for the sight of endless happiness   320
    With more desire than mine thirsts for his death.
    By all the gods that shall give ill men life,
    I am resolved chief agent in his end.
Mathias. We credit thee: join hands and ring him round;
    Kneel, on his head lay our right hands, and swear
    Vengeance against Hoffman.
All. Vengeance, vengeance, fall
    On him, or sudden death upon us all.
Saxony. Come, part; we to the cave,
    You to the court.   330
    Justice dig murder's grave.
        Exit Lorrique and Martha.
Lucibella. Nay, I'll come: my wits are mine again,
    Now faith grows firm to punish faithless men.
        Exeunt.

306 *occasion*: opportunity   311 *Mathias*: Q Lodowick
313 *redeemless*: irredeemable   324 *credit*: believe

[ACT 5

Scene 2]

Enter Hoffman, and all the train that attended the Duchess first.

Hoffman. Not to be found? Hell: which way is she gone?
Lord. Her highness charged us to call you her son,
   The mystery we know not; but we know
   You are not princely Otho of Luningberg.
Hoffman. No matter what I am; tell me the way she went
   With that Lorrique. Speak, or by heaven
   Hell shall receive you all.
     Enter Martha and Lorrique.
Lord. Be not enraged: she comes,
   And with her comes trusty Lorrique.
10 *Hoffman.* Madam, I feared you, and my heart was sick
   With doubt some over-desperate accident
   Had drawn you to melancholy paths,
   That lie within the verge of this rough scar.
Martha. Your doubt was but an embryo. I indeed
   Desired Lorrique to bring me to the place
   Where you beheld the shipwreck of my son;
   And he hath led me up and down the wood,
   But never brought me to the fatal beach.
Hoffman. It were not fit you should see the sad place,
20   That still seems dismal since the prince's death.
Lord. Dead? is our sovereign lord the prince dead?
Martha. Inquire no more of that. I will anon
   Resolve you of his fate; this time forbear,
   Esteem this gentleman, your lord and prince.
Lord. We hold him so, since you command us so.
Hoffman. Will you go forward, madam?
Martha. Willingly, so you will promise me to walk tomorrow

---

10 *feared*: worried about 14 *embryo*: in an undeveloped stage
23 *Resolve*: Settle, solve

And see the earth that gently did receive
My son's wrecked body from the churlish foam.
Hoffman. I'll wait upon your grace: set forward there   30
[*Aside*] Tricks and devices! longings! well, 'tis good:
   I'll swim to my desires through seas of blood.
     Exeunt.
Lorrique. Fox you'll be taken; hunter, you are fallen
   Into the pit you digged. I laugh to see
   How I outstripped the prince of villainy.
   Hoffman for me told such a smoothing tale,
   That had not this strange accident befallen
   In finding of the cave, I had been held
   More dear than ever in the duchess' eyes.
   But now she'll hold me hard, whate'er she say.   40
   Yet is her word passed that she'll pardon me;
     Enter Hoffman.
   And I have wealth hoard up, which I'll bear
   To some strange place: rich men live anywhere.
Hoffman. What? are you gadding sir? what moves your flight?
   Coin not excuses in your crouching: come,
   What cause have you to fly and seek strange hoards
   For your wealth gotten by my liberal gift?
Lorrique. And my desert, my lord.
Hoffman. Well, be it your desert;
   But what's the cause you'll fly this country?   50
Lorrique. As I live, my lord, I have no such intent;
   But with your leave, I was debating things,
   As if it should chance thus, and thus, why then,
   'Twere better be far off; but otherwise
   My love and life low at your service lie.
Hoffman. You are a villain damned as low as hell!
   An hypocrite, a fawning hypocrite:
   I know thy heart. Come, spaniel, up, arise:
   And think not with your antics and your lies
   To go beyond me. You have played the slave,   60

40 *hold me hard*: have a harsh opinion of me   44 *gadding*: wandering
58 *spaniel*: fawning or cringing person

Betrayed me unto the duchess, told her all,
Disappointing all my hopes with your base tongue,
O'erturned the height of my intendments;
For which I'll hurl thee from my mountain wreck,
Into the lowest cavern of pale death.
Lorrique. Alas my lord, forbear, let me be heard –
Hoffman. Thou hast betrayed me, therefore never talk.
Lorrique. By heaven –
Hoffman. O hell! why shouldst thou think on heaven?
70 *Lorrique.* Stay and believe me, think you I am mad,
So great a foe to my own happy chance?
When things are sorted to so good an end,
That all is hid, and we held in regard
After such horrid and perfidious acts:
Now to betray myself? Be reasonable,
And think how shallow such an act would seem
In me, chief agent in so many ills.
Hoffman. Thou hast a tongue as glib and smooth to lies,
As full of false inventions and base fraud,
80 As prone to circumvent believing souls,
As ever heretic or traitor used,
Whose speeches are as honey, their acts gall:
Their words raise up, but their hands ruin all.
Lorrique. By virtue's glorious soul –
Hoffman. Blasphemer peace, swear not by that thou hat'st!
Virtue and thou have no more sympathy
Than day with night, heaven with hell.
Thou knowest I know thy villainies excel.
Lorrique. Why then by villainy, by blood, by sleights,
90 By all the horrors tortures can present,
By hell, and by revenge's purple hand:
The duchess had no conference with me
But only a desire to see the place
That first received her son, whom she believes
The unrelenting waves and flinty rocks,
Had severed from sweet life after the wreck.
Hoffman. May I believe thee?
Lorrique. Have I failed you yet?

Measure my former acts, and you shall find
My soul allied to yours, wholly estranged   100
From all I ever loved.
Hoffman. No more, have done.
Th'ast won me to continue thee my friend.
But I can tell thee somewhat troubles me,
Some dreadful misadventure my soul doubts,
And I conceive it with no common thought,
But a most potent apprehension;
For it confounds imaginary sense.
Sometimes it inflames my blood, another while
Numbs all the currents that should comfort life,   110
And I remain as 'twere a senseless stone.
Lorrique. Come, come, I know the cause: you are in love;
And to be so, is to be anything.
Do you not love the duchess?
Hoffman. Yes, I do.
Lorrique. Why there's the matter, then: be ruled by me.
Tomorrow morning she desires to see
The shore that first received her sea-wrecked son,
And to be unaccompanied she loves,
Except some one or two, you and I.   120
Now when you have her near your dismal cave,
Force her. Ay, do't man: make no scruple, do't,
Else you shall never win her to your bed.
Do a man's part, please her before she go,
Or if you see that she turns violent,
Shut her perpetual prisoner in that den.
Make her a Philomel, prove Tereus:
Do't, never fear it.
Hoffman. Why she will be missed.
Lorrique. By whom? By fools: gross, dull, thick-sighted fools,   130
Whom every mist can blind. I'll sway them all
With exclamation that the grieved duchess,
When she beheld the sea that drowned her son,

---

127 *Philomel . . . Tereus*: Tereus raped Philomel in Ovid's *Metamorphoses*

Stood for a while like weeping Niobe,
As if she had been stone; and when we strived
With mild persuasions to make less her woe
She, madder than the wife of Athamas
Leapt suddenly into the troubled sea,
Whose surges greedy of so rich a prey,
140   Swallowed her up, while we in vain exclaimed
'Gainst heaven and hell, 'gainst fortune and her fate.
Hoffman. Oh my good villain! how I hug thy plots.
This shall be done: she's mine. Run swift, slow hours;
Make a short night hasten on day apace,
Rough arms wax soft, soft beauty to embrace.
Lorrique. Why so, now your fear will quickly end.
Hoffman. Thou wilt not talk of this?
Lorrique. Will I be hanged?
Ne'er take me for a blab, you'll find me none.
150   *Hoffman.* I have another secret, but –
Lorrique. Come what is't? come, this breast is yours,
My heart's your treasury.
Hoffman. Thou must be secret: 'tis a thing of weight concerns
thee near.
Lorrique. Were it as near as life, come, pray speak.
Hoffman. Hark in thine ear. I would not have the air
Be privy to this purpose: wilt thou swear?
Lorrique. What? to be secret? if the least jot I tell
Let all my hopes sink suddenly to hell.
Hoffman. Thou hast thy wish, down villain, keep this close.
                                                    [*Stabs him.*]
160   *Lorrique.* Unthankful murderer, is this my meed?
Oh slave, th'ast killed thy heart in wounding mine.
This is my day, tomorrow shall be thine.
Hoffman. Go, fool! now thou art dead, I need not fear.
Yet, as thou wert my servant just and true,

---

134 *Niobe*: punished by the gods for her pride by the murder of her
children; see also *Hamlet*, scene 2.73 and note
137 *wife of Athamas*: in Greek mythology, Ino threw herself off a cliff with
her child to escape her mad husband
142 *hug*: delight   152 *treasury*: secure store   160 *meed*: wages

I'll hide thee in the ditch: give dogs their due.
He that will prove a mercenary slave
To murder, seldom finds so good a grave.
He's gone. I can now spare him. Lorrique, farewell;
Commend me to our friends thou meet'st in hell:
Next plot for Mathias and old Saxony: 170
Their ends shall finish our black tragedy.
    Exit.

[ACT 5

Scene 3]

Enter Saxony and Mathias.

Saxony. How little care had we to let her 'scape,
  Especially on this so needful time,
  When we are vowed to wait upon revenge.
Mathias. No doubt our uncle's care will keep her safe,
  Nor is she in her fits so violent
  As she was wont. Look where my
  Uncle comes, sustaining with one hand
  A dying man, and on the other side,
  Fair Lucibel supports the fainting body.
    Enter Rodorick, and Lucibella leading Lorrique.
Lucibella. Look you here. You marvelled why I went,   10
  Why this man drew me unto him: can you help
  Him now? Hoffman has houghed him too.
Saxony. Brother, who is't you bring thus ash-pale?
  Is't not Lorrique?
Lorrique. I am, and 'tis in vain to strive for longer hope.
  I cannot – only be provident. I greatly fear
  The murderous traitor out of mere suspect
  Will plot some stratagem against the life

17 *suspect*: suspicion

Of the chaste duchess. Help her what you can,
20   Against the violence of that wicked man.
Rodorick. Hast thou not told him what we do intend?
Lorrique. No, as heaven help me in my wretched end:
        Be confident of that. Now I must fall
        Never again to rise. You know his wrongs:
        Be careful, princes to revenge them all.   [*Dies.*]
Lucibella. Well, farewell, fellow, thou art now paid home
        For all thy counselling in knavery.
        Good lord! what very fools are very knaves!
        Their cunning bodies often want due graves.
30 *Saxony.* Son, daughter, brother: follow my advice.
        Let us no longer keep this hateful plot,
        Lest we be circumvented.
Rodorick. True 'tis: to put on open arms.
Mathias. 'Tis now too late, we are beset
        With soldiers. We must fight, and since it must be;
        Let's to't valiantly.
            Enter [Martha's] Lord, with soldiers.
Lord. Princes, prepare not to resist your foes,
        We are firm as life unto your blood.
        The Duchess Martha greets old Saxony,
40   Prince Mathias, Rodorick and fair Lucibel.
        To me she hath discovered the damned plots
        Of that perfidious Hoffman, and hath sent
        These armed soldiers to attend on you.
Saxony. We thank her highness, but we think in vain
        Both you and we attend. Lorrique lies slain
        By Hoffman's sly suspicion: best be joined
        To apprehend him publicly.
Lord. There is no need. Our duchess hath apparelled
        Her speech in a green livery.
50   She salutes him fair, but her heart
        Like his actions, is attired
        In red and blue and sable ornaments.

---

33 *open arms*: fight openly   41 *discovered*: revealed
49 *green*: i.e. innocent   52 *sable*: black

Saxony. But tell us where they are?
Lord. At hand she comes with him alone her plot is:
  She comes in happy time for all your good.
Mathias. Cease words, use deeds.
  Revenge draws nigh.
Saxony. Come set his body like a scarecrow.
    [*They hang up Lorrique's body and hide behind bushes.*]
  This bush shroud you, this you.
  Stand close, true soldiers, for revenge.   60
Lucibella. Ay: do, do, do, I pray you heartily do; stand close.
    Enter Hoffman and [Martha].
Hoffman. I wonder much why you ask me for Lorrique.
  What is Lorrique to you, or what to me?
  I tell you he is damned: inquire no more,
  His name's hatefuller than death.
Martha. Heaven! what alterations these.
  Can I believe you love me as you swore,
  When you are so inconstant to your friend?
Hoffman. He is no friend of mine whom you affect.
  Pardon me, madam: such a fury reigns   70
  Over my boiling blood, that I envy
  Anyone on whom you cast an amorous eye.
Martha. What, grown so loving? marry, heaven defend,
  We shall deceive you if you dote on us,
  For I have sworn to live a widow's life,
  And never more to be termed married wife.
Hoffman. Ay, but you must.
Martha. Must? use not force, I pray.
Hoffman. Yield to my love, and then with meekest words
  And the most humble actions, I'll entreat   80
  Your sacred beauty. Deny me? I'll turn fire,
  More wild than wrath. Come then agree
  If not to marry, yet in unseen sports
  To quench these lawless heats that burn in me.
Martha. What, my adopted son become my lover?
  And make a wanton minion of his mother?
  Now fie upon you, fie, you are too obscene,
  If, like your words, your thoughts appear unclean.

Hoffman. By heaven, I do not jest: go to, believe me.
90   'Tis well you laugh. Smile on, I like this;
      Say, will you yield?
Martha. At the first? Fie, no!
      That were an abject course. But let us walk
      Into some covert; there are pretty caves
      Lucky to lovers' suits: for Virgil sings
      That Dido being driven by a sharp storm
      Into a Lybian cave, was there enticed
      By silver-tongued Aeneas to affect.
      And should you serve me so, I were undone,
100   Disgraced in Germany by every boor,
      Who in their rhymes would jest at Martha's name,
      Calling her minion to her cousin-son.
Hoffman. Fairer than Dido, or love's amorous queen:
      I know a cave, wherein the bright day's eyes
      Looked never but askance through a small crack
      Or little cranny of the fretted scar;
      There I have sometimes lived, there are fit seats
      To sit and chat, and coll and kiss, and steal
      Love's hidden pleasures. Come, are you disposed
110   To venture entrance? If you be, assay:
      'Tis death to quick desire; use no delay.
Martha. Virtue and modesty bids me say no.
      Yet trust me, Hoffman, th'art so sweet a man,
      And so beloved of me, that I must go.
Hoffman. I am crowned the king of pleasure.
Martha. [*Aside*] Slave, thou goest to meet destruction in thy
      cave.
Hoffman. 'Sdeath, who stands here?
                                   [*Discovers Lorrique's body.*]
      What's that? Lorrique's pale ghost?
      I am amazed. Nay, slave, stand off:

93 *abject*: inferior   94 *covert*: wood, shelter
95–8 *Virgil . . . Aeneas*: from the *Aeneid*, Book IV
95 *sings*: Virgil's own verb for his poetry
106 *fretted*: worn into holes   108 *coll*: embrace   110 *assay*: do, venture
118 *ghost*: corpse

Martha. [*Armed with Hoffman's sword.*] Thy weapon's sure,   120
    the prize is ours.
  Come forth dear friends, murder is in our powers.
Saxony. Yield thee, base son of shame!
Hoffman. How now: what's here? am I betrayed?
  By dotage, by the falsehood of a face?
  Oh wretched fool, fallen by a woman's hand
  From high revenge's sphere, the bliss of souls!
Saxony. Cut out the murderer's tongue.
Hoffman. What do you mean?
  Whom have I murdered; wherefore bind ye me?
Martha. They are justices to punish thy bare bones.   130
                        [*Reveals skeletons.*]
  Look with thy bloodshed eyes on these bare bones,
  And tell me that which dead Lorrique confessed
  Who is't thou villained? That least – who was't?
Hoffman. Why Otho thy son's, and that's my father's by him.
Martha. O merciless and cruel murderer
  To leave me childless!
Lucibella. And me husbandless.
Mathias. Me brotherless. Oh smooth-tongued hypocrite
  How thou didst draw me to my brother's death?
Saxony. Talk no more to him, he seeks dignity;   140
  Reason he should receive his desperate hire,
  And wear his crown made flaming hot with fire:
  Bring forth the burning crown there –
    *Enter a lord with the crown [and places it on Hoffman's
    head].*
Hoffman. Do, old dog, thou help'st to worry my dead father
  And must thou kill me too? 'tis well, 'tis fit,
  I that had sworn unto my father's soul
  To be revenged on Austria, Saxony,
  Prussia, Luningberg, and all their heirs:
  Had prospered in the downfall of some five;
  Had only three to offer to the fiends,   150
  And then must fall in love – oh, wretched eyes

133 *least*: the smaller of the skeletons

That have betrayed my heart: be you accursed,
And as the melting drops run from my brows,
So fall they on the strings that guide your heart,
Whereby their oily heat may crack them first.
Ay, so, boil on, thou foolish idle brain,
For giving entertainment to love's thoughts.
A man resolved in blood, bound by a vow
For no less vengeance than his father's death,
160   Yet become amorous of his foe's wife!
Oh sin against all conceit! worthy this shame
And all the tortures that the world can name.
Martha. Call upon heaven, base wretch, think on thy soul.
Hoffman. In charity and prayer:
To no purpose without charity.
Saxony. We pardon thee, and pray for thy soul's health.
Hoffman. So do I not yours, nor pardon you.
You killed my father, my most warlike father;
Thus as you deal by me, you did by him.
170   But I deserve it that have slacked revenge
Through fickle beauty and a woman's fraud.
But hell, the hope of all despairing men,
That wring the poor, and eat the people up
As greedy beasts the harvest of their spring;
That hell, where cowards have their seats prepared,
And barbarous asses, such as have robbed soldiers of
Reward, and punish true desert with scorned death –

                                                                    [*Dies.*]

FINIS

173 *wring*: squeeze
177 *death*: this abrupt ending may mean something is missing: one early text
in the Dyce collection, in the Victoria and Albert Museum, London, adds a
manuscript final line to complete the couplet: 'Swallow & choake you with
her sulphurous breath', but its provenance is not known

THOMAS MIDDLETON

THE REVENGER'S TRAGEDY

LIST OF CHARACTERS

VINDICE

HIPPOLITO *his brother*

CASTIZA *his sister*

MOTHER *Graziana*

DONDOLO *servant to Graziana*

DUKE

DUCHESS

LUSSURIOSO *eldest son of the duke*

NENCIO
SORDIDO } *Lussurioso's followers*

SPURIO *duke's illegitimate son*

AMBITIOSO
SUPERVACUO } *duchess' sons*
JUNIOR

ANTONIO

PIERO

2 JUDGES

Spurio's SERVANTS

NOBLEMEN

OFFICERS

GENTLEMAN

ACT 1

Scene 1

*Enter Vindice [holding a skull], the Duke, Duchess, Lussurioso
her son, Spurio the bastard, with a train; pass over the stage
with torchlight.*

Vindice. Duke: royal lecher; go, grey-haired adultery,
    And thou his son, as impious steeped as he:
    And thou his bastard true-begot in evil:
    And thou his duchess that will do with devil.
    Four excellent characters – O that marrowless age
    Would stuff the hollow bones with damned desires,
    And 'stead of heat kindle infernal fire
    Within the spendthrift veins of a dry duke.
    A parched and juiceless luxur. O God! one
    That has scarce blood enough to live upon,   10
    And he to riot it like a son and heir?
    O, the thought of that
    Turns my abused heart-strings into fret.
    Thou sallow picture of my poisoned love,
    My study's ornament, thou shell of death,
    Once the bright face of my betrothed lady;
    When life and beauty naturally filled out
    These ragged imperfections;
    When two heaven-pointed diamonds were set
    In those unsightly rings – then 'twas a face   20
    So far beyond the artificial shine
    Of any woman's bought complexion,
    That the uprightest man – if such there be,
    That sin but seven times a day – broke custom,
    And made up eight with looking after her.

4 *do*: have sex   8 *dry*: aged; impotent   9 *luxur*: lecher
11 *a son and heir*: a prodigal   13 *fret*: agitation
20 *unsightly*: unseeing; ugly   *rings*: eyesockets
22 *bought complexion*: from cosmetics

Oh, she was able to ha' made a usurer's son
Melt all his patrimony in a kiss;
And what his father fifty years told
To have consumed, and yet his suit been cold.
30   But oh, accursed palace!
Thee when thou wert apparelled in thy flesh,
The old duke poisoned,
Because thy purer part would not consent
Unto his palsy-lust; for old men lustful
Do show like young men angry, eager, violent,
Outbid like their limited performances
O 'ware an old man hot and vicious
'Age as in gold, in lust is covetous.'
Vengeance, thou murder's quit-rent, and whereby
40   Thou show'st thyself tenant to tragedy,
Oh keep thy day, hour, minute, I beseech,
For those thou hast determined. Hum: whoe'er knew
Murder unpaid? 'Faith, give revenge her due;
She's kept touch hitherto. Be merry, merry,
Advance thee, o thou terror to fat folks,
To have their costly three-piled flesh worn off
As bare as this. For banquets, ease, and laughter
Can make great men, as greatness goes by clay.
But wise men little are more great than they.
     Enter [his] brother Hippolito.
50   *Hippolito.* Still sighing o'er death's vizard?
Vindice. Brother, welcome,
     What comfort bring'st thou? how go things at court?
Hippolito. In silk and silver, brother: never braver.

26 *usurer*: moneylender   27 *Melt*: Spend   28 *told*: counted
29 *cold*: rejected   34 *palsy-lust*: paralysed or enfeebled lust
36 *Outbid*: Over-rated
38 '*Age . . . covetous*': quotation marks indicate a proverbial or quotable
phrase
39 *quit-rent*: paid by a freeholder to a landlord (here, figuratively, tragedy)
in lieu of services
42 *determined*: decided upon   46 *three-piled*: of fabric, luxurious
48 *clay*: mortal flesh   49 *little*: of low rank   49SD *[his]*: Q *her*
50 *vizard*: mask

Vindice. Puh,
    Thou play'st upon my meaning, prithee say
    Has that bald madam Opportunity
    Yet thought upon's? speak, are we happy yet?
    Thy wrongs and mine are for one scabbard fit.
Hippolito. It may prove happiness?
Vindice. What is't may prove?   60
    Give me to taste.
Hippolito. Give me your hearing then.
    You know my place at Court.
Vindice. Ay, the duke's chamber
    But 'tis a marvel thou'rt not turned out yet!
Hippolito. 'Faith I have been shoved at, but 'twas still my hap
    To hold by th' duchess' skirt, you guess at that.
    Whom such a coat keeps up can ne'er fall flat.
    But to the purpose.
    Last evening predecessor unto this,   70
    The duke's son warily inquired for me,
    Whose pleasure I attended: he began
    By policy to open and unhusk me
    About the time and common rumour.
    But I had so much wit to keep my thoughts
    Up in their built houses, yet afforded him
    An idle satisfaction without danger.
    But in the whole aim, and scope of his intent
    Ended in this: conjuring me in private
    To seek some strange-digested fellow forth,   80
    Of ill-contented nature; either disgraced
    In former times, or by new grooms displaced,
    Since his step-mother's nuptials; such a blood
    A man that were for evil only good:

55 *prithee*: I pray thee
56 *bald*: in the iconography of the period, Opportunity (Occasion) was pictured as bald, but with a long forelock to be grabbed to stop her escaping
66 *hap*: fortune   68 *coat*: petticoat   71 *warily*: watchfully
73 *policy*: craftiness   *unhusk*: strip the covering
76 *built houses*: i.e. shut away   77 *idle*: worthless
80 *strange-digested*: malcontent   82 *grooms*: manservants

To give you the true word, some base-coined pander.
Vindice. I reach you, for I know his heat is such.
    Were there as many concubines as ladies
    He would not be contained, he must fly out.
    I wonder how ill-featured, vile-proportioned
90 That one should be – if she were made for woman –
    Whom, at the insurrection of his lust,
    He would refuse for once. Heart, I think none
    Next to a skull, no more unsound than one,
    Each face he meets he strongly dotes upon.
Hippolito. Brother, y'have truly spoke him!
    He knows not you, but I'll swear you know him.
Vindice. And therefore I'll put on that knave for once,
    And be a right man then, a man a'th time;
    For to be honest is not to be i'the world.
100 Brother, I'll be that strange-composed fellow.
Hippolito. And I'll prefer you, brother.
Vindice. Go to then:
    The smallest advantage fattens wronged men.
    It may point out Occasion, if I meet her,
    I'll hold her by the fore-top fast enough;
    Or like the French mole heave up hair and all.
    I have a habit that will fit it quaintly –
    Here comes our mother.
Hippolito. And sister.
110 *Vindice.* We must coin.
    Women are apt, you know, to take false money,
    But I dare stake my soul for these two creatures.
    Only excuse excepted that they'll swallow,
    Because their sex is easy in belief. [*Enter Mother and Castiza.*]
Mother. What news from court, son Carlo?

85 *pander*: pimp, procurer   86 *reach*: understand
91 *insurrection*: rising   101 *prefer*: promote
102 *Go to*: Expression of impatience   105 *fore-top*: forelock
106 *French*: referring to venereal disease, which caused hair loss
107 *habit*: disguise   *quaintly*: in a cunning fashion
110 *coin*: invent, counterfeit   111 *take false money*: be tricked
113 *swallow*: be gullible

Hippolito. Faith, mother,
  'Tis whispered there the duchess' youngest son
  Has played a rape on Lord Antonio's wife.
Mother. On that religious lady?
Castiza. Royal blood! monster, he deserves to die,   120
  If Italy had no more hopes but he.
Vindice. Sister, y'have sentenced most direct, and true;
  The law's a woman, and would she were you.
  Mother, I must take leave of you.
Mother. Leave for what?
Vindice. I intend speedy travel.
Hippolito. That he does, Madam.
Mother. Speedy indeed!
Vindice. For, since my worthy father's funeral,
  My life's unnaturally to me, e'en compelled,   130
  As if I lived now when I should be dead.
Mother. Indeed, he was a worthy gentleman
  Had his state been fellow to his mind.
Vindice. The duke did much deject him.
Mother. Much!
Vindice. Too much.
  And through disgrace oft smothered in his spirit
  When it would mount; surely I think he died
  Of discontent, the nobleman's consumption.
Mother. Most sure he did!   140
Vindice. Did he? 'Lack – you know all
  You were his midnight secretary.
Mother. No:
  He was too wise to trust me with his thoughts.
Vindice. I'faith then father, thou wast wise indeed,
  'Wives are but made to go to bed and feed.'
  Come mother, sister: you'll bring me onward, brother?
Hippolito. I will.
Vindice. I'll quickly turn into another.   *Exeunt.*

121 *hopes*: heirs 123 *a woman*: the feminized image of Justice
130 *compelled*: forced 133 *state*: estate, money
134 *deject*: 'to lower in condition, to abase' (*OED*)
142 *secretary*: confidante

[ACT 1

Scene 2]

Enter the old Duke, Lussurioso, his son, the Duchess, the Bas-
tard, the Duchess' two sons Ambitioso and Supervacuo; the third
her youngest brought out with Officers for the rape; two judges.

Duke. Duchess, it is your youngest son: we're sorry,
   His violent act has e'en drawn blood of honour
   And stained our honours,
   Thrown ink upon the forehead of our state
   Which envious spirits will dip their pens into
   After our death, and blot us in our tombs.
   For that which would seem treason in our lives
   Is laughter when we're dead; who dares now whisper
   That dares not then speak out, and e'en proclaim
10   With loud words and broad pens our closest shame.
1 Judge. Your grace hath spoke like to your silver years,
   Full of confirmed gravity. For what is it to have
   A flattering false insculption on a tomb,
   And in men's hearts reproach? The 'bowelled corpse
   May be cered in, but with free tongue I speak:
   'The faults of great men through their cerecloths break.'
Duke. They do: we're sorry for't. It is our fate,
   To live in fear and die to live in hate.
   I leave him to your sentence. Doom him, lords –
20   The fact is great – whilst I sit by and sigh.
Duchess. [*Kneeling.*] My gracious lord, I pray: be merciful.
   Although his trespass far exceed his years,
   Think him to be your own as I am yours.
   Call him not son-in-law; the law, I fear,
   Will fall too soon upon his name and him.

10 *broad*: explicit, pronounced   13 *insculption*: carved inscription
14 *'bowelled*: disembowelled
15 *cered*: wrapped in cere- or grave-cloth; see also *Antonio's Revenge*, 2.1.1
note   19 *Doom*: Pronounce judgement   24 *son-in-law*: stepson

Temper his fault with pity?

Lussurioso. Good my lord:
   Then 'twill not taste so bitter and unpleasant
   Upon the judges' palate; for offences
   Gilt o'er with mercy, show like fairest women   30
   Good only for their beauties; which, washed off, no sin is
      uglier.

Ambitioso. I beseech your grace,
   Be soft and mild: let not relentless law,
   Look with an iron forehead on our brother.

Spurio. [*Aside*] He yields small comfort yet – hope he shall
      die –
   And if a bastard's wish might stand in force,
   Would all the court were turned into a corse.

Duchess. No pity yet? must I rise fruitless then,
   A wonder in a woman? Are my knees
   Of such low mettle that without respect –   40

1 Judge. Let the offender stand forth.
   'Tis the duke's pleasure that impartial doom
   Shall take first hold of his unclean attempt.
   A rape! Why, 'tis the very core of lust,
   Double adultery.

Junior. So, sir.

2 Judge. And which was worse,
   Committed on the Lord Antonio's wife,
   That general honest lady. Confess, my lord!
   What moved you to't?   50

Junior. Why, flesh and blood, my lord.
   What should move men unto a woman else?

Lussurioso. O do not jest thy doom, trust not an axe
   Or sword too far. The law is a wise serpent,
   And quickly can beguile thee of thy life.
   Though marriage only has made thee my brother,
   I love thee so far: play not with thy death.

Junior. I thank you, troth; good admonitions, 'faith,
   If I'd the grace now to make use of them.

---

37 *corse*: corpse   49 *general*: completely   54 *far*: much

60 *1 Judge.* That lady's name has spread such a fair wing
   Over all Italy, that if our tongues
   Were sparing toward the fact, judgement itself
   Would be condemned and suffer in men's thoughts.
Junior. Well then, 'tis done, and it would please me well
   Were it to do again. Sure she's a goddess,
   For I'd no power to see her and to live.
   It falls out true in this, for I must die:
   Her beauty was ordained to be my scaffold.
   And yet, methinks I might be easier ceased:
70 My fault being sport, let me but die in jest.
1 Judge. This be the sentence –
Duchess. O keep't upon your tongue, let it not slip,
   Death too soon steals out of a lawyer's lip.
   Be not so cruel-wise.
1 Judge. Your Grace must pardon us.
   'Tis but the justice of the law.
Duchess. The law
   Is grown more subtle than a woman should be.
Spurio. [*Aside*] Now, now he dies, rid 'em away.
80 *Duchess.* [*Aside*] O, what it is to have an old cool duke,
   To be as slack in tongue, as in performance.
1 Judge. Confirmed, this be the doom irrevocable –
Duchess. Oh!
1 Judge. Tomorrow early –
Duchess. Pray be abed, my lord.
1 Judge. Your grace much wrongs yourself.
Ambitioso. No, 'tis that tongue,
   Your too much right, does do us too much wrong.
1 Judge. Let that offender –
90 *Duchess.* Live, and be in health.
1 Judge. Be on a scaffold –
Duke. Hold, hold, my lord.
Spurio. [*Aside*] Pox on't,
   What makes my dad speak now?

80 *cool*: cold   81 *performance*: sexual potency
93 *Pox*: Expression of irritation or impatience

Duke. We will defer the judgement till next sitting.
  In the meantime let him be kept close prisoner.
  Guard bear him hence.
Ambitioso. Brother, this makes for thee;
  Fear not, we'll have a trick to set thee free.
Junior. Brother, I will expect it from you both, and in that   100
  I hope.
Supervacuo. Farewell, be merry.   *Exit [Junior] with a guard.*
Spurio. [*Aside*] Delayed, deferred, nay then, if judgement have
  cold blood,
  Flattery and bribes will kill it.
Duke. About it then my lords, with your best powers.
  More serious business calls upon our hours.
    Exeunt [all except] Duchess.
Duchess. Was ever known step-duchess was so mild,
  And calm as I? Some now would plot his death
  With easy doctors, those loose-living men,
  And make his withered grace fall to his grave,
  And keep church better?   110
  Some second wife would do this, and dispatch
  Her double-loathed lord at meat and sleep.
  Indeed, 'tis true an old man's twice a child:
  Mine cannot speak. One of his single words,
  Would quite have freed my youngest, dearest son
  From death or durance, and have made him walk
  With bold foot upon the thorny law,
  Whose prickles should bow under him. But 'tis not,
  And therefore wedlock faith shall be forgot.
  I'll kill him in his forehead, hate there feed: 120
  That wound is deepest though it never bleed.
  And here comes he whom my heart points unto:
                    [*Enter Spurio.*]
  His bastard son, but my love's true-begot.

---

98 *makes*: is advantageous   108 *easy*: ready, biddable
110 *better*: i.e. permanently   111 *dispatch*: kill   116 *durance*: imprisonment
119 *wedlock faith*: marital fidelity
120 *kill . . . forehead*: i.e. plant the cuckold's horn there

Many a wealthy letter have I sent him,
Swelled up with jewels, and the timorous man
Is yet but coldly kind.
That jewel's mine that quivers in his ear,
Mocking his master's chillness and vain fear.
He's spied me now.

130 *Spurio.* Madam? Your grace so private?
My duty upon your hand.
Duchess. Upon my hand, sir; troth, I think you'd fear,
To kiss my hand too if my lip stood there.
Spurio. Witness I would not, madam.   [*Kisses her.*]
Duchess. 'Tis a wonder,
For ceremony has made many fools.
It is as easy way unto a duchess,
As to a hatted-dame, if her love answer,
But that by timorous honours, pale respects,

140 Idle degrees of fear, men make their ways
Hard of themselves. What have you thought of me?
Spurio. Madam, I ever think of you, in duty,
Regard, and –
Duchess. Puh, upon my love I mean.
Spurio. I would 'twere love, but 'tis a fouler name
Than lust. You are my father's wife. Your grace may guess
now
What I would call it.
Duchess. Why, th'art his son but falsely;
'Tis a hard question whether he begot thee.

150 *Spurio.* I'faith 'tis true too; I'm an uncertain man
Of more uncertain woman; maybe his groom o'th'stable
begot me, you know I know not, he could ride a horse well,
a shrewd suspicion, marry – he was wondrous tall, he had
his length i'faith, for peeping over half-shut holiday windows;
men would desire him 'light. When he was afoot, he made a

124 *wealthy*: extravagant   130 *private*: solitary
138 *hatted-dame*: woman of lower class   145 *fouler name*: i.e. incest
154 *length*: bawdy pun, referring to the penis   155 *'light*: alight

goodly show under a penthouse, and when he rid, his hat
   would check the signs, and clatter barbers' basins.
Duchess. Nay, set you a-horseback once, you'll ne'er 'light off.
Spurio. Indeed, I am a beggar.
Duchess. That's the more sign thou'art great – but to our love: 160
   Let it stand firm both in thought and mind,
   That the duke was thy father, as no doubt then
   He bid fair for't, for thy injury is the more.
   For he hath cut thee a right diamond,
   Though hadst been set next in the dukedom's ring,
   When his worn self, like age's easy slave,
   Had dropped out of the collet into th'grave.
   What wrong can equal this? Canst thou be tame
   And think upon't?
Spurio. No, mad and think upon't.   170
Duchess. Who would not be revenged of such a father,
   E'en in the worst way? I would thank that sin
   That could most injury him, and be in league with it.
   Oh what a grief 'tis, that a man should live
   But once i'th' world, and then to live a bastard,
   The curse o'the womb, the thief of nature,
   Begot against the seventh commandment,
   Half-damned in the conception, by the justice
   Of that unbribed everlasting law.
Spurio. Oh I'd a hot-backed devil to my father.   180
Duchess. Would not this mad e'en patience, make blood rough?
   Who but an eunuch would not sin, his bed
   By one false minute disinherited?
Spurio. Ay, there's the vengeance that my birth was wrapped in,
   I'll be revenged for all: now hate begin,
   I'll call foul incest but a venial sin.
Duchess. Cold still? In vain then must a duchess woo?
Spurio. Madam, I blush to say what I will do.

156 *penthouse*: outhouse
156 *rid*: rode   157 *check*: knock
157 *basins*: set up outside barbers' shops
167 *collet*: setting or base of a cut diamond
177 *seventh commandment*: against adultery   186 *venial*: forgivable

Duchess. Thence flew sweet comfort, earnest, and farewell.
                                                 [*They kiss.*]
190 *Spurio.* Oh, one incestuous kiss picks open hell!
      Duchess. Faith now, old duke; my vengeance shall reach high.
      I'll arm thy brow with woman's heraldry.   *Exit.*
      Spurio. Duke, thou didst to me wrong, and by thy act
          Adultery is my nature;
          'Faith, if the truth were known, I was begot
          After some gluttonous dinner, some stirring dish
          Was my first father. When deep healths went round,
          And ladies' cheeks were painted red with wine,
          Their tongues, as short and nimble as their heels,
200   Uttering words sweet and thick; and when they rise,
          Were merrily disposed to fall again.
          In such a whispering and withdrawing hour,
          When base male-bawds kept sentinel at stairhead
          Was I stolen softly. O damnation met
          The sin of feasts. Drunken adultery,
          I feel it swell me; my revenge is just.
          I was begot in impudent wine and lust.
          Stepmother, I consent to thy desires;
          I love thy mischief well, but I hate thee,
210   And those three cubs thy sons, wishing confusion,
          Death and disgrace may be their epitaphs.
          As for my brother, the duke's only son,
          Whose birth is more beholding to report
          Then mine, and yet perhaps as falsely sown:
          Women must not be trusted with their own.
          I'll loose my days upon him, hate all I.
          Duke, on thy brow I'll draw my bastardy.
          For indeed a bastard by nature should make cuckolds,
          Because he is the son of a cuckold-maker.   *Exit.*

189 *earnest*: foretaste   197 *healths*: toasts
201 *fall*: fall down for sex or through drunkenness
202 *withdrawing*: retiring (to bed)   207 *impudent*: shameless
213 *beholding to report*: i.e. held to be legitimate   216 *loose*: devote

[ACT 1

Scene 3]

Enter Vindice and Hippolito; Vindice in disguise to attend Lord Lussurioso the Duke's son.

Vindice. What, brother? am I far enough from myself?
Hippolito. As if another man had been sent whole
  Into the world, and none wist how he came.
Vindice. It will confirm me bold: the child a'the court.
  Let blushes dwell i'th'country. Impudence,
  Thou goddess of the palace, mistress of mistresses
  To whom the costly perfumed people pray:
  Strike thou my forehead into dauntless marble,
  Mine eyes to steady sapphires, turn my visage,
  And if I must needs glow, let me blush inward   10
  That this immodest season may not spy
  That scholar in my cheeks, fool bashfulness,
  That maid in the old time, whose flush of grace
  Would never suffer to her to get good clothes.
  Our maids are wiser and are less ashamed.
  Save Grace the bawd, I seldom hear grace named!
Hippolito. Nay brother you reach out o'th'verge now.
                        [*Enter Lussurioso.*]
  'Sfoot, the duke's son: settle your looks.
Vindice. Pray let me not be doubted.
Hippolito. My lord –   20
Lussurioso. Hippolito? Be absent, leave us.
Hippolito. My lord, after long search, wary inquiries
  And politic siftings, I made choice of yon fellow,
  Whom I guess rare for many deep employments.
  This our age swims within him, and if time
  Had so much hair, I should take him for time,

---

3 *wist*: knew   8 *dauntless*: fearless   17 *out o'th'verge*: too far
18 *'Sfoot*: God's foot (oath)   23 *siftings*: searches

He is so near kin to this present minute.

Lussurioso. 'Tis enough.

    We thank thee: yet words are but great men's blanks.

30   Gold, though it be dumb, does utter the best thanks.

Hippolito. Your plenteous honour: an excellent fellow, my
    lord.

Lussurioso. So, give us leave. Welcome, be not far off, we must
    be better acquainted.

    Push, be bold with us, thy hand.

Vindice. With all my heart i'faith: how dost, sweet musk-cat?

    When shall we lie together?

Lussurioso. Wondrous knave!

    Gather him into boldness. 'Sfoot, the slave's

    Already as familiar as an ague,

    And shakes me at his pleasure. Friend, I can

40   Forget myself in private, but elsewhere,

    I pray you do remember me.

Vindice. Oh very well sir – I conster myself saucy!

Lussurioso. What hast been?

    Of what profession?

Vindice. A bone-setter.

Lussurioso. A bone-setter!

Vindice. A bawd, my lord,

    One that sets bones together.

Lussurioso. Notable bluntness!

50   Fit, fit for me, e'en trained up to my hand.

    Thou hast been scrivener to much knavery then?

Vindice. Fool, to abundance, sir. I have been witness

    To the surrenders of a thousand virgins;

    And not so little,

    I have seen patrimonies washed a-pieces

    Fruit-fields turned into bastards,

---

29 *blanks*: unsigned or incomplete payments
33 *Push*: Pish – an exclamation   34 *musk-cat*: prostitute or fop
38 *ague*: fever   40 *Forget*: Behave in a more relaxed way
41 *remember*: treat me according to my status
42 *conster*: construe, interpret   51 *scrivener*: secretary
55 *patrimonies*: inheritances

And in a world of acres,
Not so much dust due to the heir t'was left to
As would well gravel a petition.
Lussurioso. Fine villain! Troth, I like him wondrously. 60
He's e'en shaped for my purpose. Then thou knowst
I'th' world strange lust?
Vindice. O Dutch lust! fulsome lust!
Drunken procreation which begets so many drunkards.
Some father dreads not – gone to bed in wine – to slide from
the mother,
And cling the daughter-in-law.
Some uncles are adulterous with their nieces;
Brothers with brothers' wives: O hour of incest!
Any kin now next to the rim o'th' sister
Is man's meat in these days, and in the morning, 70
When they are up and dressed and their mask on,
Who can perceive this – save that eternal eye
That sees through flesh and all? Well, if anything be damned,
It will be twelve o'clock at night: that twelve
Will never 'scape;
It is the Judas of the hours, wherein
Honest salutation is betrayed to sin.
Lussurioso. In troth it is too, but let this talk glide.
It is our blood to err, though hell gaped loud.
Ladies know Lucifer fell, yet still are proud! 80
Now sir: wert thou as secret as thou'rt subtle,
And deeply fathomed into all estates
I would embrace thee for a near employment,
And thou shouldst swell in money, and be able
To make lame beggars crouch to thee.
Vindice. My lord?
Secret? I ne'er had that disease o'th' mother.
I praise my father. Why are men made close,

---

59 *gravel*: to blot ink with sand
63 *Dutch*: perhaps 'drunken' or 'excessive' 69 *rim*: limit
77 *Honest salutation*: Judas' kiss 78 *glide*: pass
80 *Lucifer*: fell from grace through pride 82 *estates*: social classes
87 *disease o'th'mother*: hysteria, gossiping

But to keep thoughts in best? I grant you this,

90   Tell but some woman a secret overnight,
Your doctor may find it in the urinal i'th' morning.
But, my lord –
Lussurioso. So, thou'rt confirmed in me
And thus I enter thee.   [*Gives him money.*]
Vindice. This Indian devil
Will quickly enter any man but a usurer.
He prevents that, by entering the devil first.
Lussurioso. Attend me: I am past my depth in lust,
And I must swim or drown. All my desires

100   Are levelled at a virgin not far from court,
To whom I have conveyed by messenger
Many waxed lines, full of my neatest spirit,
And jewels that were able to ravish her
Without the help of man; all which and more
She, foolish-chaste, sent back, the messengers,
Receiving frowns for answers.
Vindice. Possible?
'Tis a rare phoenix whoe'er she be.
If your desires be such, she so repugnant.

110   In troth, my lord, I'd be revenged, and marry her.
Lussurioso. Push: the dowry of her blood and of her fortunes
Are both too mean – good enough to be bad withal.
I'm one of that number can defend
Marriage is good: yet rather keep a friend.
Give me my bed by stealth: there's true delight.
What breeds a loathing in't, but night by night?
Vindice. A very fine religion.
Lussurioso. Therefore thus:
I'll trust thee in the business of my heart

120   Because I see thee well-experienced
In this luxurious day wherein we breathe.
Go thou, and with a smooth enchanting tongue
Bewitch her ears, and cozen her of all grace.

95 *Indian devil*: gold and silver (from the Indies)   102 *waxed*: sealed
109 *repugnant*: antagonistic   111 *blood*: status   114 *friend*: mistress
121 *luxurious*: lascivious

Enter upon the portion of her soul –
Her honour, which she calls her chastity –
And bring it into expense: for honesty
Is like a stock of money laid to sleep,
Which ne'er so little broke, does never keep.
Vindice. You have gi'en it the tang, i'faith, my lord.
  Make known the lady to me, and my brain   130
  Shall swell with strange invention; I will move it
  Till I expire with speaking, and drop down
  Without a word to save me; – but I'll work –
Lussurioso. We thank thee, and will raise thee. Receive her
  name: it is the only daughter to Madam Graziana, the late
  widow.
Vindice. [*Aside*] Oh, my sister, my sister!
Lussurioso. Why dost walk aside?
Vindice. My lord, I was thinking how I might begin,
  As thus, 'oh lady' – or twenty hundred devices: 140
  Her very bodkin will put a man in.
Lussurioso. Ay, or the wagging of her hair.
Vindice. No, that shall put you in, my lord.
Lussurioso. Shall't? Why content – dost know the daughter
  then?
Vindice. O excellent well, by sight.
Lussurioso. That was her brother
  That did prefer thee to us.
Vindice. My lord, I think so.
  I knew I had seen him somewhere –
Lussurioso. And therefore prithee let thy heart to him   150
  Be as a virgin, close.
Vindice. Oh me, good Lord.
Lussurioso. We may laugh at that simple age within him –
Vindice. Ha, ha, ha.
Lussurioso. Himself being made the subtle instrument
  To wind up a good fellow.
Vindice. That's I, my lord.

129 *tang*: flavour   134 *raise*: promote   141 *bodkin*: needle or hairpin
153 *simple*: naive   156 *wind up*: incite

Lussurioso. That's thou –

　　To entice and work his sister.

160　*Vindice.* A pure novice!

Lussurioso. 'Twas finely managed.

Vindice. Gallantly carried. A pretty-perfumed villain!

Lussurioso. I've bethought me,

　　If she prove chaste still and immovable,

　　Venture upon the mother, and with gifts

　　As I will furnish thee, begin with her.

Vindice. Oh fie, fie, that's the wrong end, my lord. 'Tis mere
　　impossible that a mother by any gifts should become a bawd
　　to her own daughter!

170　*Lussurioso.* Nay then, I see thou'rt but a puny in the subtle
　　mystery of a woman: why, 'tis held now no dainty dish. The
　　name is so in league with age that nowadays it does eclipse
　　three-quarters of a mother.

Vindice. Dost so, my lord?

　　Let me alone then to eclipse the fourth.

Lussurioso. Why, well said: come I'll furnish thee, but first
　　swear to be true in all.

Vindice. True?

Lussurioso. Nay, but swear!

180　*Vindice.* Swear? I hope your honour little doubts my faith.

Lussurioso. Yet for my humour's sake, 'cause I love swearing.

Vindice. 'Cause you love swearing, 'slud I will.

Lussurioso. Why, enough.

　　Ere long look to be made of better stuff.

Vindice. That will do well indeed, my lord.

Lussurioso. Attend me.　　　[*Exit.*]

Vindice. Oh.

　　Now let me burst, I've eaten noble poison.

　　We are made strange fellows, brother, innocent villains.

190　Wilt not be angry when thou hear'st on't, think'st thou?

　　I'faith, thou shalt. Swear me to foul my sister?

　　Sword I durst make a promise of him to thee.

170 *puny*: lightweight　172 *name*: i.e. 'bawd'　182 *'slud*: God's blood (oath)

Thou shalt dis-heir him, it shall be thine honour.
And yet now angry froth is down in me,
It would not prove the meanest policy
In this disguise to try the faith of both;
Another might have had the selfsame office,
Some slave that would have wrought effectually,
Ay, and perhaps o'erwrought 'em. Therefore I,
Being thought travelled, will apply myself   200
Unto the selfsame form, forget my nature,
As if no part about me were kin to 'em,
So touch 'em – though I durst almost for good
Venture my lands in heaven upon their good.

[ACT 1

Scene 4]

*Enter the discontented Lord Antonio, whose wife the Duchess'
youngest son ravished; he discovering the body of her, dead, to
certain Lords, [Piero] and Hippolito.*

Antonio. Draw nearer, lords, and be sad witnesses
    Of a fair comely building newly fallen,
    Being falsely undermined. Violent rape
    Has played a glorious act: behold, my lords
    A sight that strikes man out of me.
Piero. That virtuous lady.
Antonio. Precedent for wives.
Hippolito. The blush of many women, whose chaste pretence
    Would e'en call shame up to their cheeks,
    And make pale wanton sinners have good colours –   10
Antonio. Dead!
    Her honour first drunk poison, and her life,

193 *dis-heir*: prevent him from inheriting or getting heirs (by death)
OSD *discovering*: revealing   7 *Precedent*: Exemplar

Being fellows in one house did pledge her honour.

Piero. O grief of many!

Antonio. I marked not this before:
A prayerbook the pillow to her cheek,
This was her rich confection, and another
Placed in her right hand, with a leaf tucked up,
Pointing to these words:

20   *Melius virtute mori, quam per dedecus vivere.*
True and effectual it is indeed.

Hippolito. My lord, since you invite us to your sorrows,
Let's truly taste 'em, that with equal comfort,
As to ourselves we may relieve your wrongs.
We have grief too, that yet walks without tongue.
Curae leves loquuntur, majores stupent.

Antonio. You deal with truth my lord:
Lend me but your attentions, and I'll cut
Long grief into short words. Last revelling night,

30   When torchlight made an artificial moon
About the court, some courtiers in the masque
Putting on better faces than their own,
Being full of fraud and flattery: amongst whom,
The duchess' youngest son – that moth to honour –
Filled up a room, and with long lust to eat
Into my wearing, amongst all the ladies
Singled out that dear form, who ever liv'd
As cold in lust as she is now in death –
Which that step-duchess' monster knew too well –

40   And therefore in the height of all the revels,
When music was hard loudest, courtiers busiest,
And ladies great with laughter – O vicious minute!
Unfit but for relation to be spoke of –
Then with a face more impudent than his vizard

---

13 *pledge*: toast, assent   17 *confection*: medicine; sweetmeat
20 *Melius . . . vivere*: 'Better to die virtuous than live with dishonour'
26 *Curae . . . stupent*: from Seneca's *Hippolytus*: 'Small cares speak out,
greater ones are dumb'
31 *masque*: Q maske; entertainment   34 *moth*: destroyer
36 *wearing*: clothing   41 *hard*: intensely

He harried her amidst a throng of panders,
That live upon damnation of both kinds,
And fed the ravenous vulture of his lust.
O death to think on't! She, her honour forced,
Deemed it a nobler dowry for her name
To die with poison than to live with shame. 50
Hippolito. A wondrous lady of rare fire compact
Sh'as made her name an empress by that fact.
Piero. My lord, what judgement follows the offender?
Antonio. 'Faith, none, my lord: it cools and is deferred.
Piero. Delay the doom for rape?
Antonio. O you must note who 'tis should die.
The duchess' son, she'll look to be a saver,
'Judgement in this age is near kin to favour.'
Hippolito. Nay then, step forth thou bribeless officer.
[*Draws his sword.*]
I bind you all in steel to bind you surely: 60
Here let your oaths meet, to be kept and paid,
Which else will stick like rust, and shame the blade.
Strengthen my vow, that if at the next sitting,
Judgement speak all in gold and spare the blood
Of such a serpent, e'en before their seats,
To let his soul out, which long since was found
Guilty in heaven.
All. We swear it and will act it.
Antonio. Kind gentlemen, I thank you in mine ire.
Hippolito. 'Twere pity 70
The ruins of so fair a monument
Should not be dipped in the defacer's blood.
Piero. Her funeral shall be wealthy, for her name
Merits a tomb of pearl: my Lord Antonio,
For this time wipe your lady from your eyes.
No doubt our grief and yours may one day court it,
When we are more familiar with revenge.
Antonio. That is my comfort, gentleman, and I joy

45 *harried*: raped 51 *compact*: composed 58 *near*: Q ne'er
63 *sitting*: court hearing

In this one happiness above the rest,
80   Which will be called a miracle at last:
That, being an old man, I'd a wife so chaste.   *Exeunt.*

ACT 2

Scene 1

Enter Castiza the sister.

Castiza. How hardly shall that maiden be beset
Whose only fortunes are her constant thoughts,
That has no other child's part but her honour,
That keeps her low, and empty in estate.
Maids and their honours are like poor beginners,
Were not sin rich there would be fewer sinners.
Why had not virtue a revenue? Well,
I know the cause: would have impoverished hell.
                                        [*Enter Dondolo.*]
How now, Dondolo.
10   *Dondolo.* Madonna, there is one, as they say, a thing of flesh
and blood: a man I take him, by his beard, that would very
desirously mouth to mouth with you.
Castiza. What's that?
Dondolo. Show his teeth in your company.
Castiza. I understand thee not.
Dondolo. Why speak with you, madonna!
Castiza. Why, say so madman, and cut a great deal of dirty
way. Had it not been better spoke in ordinary words that one
would speak with me?
20   *Dondolo.* Ha, ha, that's as ordinary as two shillings! I would
strive a little to show myself in my place: a gentleman-usher
scorns to use the phrase and fancy of a servingman.

---

1 *hardly*: severely   10 *Madonna*: Respectful term for an Italian woman
21 *gentleman-usher*: a higher rank of attendant

Castiza. Yours be your own, sir: go direct him hither.
  I hope some happy tidings from my brother
  That lately travelled, whom my soul affects.
  Here he comes.
    Enter Vindice her brother disguised.
Vindice. Lady, the best of wishes to your sex.
  Fair skins and new gowns.
Castiza. Oh they shall thank you sir.   [*He gives her a letter.*]
  Whence thus?   30
Vindice. Oh from a dear and worthy friend, mighty.
Castiza. From whom?
Vindice. The duke's son.
Castiza. Receive that!   *A box o'th' ear to her Brother.*
  I swore I'd put anger in my hand
  And pass the virgin limits of my self,
  To him that next appeared in that base office,
  To be his sins' attorney. Bear to him
  That figure of my hate upon thy cheek
  Whilst 'tis yet hot, and I'll reward thee for't.   40
  Tell him my honour shall have a rich name,
  When several harlots shall share his with shame.
  Farewell, commend me to him in my hate!   *Exit.*
Vindice. It is the sweetest box
  That e'er my nose came nigh,
  The finest drawn-work cuff that e'er was worn.
  I'll love this blow forever, and this cheek
  Shall still hence forward take the wall of this.
  Oh I'm above my tongue! Most constant sister,
  In this thou hast right honourable shown;   50
  Many are called by their honour that have none,
  Thou art approved forever in my thoughts.
  It is not in the power of words to taint thee.
  And yet for the salvation of my oath,
  As my resolve in that point, I will lay
  Hard siege unto my mother – though I know

23 *own*: Q one 38 *attorney*: representative 46 *drawn-work*: decorated
48 *take the wall*: allow the privilege of walking protected on the wall-side

A siren's tongue could not bewitch her so.   [*Enter Mother.*]
Mass, fitly here she comes; thanks my disguise.
Madam, good afternoon.
60 *Mother.* Y'are welcome sir.
Vindice. The next of Italy commends him to you:
Our mighty expectation, the duke's son.
Mother. I think myself much honoured, that he pleases
To rank me in his thoughts.
Vindice. So may you, lady.
One that is like to be our sudden duke,
The crown gapes for him every tide, and then
Commander o'er us all: do but think on him.
How blest were they now that could pleasure him
70 E'en with anything, almost.
Mother. Ay, save their honour.
Vindice. Tut, one would let a little of that go too
And ne'er be seen in't: ne'er be seen in't, mark you,
I'd wink and let it go –
Mother. Marry, but I would not.
Vindice. Marry, but I would, I hope; I know you would too,
If you'd that blood now which you gave your daughter.
To her indeed 'tis this wheel comes about.
That man that must be all this – perhaps ere morning
80 For his white father does but mould away –
Has long desired your daughter.
Mother. Desired?
Vindice. Nay, but hear me,
He desires now that will command hereafter,
Therefore be wise: I speak more as a friend
To you then him. Madam, I know y'are poor,
And 'lack the day, there are too many poor ladies already.
Why should you vex the number? 'Tis despised.

---

57 *siren*: in Greek mythology, mermaids with beautiful singing voices who
lured sailors to their death
58 *Mass*: Used in oaths
61 *next*: heir   66 *sudden*: imminent   67 *tide*: hour
74 *wink*: nod, shut (my) eyes to   80 *white*: aged   *mould*: decline
87 *'lack the day*: lackaday: unfortunately   88 *vex*: aggravate

Live wealthy, rightly understand the world,
And chide away that foolish country girl   90
Keeps company with your daughter: chastity.
Mother. Oh fie, fie, the riches of the world cannot hire a mother
    to such a most unnatural task!
Vindice. No, but a thousand angels can.
    Men have no power; angels must work you to it.
    The world descends into such baseborn evils
    That forty angels can make fourscore devils.
    There will be fools still, I perceive, still fool.
    Would I be poor, dejected, scorned of greatness,
    Swept from the palace, and see other daughters   100
    Spring with the dew o'th court, having mine own
    So much desired and loved – by the duke's son?
    No, I would raise my state upon her breast
    And call her eyes my tenants; I would count
    My yearly maintenance upon her cheeks;
    Take coach upon her lip; and all her parts
    Should keep men after men; and I would ride
    In pleasure upon pleasure:
    You took great pains for her once when it was:
    Let her requite it now, though it be but some.   110
    You brought her forth, she may well bring you home.
Mother. O heavens! This overcomes me.
Vindice. [*Aside*] Not, I hope, already?
Mother. It is too strong for me. Men know that know us,
    We are so weak their words can overthrow us.
    He touched me nearly, made my virtues 'bate
    When his tongue struck upon my poor estate.
Vindice. [*Aside*] I e'en quake to proceed. My spirit turns edge?
    I fear me she's unmothered, yet I'll venture:
    'That woman is all male, whom none can enter.'   120
    What think you now, lady: speak, are you wiser?
    What said advancement to you? Thus it said:
    The daughter's fall lifts up the mother's head:

94 *angels*: gold coins   103 *state*: estate
107 *keep men*: keep servants; lovers   116 *nearly*: deeply   *'bate*: abate
118 *turns edge*: is blunted   119 *unmothered*: unmotherly

Did it not, madam? but I'll swear it does
In many places. Tut, this age fears no man –
''Tis no shame to be bad, because 'tis common.'
Mother. Ay, there's the comfort on't.
Vindice. The comfort on't!
I keep the best for last: can these persuade you
130   To forget heaven – and –   [*Gives her money.*]
Mother. Ay, these are they –
Vindice. Oh!
Mother. That enchant our sex.
These are the means that govern our affections. That woman
will not be troubled with the mother long, that sees the
comfortable shine of you. I blush to think what for your
sakes I'll do!
Vindice. [*Aside*] Oh suffering heaven with thy invisible finger
E'en at this instant turn the precious side
140   Of both mine eyeballs inward, not to see myself.
Mother. Look you sir.
Vindice. Holla.
Mother. Let this thank your pains.   [*Gives him money.*]
Vindice. O, you're a kind madam;
Mother. I'll see how I can move.
Vindice. Your words will sting.
Mother. If she be still chaste, I'll ne'er call her mine.
Vindice. [*Aside*] Spoke truer than you meant it,
Mother. Daughter Castiza?   [*Enter Castiza.*]
150 *Castiza.* Madam?
Vindice. O she's yonder. Meet her.
[*Aside*] Troops of celestial soldiers guard her heart,
Yon dam has devils enough to take her part.
Castiza. Madam, what makes yon evil-officed man
In presence of you?
Mother. Why?
Castiza. He lately brought
Immodest writing sent from the duke's son

142 *Holla*: Exclamation meaning 'Stop!'   144 *madam*: Q Mad-man
153 *dam*: mother

To tempt me to a dishonourable act.
Mother. Dishonourable act? Good honourable fool,   160
    That wouldst be honest 'cause thou wouldst be so,
    Producing no one reason but thy will.
    And 't'as a good report, prettily commended,
    But pray, by whom? Mean people, ignorant people:
    The better sort I'm sure cannot abide it.
    And by what rule shouldst we square our lives,
    But by our betters' actions? Oh if thou knewest
    What t'were to lose it, thou would never keep it.
    But there's a cold curse laid upon all maids,
    Whilst other clip the sun, they clasp the shades!   170
    Virginity is paradise locked up.
    You cannot come by yourselves without fee,
    And it was decreed that man should keep the key.
    Deny advancement, treasure, the duke's son?
Castiza. I cry you mercy, lady. I mistook you:
    Pray, did you see my mother? which way went you?
    Pray God I have not lost her.
Vindice. [*Aside*] Prettily put by.
Mother. Are you as proud to me as coy to him?
    Do you not know me now?   180
Castiza. Why are you she?
    The world's so changed, one shape into another,
    It is a wise child now that knows her mother!
Vindice. Most right i'faith.
Mother. I owe your cheek my hand,
    For that presumption now, but I'll forget it.
    Come, you shall leave those childish haviours,
    And understand your time. Fortunes flow to you.
    What, will you be a girl?
    If all feared drowning that spy waves ashore,   190
    Gold would grow rich, and all the merchants poor.
Castiza. It is a pretty saying of a wicked one, but methinks now
    It does not show so well out of your mouth:

170 *clip*: embrace   176 *mother*: in the proverbial saying, 'father'
187 *haviours*: behaviours   190 *ashore*: from the shore

Better in his.
Vindice. [*Aside*] I'faith bad enough in both,
Were I in earnest as I'll seem no less?
I wonder, lady, your own mother's words,
Cannot be taken, nor stand in full force.
'Tis honesty you urge; what's honesty?
200 'Tis but heaven's beggar: and what woman is so foolish to
keep honesty
And be not able to keep herself? No,
Times are grown wiser and will keep less charge.
A maid that has small portion now intends
To break up house, and live upon her friends.
How blest are you: you have happiness alone.
Others must fall to thousands, you to one,
Subservient in himself to make your forehead
Dazzle the world with jewels, and petitionary people
Start at your presence.
210 *Mother.* Oh if I were young, I should be ravished.
Castiza. Ay, to lose your honour.
Vindice. 'Slid, how can you lose your honour
To deal with my lord's grace?
He'll add more honour to it by his title:
Your mother will tell you how.
Mother. That I will.
Vindice. O, think upon the pleasure of the palace:
Secured ease and state; the stirring meats
Ready to move out of the dishes that e'en now quicken when
they're eaten;
220 Banquets abroad by torchlight; music, sports,
Bare-headed vassals, that had ne'er the fortune
To keep on their own hats, but let horns wear 'em;
Nine coaches waiting – hurry, hurry, hurry.
Castiza. Ay, to the devil.

203 *portion*: money   204 *friends*: lovers
207–8 *forehead . . . jewels*: fashionable jewellery for the forehead
208 *petitionary people*: commoners presenting petitions at court
212 *'Slid*: God's eyelid (oath)   221 *vassals*: servants
222 *horns*: i.e. of cuckoldry

Vindice. [*Aside*] Ay, to the devil – to th'duke by my faith.

Mother. Ay, to the duke: daughter you'd scorn to think o'th'
   Devil and you were there once.

Vindice. True, for most there are as proud as he for his heart
   i'faith.
   Who'd sit at home in a neglected room,
   Dealing her short-lived beauty to the pictures   230
   That are as useless as old men, when those
   Poorer in face and fortune than herself,
   Walk with a hundred acres on their backs,
   Fair meadows cut into green foreparts – oh,
   It was the greatest blessing ever happened to women;
   When farmers' sons agreed and met again
   To wash their hands, and come up gentlemen.
   The commonwealth has flourished ever since.
   Lands that were mete by the rod, that labour's spared:
   Tailors ride down, and measure 'em by the yard.   240
   Fair trees, those comely foretops of the field
   Are cut to maintain head-tires. Much untold,
   All thrives but chastity: she lies a-cold.
   Nay shall I come nearer to you? mark but this:
   Why there are so few honest women, but because 'tis the
   poorer profession. That's accounted best, that's best fol-
   lowed; least in trade, least in fashion; and that's not honesty,
   believe it, and do but note the love and dejected price of it:
   'Lose but a pearl, we search and cannot brook it.   250
   But that once gone, who is so mad to look it?'

Mother. Troth, he says true.

Castiza. False, I defy you both.
   I have endured you with an ear of fire.
   Your tongues have struck hot irons on my face.
   Mother, come from that poisonous woman there.

Mother. Where?

Castiza. Do you not see her? she's too inward then.

---

233 *hundred acres*: i.e. in clothes of great equivalent value
234 *foreparts*: ornamental breast-covering   239 *mete*: measured
239 *rod*: land measure   242 *head-tires*: fashionable headdresses
242 *untold*: not counted   251 *look*: worry   258 *inward*: internal

Slave, perish in thy office: you heavens please
260   Henceforth to make the mother a disease
       Which first begins with me; yet I've outgone you.   *Exit.*
Vindice. [*Aside*] O angels, clap your wings upon the skies,
       And give this virgin crystal plaudities!
Mother. Peevish, coy, foolish! But return this answer:
       My lord shall be most welcome, when his pleasure
       Conducts him this way. I will sway mine own;
       Women with women can work best alone.   *Exit.*
Vindice. Indeed I'll tell him so.
       O more uncivil, more unnatural,
270   Than those base-titled creatures that look downward:
       Why does not heaven turn black, or with a frown
       Undo the world? why does not earth start up,
       And strike the sins that tread upon't? oh:
       Wer't not for gold and women, there would be no damnation;
       Hell would look like a lord's great kitchen without fire in't.
       But, 'twas decreed before the world began,
       That they should be the hooks to catch at man.   *Exit.*

ACT 2

Scene 2

Enter Lussurioso, with Hippolito, Vindice's brother.

Lussurioso. I much applaud thy judgement: thou art well-read
       in a fellow,
       And 'tis the deepest art to study man.
       I know this, which I never learnt in schools,
       The world's divided into knaves and fools.
Hippolito. [*Aside*] Knave in your face, my lord behind your back.
Lussurioso. And I much thank thee, that thou hast preferred

263 *plaudities*: applause   270 *base-titled creatures*: beasts

A fellow of discourse, well-mingled,
And whose brain time hath seasoned.
Hippolito. True my lord,
We shall find season once I hope. [*Aside*] O villain!   10
    To make such an unnatural slave of me, but –
                                            [*Enter Vindice, disguised.*]
Lussurioso. Mass, here he comes.
Hippolito. [*Aside*] And now shall I have free leave to depart.
Lussurioso. Your absence, leave us.
Hippolito. Are not my thoughts true?
    I must remove, but brother you may stay.
    Heart, we are both made bawds a new-found way.   *Exit.*
Lussurioso. Now, we're an even number! A third man's
        dangerous,
    Especially her brother. Say, be free;
    Have I a pleasure toward?   20
Vindice. Oh, my lord.
Lussurioso. Ravish me in thine answer, art thou rare,
    Hast thou beguiled her of salvation
    And rubbed hell o'er with honey? Is she a woman?
Vindice. In all but desire.
Lussurioso. Then she's in nothing. I bate in courage now.
Vindice. The words I brought
    Might well have made indifferent honest naught.
    A right good woman in these days is changed
    Into white money with less labour far;   30
    Many a maid has turned to Mahomet,
    With easier working; I durst undertake
    Upon the pawn and forfeit of my life,
    With half those words to flat a Puritan's wife;
    But she is close and good. Yet 'tis a doubt by this time? oh
        the mother, the mother!
Lussurioso. I never thought their sex had been a wonder
    Until this minute. What fruit from the mother?
Vindice. [*Aside*] Now must I blister my soul, be forsworn,

---

7 *discourse*: conversation   20 *toward*: future   26 *bate*: cease
30 *white money*: silver   31 *Mahomet*: Islam   34 *flat*: seduce
35 *close*: reserved

40   Or shame the woman that received me first.
        I will be true, thou livest not to proclaim;
        Spoke to a dying man, shame has no shame.
        My lord.
Lussurioso. Who's that?
Vindice. Here's none but I, my lord.
Lussurioso. What would thou haste utter?
Vindice. Comfort.
Lussurioso. Welcome.
Vindice. The maid being dull, having no mind to travel
50   Into unknown land, what did me I straight,
        But set spurs to the mother? Golden spurs
        Will put her to a false gallop in a trice.
Lussurioso. Is't possible that in this
        The mother should be damned before the daughter?
Vindice. Oh, that's good manners my lord: the mother for her
        age must go foremost, you know.
Lussurioso. Thou'st spoke that true, but where comes in this
            comfort?
Vindice. In a fine place my lord: the unnatural mother,
60   Did with her tongue so hard beset her honour,
        That the poor fool was struck to silent wonder.
        Yet still the maid, like an unlighted taper,
        Was cold and chaste, save that her mother's breath,
        Did blow fire on her cheeks. The girl departed,
        But the good ancient madam, half-mad, threw me
        These promising words, which I took deeply note of:
        'My lord shall be most welcome –'
Lussurioso. 'Faith, I thank her.
Vindice. '– when his pleasure conducts him this way.'
70 *Lussurioso.* That shall be soon, i'faith.
Vindice. 'I will sway mine own.'
Lussurioso. She does the wiser; I commend her for't.
Vindice. 'Women with women can work best alone.'

40 *received*: greeted
52 *false gallop*: canter   62 *taper*: candle

Lussurioso. By this light and so they can, give 'em their due;
   men are not comparable to 'em.

Vindice. No that's true, for you shall have one woman knit
   more in an hour than any man can ravel again in seven and
   twenty year.

Lussurioso. Now my desires are happy, I'll make 'em freemen
   now.
   Thou art a precious fellow, 'faith I love thee.   80
   Be wise and make it thy revenue: beg, leg,
   What office couldst thou be ambitious for?

Vindice. Office, my lord? Marry, if I might have my wish
   I would have one that was never begged yet.

Lussurioso. Nay, then thou canst have none.

Vindice. Yes my lord, I could pick out another office yet, nay
   and keep a horse and drab upon't.

Lussurioso. Prithee good bluntness, tell me.

Vindice. Why I would desire but this my lord: to have all the
   fees behind the arras, and all the farthingales that fall plump   90
   about twelve o'clock at night upon the rushes.

Lussurioso. Thou'rt a mad apprehensive knave; dost think to
   make any great purchase of that?

Vindice. Oh 'tis an unknown thing, my lord; I wonder 't'as
   been missed so long.

Lussurioso. Well this night I'll visit her, and 'tis till then
   A year in my desires. Farewell, attend;
   Trust me with thy preferment.   *Exit.*

Vindice. My loved lord.
   Oh, shall I kill him a th' wrong side now? No!   100
   Sword, thou wast never a back-biter yet.
   I'll pierce him to his face; he shall die looking upon me.
   Thy veins are swelled with lust; this shall unfill 'em,
   Great men were gods; if beggers could not kill 'em.
   Forgive me heaven, to call my mother wicked.

---

77 *ravel*: unravel 81 *leg*: bow 87 *drab*: whore
90 *fees behind the arras*: fees for arranging liaisons behind the tapestry or
arras (a joke about Jacobean monopolies)
90 *farthingales*: hooped skirts 92 *apprehensive*: quick, intelligent
93 *purchase*: profit 100 *wrong side*: i.e. in the back

Oh, lessen not my days upon the earth.
I cannot honour her, by this I fear me
Her tongue has turned my sister into use.
I was a villain not to be forsworn
To this our lecherous hope, the duke's son;
For lawyers, merchants, some divines and all,
Count beneficial perjury a sin small.
It shall go hard yet, but I'll guard her honour
And keep the ports sure.   *Enter Hippolito.*
Hippolito. Brother, how goes the world? I would know news of
      you,
      But I have news to tell you.
Vindice. What, in the name of knavery?
Hippolito. Knavery, 'faith.
      This vicious old duke's worthily abused:
      The pen of his bastard writes him cuckold!
Vindice. His bastard?
Hippolito. Pray believe it, he and the duchess
      By night meet in their linen; they have been seen
      By stairfoot panders!
Vindice. Oh sin foul and deep;
      Great faults are winked at when the duke's asleep.
                                 [*Enter Spurio and servants.*]
      See, see here comes the Spurio.
Hippolito. Monstrous luxur!
Vindice. Unbraced; two of his valiant bawds with him.
      O there's a wicked whisper. Hell is in his ear.
      Stay: let's observe his passage –   [*They remain unobserved.*]
Spurio. Oh, but are you sure on't?
Servant. My lord, most sure on't, for 'twas spoke by one
      That is most inward with the duke's son's lust:
      That he intends within this hour to steal
      Unto Hippolito's sister, whose chaste life
      The mother has corrupted for his use.

110

120

130

---

108 *use*: prostitution   112 *beneficial perjury*: lies for a good motive
114 *ports*: gates   119 *worthily*: appropriately   120 *pen*: penis
129 *Unbraced*: Clothes loosened   134 *inward*: intimate

Spurio. Sweet word, sweet occasion; 'faith then, brother:
  I'll disinherit you in as short time
  As I was when I was begot in haste.   140
  I'll damn you at your pleasure; a precious deed
  After your lust. Oh, 'twill be fine to bleed.
  Come, let our passing out be soft and wary.   *Exeunt.*
Vindice. Mark, there, there, that step now to the duchess.
  This their second meeting writes the duke cuckold
  With new additions; his horns newly revived.
  Night! thou that look'st like funeral heralds' fees
  Torn down betimes i'th' morning, thou hang'st fittly
  To grace those sins that have no grace at all.
  Now 'tis full sea abed over the world;   150
  There's juggling of all sides. Some that were maids
  E'en at sunset are now perhaps i'th' toll-book.
  This woman in immodest thin apparel
  Lets in her friend by water; here a dame
  Cunning, nails leather hinges to a door,
  To avoid proclamation.
  Now cuckolds are a-coining: apace, apace, apace, apace!
  And careful sisters spin that thread i'th'night
  That does maintain them and their bawds i'th'day!
Hippolito. You flow well, brother.   160
Vindice.   Puh, I'm shallow yet,
  Too sparing and too modest. Shall I tell thee,
  If every trick were told that's dealt by night
  There are few here that would not blush outright.
Hippolito. I am of that belief too.
Vindice. Who's this comes?   [*Enter Lussurioso.*]
  The duke's son up so late! Brother, fall back,
                         [*Hippolito hides.*]

---

146 *additions*: passages   150 *full sea*: high tide
151 *juggling*: sexual behaviour
152 *toll-book*: record of animals sold at market and, thus, prostituted
154 *by water*: i.e. by boat
156 *proclamation*: squeaking hinges giving away the secret
157 *a-coining*: being coined   160 *flow*: talk smoothly

And you shall learn some mischief. My good lord.
Lussurioso. Piato, why the man I wished for. Come:
170 I do embrace this season for the fittest
 To taste of that young lady.
Vindice. [*Aside*] Heart and hell.
Hippolito. [*Aside*] Damned villain.
Vindice. [*Aside*] I have no way now to cross it, but to kill him.
Lussurioso. Come, only thou and I.
Vindice. My lord, my lord.
Lussurioso. Why dost thou start thus?
Vindice. I'd almost forgot – the bastard!
Lussurioso. What of him?
180 *Vindice.* This night, this hour – this minute now!
Lussurioso. What? What?
Vindice. Shadows the duchess –
Lussurioso. Horrible word!
Vindice. And, like strong poison, eats
 Into the duke your father's forehead.
Lussurioso. Oh!
Vindice. He makes horn royal.
Lussurioso. Most ignoble slave!
Vindice. This is the fruit of two beds.
190 *Lussurioso.* I am mad!
Vindice. That passage he trod warily –
Lussurioso. He did?
Vindice. And hushed his villains every step he took.
Lussurioso. His villains? confound them!
Vindice. Take 'em finely, finely now.
Lussurioso. The duchess' chamber door shall not control me!
             Exeunt.
Hippolito. Good, happy, swift: there's gunpowder i'th' court,
 Wild-fire at midnight in this heedless fury.
 He may show violence to cross himself:
200 I'll follow the event. *Exit.*

169 *Piato*: Vindice's alter ego; the word means, according to Florio's *Worlde of Wordes* (1598): 'made flat, razed or level to the ground, hidden, squatted, close, hushed, secret, lurking, cowering down flat'
182 *Shadows*: Covers 191 *warily*: secretly 199 *cross*: thwart

ACT 2

Scene 3

*[The Duke and Duchess in bed.] Enter again [Lussurioso and
Vindice].*

Lussurioso. Where is that villain?
Vindice. Softly, my lord, and you may take 'em twisted.
Lussurioso. I care not how!
Vindice. Oh 'twill be glorious,
  To kill 'em doubled, when they're heaped. Be soft, my lord.
Lussurioso. Away, my spleen is not so lazy: thus and thus,
  I'll shake their eyelids ope, and with my sword
  Shut 'em again for ever. Villain, strumpet!
Duke. You upper guard defend us!
Duchess. Treason, treason!   10
Duke. Oh take me not in sleep! I have great sins, I must have
    days,
  Nay months, dear son, with penitential heaves
  To lift 'em out, and not to die unclear.
  O thou wilt kill me both in heaven and here!
Lussurioso. I am amazed to death.
Duke. Nay villain, traitor –
  Worse than the foulest epithet – now I'll grip thee
  E'en with the nerves of wrath, and throw thy head
  Amongst the lawyers. Guard!
    *Enter [Hippolito], Nobles and sons [Supervacuo and
    Ambitioso].*
1 Noble. How comes the quiet of your grace disturbed?   20
Duke. This boy that should be myself after me,
  Would be myself before me; and in heat
  Of that ambition bloodily rushed in
  Intending to depose me in my bed!

---

2 *twisted*: entwined 7 *ope*: open 12 *heaves*: groans
14 *in heaven*: i.e. kill my soul because unconfessed

2 Noble. Duty and natural loyalty forfend!

Duchess. He called his father villain; and me strumpet,
    A word that I abhor to 'file my lips with.

Ambitioso. That was not so well done, brother.

Lussurioso. I am abused. I know there's no excuse can do me
    good.

30 *Vindice.* [*Aside*] 'Tis now good policy to be from sight.
    His vicious purpose to our sister's honour
    Is crossed beyond our thought.

Hippolito. [*Aside*] You little dreamed his father slept here?

Vindice. [*Aside*] Oh 'twas far beyond me,
    But since it fell so without frightful word –
    Would he had killed him; would have eased our sword.

Duke. Be comforted, our duchess, he shall die.

                    [*Vindice and Hippolito*] *dissemble a flight.*

Lussurioso. Where's this slave-pander now? Out of mine eye,
    Guilty of this abuse.

        Enter Spurio with his villains.

40 *Spurio.* Y'are villains, fablers,
    You have knaves' chins and harlots' tongues, you lie,
    And I will damn you with one meal a day!

1 Servant. O good my lord!

Spurio. 'Sblood, you shall never sup.

2 Servant. O, I beseech you sir.

Spurio. To let my sword catch cold so long and miss him.

1 Servant. Troth my lord – 'twas his intent to meet there.

Spurio. Heart he's yonder.
    Ha? what news here? Is the day out o'th' socket

50 That it is noon at midnight, the court up?
    How comes the guard so saucy with his elbows?

Lussurioso. The bastard here?
    Nay then the truth of my intent shall out.
    My lord and father hear me –

Duke. Bear him hence.

25 *forfend*: forbid
26 *strumpet*: 'a debauched or unchaste woman' (*OED*)   27 *'file*: defile
37SD *dissemble a flight*: leave stealthily   49 *out o'th' socket*: out of joint

Lussurioso. I can with loyalty excuse –
Duke. Excuse? To prison with the villain,
  Death shall not long lag after him.
Spurio. Good, i'faith; then 'tis not much amiss.
Lussurioso. Brothers, my best release lies on your tongues.   60
  I pray persuade for me.
Ambitioso. It is our duties: make yourself sure of us.
Supervacuo. We'll sweat in pleading.
Lussurioso. And I may live to thank you.   *Exeunt.*
Ambitioso. No, thy death shall thank me better.
Spurio. He's gone: I'll after him
  And know his trespass, seem to bear a part
  In all his ills, but with a Puritan heart.   *Exit.*
Ambitioso. Now brother, let our hate and love be woven
  So subtly together, that in speaking one word for his life,   70
  We may make three for his death.
  The craftiest pleader gets most gold for breath.
Supervacuo. Set on, I'll not be far behind you, brother.
Duke. Is't possible a son should be disobedient as far as the
  sword? It is the highest; he can go no farther.
Ambitioso. My gracious lord, take pity –
Duke. Pity, boys?
Ambitioso. Nay we'd be loath to move your grace too much;
  We know the trespass is unpardonable,
  Black, wicked, and unnatural,   80
Supervacuo. In a son, oh monstrous!
Ambitioso. Yet my lord,
  A duke's soft hand strokes the rough head of law,
  And makes it lie smooth.
Duke. But my hand shall ne'er do't.
Ambitioso. That as you please, my lord.
Supervacuo. We must needs confess,
  Some father would have entered into hate
  So deadly pointed, that before his eyes
  He would have seen the execution sound   90

68 *Puritan*: Hypocritical 90 *sound*: complete

Without corrupted favour.

Ambitioso. But my lord,
Your grace may live the wonder of all times,
In pardoning that offence which never yet
Had face to beg a pardon.

Duke. Honey, how's this?

Ambitioso. Forgive him, good my lord: he's your own son,
And I must needs say 'twas the vildlier done.

Supervacuo. He's the next heir: yet this true reason gathers,
100   None can possess that dispossess their fathers.
Be merciful –

Duke. [*Aside*] Here's no stepmother's wit;
I'll try 'em both upon their love and hate.

Ambitioso. Be merciful – although –

Duke. You have prevailed.
My wrath like flaming wax hath spent itself.
I know 'twas but some peevish moon in him: go, let him be
released.

Supervacuo. [*Aside*] 'Sfoot, how now brother?

Ambitioso. Your grace doth please to speak beside your spleen.
110   I would it were so happy.

Duke. Why, go release him.

Supervacuo. O my good lord, I know the fault's too weighty,
And full of general loathing; too inhuman.
Rather by all men's voices, worthy death.

Duke. 'Tis true too; here then, receive this signet. Doom
shall pass.
Direct it to the judges: he shall die
Ere many days. Make haste.

Ambitioso. All speed that may be,
We could have wished his burden not so sore,
120   We knew your grace did but delay before.   *Exeunt.*

Duke. Here's envy with a poor thin cover o'er't,
Like scarlet hid in lawn, easily spied through.

95 *face*: boldness   96 *Honey*: Sweet words   98 *vildlier*: more vilely
107 *moon*: temporary madness   122 *lawn*: thin linen

This their ambition by the mother's side
Is dangerous, and for safety must be purged.
I will prevent their envies, for sure it was
But some mistaken fury in our son,
Which these aspiring boys would climb upon.
He shall be released suddenly.   *Enter Nobles.*
1 Noble. Good morning to your grace.
Duke. Welcome, my lords.   130
2 Noble. Our knees shall take away the office of our feet
    for ever,
  Unless your grace bestow a father's eye
  Upon the clouded fortunes of your son;
  And in compassionate virtue grant him that
  Which makes e'en mean men happy; liberty.
Duke. [*Aside*] How seriously their loves and honours woo
  For that, which I am about to pray them to do.
  Which, rise, my lords: your knees sign his release.
  We freely pardon him.
1 Noble. We owe your grace much thanks, and he much duty.   140
                                                 Exeunt.
Duke. It well becomes that judge to nod at crimes,
  That does commit greater himself and lives.
  I may forgive a disobedient error,
  That expect pardon for adultery
  And in my old days am a youth in lust.
  Many a beauty have I turned to poison
  In the denial, covetous of all.
  Age hot is like a monster to be seen:
  My hairs are white, and yet my sins are green.

128 *suddenly*: immediately   147 *denial*: rejection
148 *hot*: lecherous   149 *green*: youthful

ACT 3

Scene 1

Enter Ambitioso and Supervacuo.

Supervacuo. Brother, let my opinion sway you once.
   I speak it for the best, to have him die
   Surest and soonest. If the signet come
   Unto the judge's hands, why then his doom,
   Will be deferred till sittings and court days:
   Juries and further; faiths are bought and sold,
   Oaths in these days are but the skin of gold.
Ambitioso. In troth, 'tis true too.
Supervacuo. Then let's set by the judges
10   And fall to the officers. 'Tis but mistaking
   The duke our father's meaning, and where he named
   'Ere many days', 'tis but forgetting that
   And have him die i'th'morning.
Ambitioso. Excellent.
   Then am I heir – duke in a minute!
Supervacuo. [*Aside*] Nay,
   And he were once puffed out, here is a pin
   Should quickly prick your bladder.
Ambitioso. Blest occasion!
20   He being packed, we'll have some trick and wile
   To wind our younger brother out of prison,
   That lies in for the rape. The lady's dead,
   And people's thoughts will soon be buried.
Supervacuo. We may with safety do't, and live and feed:
   The duchess' sons are too proud to bleed.
Ambitioso. We are i'faith to say true: come let's not linger.
   I'll to the officers, go you before,
   And set an edge upon the executioner.

7 *skin*: covering 9 *set by*: put aside 19 *occasion*: opportunity
20 *packed*: finished off 28 *set an edge*: prepare

Supervacuo. Let me alone to grind him.   *Exit.*
Ambitioso. Meet: farewell.   30
   I am next now. I rise just in that place,
   Where thou'rt cut off. Upon thy neck, kind brother,
   The falling of one head lifts up another.   *Exit.*

ACT 3

Scene 2

Enter with the Nobles, Lussurioso from prison.

Lussurioso. My lords: I am so much indebted to your loves,
   For this, O this delivery.
1 Noble. But our duties, my lord, unto the hopes that grow in
    you.
Lussurioso. If ere I live to be myself, I'll thank you.
   O liberty, thou sweet and heavenly dame;
   But hell for prison is too mild a name.   *Exeunt.*

ACT 3

Scene 3

Enter Ambitioso and Supervacuo with Officers.

Ambitioso. Officers? Here's the duke's signet, your firm
   warrant,
   Brings the command of present death along with it
   Unto our brother, the duke's son. We are sorry
   That we are so unnaturally employed
   In such an unkind office, fitter far

2 *present*: immediate

For enemies than brothers.
Supervacuo. But you know
   The duke's command must be obeyed.
1 Officer. It must and shall, my lord. This morning then,
10   So suddenly?
Ambitioso. Ay, alas poor – good – soul.
   He must break fast betimes: the executioner
   Stands ready to put forth his cowardly valour.
2 Officer. Already?
Supervacuo. Already i'faith. O sir, destruction hies,
   And that is least impudent, soonest dies.
1 Officer. Troth, you say true my lord. We take our leaves,
   Our office shall be sound; we'll not delay
   The third part of a minute.
20 *Ambitioso.* Therein you show
   Yourselves good men and upright officers.
   Pray let him die as private as he may.
   Do him that favour, for the gaping people
   Will but trouble him at his prayers,
   And make him curse, and swear, and so die black.
   Will you be so far kind?
1 Officer. It shall be done, my lord.
Ambitioso. Why we do thank you, if we live to be,
   You shall have a better office.
30 *2 Officer.* Your good lordship.
Supervacuo. Commend us to the scaffold in our tears.
1 Officer. We'll weep and do your commendations.
                                   Exeunt [Officers].

Ambitioso. Fine fools in office!
Supervacuo. Things fall out so fit.
Ambitioso. So happily, come brother: ere next clock,
   His head will be made serve a bigger block. *Exeunt.*

12 *betimes*: early   15 *hies*: comes near   25 *black*: sinful

ACT 3

Scene 4

Enter in prison, Junior Brother.

Junior. Keeper.   [*Enter Keeper.*]
Keeper. My lord.
Junior. No news lately from our brothers?
   Are they unmindful of us?
Keeper. My lord, a messenger came newly in and brought this
   from 'em.   [*Gives him a letter.*]
Junior. Nothing but paper comforts?
   I looked for my delivery before this,
   Had they been worth their oaths. Prithee be from us.
                                             [*Exit.*]
   Now what you say forsooth: speak out I pray.   10
[*Reads*] *Letter*: 'Brother be of good cheer,' –
   'Slid, it begins like a whore with good cheer –
   'Thou shalt not be long a prisoner.'
   Not five and thirty year like a bankrupt, I think so.
   'We have thought upon a device to get thee out by a trick!'
   By a trick, pox o'your trick, and it be so long a-playing.
   'And so rest comforted, be merry and expect it suddenly.'
   Be merry? Hang merry; draw and quarter merry, I'll be mad.
   Is't not strange that a man should lie in a whole month for a
   woman? Well, we shall see how sudden our brothers will be   20
   in their promise: I must expect still a trick! I shall not be long
   a prisoner. [*Enter Keeper.*] How now, what news?
Keeper. Bad news, my lord: I am discharged of you.
Junior. Slave call'st thou that bad news? I thank you, brothers.
Keeper. My lord 'twill prove so: here come the officers
   Into whose hands I must commit you.   [*Enter Officers.*]

---

4 *unmindful*: forgetful   7 *delivery*: release
19 *lie in*: with a pun on childbirth

Junior. Ha, officers? what, why?

1 Officer. You must pardon us, my lord.
Our office must be sound: here is our warrant
30   The signet from the duke. You must straight suffer.

Junior. Suffer? I'll suffer you to be gone; I'll suffer you
To come no more; what would you have me suffer?

2 Officer. My lord, those words were better changed to prayers.
The time's but brief with you: prepare to die.

Junior. Sure, 'tis not so.

3 Officer. It is too true, my lord.

Junior. I tell you 'tis not, for the duke my father
Deferred me till next sitting, and I look
E'en every minute, threescore times an hour.
40   For a release, a trick wrought by my brothers.

1 Officer. A trick, my lord? If you expect such comfort,
Your hope's as fruitless as a barren woman.
Your brothers were the unhappy messengers
That brought this powerful token for your death.

Junior. My brothers? No, no!

2 Officer. 'Tis most true, my lord.

Junior. My brothers to bring a warrant for my death?
How strange this shows.

3 Officer. There's no delaying time.

50   *Junior.* Desire 'em hither. Call 'em up, my brothers?
They shall deny it to your faces.

1 Officer. My lord,
They're far enough by this, at least at court,
And this most strict command they left behind 'em.
When grief swum in their eyes they showed like brothers,
Brimful of heavy sorrow: but the duke
Must have his pleasure.

Junior. His pleasure?

1 Officer. These were their last words which my memory bears:
60   'Commend us to the scaffold in our tears.'

Junior. Pox! dry their tears, what should I do with tears?
I hate 'em worse than any citizen's son

Can hate salt water. Here came a letter now,
New-bleeding from their pens, scarce stinted yet.
Would I'd been torn in pieces when I tore it!
Look, you officious whoresons! Words of comfort:
'Not long a prisoner.'
1 Officer. It says true in that, sir, for you must suffer
    presently.
Junior. A villainous Duns upon the letter: knavish exposition!
    Look you then here sir: 'we'll get you out by a trick' says he.   70
2 Officer. That may hold too sir, for you know a trick is
    commonly four cards, which was meant by us four officers.
Junior. Worse and worse dealing.
1 Officer. The hour beckons us,
    The headsman waits. Lift up your eyes to heaven.
Junior. I thank you, faith: good pretty wholesome counsel.
    I should look up to heaven as you said,
    Whilst he behind me cozens me of my head:
    Ay, that's the trick.
3 Officer. You delay too long, my lord.   80
Junior. Stay, good authority's bastards. Since I must
    Through brothers' perjury die, O let me venom
    Their souls with curses.
1 Officer. Come, 'tis no time to curse.
Junior. Must I bleed then, without respect of sign? well –
    My fault was sweet sport, which the world approves,
    I die for that which every woman loves.   *Exeunt.*

63 *hate salt water*: because of the dangers and unfamiliarity of the sea
69 *Duns*: Duns Scotus, medieval theologian associated with specious
arguments   75 *headsman*: executioner   78 *cozens*: tricks
81 *Stay*: Hold   85 *sign*: astrological sign

ACT 3

Scene 5

Enter Vindice with Hippolito his brother.

Vindice. O sweet, delectable, rare, happy, ravishing!
Hippolito. Why, what's the matter, brother?
Vindice. O, 'tis able to make a man spring up and knock
   his forehead
  Against yon silver ceiling.
Hippolito. Prithee tell me,
  Why may I not partake with you? You vowed once
  To give me share to every tragic thought.
Vindice. By th'mass, I think I did too.
  Then I'll divide it to thee: the old duke,
10 Thinking my outward shape and inward heart
  Are cut out of one piece – for he that prates his secrets,
  His heart stands o'th'outside – hires me by price,
  To greet him with a lady,
  In some fit place, veiled from the eyes o'th'court,
  Some darkened blushless angle, that is guilty
  O'his forefather's lusts, and great folks' riots.
  To which I easily, to maintain my shape,
  Consented, and did wish his impudent grace
  To meet her here in this unsunned lodge,
20 Wherein 'tis night at noon; and here the rather
  Because, unto the torturing of his soul,
  The bastard and the duchess have appointed
  Their meeting too in this luxurious circle,
  Which most afflicting sight will kill his eyes
  Before we kill the rest of him.
Hippolito. 'Twill i'faith, most dreadfully digested:
  I see not how you could have missed me, brother.

---

4 *ceiling*: sky 11 *prates*: babbles 15 *blushless*: shameless
17 *shape*: disguise 27 *missed me*: left me out

Vindice. True, but the violence of my joy forgot it.
Hippolito. Ay, but where's that lady now?
Vindice. Oh, at that word   30
  I'm lost again: you cannot find me yet.
  I'm in a throng of happy apprehensions.
  He's suited for a lady. I have took care
  For a delicious lip, a sparkling eye.
  You shall be witness brother;
  Be ready stand with your hat off.   *Exit.*
Hippolito. Troth, I wonder what lady it should be?
  Yet 'tis no wonder, now I think again,
  To have a lady stoop to a duke, that stoops unto his men.
  'Tis common to be common through the world: 40
  And there's more private common shadowing vices,
  Than those who are known both by their names and prices.
  'Tis part of my allegiance to stand bare
  To the duke's concubine – and here she comes.
    Enter Vindice, with the skull of his love dressed up in tires.
Vindice. Madam, his grace will not be absent long.
  Secret? Ne'er doubt us, madam. 'Twill be worth
  Three velvet gowns to your ladyship. Known?
  Few ladies respect that. Disgrace? A poor thin shell;
  'Tis the best grace you have to do it well.
  I'll save your hand that labour: I'll unmask you.   50
Hippolito. Why brother, brother.
Vindice. Art thou beguiled now? Tut, a lady can
  At such, all hid, beguile a wiser man.
  Have I not fitted the old surfeiter
  With a quaint piece of beauty? Age and bare bone
  Are e'er allied in action. Here's an eye
  Able to tempt a great man – to serve God;
  A pretty hanging lip, that has forgot now to dissemble –
  Methinks this mouth should make a swearer tremble,
  A drunkard clasp his teeth, and not undo 'em,   60
  To suffer wet damnation to run through 'em.

---

39 *stoop*: submit   40 *be common*: be sexually experienced
43 *bare*: bareheaded   44SD *tires*: costume   54 *surfeiter*: indulger

Here's a cheek keeps her colour: let the wind go whistle,
Spout rain, we fear thee not; be hot or cold,
All's one with us; and is not he absurd,
Whose fortunes are upon their faces set,
That fear no other God but wind and wet?
Hippolito. Brother, y'have spoke that right.
Is this the form that living shone so bright?
Vindice. The very same.

70 And now methinks I could e'en chide myself,
For doting on her beauty, though her death
Shall be revenged after no common action.
Does the silkworm expend her yellow labours
For thee? For thee does she undo herself?
Are lordships sold to maintain ladyships
For the poor benefit of a bewitching minute?
Why does yon fellow falsify highways
And put his life between the judge's lips.
To refine such a thing, keeps horse and men

80 To beat their valours for her?
Surely we're all mad people, and they
Whom we think are, are not: we mistake those.
'Tis we are mad in sense, they but in clothes.
Hippolito. Faith and in clothes too we, give us our due.
Vindice. Does every proud and self-affecting dame
Camphor her face for this, and grieve her maker
In sinful baths of milk, when many an infant starves,
In her superfluous outside, for all this?
Who now bids twenty pound a night, prepares

90 Music, perfumes, and sweetmeats: all are hushed.
Thou mayst lie chaste now! It were fine, methinks,
To have thee seen at revels, forgetful feasts,

75 *lordships*: estates
77 *falsify highways*: obscure, perhaps suggesting highway robbery or
impersonating the higher classes
79 *refine*: make more refined   80 *valours*: strengths
85 *self-affecting*: vain
86 *Camphor*: White, scented substance used as a cosmetic
88 *superfluous*: excessive   92 *forgetful*: not conscious of death

And unclean brothels. Sure, 'twould fright the sinner
And make him a good coward, put a reveller
Out off his antic amble,
And cloy an epicure with empty dishes!
Here might a scornful and ambitious woman,
Look through and through herself – see ladies, with false
    forms,
You deceive men, but cannot deceive worms.
Now to my tragic business. Look you, brother,   100
I have not fashioned this only for show
And useless property; no, it shall bear a part
E'en in its own revenge. This very skull,
Whose mistress the duke poisoned, with this drug,
The mortal curse of the earth, shall be revenged
In the like strain, and kiss his lips to death.
As much as the dumb thing can, he shall feel:
What fails in poison, we'll supply in steel.
Hippolito. Brother, I do applaud thy constant vengeance,
    The quaintness of thy malice, above thought.   110
Vindice. So 'tis laid on: now come and welcome, duke,
    I have her for thee. I protest it, brother:
    Methinks she makes almost as fair a sign
    As some old gentlewoman in a periwig.
    Hide thy face now for shame, thou hadst need have a mask
        now.
    'Tis vain when beauty flows, but when it fleets,
    This would become graves better than the streets.
Hippolito. You have my voice in that. Hark, the duke's come.
Vindice. Peace, let's observe what company he brings,
    And how he does absent 'em, for you know   120
    He'll wish all private. Brother, fall you back a little
    With the bony lady.
Hippolito. That I will.
Vindice. So, so, now nine years' vengeance crowd into a minute!
    [*Enter Duke with Gentleman.*]

102 *property*: stage prop   110 *quaintness*: cunning   113 *sign*: show
116 *fleets*: leaves

Duke. You shall have leave to leave us, with this charge,
  Upon your lives, if we be missed by the duchess
  Or any of the nobles, to give out
  We're privately rid forth.
Vindice. [*Aside*] Oh happiness!
130 *Duke.* With some few honourable gentlemen you may say:
  You may name those that are away from court.
Gentleman. Your will and pleasure shall be done my lord.
                                                                    [*Exit.*]
Vindice. [*Aside*] 'Privately rid forth',
  He strives to make sure work on't. Your good grace?
Duke. Piato, well done. Hast brought her; what lady is't?
Vindice. 'Faith my lord, a country lady: a little bashful at first
  as most of them are, but after the first kiss, my lord, the
  worst is past with them. Your grace knows now what you
  have to do. She's somewhat a grave look with her – but –
140 *Duke.* I love that best: conduct her.
Vindice. [*Aside*] Have at all!
                                    [*Brings forward the dressed skull.*]
Duke. In gravest looks the greatest faults seem less:
  Give me that sin that's robed in holiness.
Vindice. [*Aside*] Back with the torch; brother raise the perfumes.
Duke. How sweet can a duke breathe? Age has no fault.
  Pleasure should meet in a perfumed mist.
  Lady, sweetly encountered. I came from court; I must be bold
    with you –   [*Kisses the skull.*]
  Oh, what's this, oh!
Vindice. Royal villain, white devil!
150 *Duke.* Oh!
Vindice. Brother, place the torch here, that his affrighted eyeballs
  May start into those hollows. Duke, dost know
  Yon dreadful vizard? View it well, 'tis the skull
  Of Gloriana whom thou poisonedst last.
Duke. Oh, 't'as poisoned me.
Vindice. Didst not know that till now?
Duke. What are you two?

149 *white devil*: hypocrite

Vindice. Villains all three. The very ragged bone
  Has been sufficiently revenged.
Duke. Oh Hippolito? call treason.   160
Hippolito. Yes, my good lord. Treason, treason, treason.
                                   Stamping on him.
Duke. Then I'm betrayed.
Vindice. Alas, poor lecher in the hands of knaves;
  A slavish duke is baser than his slaves.
Duke. My teeth are eaten out.
Vindice. Hadst any left?
Hippolito. I think but few.
Vindice. Then those that did eat are eaten.
Duke. O my tongue!
Vindice. Your tongue? 'twill teach you to kiss closer,   170
  Not like a slobbering Dutchman. You have eyes still:
  Look monster, what a lady hast thou made me,
  My once-betrothed wife.
Duke. Is it thou, villain, nay then –
Vindice. 'Tis I, 'tis Vindice, 'tis I.
Hippolito. And let this comfort thee: our lord and father
  Fell sick upon the infection of thy frowns,
  And died in sadness. Be that thy hope of life.
Duke. Oh!
Vindice. He had his tongue, yet grief made him die speechless.   180
  Puh, 'tis but early yet. Now I'll begin
  To stick thy soul with ulcers; I will make
  Thy spirit grievous sore: it shall not rest,
  But like some pestilent man toss in thy breast. Mark me, duke:
  Thou'rt a renowned, high, and mighty cuckold.
Duke. Oh!
Vindice. Thy bastard, thy bastard rides a-hunting in thy brow.
Duke. Millions of deaths!
Vindice. Nay to afflict thee more,
  Here in this lodge they meet for damned clips.   190
  Those eyes shall see the incest of their lips.

171 *slobbering*: Q flobbering   177 *frowns*: disfavour
187 *brow*: location of the cuckold's horns

Duke. Is there a hell besides this, villains?
Vindice. Villain?
　　Nay heaven is just; scorns are the hires of scorns.
　　I ne'er knew yet adulterer without horns.
Hippolito. Once ere they die, 'tis quitted.　　[*Music within.*]
Vindice. Hark the music:
　　Their banquet is prepared, they're coming –
Duke. Oh, kill me not with that sight.
200　*Vindice.* Thou shalt not lose that sight for all thy dukedom.
Duke. Traitors, murderers!
Vindice. What? Is not thy tongue eaten out yet?
　　Then we'll invent a silence. Brother, stifle the torch.
Duke. Treason, murder!
Vindice. Nay 'faith, we'll have you hushed. Now with thy
　　　　dagger
　　Nail down his tongue, and mine shall keep possession
　　About his heart, if he but gasp he dies.
　　We dread not death to quittance injuries, brother.
　　If he but wink, not brooking the foul object,
210　Let our two other hands tear up his lids,
　　And make his eyes, like comets, shine through blood.
　　When the bad bleeds, then is the tragedy good.
Hippolito. Whist, brother, music's at our ear: they come.
　　　　Enter the bastard [Spurio] meeting the Duchess.
Spurio. Had not that kiss a taste of sin, 'twere sweet.
Duchess. Why there's no pleasure sweet but it is sinful.
Spurio. True, such a bitter sweetness fate hath given,
　　Best side to us, is the worst side to heaven.
Duchess. Push, come: 'tis the old duke thy doubtful father,
　　The thought of him rubs heaven in thy way;
220　But I protest by yonder waxen fire,
　　Forget him, or I'll poison him.
Spurio. Madam, you urge a thought which ne'er had life.
　　So deadly do I loathe him for my birth
　　That if he took me hasped within his bed,

196 *quitted*: requited　208 *quittance*: repay　209 *wink*: close his eyes
209 *brooking*: bearing　213 *Whist*: Hush　218 *doubtful*: uncertain
224 *hasped*: embraced

I would add murder to adultery,
    And with my sword give up his years to death.
Duchess. Why, now thou'rt sociable, let's in and feast.
    Loudest music sound; pleasure is banquet's guest.   *Exeunt.*
Duke. I cannot brook –
Vindice. The brook is turned to blood.   230
Hippolito. Thanks to loud music.
Vindice. 'Twas our friend indeed,
    'Tis state, in music for a duke to bleed:
    The dukedom wants a head, though yet unknown:
    As fast as they peep up, let's cut 'em down.   *Exeunt.*

ACT 3

Scene 6

Enter the Duchess' two sons, Ambitioso and Supervacuo.

Ambitioso. Was not his execution rarely plotted?
    We are the duke's sons now.
Supervacuo. Ay, you may thank my policy for that.
Ambitioso. Your policy, for what?
Supervacuo. Why wast not my invention, brother,
    To slip the judges? And in lesser compass,
    Did not I draw the model of his death,
    Advising you to sudden officers,
    And e'en extemporal execution?
Ambitioso. Heart, 'twas a thing I thought on too.   10
Supervacuo. You thought on't too: 'sfoot, slander not your
        thoughts
    With glorious untruth. I know 'twas from you.
Ambitioso. Sir I say, 'twas in my head.
Supervacuo. Ay, like your brains then,
    Ne'er to come out as long as you lived.

233 *state*: stately   234 *head*: leader   3 *policy*: strategy

Ambitioso. You'd have the honour on't forsooth, that your wit
    Lead him to the scaffold.
Supervacuo. Since it is my due,
    I'll publish't, but I'll ha't in spite of you.
20 *Ambitioso.* Methinks y'are much too bold, you should a little
    Remember us, brother: next to be honest duke.
Supervacuo. Ay, it shall be as easy for you to be duke,
    As to be honest, and that's never, i'faith.
Ambitioso. Well, cold he is by this time, and because
    We're both ambitious, be it our amity,
    And let the glory be shared equally.
Supervacuo. I am content to that.
Ambitioso. This night our younger brother shall out of prison.
    I have a trick.
30 *Supervacuo.* A trick, prithee what is't?
Ambitioso. We'll get him out by a wile.
Supervacuo. Prithee, what wile?
Ambitioso. No sir, you shall not know it, till't be done,
    For then you'd swear 'twere yours.
                    [*Enter an officer carrying a decapitated head.*]
Supervacuo. How now, what's he?
Ambitioso. One of the officers.
Supervacuo. Desired news.
Ambitioso. How now, my friend?
Officer. My lords, under your pardon, I am allotted
40   To that desertless office, to present you
    With the yet bleeding head.
Supervacuo. [*Aside*] Ha, ha, excellent!
Ambitioso. [*Aside*] All's sure our own. Brother, canst weep,
        think'st thou?
    'Twould grace our flattery much. Think of some dame,
    'Twill teach thee to dissemble.
Supervacuo. I have thought – now for yourself.
Ambitioso. Our sorrows are so fluent,
    Our eyes o'erflow our tongues, words spoke in tears
    Are like the murmurs of the waters, the sound
50   Is loudly heard, but cannot be distinguished.
Supervacuo. How died he, pray?

Officer. O, full of rage and spleen.
Supervacuo. He died most valiantly then; we're glad to hear it.
Officer. We could not woo him once to pray.
Ambitioso. He showed himself a gentleman in that: give him
    his due.
Officer. But in the stead of prayer, he drew forth oaths.
Supervacuo. Then did he pray, dear heart,
    Although you understood him not.
Officer. My lords,
    E'en at his last – with pardon be it spoke –   60
    He cursed you both.
Supervacuo. He cursed us? 'Las, good soul.
Ambitioso. It was not in our powers, but the duke's pleasure,
[*Aside*] Finely dissembled o'both sides, sweet fate,
    O happy opportunity!
      Enter Lussurioso.
Lussurioso. Now my lords.
Both. Oh!
Lussurioso. Why do you shun me, brothers?
    You may come nearer now;
    The savour of the prison has forsook me.   70
    I thank such kind lords as yourselves, I'm free.
Ambitioso. Alive!
Supervacuo. In health!
Ambitioso. Released?
    We were both e'en amazed with joy to see it.
Lussurioso. I am much to thank you.
Supervacuo. 'Faith, we spared no tongue unto my lord the duke.
Ambitioso. I know your delivery, brother,
    Had not been half so sudden but for us.
Supervacuo. O, how we pleaded.   80
Lussurioso. Most deserving brothers.
      In my best studies I will think of it. *Exit Lussurioso.*
Ambitioso. O death and vengeance!
Supervacuo. Hell and torments!
Ambitioso. Slave, cam'st thou here to delude us?

54 *woo*: persuade   62 *'Las*: Alas   70 *savour*: smell

Officer. Delude you my lords?

Supervacuo. Ay, villain, where's this head now?

Officer. Why here, my lord:

   Just after his delivery, you both came

90   With warrant from the duke to behead your brother.

Ambitioso. Ay, our brother, the duke's son.

Officer. The duke's son, my lord, had his release before you came.

Ambitioso. Whose head's that then?

Officer. His whom you left command for, your own brother's.

Ambitioso. Our brother's? O furies –

Supervacuo. Plagues!

Ambitioso. Confusions!

Supervacuo. Darkness!

Ambitioso. Devils!

100 *Supervacuo.* Fell it out so accursedly?

Ambitioso. So damnedly?

Supervacuo. Villain, I'll brain thee with it.

Officer. O, my good lord!

Supervacuo. The devil overtake thee.

Ambitioso. O fatal!

Supervacuo. O prodigious to our bloods!

Ambitioso. Did we dissemble?

Supervacuo. Did we make our tears women for thee?

Ambitioso. Laugh and rejoice for thee?

110 *Supervacuo.* Bring warrant for thy death?

Ambitioso. Mock off thy head?

Supervacuo. You had a trick, you had a wile forsooth.

Ambitioso. A murrain meet 'em, there's none of these wiles

   that ever come to good. I see now, there is nothing sure in

   mortality, but mortality. Well, no more words; shalt be

   revenged, i'faith.

   Come, throw off clouds now, brother: think of vengeance,

   And deeper settled hate. Sirrah, sit fast,

   We'll pull down all, but thou shalt down at last.   *Exeunt.*

113 *murrain*: plague

ACT 4

Scene 1

Enter Lussurioso with Hippolito.

Lussurioso. Hippolito.
Hippolito. My lord.
  Has your good lordship aught to command me in?
Lussurioso. I prithee, leave us.
Hippolito. [*Aside*] How's this? come and leave us?
Lussurioso. Hippolito.
Hippolito. Your honour – I stand ready for any duteous
    employment.
Lussurioso. Heart, what mak'st thou here?
Hippolito. [*Aside*] A pretty lordly humour.
  He bids me to be present, to depart. Something has stung his   10
  honour?
Lussurioso. Be nearer, draw nearer:
  Ye're not so good methinks. I'm angry with you.
Hippolito. With me, my lord? I'm angry with my self for't.
Lussurioso. You did prefer a goodly fellow to me:
  'Twas wittily elected; 'twas, I thought
  Had been a villain; and he proves a knave?
  To me a knave.
Hippolito. I chose him for the best, my lord.
  'Tis much my sorrow, if neglect in him breed discontent
  in you.
Lussurioso. Neglect? 'Twas will: judge of it.   20
  Firmly to tell, an incredible act
  Not to be thought, less to be spoken of
  'Twixt my stepmother and the bastard, oh,
  Incestuous sweets between 'em.
Hippolito. Fie my lord.

---

9 *humour*: mood   14 *prefer*: recommend   15 *wittily*: wisely
20 *will*: intentional   25 *Fie*: Exclamation expressing disgust or reproach

Lussurioso. I in kind loyalty to my father's forehead
Made this a desperate arm, and in that fury,
Committed treason on the lawful bed;
And with my sword e'en rac'd my father's bosom,
30   For which I was within a stroke of death.
Hippolito. Alack, I'm sorry: [*Aside*] 'sfoot, just upon the stroke
Jars in my brother, 'twill be villainous music.
      Enter Vindice.
Vindice. My honoured lord.
Lussurioso. Away! Prithee forsake us: hereafter we'll not know
thee.
Vindice. Not know me, my lord? Your lordship cannot choose.
Lussurioso. Begone I say; thou art a false knave.
Vindice. Why the easier to be known, my lord.
Lussurioso. Push, I shall prove too bitter with a word;
Make thee a perpetual prisoner,
40   And lay this iron age upon thee.
Vindice. [*Aside*] Mum, for there's a doom would make a
woman dumb.
Missing the bastard next him: the wind's come about;
Now 'tis my brother's turn to stay, mine to go out.
                                             Exit Vindice.
Lussurioso. Has greatly moved me.
Hippolito. Much to blame, i'faith.
Lussurioso. But I'll recover to his ruin. 'Twas told me lately,
I know not whether falsely, that you'd a brother.
Hippolito. Who, I? Yes, my good lord, I have a brother.
Lussurioso. How chance the court ne'er saw him? of what
nature?
50   How does he apply his hours?
Hippolito. 'Faith, to curse fates,
Who, as he thinks, ordained him to be poor;
Keeps at home full of want and discontent.
Lussurioso. There's hope in him, for discontent and want
Is the best clay to mould a villain of.
Hippolito, with him repair to us;

29 *rac'd*: scratched   40 *iron age*: fetters   50 *apply*: spend

If there be aught in him to please our blood,
For thy sake we'll advance him, and build fair
His meanest fortunes: for it is in us
To rear up towers from cottages.   60
Hippolito. It is so my lord: he will attend your honour,
  But he's a man in whom much melancholy dwells.
Lussurioso. Why the better: bring him to court.
Hippolito. With willingness and speed,
  Whom he cast off e'en now must now succeed.
[*Aside*] Brother, disguise must off;
  In thine own shape now, I'll prefer thee to him:
  How strangely does himself work to undo him.   *Exit.*
Lussurioso. This fellow will come fitly: he shall kill
  That other slave that did abuse my spleen,   70
  And made it swell to treason. I have put
  Much of my heart into him; he must die.
  He that knows great men's secrets and proves slight,
  That man ne'er lives to see his beard turn white:
  Ay, he shall speed him. I'll employ thee, brother,
  Slaves are but nails, to drive out one another.
  He being of black condition, suitable
  To want and ill content, hope of preferment
  Will grind him to an edge –   *The Nobles enter.*
1 Noble. Good days unto your honour.   80
Lussurioso. My kind lords, I do return the like.
2 Noble. Saw you my lord the duke?
Lussurioso. My lord and father, is he from court?
1 Noble. He's sure from court,
  But where, which way, his pleasure took we know not,
  Nor can we hear on't.
Lussurioso. Here come those should tell.
  Saw you my lord and father?
3 Noble. Not since two hours before noon, my lord,
  And then he privately rid forth.   90
Lussurioso. O, he's rode forth.
1 Noble. 'Twas wondrous privately.

64 *speed*: kill

2 *Noble.* There's none i'th'court had any knowledge on't.
Lussurioso. His grace is old and sudden: 'tis no treason
  To say the duke my father has a humour,
  Or such a toy about him. What in us
  Would appear light, in him seems virtuous.
3 *Noble.* 'Tis oracle, my lord.   *Exeunt.*

ACT 4

Scene 2

Enter Vindice and Hippolito, Vindice out of his disguise.

Hippolito. So, so, all's as it should be; y'are yourself.
Vindice. How that great villain puts me to my shifts.
Hippolito. He that did lately in disguise reject thee,
  Shalt now thou art thyself as much respect thee.
Vindice. 'Twill be the quainter fallacy; but brother,
  'Sfoot, what use will he put me to now, think'st thou?
Hippolito. Nay, you must pardon me in that, I know not.
  H'as some employment for you, but what 'tis
  He and his secretary the devil knows best.
10 *Vindice.* Well, I must suit my tongue to his desires,
  What colour soe'er they be; hoping at last
  To pile up all my wishes on his breast.
Hippolito. 'Faith, brother, he himself shows the way.
Vindice. Now the duke is dead, the realm is clad in clay.
  His death being not yet known, under his name
  The people still are governed; well, thou his son
  Art not long-lived, thou shalt not joy his death.
  To kill thee then, I should most honour thee;
  For 'twould stand firm in every man's belief,
20   Thou'st a kind child, and only died'st with grief.

96 *toy*: whim 97 *light*: foolish 98 *oracle*: truth
2 *shifts*: roles; plots 5 *fallacy*: error 10 *tongue*: speech
14 *clad in clay*: buried 17 *joy*: enjoy

Hippolito. You fetch about well, but let's talk in present.
  How will you appear in fashion different,
  As well as in apparel, to make all things possible?
  If you be but once tripped, we fall forever.
  It is not the least policy to be doubtful,
  You must change tongue: familiar was your first.
Vindice. Why I'll bear me in some strain of melancholy,
  And string myself with heavy-sounding wire,
  Like such an instrument that speaks merry things sadly.
Hippolito. Then 'tis as I meant,   30
  I gave you out at first in discontent.
Vindice. I'll turn myself and then –
Hippolito. 'Sfoot here he comes: hast thought upon't?
                              [*Enter Lussurioso.*]
Vindice. Salute him, fear not me.
Lussurioso. Hippolito.
Hippolito. Your lordship.
Lussurioso. What's he yonder?
Hippolito. 'Tis Vindice, my discontented brother,
  Whom, 'cording to your will, I'ave brought to court.
Lussurioso. Is that thy brother? Beshrew me, a good presence.   40
  I wonder h'as been from the court so long.
  Come nearer.
Hippolito. Brother, Lord Lussurioso, the duke's son.
    [*Vindice*] *snatches off his hat and makes legs to him.*
Lussurioso. Be more near to us; welcome, nearer yet.
Vindice. How don you? God you god den.
Lussurioso. We thank thee.
  How strangely such a court-homely salute,
  Shows in the palace, where we greet in fire.
  Nimble and desperate tongues, should we name,
  God in a salutation, 'twould ne'er be stood on't. Heaven!   50
  Tell me, what has made thee so melancholy?
Vindice. Why, going to law.
Lussurioso. Why, will that make a man melancholy?

21 *fetch about*: digress 24 *tripped*: caught out 25 *doubtful*: careful
40 *Beshrew me*: The devil take me 43SD *legs*: bows
45 *don*: Vindice's country accent

Vindice. Yes, to look long upon ink and black buckram – I
went me to law in *Anno quadragesimo secundo*, and I waded
out of it, in *Anno sextagesimo tertio*.
Lussurioso. What, three and twenty years in law?
Vindice. I have known those that have been five and fifty, and
all about pullin and pigs.
60 *Lussurioso.* May it be possible such men should breathe,
To vex the terms so much?
Vindice. 'Tis food to some, my lord.
There are old men at the present, that are so poisoned with
the affectation of law-words – have had many suits canvassed –
that their common talk is nothing but Barbary Latin. They
cannot so much as pray, but in law, that their sins may be
removed, with a writ of error; and their souls fetched up on
heaven with a sasarara.
Hippolito. It seems most strange to me,
70 Yet all the world meets round in the same bent:
Where the heart's set, there goes the tongue's consent.
How dost apply thy studies, fellow?
Vindice. Study? Why, to think how a great rich man lies a-dying,
and a poor cobbler tolls the bell for him? How he cannot depart
the world, and see the great chest stand before him; when he lies
speechless, how he will point you readily to all the boxes; and
when he is past all memory, as the gossips guess, then thinks he
of forfeitures and obligations; nay when to all men's hearings he
80 whirls and rattles in the throat, he's busy threatening his poor
tenants? And this would last me now some seven years' thinking
or thereabouts. But I have a conceit a-coming in picture upon
this: I draw it myself, which i'faith la I'll present to your honour.
You shall not choose but like it, for your lordship shall give me
nothing for it.

55 *Anno quadragesimo secundo*: forty-second year
56 *Anno sextagesimo tertio*: sixty-third year   59 *pullin*: poultry
61 *terms*: Law Court sessions   64 *canvassed*: heard before a judge
65 *Barbary*: barbarous
68 *sasarara*: legal term for an appeal to the highest court
70 *bent*: tendency   75 *chest*: treasury
78 *obligations*: promissory notes for payment of money

Lussurioso. Nay you mistake me then,
   For I am published bountiful enough.
   Let's taste of your conceit.
Vindice. In picture, my lord.
Lussurioso. Ay, in picture.
Vindice. Marry this it is – 'a usuring father to be boiling in hell,   90
   and his son and heir with a whore dancing over him.'
Hippolito. [*Aside*] H'as pared him to the quick.
Lussurioso. The conceit's pretty, i'faith,
   But tak't upon my life, 'twill ne'er be liked.
Vindice. No? Why, I'm sure the whore will be liked well enough.
Hippolito. [*Aside*] Ay, if she were out o'th' picture, he'd like her
   then himself.
Vindice. And as for the son and heir, he shall be an eyesore to
   no young revellers, for he shall be drawn in cloth of gold
   breeches.   100
Lussurioso. And thou hast put my meaning in the pockets,
   And canst not draw that out: my thought was this,
   To see the picture of a usuring father
   Boiling in hell, our rich men would ne'er like it.
Vindice. O true, I cry you heartily mercy. I know the reason, for
   some of 'em had rather be damned indeed, than damned in
   colours.
Lussurioso. [*Aside*] A parlous melancholy has wit enough
   To murder any man, and I'll give him means.
   I think thou art ill monied.   110
Vindice. Money, ho, ho,
   'T'as been my want so long, 'tis now my scoff.
   I've eve' forgot what colour silver's of.
Lussurioso. [*Aside*] It hits as I could wish.
Vindice. I get good clothes,
   Of these those that dread my humour, and for table-room,
   I feed on those that cannot be rid of me.
Lussurioso. Somewhat to set thee up withal.
                                                  [*Gives him money.*]
Vindice. O mine eyes –

86 *published*: reputed   107 *colours*: painting

120   *Lussurioso.* How now man?
       Vindice. Almost struck blind,
           This bright unusual shine to me seems proud.
           I dare not look till the sun be in a cloud.
       Lussurioso. [*Aside*] I think I shall affect his melancholy.
           How are they now?
       Vindice. The better for your asking.
       Lussurioso. You shall be better yet if you but fasten
           Truly on my intent. Now y'are both present
           I will unbrace such a close private villainy
130   Unto your vengeful swords, the like ne'er heard of,
           Who hath disgraced you much and injured us.
       Hippolito. Disgraced us, my lord?
       Lussurioso. Ay, Hippolito.
           I kept it here till now, that both your angers
           Might meet him at once.
       Vindice. I'm covetous
           To know the villain.
       Lussurioso. You know him: that slave-pander,
           Piato whom we threatened last
140   With irons in perpetual prisonment.
       Vindice. [*Aside*] All this is I.
       Hippolito. Is't he, my lord?
       Lussurioso. I'll tell you: you first preferred him to me.
       Vindice. Did you brother?
       Hippolito. I did indeed.
       Lussurioso. And the ingrateful villain
           To quit that kindness, strongly wrought with me –
           Being as you see a likely man for pleasure –
           With jewels to corrupt your virgin sister.
150   *Hippolito.* O villain!
       Vindice. He shall surely die that did it!
       Lussurioso. I, far from thinking any virgin harm,
           Especially knowing her to be as chaste
           As that part which scarce suffers to be touched,
           Th'eye, would not endure him.

       129 *unbrace*: reveal   147 *quit*: requite   *wrought*: worked, persuaded

Vindice. Would you not my lord?
  'Twas wondrously honourably done.
Lussurioso. But with some five frowns kept him out.
Vindice. [*Aside*] Out, slave.
Lussurioso. What did me he, but in revenge of that,   160
  Went of his own free will to make infirm
  Your sister's honour, whom I honour with my soul,
  For chaste respect, and not prevailing there
  – As 'twas but desperate folly to attempt it –
  In mere spleen, by the way, waylays your mother,
  Whose honour being a coward as it seems,
  Yielded by little force.
Vindice. Coward indeed!
Lussurioso. He proud of their advantage, as he thought,
  Brought me these news for happy, but I, heaven forgive 170
    me for't –
Vindice. What did your honour?
Lussurioso. In rage pushed him from me,
  Trampled beneath his throat, spurned him, and bruised:
  Indeed I was too cruel to say, troth.
Hippolito. Most nobly managed.
Vindice. [*Aside*] Has not heaven an ear? is all the lightning
    wasted?
Lussurioso. If I now were so impatient in a modest cause,
  What should you be?
Vindice. Full mad, he shall not live
  To see the moon change.   180
Lussurioso. He's about the palace.
  Hippolito entice him this way, that thy brother
  May take full mark of him.
Hippolito. Heart? That shall not need, my lord,
  I can direct him so far.
Lussurioso. Yet for my hate's sake,
  Go wind him this way? I'll see him bleed myself.
Hippolito. [*Aside*] What now, brother?
Vindice. [*Aside*] Nay e'en what you will – y'are put to't brother?

183 *mark*: sight

190   *Hippolito.* [*Aside*] An impossible task, I'll swear,
       To bring him hither that's already here.   *Exit Hippolito.*
       Lussurioso. Thy name: I have forgot it.
       Vindice. Vindice, my lord.
       Lussurioso. 'Tis a good name that.
       Vindice. Ay, a revenger.
       Lussurioso. It does betoken courage; th'one should'st be valiant,
           And kill thine enemies.
       Vindice. That's my hope, my lord.
       Lussurioso. This slave is one.
200   *Vindice.* I'll doom him.
       Lussurioso. Then I'll praise thee.
           Do thou observe me best, and I'll best raise thee.
                                                        Enter Hippolito.
       Vindice. Indeed, I thank you.
       Lussurioso. Now Hippolito, where's the slave-pander?
       Hippolito. Your good lordship
           Would have a loathsome sight of him, much offensive.
           He's not in case now to be seen, my lord:
           The worst of all the deadly sins is in him:
           That beggarly damnation, drunkenness.
210   *Lussurioso.* Then he's a double slave.
       Vindice. [*Aside*] 'Twas well conveyed, upon a sudden wit.
       Lussurioso. What, are you both
           Firmly resolved? I'll see him dead myself.
       Vindice. Or else, let us not live.
       Lussurioso. You may direct your brother to take note of him.
       Hippolito. I shall.
       Lussurioso. Rise but in this, and you shall never fall.
       Vindice. Your honour's vassals.
       Lussurioso. This was wisely carried.
220   Deep policy in us makes fools of such:
           Then must a slave die when he knows too much.
                                                        Exit Lussurioso.
       Vindice. O thou almighty patience, 'tis my wonder,
           That such a fellow, impudent and wicked,

218 *vassals*: feudal tenants

Should not be cloven as he stood,
Or with a secret wind burst open!
Is there no thunder left, or is it all kept up
In stock for heavier vengeance? [*Thunder.*] There it goes!
Hippolito. Brother, we lose ourselves.
Vindice. But I have found it,
  'Twill hold, 'tis sure, thanks, thanks to any spirit   230
  That mingled it 'mongst my inventions.
Hippolito. What is't?
Vindice. 'Tis sound, and good; thou shalt partake it.
  I'm hired to kill myself.
Hippolito. True.
Vindice. Prithee, mark it,
  And the old duke being dead, but not conveyed,
  For he's already missed too, and you know:
  Murder will peep out of the closest husk.
Hippolito. Most true!   240
Vindice. What say you then to this device:
  If we dressed up the body of the duke –
Hippolito. – in that disguise of yours.
Vindice. Y're quick, y'ave reached it.
Hippolito. I like it wondrously.
Vindice. And being in drink, as you have published him,
  To lean him on his elbow, as if sleep had caught him,
  Which claims most interest in such sluggy men.
Hippolito. Good yet, but here's a doubt.
  We, thought by th'duke's son to kill that pander,   250
  Shall, when he is known, be thought to kill the duke.
Vindice. Neither, O thanks, it is substantial;
  For that disguise being on him, which I wore.
  It will be thought I, which he calls the pander, did kill the
  duke, and fled away in his apparel, leaving him so disguised,
  to avoid swift pursuit.
Hippolito. Firmer, and firmer.

---

224 *cloven*: hoofed, like the devil
237 *conveyed*: transported; communicated   248 *sluggy*: sluggish
252 *substantial*: sound

Vindice. Nay doubt not, 'tis in grain. I warrant it hold colour.
Hippolito. Let's about it.
260 *Vindice.* But by the way too, now I think on't, brother,
        Let's conjure that base devil out of our mother.   *Exeunt.*

ACT 4

Scene 3

Enter the Duchess arm in arm with [Spurio] the Bastard: he seemeth lasciviously to her; after them, enter Supervacuo, running with a rapier; his brother [Ambitioso] stops him.

Spurio. Madam, unlock yourself, should it be seen,
    Your arm would be suspected.
Duchess. Who is't that dares suspect, or this, or these?
    May we not deal our favours where we please?
Spurio. I'm confident, you may.   *Exeunt.*
Ambitioso. 'Sfoot, brother hold.
Supervacuo. Wouldst let the bastard shame us?
Ambitioso. Hold, hold brother! There's fitter time than now.
Supervacuo. Now, when I see it.
10 *Ambitioso.* 'Tis too much seen already.
Supervacuo. Seen and known,
    The nobler she's, the baser is she grown.
Ambitioso. If she were bent lasciviously, the fault
    Of mighty women, that sleep soft – O death,
    Must she needs choose such an unequal sinner
    To make all worse?
Supervacuo. A bastard, the duke's bastard; shame heaped on
        shame.
Ambitioso. O our disgrace.
    Most women have small waist the world throughout.

---

258 *in grain*: engrained, firm   OSD *seemeth*: acts   13 *bent*: inclined
14 *soft*: in comfort

But their desires are thousand miles about.   20
Supervacuo. Come, stay not here, let's after, and prevent.
Or else they'll sin faster than we'll repent.   *Exeunt.*

ACT 4

Scene 4

Enter Vindice and Hippolito, bringing out their mother one by one shoulder, and the other by the other, with daggers in their hands.

Vindice. O, thou for whom no name is bad enough.
Mother. What means my sons? What, will you murder me?
Vindice. Wicked, unnatural parents.
Hippolito. Fiend of women.
Mother. Oh! are sons turned monsters? Help!
Vindice. In vain.
Mother. Are you so barbarous to set iron nipples
   Upon the breast that gave you suck?
Vindice. That breast
   Is turned to quarled poison.   10
Mother. Cut not your days for't. Am not I your mother?
Vindice. Thou dost usurp that title now by fraud,
   For in that shell of mother breeds a bawd.
Mother. A bawd? O name far loathsomer than hell!
Hippolito. It should be so, knew'st thou thy office well.
Mother. I hate it.
Vindice. Ah is't possible? Thou only? You powers on high,
   That women should dissemble when they die.
Mother. Dissemble?
Vindice. Did not the duke's son direct   20
   A fellow of the world's condition hither,
   That did corrupt all that was good in thee,

7 *iron nipples*: daggers   10 *quarled*: soured   11 *Cut*: Shorten

Made thee uncivilly to forget thyself,
And work our sister to his lust?
Mother. Who, I?
　　That had been monstrous: I defy that man
　　For any such intent. None lives so pure
　　But shall be soiled with slander: good son, believe it not.
Vindice. Oh I'm in doubt
30　　Whether I'm myself, or no:
　　Stay, let me look again upon this face.
　　Who shall be saved when mothers have no grace?
Hippolito. 'Twould make one half despair.
Vindice. I was the man.
　　Defy me now? Let's see, do't modestly.
Mother. O hell unto my soul!
Vindice. In that disguise, I sent from the duke's son,
　　Tried you, and found you base metal
　　As any villain might have done.
40　*Mother.* O no, no tongue but yours could have bewitched
　　　me so!
Vindice. O nimble in damnation, quick in tune,
　　There is no devil could strike fire so soon:
　　I am confuted in a word.
Mother. O son, forgive me: to myself I'll prove more true.
　　You that should honour me, I kneel to you.
Vindice. A mother to give aim to her own daughter.
Hippolito. True brother, how far beyond nature 'tis,
　　Though many mothers do it.
Vindice. Nay and you draw tears once: go you to bed.
50　　Wet will make iron blush and change to red.
　　Brother, it rains; 'twill spoil your dagger, house it.
Hippolito. 'Tis done.
Vindice. I'faith 'tis a sweet shower, it does much good.
　　The fruitful grounds and meadows of her soul
　　Has been long dry: pour down, thou blessed dew.
　　Rise, mother; troth, this shower has made you higher.

41 *nimble*: quick-witted　43 *confuted*: silenced; disproved
46 *give aim*: in archery, to guide one in their aim

Mother. O you heavens. Take this infectious spot out of my
    soul,
  I'll rinse it in seven waters of mine eyes;
  Make my tears salt enough to taste of grace.
  To weep is to our sex naturally given: 60
  But to weep truly, that's a gift from heaven.
Vindice. Nay I'll kiss thee now: kiss her brother.
  Let's marry her to our souls wherein's no lust,
  And honourably love her.
Hippolito. Let it be.
Vindice. For honest women are so seld and rare,
  'Tis good to cherish those poor few that are.
  Oh you of easy wax, do but imagine,
  Now the disease has left you, how leprously
  That office would have clinged to your forehead.   70
  All mothers that had any graceful hue
  Would have worn masks to hide their face at you.
  It would have grown to this: at your foul name,
  Green-coloured maids would have turned red with shame.
Hippolito. And then our sister full of hire and baseness.
Vindice. There had been boiling lead again:
  The duke's son's great concubine,
  A drab of state, a cloth-o'-silver slut,
  To have her train born up, and her soul trail i'th'dirt: great!
Hippolito. To be miserably great; rich, to be eternally wretched.   80
Vindice. O common madness.
  Ask but the thriving'st harlot in cold blood,
  She'd give the world to make her honour good.
  Perhaps you'll say, but only to the duke's son
  In private; why, she first begins with one,
  Who afterward to thousand proves a whore.
  Break ice in one place, it will crack in more.
Mother. Most certainly applied.
Hippolito. Oh brother, you forget our business.

---

57 *infectious*: infected   66 *seld*: seldom
68 *wax*: impressionable, malleable   74 *Green-coloured*: Virginal
75 *hire*: prostitution   82 *cold blood*: calm reflection

90   *Vindice.* And well remembered: joy's a subtle elf.
      I think man's happiest when he forgets himself.
      Farewell, once dried, now holy-watered mead;
      Our hearts wear feathers, that before wore lead.
     Mother. I'll give you this, that one I never knew
      Plead better, for, and 'gainst the devil, than you.
     Vindice. You make me proud on't.
     Hippolito. Commend us in all virtue to our sister.
     Vindice. Ay, for the love of heaven, to that true maid.
     Mother. With my best words.
100 *Vindice.* Why that was motherly said.   *Exeunt.*
     Mother. I wonder now what fury did transport me?
      I feel good thoughts begin to settle in me.
      Oh, with what forehead can I look on her?
      Whose honour I've so impiously beset.   [*Enter Castiza.*]
      And here she comes.
     Castiza. Now mother, you have wrought with me so strongly,
      That what for my advancement, as to calm
      The trouble of your tongue – I am content.
     Mother. Content to what?
110 *Castiza.* To do as you have wished me.
      To prostitute my breast to the duke's son:
      And put myself to common usury.
     Mother. I hope you will not so.
     Castiza. Hope you I will not?
      That's not the hope you look to be saved in.
     Mother. Truth, but it is.
     Castiza. Do not deceive yourself.
      I am as you e'en out of marble wrought,
      What would you now? Are ye not pleased with me?
120   You shall not wish me to be more lascivious
      Than I intend to be.
     Mother. Strike me not cold!
     Castiza. How often have you charged me on your blessing
      To be a cursed woman? When you knew

90 *elf*: spirit   103 *forehead*: countenance, expression
112 *usury*: associating prostitution with moneylending at interest

Your blessing had no force to make me lewd,
You laid your curse upon me: that did more.
The mother's curse is heavy, where that fights,
Sons set in storm, and daughters lose their lights.
Mother. Good child, dear maid: if there be any spark
   Of heavenly intellectual fire within thee, oh let my breath   130
   Revive it to a flame.
   Put not all out, with woman's wilful follies.
   I am recovered of that foul disease
   That haunts too many mothers: kind, forgive me;
   Make me not sick in health? If then
   My words prevailed when they were wickedness,
   How much more now when they are just and good?
Castiza. I wonder what you mean: are not you she
   For whose infect persuasions I could scarce
   Kneel out my prayers, and had much ado   140
   In three hours' reading, to untwist so much
   Of the black serpent as you wound about me?
Mother. 'Tis unfruitful, held tedious to repeat what's past.
   I'm now your present mother.
Castiza. Push, now 'tis too late.
Mother. Bethink again: thou knowst not what thou sayst.
Castiza. No: deny advancement, treasure, the duke's son?
Mother. O see, I spoke those words, and now they poison me!
   What will the deed do then?
   Advancement? True, as high as shame can pitch   150
   For treasure: who e'er knew a harlot rich?
   Or could build by the purchase of her sin,
   An hospital to keep their bastards in? The duke's son:
   Oh, when women are young courtiers, they are sure to be old
     beggars to know the miseries most harlots taste.
   Thou'dst wish thyself unborn, when thou art unchaste.
Castiza. O mother, let me twine about your neck,
   And kiss you till my soul melt on your lips.
   I did but this to try you!
Mother. O, speak truth.

130 *intellectual*: spiritual 144 *present*: true 158 *try*: test

160 *Castiza*. Indeed I did not, for no tongue has force to alter me
          from honest.
       If maidens would, men's words could have no power:
       A virgin honour is a crystal tower
       Which, being weak, is guarded with good spirits,
       Until she basely yields, no ill inherits.
    Mother. O happy child! Faith and thy birth hath saved me,
       'Mongst thousand daughters happiest of all others,
       Be thou a glass for maids, and I for mothers.   *Exeunt*.

ACT 5

Scene 1

Enter Vindice and Hippolito[, arranging the corpse of the Duke dressed as Piato].

Vindice. So, so, he leans well; take heed you wake him not,
       brother.
Hippolito. I warrant you, my life for yours.
Vindice. That's a good lay, for I must kill myself!
       Brother, that's I: that fits for me, do you mark it,
       And I must stand ready here to make away myself yonder. I
       must be fit to be killed, and stand to kill myself. I could vary
       if not so little as thrice over again: 't'as some eight returns
       like Michaelmas term.
10 *Hippolito*. That's enow, o'conscience.
Vindice. But sirrah, does the duke's son come single?
Hippolito. No, there's the hell on't: his faith's too feeble to go
       alone. He brings flesh-flies after him, that will buzz against
       suppertime, and hum for his coming out.

---

167 *Be*: Q buy   *glass*: example   4 *lay*: reckoning
9 *Michaelmas term*: the law term had eight weeks; Vindice seems to imagine
eight versions of their situation
10 *enow*: enough   11 *single*: alone   13 *flesh-flies*: bluebottles; flatterers

Vindice. Ah, the fly-flop of vengeance beat 'em to pieces! Here
  was the sweetest occasion, the fittest hour, to have made my
  revenge familiar with him; show him the body of the duke
  his father, and how quaintly he died, like a politician in
  hugger-mugger; made no man acquainted with it, and in
  catastrophe, slain him over his father's breast, and oh, I'm   20
  mad to lose such a sweet opportunity.
Hippolito. Nay pish, prithee be content! There's no remedy
  present: may not hereafter times open in as fair faces as this?
Vindice. They may if they can paint so well.
Hippolito. Come, now to avoid all suspicion, let's forsake this
  room, and be going to meet the duke's son.
Vindice. Content: I'm for any weather. Heart, step close; here
  he comes.   *Enter Lussurioso.*
Hippolito. My honoured lord?
Lussurioso. Oh me, you both present?   30
Vindice. E'en newly my lord, just as your lordship entered now.
  About this place we had notice given he should be, but in
  some –
Hippolito. Came your honour private?
Lussurioso. Private enough for this: only a few
  Attend my coming out.
Hippolito. [*Aside*] Death rot those few.
Lussurioso. Stay, yonder's the slave.
Vindice. Mass, there's the slave indeed, my lord.
  [*Aside*] 'Tis a good child: he calls his father slave.   40
Lussurioso. Ay, that's the villain, the damned villain: softly,
  Tread easy.
Vindice. Puh, I warrant you my lord; we'll stifle in our breaths.
Lussurioso. That will do well.
  Base rogue, thou sleepest thy last. [*Aside*] 'Tis policy
  To have him killed in's sleep, for if he waked
  He would betray all to them.
Vindice. But my lord.
Lussurioso. Ha, what sayst?

15 *fly-flop*: perhaps a fly-swat   19 *hugger-mugger*: secretly
20 *catastrophe*: the end of a tragedy   24 *paint*: use make-up

50   *Vindice.* Shall we kill him now he's drunk?
      Lussurioso. Ay, best of all.
      Vindice. Why then he will ne'er live to be sober?
      Lussurioso. No matter, let him reel to hell.
      Vindice. But being so full of liquor, I fear he will put out all the
          fire.
      Lussurioso. Thou art a mad breast!
      Vindice. [*Aside*] And leave none to warm your lordship's golls
          withal; for he that dies drunk falls into hell-fire like a bucket
          o'water, qush, qush.
60   *Lussurioso.* Come be ready: nake your swords; think of your
          wrongs.
          This slave has injured you.
      Vindice. Troth, so he has [*Aside*] and he has paid well for't.
      Lussurioso. Meet with him now.
      Vindice. You'll bear us out, my lord?
      Lussurioso. Puh, am I a lord for nothing, think you?
          Quickly now.
      Vindice. Sa, sa, sa: [*Stabs the corpse.*] thump, there he lies.
      Lussurioso. Nimbly done, ha? Oh villains, murderers!
70   'Tis the old duke my father.
      Vindice. [*Aside*] That's a jest.
      Lussurioso. What, stiff and cold already?
          O pardon me to call you from your names,
          'Tis none of your deed. That villain Piato,
          Whom you thought now to kill, has murdered him
          And left him thus disguised.
      Hippolito. And not unlikely.
      Vindice. O rascal, was he not ashamed
          To put the duke into a greasy doublet?
80   *Lussurioso.* He has been cold and stiff – who knows how long?
      Vindice. [*Aside*] Marry, that do I.
      Lussurioso. No words, I pray, of anything intended.
      Hippolito. I would fain have your lordship think that we have
          small reason to prate.

      57 *golls*: hands   60 *nake*: unsheathe   65 *bear us out*: support us

Lussurioso. 'Faith, thou sayest true. I'll forthwith send to court,
   For all the nobles, bastard, duchess all,
   How here by miracle we found him dead,
   And in his raiment that foul villain fled.
Vindice. That will be the best way my lord, to clear us all: let's
   cast about to be clear.   90
Lussurioso. Ho, Nencio, Sordido, and the rest.
                    Enter [Nencio, Sordido and servants].
Sordido. My lord.
Nencio. My lord.
Lussurioso. Be witnesses of a strange spectacle:
   Choosing for private conference that sad room
   We found the duke my father geal'd in blood.
Sordido. My lord the duke! Run, hie thee, Nencio.
   Startle the court by signifying so much.   [*Exit Nencio.*]
Vindice. [*Aside*] Thus much by wit a deep revenger can,
   When murders known, to be the clearest man;   100
   We're furthest off, and with as bold an eye,
   Survey his body as the standers by.
Lussurioso. My royal father, too basely let blood,
   By a malevolent slave.
Hippolito. [*Aside*] Hark? he calls thee slave again.
Vindice. [*Aside*] H'as lost, he may.
Lussurioso. Oh sight, look hither! See, his lips are gnawn with
   poison.
Vindice. How – his lips? By th'mass, they be.
Lussurioso. O villain – O rogue – O slave – O rascal!   110
Hippolito. O good deceit, he quits him with like terms.
        [*Enter Nobles, Gentleman, Ambitioso and Supervacuo.*]
1 Noble. Where?
2 Noble. Which way?
Ambitioso. Over what roof hangs this prodigious comet
   In deadly fire?
Lussurioso. Behold, behold my lords: the duke my father's mur-
   dered by a vassal, that owes this habit, and here left disguised.

88 *raiment*: clothes   96 *geal'd*: congealed   114 *prodigious*: unlucky

[*Enter Duchess and Spurio.*]

Duchess. My lord and husband!

2 Noble. Reverent majesty.

120 *1 Noble.* I have seen these clothes often attending on him.

Vindice. [*Aside*] That nobleman hath been i'th' country, for he
    does not lie.

Supervacuo. [*Aside*] Learn of our mother let's dissemble too.
    I'm glad he's vanished; so I hope are you?

Ambitioso. [*Aside*] Ay, you may take my word for't.

Spurio. [*Aside*] Old dad, dead?
    Ay, one of his cast sins will send the fates
    Most hearty commendations by his own son.
    I'll tug in the new stream, till strength be done.

Lussurioso. Where be those two, that did affirm to us

130   My lord the duke was privately rid forth?

Gentleman. O pardon us, my lords: he gave that charge
    Upon our lives, if he were missed at Court
    To answer so; he rode not anywhere,
    We left him private with that fellow here?

Vindice. [*Aside*] Confirmed.

Lussurioso. O heavens, that false charge was his death.
    Impudent beggars, durst you to our face
    Maintain such a false answer? Bear him straight to execution.

Gentleman. My lord?

140 *Lussurioso.* Urge me no more.
    In this the excuse may be called half the murder.

Vindice. You've sentenced well.

Lussurioso. Away, see it be done.

                    [*Exit Gentleman under guard.*]

Vindice. [*Aside*] Could you not stick; see what confession doth?
    Who would not lie when men are hanged for truth?

Hippolito. [*Aside*] Brother, how happy is our vengeance.

Vindice. [*Aside*] Why it hits past the apprehension of
    indifferent wits.

Lussurioso. My lord, let post-horse be sent
    Into all places to entrap the villain.

126 *cast*: rejected   148 *post-horse*: swift couriers

Vindice. [Aside] Post-horse, ha ha.   150
Nobles. My lord, we're something bold to know our duty.
    Your father's accidentally departed:
    The titles that were due to him meet you.
Lussurioso. Meet me? I'm not at leisure, my good lord,
    I've many griefs to dispatch out o'th'way.
[Aside] Welcome, sweet titles: talk to me, my lords,
    Of sepulchres and mighty emperors' bones;
    That's thought for me.
Vindice. [Aside] So, one may see by this,
    How foreign markets go: 160
    Courtiers have feet o'th' nines, and tongues o'th' twelves;
    They flatter dukes, and dukes flatter themselves.
2 Noble. My lord, it is your shine must comfort us.
Lussurioso. Alas I shine in tears, like the sun in April.
1 Noble. You're now my lord's grace.
Lussurioso. My lord's grace? I perceive you'll have it so.
2 Noble. 'Tis but your own.
Lussurioso. Then heavens give me grace to be so.
Vindice. [Aside] He prays well for himself.
2 Noble. Madam, all sorrows   170
    Must run their circles into joys; no doubt but time
    Will make the murderer bring forth himself.
Vindice. [Aside] He were an ass then i'faith.
1 Noble. In the mean season,
    Let us bethink the latest funeral honours
    Due to the duke's cold body – and withal,
    Calling to memory our new happiness
    Spread in his royal son: lords, gentlemen,
    Prepare for revels.
Vindice. Revels!   180
1 Noble. Time hath several falls;
    Griefs lift up joys, feasts put down funerals.
Lussurioso. Come then, my lords: my favours to you all.
[Aside] The duchess is suspected, fouly bent;
    I'll begin dukedom with her banishment.

161 *feet ... twelves*: tongues bigger than their feet

Exeunt [Lussurioso as] Duke, Nobles and Duchess.

Hippolito. Revels.

Vindice. Ay, that's the word, we are firm yet.

    Strike one strain more, and then we crown our wit.

                                       Exeunt brothers.

Spurio. Well, have the fairest mark – so said the duke when

    he begot me –

190   And if I miss his heart or near about,

    Then have at any, a bastard scorns to be out.   *[Exit.]*

Supervacuo. Not'st thou that Spurio, brother?

Ambitioso. Yes, I note him to our shame.

Supervacuo. He shall not live, his hair shall not grow much

    longer. In this time of revels, tricks may be set afoot. Seest

    thou yon new moon? It shall outlive the new duke by much;

    this hand shall dispossess him, then we're mighty.

    A mask is treason's licence – that build upon.

    'Tis murder's best face when a vizard's on.

                                  Exit Supervacuo.

200 *Ambitioso.* Is't so, it's very good.

    And do you think to be duke then, kind brother?

    I'll see fair play, drop one and there lies t'other.

                                     Exit Ambitioso.

ACT 5

Scene 2

Enter Vindice and Hippolito, with Piero and other Lords.

Vindice. My lords, be all of music: strike old griefs into other

    countries

    That flow in too much milk, and have faint livers,

    Not daring to stab home their discontents.

187 *firm*: secure

Let our hid flames break out, as fire, as lightning,
To blast this villainous dukedom, vexed with sin:
Wind up your souls to their full height again.
Piero. How?
1 Lord. Which way?
2 Lord. We cannot justly be revenged too much.
Vindice. You shall have all enough. Revels are toward,   10
And those few nobles that have long suppressed you,
Are busied to the furnishing of a masque,
And do affect to make a pleasant tale on't.
The masquing suits are fashioning; now comes in
That which must glad us all – we to take pattern
Of all those suits: the colour, trimming, fashion,
E'en to an undistinguished hair almost;
Then, entering first, observing the true form,
Within a strain or two we shall find leisure
And steal our swords out handsomely.   20
And, when they think their pleasure sweet and good,
In midst of their joys, they shall sigh blood.
Piero. Weightily, effectually.
1 Noble. Before the other masquers come.
Vindice. We're gone, all done and past.
Piero. But how for the duke's guard?
Vindice. Let that alone.
By one and one their strengths shall be drunk down.
Hippolito. There are five hundred gentlemen in the action,
That will apply themselves and not stand idle.   30
Piero. Oh, let us hug your bosoms.
Vindice. Come, my lords:
Prepare for deeds, let other times have words.   *Exeunt.*

---

10 *toward*: imminent   15 *pattern*: copy   19 *strain*: of music
23 *Weightily*: Heavily   *effectually*: effectively

ACT 5

Scene 3

In a dumb show, the possessing of the young Duke with all his Nobles; then sounding music, a furnished table is brought forth; then enters the Duke and his Nobles to the banquet. A blazing star appeareth.

1 Noble. Many harmonious hours and choicest pleasures
   Fill up the royal numbers of your years.
Lussurioso. My lords we're pleased to thank you – though we know
   'Tis but your duty now to wish it so.
2 Noble. That shine makes us all happy.
3 Noble. [*Aside*] His grace frowns?
2 Noble. [*Aside*] Yet we must say he smiles.
3 Noble. [*Aside*] I think we must.
Lussurioso. [*Aside*] That foul incontinent duchess we
   have banished,

10   The bastard shall not live: after these revels
   I'll begin strange ones. He and the stepsons
   Shall pay their lives for the first subsidies,
   We must not frown so soon, else 't'ad been now.
1 Noble. My gracious lord please you prepare for pleasure.
   The masque is not far off.
Lussurioso. We are for pleasure.
   Beshrew thee, what art thou? Mad'st me start!
   Thou hast committed treason – a blazing star.
2 Noble. A blazing star, O where, my lord?
20 *Lussurioso.* Spy out.
2 Noble. See, see, my lords, a wondrous dreadful one.
Lussurioso. I am not pleased at that ill-knotted fire,
   That bushing staring star – am not I duke?

OSD *possessing*: installation   *blazing star*: comet
9 *incontinent*: lascivious   12 *subsidies*: contributions
23 *bushing*: spreading like a bush

It should not quake me now. Had it appeared
Before it, I might then have justly feared.
But yet they say, whom art and learning weds:
When stars wear locks, they threaten great men's heads.
Is it so? You are read, my lords.
2 Noble. May it please your grace,
  It shows great anger.   30
Lussurioso. That does not please our grace.
1 Noble. Yet here's the comfort, my lord: many times
  When it seems most it threatens farthest off.
Lussurioso. 'Faith, and I think so too.
2 Noble. Beside, my lord,
  You're gracefully established with the loves
  Of all your subjects; and for natural death,
  I hope it will be threescore years a-coming.
Lussurioso. True, no more but threescore years.
1 Noble. Fourscore I hope, my lord.   40
2 Noble. And fivescore, I.
3 Noble. But 'tis my hope, my lord, you shall ne'er die.
Lussurioso. Give me thy hand: these others I rebuke.
  He that hopes so, is fittest for a duke.
  Thou shalt sit next me. Take your places, lords;
  We're ready now for sports, let 'em set on.
  You thing, we shall forget you quite anon!
3 Noble. I hear 'em coming, my lord.
    Enter the Masque of Revengers the two brothers [Vindice
    and Hippolito] and two Lords more.
Lussurioso. [Aside] Ah, 'tis well:
  Brothers, and bastard, you dance next in hell.   50
    The Revengers dance. At the end steal out their swords,
    and those four kill the four at the table, in their chairs. It
    thunders.
Vindice. Mark, thunder.
  Does know thy cue, thou big-voiced crier?
  Duke's groans are thunder's watchwords.
Hippolito. So my lords, you have enough.

27 *locks*: the tail of the comet, like hair

Vindice. Come let's away, no lingering.
Hippolito. Follow, go?   *Exeunt [except Vindice].*
Vindice. No power is angry when the lustful die.
   When thunder claps, heaven likes the tragedy.
                                     Exit Vindice.
Lussurioso. Oh, oh!
   Enter the other Masque of intended murderers: stepsons,
   Bastard, and a fourth man, coming in dancing. The
   Duke recovers a little in voice and groans – calls a guard,
   Treason. At which they all start out of their measure,
   and turning towards the table, they find them all to be
   murdered.
60 *Spurio.* Whose groan was that?
Lussurioso. Treason, a guard!
Ambitioso. How now? All murdered!
Supervacuo. Murdered!
4 Noble. And those his nobles?
Ambitioso. [*Aside*] Here's a labour saved;
   I thought to have sped him. 'Sblood, how came this?
Supervacuo. Then I proclaim myself: now I am duke.
Ambitioso. Thou duke! Brother, thou liest.
                              [*Stabs Supervacuo*]
Spurio. Slave, so dost thou!   [*Stabs Ambitioso*]
70 *4 Noble.* Base villain, hast thou slain my lord and master?
                                   [*Stabs Spurio.*]
   Enter the first men [Vindice, Hippolito and the masquers,
   with Antonio].
Vindice. Pistols, treason, murder! Help, guard my lord the duke.
Hippolito. Lay hold upon this traitors!
Lussurioso. Oh!
Vindice. Alas, the duke is murdered!
Hippolito. And the nobles.
Vindice. Surgeons, surgeons! [*Aside*] Heart, does he breathe so
   long.
Antonio. A piteous tragedy, able to wake
   An old man's eyes: bloodshot.

59SD *measure*: stately dance

Lussurioso. Oh!

Vindice. Look to my lord the duke. [*Aside*] A vengeance throttle   80
him!

Confess thou murderous and unhallowed man,

Didst thou kill all these?

4 Noble. None but the bastard, I.

Vindice. How came the duke slain then?

4 Noble. We found him so.

Lussurioso. O villain!

Vindice. Hark!

Lussurioso. Those in the masque did murder us.

Vindice. Law you now sir,

O marble impudence! Will you confess now?   90

4 Noble. 'Sblood, 'tis all false!

Antonio. Away with that foul monster,

Dipped in a prince's blood.

4 Noble. Heart, 'tis a lie.

Antonio. Let him have bitter execution.

[*Exit 4 Noble under guard.*]

Vindice. [*Aside*] New marrow! No, I cannot be expressed.

How fares my lord the duke?

Lussurioso. Farewell to all.

He that climbs highest has the greatest fall:

My tongue is out of office.   100

Vindice. Air, gentlemen, air.

[*Whispers*] Now thou'lt not prate on't, 'twas Vindice murdered
thee.   [*Stabs Lussurioso.*]

Lussurioso. Oh!

Vindice. Murdered thy father.

Lussurioso. Oh!

Vindice. And I am he. Tell nobody. [*Lussurioso dies.*] So so,
the duke's departed.

Antonio. It was a deadly hand that wounded him.

The rest, ambitious who should rule and sway,

After his death were so made all away.   110

---

89 *Law*: Expression of surprise   96 *marrow*: food for revenge

Vindice. My lord was unlikely.

Hippolito. Now, the hope
Of Italy lies in your reverend years.

Vindice. Your hair will make the silver age again,
When there was fewer but more honest men.

Antonio. The burden's weighty and will press age down.
May I so rule that heaven may keep the crown.

Vindice. The rape of your good lady has been 'quited,
With death on death.

120 *Antonio.* Just is the law above.
But of all things it puts me most to wonder,
How the old duke came murdered.

Vindice. Oh, my lord.

Antonio. It was the strangeliest carried: I not heard of the like.

Hippolito. 'Twas all done for the best, my lord.

Vindice. All for your grace's good. We may be bold to speak
it now:
'Twas somewhat witty carried though we say it.
'Twas we two murdered him.

Antonio. You two?

130 *Vindice.* None else, i'faith my lord, nay 'twas managed.

Antonio. Lay hands upon those villains!

Vindice. How? On us?

Antonio. Bear 'em to speedy execution.

Vindice. Heart, wast not for your good, my lord?

Antonio. My good? Away with 'em. Such an old man as he,
You that would murder him would murder me.

Vindice. Is't come about –

Hippolito. 'Sfoot, brother, you begun.

Vindice. May we not set so well as the duke's on,
140   Thou hast no conscience; are we not revenged?
Is there one enemy left alive amongst those?
'Tis time to die, when we ourselves our foes.
When murders shut deeds close, this curse does seal 'em;
If none disclose 'em, they themselves reveal 'em!

111 *unlikely*: unsuited   114 *silver age*: in Greek mythology, an age of peace
140 *conscience*: moral qualms

This murder might have slept in tongueless brass,
But for ourselves, and the world died an ass.
Now I remember too, here was Piato
Brought forth a knavish sentence once, no doubt, said he,
    but time
Will make the murderer bring forth himself?
'Tis well he died, he was a witch.   150
And now my lord, since we are in for ever:
This work was ours which else might have been slipped;
And if we list, we could have nobles clipped,
And go for less than beggars; but we hate
To bleed so cowardly. We have enough,
I'faith: we're well, our mother turned, our sister true,
We die after a nest of dukes, adieu.   *Exeunt [under guard].*
Antonio. How subtly was that murder closed. Bear up
    Those tragic bodies, 'tis a heavy season:
    Pray heaven their blood may wash away all treason.   160
                                                 Exeunt.

FINIS

150 *witch*: predictor of the future   153 *clipped*: beheaded
158 *closed*: concealed

FINIS

Appendix
Hamlet (or *Hamlets*)

The text published here as *Hamlet (1603)* was not rediscovered until the nineteenth century. Its title-page describes the quarto pamphlet as 'The / Tragicall Historie of / Hamlet / Prince of Denmarke / By William Shake-speare / As it hath beene diverse times acted by his Highnesse ser- / vants in the Cittie of London : as also in the two U- / niversities of Cambridge and Oxford, and else-where', and gives the date of publication of 1603. In 1604, another quarto was published: 'The / Tragicall Historie of / Hamlet, / Prince of Denmarke. / By William Shakespeare. / Newly imprinted and enlarged to almost as much / againe as it was, according to the true and perfect / Coppie.' The play was printed again in the complete collected works of Shakespeare, the First Folio of 1623. Textual critics call these three versions of *Hamlet* Q1, Q2 and F, respectively (Q1 is referred to as 'Q' in the annotation in this volume).

While Q2 and F differ in some details, Q1 is radically different from them, even though it shares plot, characters and, in outline at least, many of the speeches. But Q1 is about half the length of Q2 and F, and thus is the only one of the three extant versions that could feasibly have been performed in its entirety on the early modern stage. The names of some characters are slightly different, and the king's councillor is called Corambis, rather than Polonius as in the later texts. It also has a different role for Hamlet's mother, who has an unique scene (14) in which she vows with Horatio to support her son against her husband.

There has been extensive scholarly discussion of the nature of the differences between the texts and their possible provenance without any clearcut conclusion, although almost all modern editors of *Hamlet* base their text on either Q2 or F. The theory that Q1 represents a so-called 'bad quarto' – the phrase comes from the bibliographer A. W. Pollard writing at the beginning of the twentieth century, whose variations from later texts are the mangled signs of piracy, corruption and misremembering – has been challenged on several fronts in recent years. For example, one group of scholars has been interested in the ways Q1 might represent a theatrical text and thus give us information about the *Hamlet* performed at the Globe Theatre at the turn of the seventeenth century, and particular descriptive stage directions such as '*Enter Ofelia playing on a lute, and her hair down, singing*' (scene 13) may support this view. For another, renewed interest in the idea that Shakespeare might have revised his own works, particularly *King Lear*, has led to speculation that Q1 represents Shakespeare's own theatrical abridgement of a longer text (Q2) intended for reading (see Erne). On the other hand, there are marks in Q1 designed to help readers identify commonplaces, or extract lines or sentiments that might be used in other contexts, which would suggest it was at least in part prepared as a reading text (Lesser and Stallybrass).

So far, the textual discussion of the *Hamlet*s has been trapped in comparisons: looking at how characters, speeches and stage business are differently enacted across two or three versions, largely to the detriment of the earliest text. In printing Q1 alongside the revenge plays with which it is clearly akin, this edition tries to break out of that Shakespeare-centric comparative model. Edited alongside, for example, Chettle's *Hoffman*, the textual problems of Q1 seem much less troublesome than they do by endless comparison to the Q2 and F, still implicitly perceived to be 'better' texts. The logic of disentangling those earlier texts which previous editors conflated into a supra-*Hamlet* – as in, for example, the Arden text edited by Ann Thompson and Neil Taylor – must now be that the three distinct versions which emerge have their own autonomous life, in dialogue less with narcissistic versions of the same play but with dramatic imaginings of similar scenarios by different authors. This edition gives readers the opportunity to read *Hamlet* as it first appeared in 1603, before it was overshadowed by Q2's boastful self-presentation as the 'true and perfect' copy, and to read it alongside other revenge plays of the period.

Further Reading

Exploring the textual issues around *Hamlet* can quickly become overwhelming. The Arden edition by Ann Thompson and Neil Taylor (2006) publishes Q2 in one volume, with a supplementary volume for Q1 and F. Aspects of printing and play publication are usefully considered in Part 7 of David Scott Kastan's *A Companion to Shakespeare* (1999), and his *Shakespeare and the Book* (2001) is lucid and engaging on the issues, rather than the detail. Lukas Erne gives a clear idea of its revisionist thesis in his title: *Shakespeare as Literary Dramatist* (2003). Also of interest is Zachary Lesser and Peter Stallybrass, 'The First Literary *Hamlet* and the Commonplacing of Professional Plays', *Shakespeare Quarterly* 59 (2008), 371–42.

PENGUIN CLASSICS

THE COMPLETE PLAYS
CHRISTOPHER MARLOWE

Dido, Queen of Carthage/Tamburlaine the Great, Parts One and Two/The Jew of Malta/Doctor Faustus/Edward the Second/The Massacre at Paris

> 'When I behold the heavens, then I repent,
>
> And curse thee, wicked Mephistopheles'

Christopher Marlowe – a possible spy with a reputation for atheism who was murdered in mysterious circumstances – courted danger throughout his life. A sense of dark forces operating in all social and political relationships underlies his work. In *Dr Faustus*, a man of great intellect and even greater ambition craves knowledge, and is prepared to sell his soul to the Devil to achieve it. Tamburlaine attempts to satisfy his desire for greatness through his domination over an ever-growing empire, while Edward II upsets the delicate balance of power in the land and plants the seed of his own murder. All the plays here show Marlowe's fascination with the tension between weak and strong, sacred and profane.

Frank Romany's introduction relates the plays to Marlowe's turbulent religious world. The fully modernized texts have been newly edited from the earliest editions, and the full commentary on each play is supplemented with a glossary and an appendix of mythological and historical allusions.

Edited by Frank Romany and Robert Lindsey

PENGUIN CLASSICS

SIDNEY'S 'THE DEFENCE OF POESY' AND SELECTED RENAISSANCE LITERARY CRITICISM

'The poet with that same hand of delight doth draw the mind more effectually than any other art doth'

Out of the intellectual ferment of the English Renaissance came a number of outstanding critical works that sought to define and defend the role of literature in society and to comment on the craft of writing. Foremost among these is Sir Philip Sidney's *The Defence of Poesy*: an eloquent argument for fiction as a means of inspiring its readers to virtuous action. George Puttenham's *The Art of English Poesy* is an entertaining examination of poetry, verse form and rhetoric, while Samuel Daniel's *A Defence of Rhyme* considers the practice of versification and praises the English literary tradition. Along with pieces by such writers as Sir John Harrington, Francis Bacon and Ben Jonson, these works reveal the emergence of new critical ideas and approaches, and celebrate the possibilities of the English language.

Gavin Alexander's introduction sets these writings in the context of the Renaissance and discusses the traditions of humanist literary criticism and rhetoric. This edition also includes detailed notes on each work, further reading, glosses and a chronology.

Edited with an introduction and notes by Gavin Alexander

PENGUIN CLASSICS

THE FAERIE QUEENE
EDMUND SPENSER

'Great Lady of the greatest Isle, whose light
Like Phoebus lampe throughout the world doth shine'

The Faerie Queene was one of the most influential poems in the English language.
Dedicating his work to Elizabeth I, Spenser brilliantly united Arthurian romance
and Italian renaissance epic to celebrate the glory of the Virgin Queen. Each book
of the poem recounts the quest of a knight to achieve a virtue: the Red Crosse
Knight of Holinesse, who must slay a dragon and free himself from the witch
Duessa; Sir Guyon, Knight of Temperance, who escapes the Cave of Mammon
and destroys Acrasia's Bowre of Bliss; and the lady-knight Britomart's search for
her Sir Artegall, revealed to her in an enchanted mirror. Although composed as a
moral and political allegory, *The Faerie Queene's* magical atmosphere captivated
the imaginations of later poets from Milton to the Victorians.

This edition includes the letter to Raleigh, in which Spenser declares his intentions
for his poem, the commendatory verses by Spenser's contemporaries and his
dedicatory sonnets to the Elizabethan court, and is supplemented by a table of
dates and a glossary.

Edited by Thomas P. Roche, Jr, with C. Patrick O'Donnell, Jr

PENGUIN CLASSICS

OROONOKO, THE ROVER AND OTHER WORKS
APHRA BEHN

> 'Behold Oroonoko, the most wretched,
> and abandoned by fortune of all the creation of the gods'

Aphra Behn's short novel *Oroonoko* tells the story of a noble African prince who is betrayed and sold into slavery. Using the author's own experiences in Surinam, it depicts the tragedy of a man born to command brought to a position of abject powerlessness. Behn's bawdy Restoration drama *The Rover* centres on the dissolute Cavalier Willmore, a follower of the exiled Charles II, and the attempts of two spirited women, Angellica Bianca and Hellena, the cross-dressing virgin, to woo him. The other works collected here include poems, letters, prose and the play *The Widow Ranter*, the first play to be set in the American colonies. Together they demonstrate the versatility and sophistication of one of the most innovative, wide-ranging authors of the seventeenth century.

In her introduction, Janet Todd explores the social changes that have influenced Aphra Behn's reputation over the centuries. This edition also contains notes on all the texts.

'All women together ought to let flowers fall upon the tomb of Aphra Behn, for it was she who earned them the right to speak their minds' Virginia Woolf

Edited with an introduction and notes by Janet Todd

PENGUIN CLASSICS

THE METAPHYSICAL POETS

> 'Death be not proud, though some have called thee
> Mighty and dreadfull, for, thou art not soe'

With their intricate arguments, startling conceits and dazzling wit, the seventeenth-century poets who became known as 'metaphysical' brought a new ingenuity and energy to English verse. John Donne's poems are some of the most passionate and profound to be written on both secular and spiritual love, from the playful eroticism of 'To his Mistris Going to Bed' to the dramatic force of his Holy Sonnets. George Herbert's religious verse, including 'Easter-wings', drew on unusual images such as music and money to create works that are intensely personal and devotional. And Andrew Marvell encompassed love poetry like 'To His Coy Mistress', philosophical dialogues, public odes and pastoral verse. All the poets collected here, who also include Henry Vaughan, Thomas Traherne and Richard Crashaw, can be seen fusing intellect and learning with powerful emotion to create some of the most individual and original poetry in the language.

Helen Gardner's acclaimed edition contains an introduction placing works in their historical context, biographical notes for each poet and indexes of first lines and authors.

Edited with an introduction by Helen Gardner

PENGUIN CLASSICS

THE COMPLETE POEMS
JOHN MILTON

'I may assert Eternal Providence
And justify the ways of God to men'

John Milton was a master of almost every type of verse, from the classical to the religious and from the lyrical to the epic. His early poems include the devotional 'On the Morning of Christ's Nativity', 'Comus', a masque, and the pastoral elegy 'Lycidas'. After Cromwell's death and the dashing of Milton's political hopes, he began composing *Paradise Lost*, which reflects his profound understanding of politics and power. Written when Milton was at the height of his abilities, this great masterpiece fuses the Christian with the classical in its description of the Fall of Man. In *Samson Agonistes*, Milton's last work, the poet draws a parallel with his own life in the hero's struggle to renew his faith in God.

In this edition of the *Complete Poems*, John Leonard draws attention to words coined by Milton and those that have changed their meaning since his time. He also provides full notes to elucidate biblical, classical and historical allusions and has modernized spelling, capitalization and punctuation.

Edited with a preface and notes by John Leonard

PENGUIN CLASSICS

THE COMPLETE POEMS
ANDREW MARVELL

'Thus, though we cannot make our sun
Stand still, yet we will make him run'

Member of Parliament, tutor to Oliver Cromwell's ward, satirist and friend of
John Milton, Andrew Marvell was one of the most significant poets of the
seventeenth century. *The Complete Poems* demonstrates his unique skill and
immense diversity, and includes lyrical love-poetry, religious works and biting
satire. From the passionately erotic 'To his Coy Mistress', to the astutely political
Cromwellian poems and the prescient 'Garden' and 'Mower' poems, which
consider humankind's relationship with the environment, these works are
masterpieces of clarity and metaphysical imagery. Eloquent and compelling, they
remain among the most vital and profound works of the era – works by a figure
who, in the words of T. S. Eliot, 'speaks clearly and unequivocally with the voice
of his literary age'.

This edition of Marvell's complete poems is based on a detailed study of the extant
manuscripts, with modern translations provided for Marvell's Greek and Latin
poems. This edition also includes a chronology, further reading, appendices, notes
and indexes of titles and first lines, with a new introduction by Jonathan Bate.

Edited by Elizabeth Story Donno

With an introduction by Jonathan Bate

PENGUIN CLASSICS

PARADISE LOST
JOHN MILTON

'Better to reign in Hell, than serve in Heav'n ...'

In *Paradise Lost* Milton produced a poem of epic scale, conjuring up a vast, awe-inspiring cosmos and ranging across huge tracts of space and time. And yet, in putting a charismatic Satan and naked Adam and Eve at the centre of this story, he also created an intensely human tragedy on the Fall of Man. Written when Milton was in his fifties – blind, bitterly disappointed by the Restoration and briefly in danger of execution – *Paradise Lost*'s apparent ambivalence towards authority has led to intense debate about whether it manages to 'justify the ways of God to men', or exposes the cruelty of Christianity.

John Leonard's revised edition of *Paradise Lost* contains full notes, elucidating Milton's biblical, classical and historical allusions and discussing his vivid, highly original use of language and blank verse.

'An endless moral maze, introducing literature's first Romantic, Satan' John Carey

Edited with an introduction and notes by John Leonard

PENGUIN CLASSICS

THE DIARIES OF SAMUEL PEPYS: A SELECTION
SAMUEL PEPYS

> 'But Lord, what a sad sight it was by moonlight
> to see the whole City almost on fire'

The 1660s represent a turning point in English history, and for the main events – the Restoration, the Dutch War, the Great Plague and the Fire of London – Pepys provides a definitive eyewitness account. As well as recording public and historical events, Pepys paints a vivid picture of his personal life, from his socializing and amorous entanglements, to theatre going and his work at the Navy Board. Unequalled for its frankness, high spirits and sharp observations, the diary is both a literary masterpiece and a marvellous portrait of seventeenth-century life.

'This prince of Diarists, this most amiable and admirable of men, has at last been worthily served' Paul Johnson, *Spectator*

PREVIOUSLY PUBLISHED AS *THE SHORTER PEPYS*

Selected and edited by Robert Latham

PENGUIN SHAKESPEARE

HAMLET
WILLIAM SHAKESPEARE

WWW.PENGUINSHAKESPEARE.COM

A young Prince meets with his father's ghost, who alleges that his own brother, now married to his widow, murdered him. The Prince devises a scheme to test the truth of the ghost's accusation, feigning wild madness while plotting a brutal revenge. But his apparent insanity soon begins to wreak havoc on innocent and guilty alike.

This book includes a general introduction to Shakespeare's life and the Elizabethan theatre, a separate introduction to *Hamlet*, a chronology of his works, suggestions for further reading, an essay discussing performance options on both stage and screen by Paul Prescott, and a commentary.

Edited by T. J. B. Spencer

With an introduction by Alan Sinfield

General Editor: Stanley Wells

PENGUIN SHAKESPEARE

OTHELLO
WILLIAM SHAKESPEARE

WWW.PENGUINSHAKESPEARE.COM

A popular soldier and newly married man, Othello seems to be in an enviable position. And yet, when his supposed friend sows doubts in his mind about his wife's fidelity, he is gradually consumed by suspicion. In this powerful tragedy, innocence is corrupted and trust is eroded as every relationship is drawn into a tangled web of jealousies.

This book includes a general introduction to Shakespeare's life and the Elizabethan theatre, a separate introduction to *Othello*, a chronology of Shakespeare's works, suggestions for further reading, an essay discussing performance options on both stage and screen, and a commentary.

Edited by Kenneth Muir

With an introduction by Tom McAlindon

General Editor: Stanley Wells

Penguin Shakespeare

KING LEAR
WILLIAM SHAKESPEARE

WWW.PENGUINSHAKESPEARE.COM

An ageing king makes a capricious decision to divide his realm among his three daughters according to the love they express for him. When the youngest daughter refuses to take part in this charade, she is banished, leaving the king dependent on her manipulative and untrustworthy sisters. In the scheming and recriminations that follow, not only does the king's own sanity crumble, but the stability of the realm itself is also threatened.

This book includes a general introduction to Shakespeare's life and the Elizabethan theatre, a separate introduction to *King Lear*, a chronology of his works, suggestions for further reading, an essay discussing performance options on both stage and screen, and a commentary.

Edited by George Hunter

With an introduction by Kiernan Ryan

General Editor: Stanley Wells

PENGUIN SHAKESPEARE

MACBETH
WILLIAM SHAKESPEARE

WWW.PENGUINSHAKESPEARE.COM

Promised a golden future as ruler of Scotland by three sinister witches, Macbeth murders the king to ensure his ambitions come true. But he soon learns the meaning of terror – killing once, he must kill again and again, and the dead return to haunt him. A story of war, witchcraft and bloodshed, *Macbeth* also depicts the relationship between husbands and wives, and the risks they are prepared to take to achieve their desires.

This book includes a general introduction to Shakespeare's life and the Elizabethan theatre, a separate introduction to *Macbeth*, a chronology of Shakespeare's works, suggestions for further reading, an essay discussing performance options on both stage and screen, and a commentary.

Edited by George Hunter

With an introduction by Carol Rutter

General Editor: Stanley Wells

THE STORY OF PENGUIN CLASSICS

Before 1946 ... 'Classics' are mainly the domain of academics and students; readable editions for everyone else are almost unheard of. This all changes when a little-known classicist, E. V. Rieu, presents Penguin founder Allen Lane with the translation of Homer's *Odyssey* that he has been working on in his spare time.

1946 Penguin Classics debuts with *The Odyssey*, which promptly sells three million copies. Suddenly, classics are no longer for the privileged few.

1950s Rieu, now series editor, turns to professional writers for the best modern, readable translations, including Dorothy L. Sayers's *Inferno* and Robert Graves's unexpurgated *Twelve Caesars*.

1960s The Classics are given the distinctive black covers that have remained a constant throughout the life of the series. Rieu retires in 1964, hailing the Penguin Classics list as 'the greatest educative force of the twentieth century.'

1970s A new generation of translators swells the Penguin Classics ranks, introducing readers of English to classics of world literature from more than twenty languages. The list grows to encompass more history, philosophy, science, religion and politics.

1980s The Penguin American Library launches with titles such as *Uncle Tom's Cabin*, and joins forces with Penguin Classics to provide the most comprehensive library of world literature available from any paperback publisher.

1990s The launch of Penguin Audiobooks brings the classics to a listening audience for the first time, and in 1999 the worldwide launch of the Penguin Classics website extends their reach to the global online community.

The 21st Century Penguin Classics are completely redesigned for the first time in nearly twenty years. This world-famous series now consists of more than 1300 titles, making the widest range of the best books ever written available to millions – and constantly redefining what makes a 'classic'.

The Odyssey continues ...

The best books ever written

PENGUIN 🐧 CLASSICS

SINCE 1946